Adolf Hitler

3

Adolf Hitler

by

COLIN CROSS

HODDER AND STOUGHTON
LONDON SYDNEY AUCKLAND TORONTO

Copyright © *1973 by Colin Cross. First printed 1973. 2nd impression 1973. ISBN 0 340 10911 4. All rights reserved. No part of this publication may be reproduced or transmitted in any form or by any means, electronic or mechanical, including photocopy, recording or any information storage and retrieval system, without permission in writing from the publisher. Printed in Great Britain for Hodder and Stoughton Limited, St. Paul's House, Warwick Lane, London EC4P 4AH by T. & A. Constable Ltd., Hopetoun Street, Edinburgh EH7 4NF.*

To P.

Illustrations

'Who escapes from criticism? I myself, if I disappear today, realise that a time will come, in a hundred years perhaps, when I shall be violently attacked. History will make no exception in my favour.'

ADOLF HITLER, DECEMBER 28TH, 1941.

FRONTIER CHANGES IN EASTERN EUROPE
1938 – 41

AREAS ACQUIRED BY:-
RUSSIA
GERMANY
HUNGARY
ITALY
BULGARIA
LITHUANIA
1938 FRONTIERS

FINLAND

E. KARELIA

Helsinki

Leningrad

Stockholm

Tallinn

ESTONIA

DENMARK

BALTIC SEA

Memel

Riga

LATVIA

LITHUANIA

Kaunas

Vilna

U S S R

Hamburg

Danzig

E. PRUSSIA

Berlin

Warsaw

EAST POLAND

GERMANY

POLAND

Breslau

Prague

SUDETENLAND

BOHEMIA

Cracow

Lvov

MORAVIA

Munich

Vienna

SLOVAKIA

RUTHENIA

BESSARABIA

AUSTRIA

Budapest

HUNGARY

N TRANSYLVANIA

Zagreb

BAČKA

RUMANIA

Bucharest

YUGOSLAVIA

Belgrade

S DOBRUJA

BLACK SEA

CROATIA

ITALY

SERBIA

BULGARIA

ADRIATIC SEA

Sofia

Rome

ALBANIA

TYRRHENIAN SEA

GREECE

AEGEAN SEA

Introduction

Adolf Hitler saw his first movie in 1904, when he was aged fourteen. It impressed him deeply and for the rest of his life he was a cinema (as well as an opera) fan: as Chancellor of Germany he enjoyed repeated private showings of *Lives of a Bengal Lancer,* which showed British-occupied India. Given his particular artistic skills and his historical sense, it is a tragedy that Hitler failed to find his way to the Hollywood of the 1920s. He might have become a great producer of popular films, in the Cecil B. de Mille style, with plenty of colour and spectacle. On celluloid his autocracy and imagination would have been untrammelled by practical political facts. In real life, however, the same qualities led to disaster. It is an amazing fact that in such a country as Germany such a man as Hitler could ever have won power and this book lays particular stress on an attempt to analyse the exceptional circumstances in which Hitler was able to squeeze into office and to convert a constitutional chancellorship into absolute dictatorship.

I have attempted to treat Hitler as an historical figure who belonged to the mid and early twentieth-century period in Germany and Europe. He is fascinating because of the vast results achieved. He became, although only briefly, the most powerful figure in Europe since Napoleon Bonaparte. But in the long run his achievements were mostly the opposite of what he had aimed at. Thus he wanted the German Reich to extend far into Russia but he ended up with the Russians in Berlin. He wanted to exterminate the Jewish people but in fact was the final stimulus in the erection of the first independent Jewish state in 2,000 years. A good deal of non-academic writing about Hitler and the German National Socialists has hitherto been based on what can be termed the 'Nuremberg' approach, an attempt to assemble every unfavourable fact so as to form a prosecution case. Some 'facts' about

11

Hitler and the Nazis, especially those dating from the mid-1930s, were actual inventions. The Communist Willi Münzenberg ran a lie factory in Paris which was just as efficient as Goebbels's in Berlin. This was legitimate in that Hitler was not the kind of person who could be fought with kid gloves on, and he needed to be fought because he himself started fights. His enemies saw him as the devil incarnate. In the perspective of history, however, he can surely be treated as he really was. He was a loser who ruined his country and tainted the achievements of his fighting men. In one aspect, World War II was a struggle between Hitler and Stalin to decide who should be paramount in eastern Europe. Stalin won and it would be difficult, in my view, to draw much moral distinction between the two men. Stalin was abler, luckier and more realistic but—in actual numbers involved—his purges, deportations and executions, were even bigger atrocities than Hitler's. On the other hand, Hitler rather than Stalin was the prime mover in World War II and this was an extraordinary episode which cost something like forty million lives. Europe has never been the same since, although some of the ultimate changes have been for the better.

Hitler was an unsophisticated, self-taught thinker who fastened on to prejudices which were quite common among the ordinary people in the street in Germany, and in Europe generally, in the early twentieth century. He was earnestly patriotic and believed his own people to be better than any others. He took it utterly for granted that the 'white' races, and particularly the northern Europeans, were superior beings. He was anti-Semitic. He greeted World War I with a sense of joy and liberation but four years of almost unbroken service as an ordinary soldier on the Western Front killed the glamour. He believed his own side had a just cause and would win. He was shattered by defeat and attributed it to faulty leadership by the old upper classes, together with sabotage from Marxist revolutionaries.

All this was commonplace fifty and sixty years ago. Every nationality was banging its drums. As late as 1928 the British Prime Minister, Stanley Baldwin, was observing quite seriously in a speech: 'When God wants something difficult done, he sends for his Englishmen.' Where Hitler differed from ordinary people was not in sophistication of thought but in his power to pick up commonplace ideas and to take them to extremes in practical action. In so doing he put them into lasting discredit, at least in Europe. It is far from wholly coincidence that the British world-empire, which Hitler respected and desired to emulate, vanished within twenty years of Hitler's passing.

12

There were special factors in German politics in the 1920s and 1930s which made the rise of somebody of Hitler's type almost inevitable. The loss of the war, the 1923 inflation and the 1929 depression, plus class and regional conflicts, made Germany fertile for a populist politician of Hitler's type. He was a considerable orator with an air of passionate, innocent sincerity. What was not inevitable, however, was that the populist should actually win power and that he should use power in the way Hitler did. It was in these two matters that Hitler, as a person, was a decisive force in history. In particular, he proved himself a brilliant tactician, first at edging himself into the chancellorship (he had never won a majority of the electorate and his mushroom party was showing signs of decline at the time), and then in converting the chancellorship into absolute dictatorship.

Hitler rose into prominence very suddenly. Up to 1930 he was only a fringe politician but by 1932 he had become a candidate for power. One aspect of this was that he and his party seemed to represent youth. He was in power at the age of forty-three and most of his associates were younger than himself. He was a good deal younger than most of the international statesmen with whom he came into contact. He was twenty years younger than Neville Chamberlain, fifteen years younger than Winston Churchill, ten years younger than Joseph Stalin, seven years younger than Franklin D. Roosevelt, six years younger than Benito Mussolini and one year older than Charles de Gaulle. His successors in the political leadership of Germany, Konrad Adenauer and Wilhelm Pieck, were both thirteen years older than himself. Had he managed things better and kept his health, he might still, as a 'grand old man', have been ruling Germany in the 1970s.

Hitler suffered acutely from the politician's occupational disease, megalomania. He lacked even a wife and family as a means of keeping in touch with normality. He felt a sense of divine mission. In youth he had lacked sense of direction but in middle age he had suddenly become an all-powerful dictator. He had used the mechanisms of liberal democracy to achieve this but he did not believe in liberal democracy. The only explanation he could think of, as success followed success, must be that he had a kind of divine right, akin to the old divine right of kings. Hitler's was in any event an odd personality, limited in ordinary affections and possibly (although the evidence for this is only tenuous) streaked with pathological sadism. Politically, he became virtually insane and he seriously believed that through faith and will-power he could accomplish anything. His megalomania was strengthened by his banning of any criticism, or even discussion of his policies.

13

His downfall illustrates with some clarity that an autocratic state, with opposition banned, has inbuilt weaknesses which can lead to false decisions being taken, even against its own interests. Hitler's policies could have survived no form of open discussion.

Above all, and this is the single most significant fact about Hitler, he had an artistic temperament. He preferred to work only as and when the mood took him. He preferred intuition to reason. When he wanted, or it was necessary, he had the mental equipment for following a logical argument and answering it. He had above-average reasoning power and a superb memory. But this was not his genius. What drove him was faith in his intuition and he made the great decisions of his life on an irrational basis. He gloried in this and went so far as to claim in a public speech that he was like a 'sleepwalker'. This makes him difficult to pin down on his intentions and on his personal honesty. He was not a cold man, scheming from the 1920s onwards how he would dominate the world. He had no detailed advance programme at all, only vague outlines. He was a warm, emotional man, operating opportunistically and by 'feel'. He was particularly expert at getting the 'feel' of individuals with whom he came into contact.

The nearest equivalent to Hitler as an individual who in the twentieth century personally changed the course of history is Lenin. It is arguable that without Lenin the Communist Party would not have seized power in Petrograd in 1917 and would not have won the subsequent civil war. Prior to 1917, Russia was not a country which Marxists had expected to be the first to fall to their doctrines. However, Lenin did not stand so alone as Hitler. Lenin depended greatly upon such colleagues as Trotsky, whereas Hitler's colleagues, even Göring, were scarcely more than tools. Lenin belonged to a real and continuing tradition, whereas Hitler stood alone. Lenin achieved at least something of what he wanted, whereas Hitler, in the long run, was a total failure. One of the few who met both Lenin and Hitler was the English socialist, Lord Allen of Hurtwood. Allen met Lenin in 1920 and Hitler in 1935. In a private note comparing the two men, Allen judged that Lenin gave the impression of being 'academic' whereas Hitler gave the impression of 'immense vitality'.*

Hitler can be compared, also, with his two immediate contemporaries as dictators, Mussolini and Stalin.

Mussolini was a more normal human being than the other two. He was intelligent, pushful and capable, on occasion, of being extraordinarily silly. He worried about prestige and for bombastic rather than realistic reasons wanted to expand Italian power.

* Quoted by Arthur Marwick, *Clifford Allen* (Edinburgh/London, 1964).

(Hitler, in contrast, did not want fresh territories for prestige but as colonies to be exploited to build up the power and population of Germany.) Mussolini could be rough when crossed but he did not commit atrocities on the Hitler–Stalin scale. He was of some significance in Hitler's early career in that he had won power in Italy just after Hitler had started in politics. He was, therefore, an example of what could be achieved. Part of the inspiration behind Hitler's 1923 attempted *coup d'état* in Munich was Mussolini's 'march on Rome'. Later, in the 1930s, Mussolini took an instinctive dislike to Hitler at first sight, but by various methods, including the sheer force of Hitler's personality, was driven into junior partnership.

Stalin and Hitler never met and knew little about each other personally. They had it in common that they were both, to some extent, 'outsiders' in the countries they ruled; Hitler had been born an Austrian and Stalin a Georgian. Possibly, but not certainly, this gave them a little extra insight, from a semi-detached position, into the mentalities of their subjects. Stalin was more of a cold calculator than Hitler. In August 1939 they did a deal, carving up Eastern Europe between them, but they were both cynical enough to recognise that the friendship was unlikely to be permanent. Stalin, using often atrocious methods, built an industrial system and an empire which survived long after his death and so he was more successful than Hitler. Against this, Stalin, unlike Hitler, was working within a political system which, in the last resort, was stronger than himself and ultimately able to repudiate him. No second or third generation National Socialist government, had such a thing ever existed, would have been able to repudiate Hitler without losing its *raison d'être;* he was the Marx, Lenin and Stalin of National Socialism, rolled into one.

Underlying the whole of Hitler's ideas and methods was a streak of ruthlessness and cruelty which was almost an end in itself. He started life as a highly imaginative boy who did badly at high school. He lived, in his teens, on illusions. In Vienna, where he was appalled to encounter 'Jews' and 'foreigners' in a 'German' city, he encountered further failure and suffered some degree of economic hardship, although certainly not so great as he subsequently liked to make out. This hardened him without weakening his illusions. His war experiences in 1914–18 must have hardened him yet further, and brought him finally to the view that ruthless struggle between races was the law of nature. Save in a few temporary, tactical situations, it was not in his nature to try to win his way by concessions. His answer was always to strike down an opponent before the opponent struck first. He

15

sneered at softness. The world was like a jungle in which the rule was to kill or be killed. Whenever things went badly for him, his thoughts turned readily to suicide.

He had a love of architecture, of some forms of music and of animals. He could be courteous and well-mannered. He was a vegetarian, a teetotaller and a non-smoker. He suffered from insomnia. He had a passion for Germany and brought her to ruin, materially and morally. So far as this book has a hero it is not Hitler but the men and women of the German resistance, and in particular Claus Philipp Maria Schenk, Count von Stauffenberg.

1

In social background, Adolf Hitler belonged to the prosperous lower middle class of the German-speaking fringe of the Austro-Hungarian Empire. His childhood was somewhat unusual in that he began as an exceptionally clever little boy at primary school but fell off completely in his teens and virtually failed high school. He changed from being a leader among his fellows into a brooding solitary. As a young man he became a drifting artist, picking up on the way a wide practical experience of human behaviour. While material is lacking for any close analysis of his early psychology, one governing factor is that he possessed a wholly exceptional power of imagination and drifted easily into fantasy.

Essentially his family background was petty bourgeois and well within the bounds of normality. However it did have certain special features.

Both his father, Alois Hitler, and his mother, Klara Hitler, sprang from the backward peasantry of the Waldviertel area of Upper Austria, on the frontier with what is now Czechoslovakia. Alois, who was fifty-one when Adolf was born, had worked himself up from peasant origins to be a senior customs official and, in his sphere, a person of weight and authority. However there is mystery about Alois in that it cannot be established for certain who his father, Adolf's grandfather, was. Alois had been born Alois Schickelgruber, the illegitimate son of a spinster peasant woman, Maria Schickelgruber; she had produced him as her only child at the late age of forty-two. The birth took place in the Waldviertel and the assumption would normally be that the father would have been an ordinary Waldviertel peasant.

However the interesting rumour has existed that Alois's father was a bourgeois called Frankenberger, of Jewish faith or origin, in the city of Graz, Austrian Styria. The story went that Maria

fahrs dad.

Schickelgruber had been employed by the Frankenbergers as a domestic servant and that although she had left them on becoming pregnant and returned home, they paid her alimony for the child for the first fourteen years of its life. This would indicate that a member of the Frankenberger family had been the father and that Alois Hitler, consequently, was half-Jewish and Adolf Hitler was quarter-Jewish. This is significant, of course, in view of the fact that Adolf Hitler preached that Jewish 'blood' was a corrupting force; under his regime, possession of a single Jewish grandparent was sufficient to bar a person from public office. The evidence for the story is, however, late and extremely thin.* But it can only have made Hitler uneasy—the story that he was Jewish was being bruited around in Munich as early as 1921—and it may well have affected his policy towards the Jews. A more embellished version which appeared first in 1933, was that Maria had been employed by the Rothschilds in Vienna as a servant and had become pregnant by one of them. The 1935 Nuremberg laws made a point of forbidding Jewish households to employ 'Aryan' female servants of child-bearing age.

From early infancy, Alois Schicklgruber† was put out to fostering in the home of Nepomuk Hüttler, a Waldviertel small farmer. From this, the probability obviously arises that Nepomuk was the true father; he was a married man with daughters living but no legitimate son. When Alois was six, his mother, Maria Schickelgruber, married Nepomuk's elder brother Georg Hiedler, a widower and a journeyman miller. Adolf Hitler grew up in the belief that Georg Hiedler had been his grandfather, and this could be correct, but in fact, even after Maria and Georg were married, young Alois continued to live with Nepomuk Hüttler and to bear the name Alois Schicklgruber. Had Georg Hiedler been the father, or declared himself to be the father, he could, on his subsequent marriage to Maria, have taken steps to legitimise Alois and to change his name to Hiedler; he did not do so. There was at this time much illegitimacy among the Waldviertel peasantry and retrospective legitimisations were commonplace.

Alois Schicklgruber grew up to be a man of exceptional energy

---

* The best authority for it is *At the Foot of the Gallows*, a book by the National Socialist lawyer, Hans Frank. As its title indicates, it was written shortly before his execution. In the book, Frank asserts that in 1930 he saw letters proving that the Frankenbergers had paid maintenance for fourteen years for Alois Hitler and, further, that Hitler at this time said he knew about the payments, although denying to Frank that he had Jewish blood. No trace of such letters now exists and the Graz Hebrew congregation had no 'Frankenberger' among its members at the relevant time.

† Maria's name is recorded Schickelgruber, but Alois spelled himself Schicklgruber.

and ambition. After what can only have been the sketchiest of primary educations, he was apprenticed to a bootmaker. At eighteen he joined the customs service as a frontier guard, with a status somewhere between that of a policeman and a private soldier. He rose to be a non-commissioned officer in the guard and then to be an actual customs officer, which involved passing an examination. He must have had expert clerical skills and during a forty years' career he rose as far as was open to him, ending up with the grade of higher collector. Surviving recollections of him indicate that he was a disciplinarian, strict at enforcing exact hours of duty for himself and his subordinates. A surviving letter by him gives advice to one of his relations who was considering joining the service; he wrote of a customs officer: 'First he is required to render absolute obedience to his supervisors at every level. Then there is much to learn, especially for one who hasn't any prior education. Drinkers, debtors, card players and other types that lead immoral lives cannot last. Then, of course, one must go out on duty in every kind of weather, day and night.' Off-duty, Alois had a passion for bee-keeping—Adolf Hitler used to recall how in his childhood his father would come in from the hives smothered in stings which did not bother him at all. Alois also enjoyed an evening in the tavern with his friends and, especially as he got older and rose in his service, he tended to be dogmatic in putting forward his views; a higher collector of customs was a man of standing in a small frontier town and could expect to be heard with respect. Alois was strongly in favour of free education and he had a definitely anti-clerical bent. But he was loyal to the Hapsburg monarchy, the uniform of which he wore, and like many other officials grew whiskers modelled on those of the Emperor, Franz Josef. He went to church only once a year and that was on the Emperor's birthday, when he attended, a prominent figure, in full uniform, with white trousers and elaborate plumed hat. His income by middle life was that of the lower middle class, being rather above that of a primary school principal.

His private life was less orderly. While in his twenties Alois fathered an illegitimate son by one Therese Schmidt. He remained a bachelor until he was thirty-six and then married Anna Glassl, a woman of fifty, the daughter of an official in the imperial tobacco monopoly; the usual explanation is that he must have done so for money and social position. Aged thirty-nine, he changed his surname from Schicklgruber to Hitler, on the basis that Georg Hiedler had been his father, and the civil service records were adjusted accordingly although, technically, he did not fully legitimise himself. Both Georg Hiedler and his mother, Maria Schickelgruber Hiedler, were both then long dead but the foster-father Nepomuk Hüttler was still living and, since he had no legitimate sons, may have wanted his name to be carried on by Alois, with property to go with it. However it is a curiosity that Alois chose to call himself 'Hitler' rather than 'Hiedler'. The name is of possibly Czech origin and can be traced through the centuries in various spellings, including 'Hüttler', 'Hiedler', 'Hittler' and 'Hitler': it long depended on how a parish priest chose to write down a name given by an illiterate peasant. But by the time of Alois's change of name, Nepomuk was definitely 'Hüttler' and Alois in his daily work was thoroughly accustomed to getting names right. Surviving letters in his hand show him using both perfect spelling and perfect grammar. He could not have called himself 'Hitler' by mistake. Perhaps he did so because 'Hitler' was a compromise between 'Hüttler' and 'Hiedler'. His son, Adolf, came to approve of the choice; as a teenager Adolf mused that Schicklgruber as a name was peasant-like and that Hiedler sounded weak but that Hitler had a good ring to it.

Alois, now Alois Hitler, was not content with his wife fourteen years older than himself and some air of scandal existed around his household. He had a teenage granddaughter of Nepomuk Hüttler, Klara Pölzl, to work as a maidservant but she went off suddenly to become a servant in Vienna in circumstances that apparently caused gossip. At the same time he got mixed up with a hotel maid, another teenager, called Franziska Matzelberger and his wife successfully sued him for a judicial separation—divorce was not an option. Alois thereafter lived with Franziska and by her, in 1882, had a son named Alois after himself. On the death of his first wife in 1883, Alois immediately married Franziska and a month after the wedding she gave birth to a daughter, Angela.

Aged forty-six, newly-married to a wife twenty-four years younger than himself and the father of two children, Alois ought to have been settled for life, with his bees as his only extra-curricular interest. But almost immediately after the marriage there came the disaster of Franziska falling mortally ill with tuberculosis and Alois had to make further arrangements. He brought back his Hüttler cousin, Klara Pölzl, to look after his family and she evidently became his lover also. Klara became pregnant by Alois at about the moment of Franziska's death in August 1884.

Thus it was that the parents of Adolf Hitler came together. Although they were living with each other from before Franziska's death, and Klara was running the household, they were at first unable to marry. This was because Alois had declared himself to be Georg Hiedler's son and thus Klara, as Nepomuk Hüttler's granddaughter, was his second cousin and within the degrees of prohibited affinity. The true relationship could have been even closer—on the basis that Nepomuk rather than Georg had been Alois's natural father, they were uncle and niece. On the other hand, if Alois's father had not been a Hiedler, but, say a Frankenberger at Graz, then there was no blood relationship at all. The matter is so uncertain that it would be unsafe to draw any conclusions about the influence of Adolf Hitler's heredity on his character; like many things about him, it is a matter of extremes —he might have been exceptionally in-bred or he could conceivably have had a strain in him outside that of the Waldviertel peasantry.

To get a dispensation to marry as second cousins, Alois and Klara had to apply, through the local bishop, to Rome itself and this took four months. Not until January 1885 were they able to marry. Klara used wryly to recall, with only slight exaggeration, that the wedding had taken place at six-thirty in the morning and that Alois had been back on duty at the customs house by seven. Klara was then aged twenty-four and four months pregnant; Alois was forty-eight.

Klara Hitler was a tall, good-looking woman with brown hair and she was a diligent housewife. In many ways her marriage to Alois Hitler was an advantageous one to her, giving her a position she might not otherwise have attained—she had no dowry. They had a comfortable home in a top floor flat over the Pommer tavern in Braunau, with a maid living in, and Alois was a man of sound social position, with a secure income. No further scandal occurred. Alois was obviously an authoritarian husband but that was normal for the time and especially to be expected in view of his twenty-four years seniority in age. Long after the marriage, Klara was still on occasion slipping back to addressing him as 'uncle'. Unlike her husband, Klara was a practising church-goer. She got on well with the two children from the previous marriage, particularly with Angela, with whom she had a virtually complete mother-daughter relationship. But her own family life was a tragic one. Her first child, Gustav, born five months after the marriage, died in his second year. Then came a daughter, Ida, who also died in her second year. Then came the remarkable Adolf, who was to be the first of Klara's children to grow to maturity. The next child, Edmund, died of measles aged six. Finally came a daughter, Paula, who lived from 1896 to 1960. Paula kept in the background during Adolf's public career and remained unmarried; she seems to have been weak mentally.

Adolf Hitler was born at six-thirty in the evening on Easter

Eve, April 20th, 1889, in the family flat above the Pommer tavern —within half a century his alleged natal bed had been broken up and sold to tourists at twenty marks a splinter. According to custom he was baptised the day after his birth and he was given the sole Christian name of Adolf. (His surname, of course, was Hitler—his father had ceased to be Schicklgruber fourteen years before Adolf's birth.) While in his ideas Hitler was to diverge far from Roman Catholic orthodoxy and he never after his childhood attended church except for weddings and funerals, he never formally apostasised; as late as 1945 he was still, according to protocol, a Roman Catholic Head of State and on his death official requiem masses were offered for him at least in Dublin and Lisbon. (It was then believed that he had died in action, not by suicide.)

Given the fact that three of her children had died in infancy, it can only be assumed that Klara Hitler surrounded baby Adolf with much love and care and that his first years must have been happy ones. Every account agrees that Klara was a good mother and there was certainly enough money to look after him properly.

As a politician, Hitler was to attach high symbolic importance to the fact that he had been born at Braunau, on the frontier between Austria and Germany. To his way of thinking, it symbolised his 'destiny' of bringing about the unification of the two countries. He started his book *My Struggle* with an emotional plea to this end: 'The same blood belongs in the same Reich.' However Hitler could have had few or no actual memories of Braunau. When he was aged three his father, on promotion, was posted away to Passau, Bavaria, on the German side of the frontier and his family went with him. There was no more feeling of him being sent to a 'foreign' country than if a modern United States customs officer were, for convenience, to happen to operate just over the border of Canada. Bavarians and German-Austrians had a common language, common religion and common social standards; the frontier was a political accident rather than a dividing line between nations. The Hitlers were three years at Passau and Adolf, playing with the local children, picked up the local accent, and this remained, indeed, at the basis of his way of speaking for the rest of his life. He declared he always felt somehow back at home when he heard Bavarian voices.

After three years in Passau, the family moved again, Alois Hitler, at fifty-eight, having produced medical evidence that he was no longer fit to work. Since he had been forty years in the civil service he was eligible for full pension. The retirement terms were generous—he simply went on drawing his former salary without having to work for it. For his retirement Alois had bought a small holding in Austria at Hafeld, a hamlet about thirty miles south-west of Linz. It was a good little estate of about nine acres, with a decent two-storey house commanding wide views over the countryside. In the values of the time, it would have cost about 10,000 crowns, equivalent to about £430, or to well over £4,000 in the purchasing power of the 1970s. While it was not a rich man's home, it certainly was not a place of poverty either. There was plenty of space for Alois's beehives plus fruit trees and a market garden for him to cultivate; the children had fresh air and plenty of space. Any living to be earned from it would have been a narrow one and sufficient only for the standards of the poorest peasant-proprietor. But Alois also had full salary, 2,200 crowns a year—about £108 in the exchange values of the time. This was about double the wage of a skilled factory worker in Austria then. His standing would have been equivalent to that of a £3,000 a year man in the 1970s, or even better, and he had complete security. Considering that he had started with nothing and as an illegitimate, Alois Hitler had done well for himself.

While the family was at Hafeld, six-year-old Adolf started his education, trotting across the fields clutching Angela's hand to a little rural primary school. It had only one teacher for all ages and he, forty years later, was recalling how neat and tidy Adolf and Angela had been. Socially the Hitler children ranked rather above their mostly peasant schoolmates and Adolf seems to have been quick with his figures and at learning to read. But the influence of this school must have been slight because after only two years the family moved again. The reasons for Alois Hitler quitting what should have been his idyllic retirement home are not clear. Probably he was bored and found that the smallholding took more work than he had anticipated. Also he may well have wanted to get Adolf into a better school. Then there seems to have been a certain wanderlust in him, a distaste for putting down roots. At any rate, Alois sold up and moved his household to a rented flat in the nearby small market town of Lambach.

At Lambach Adolf entered a more sophisticated type of primary school and continued to do well at his work. He also began to emerge as something of a gang leader in children's games. He acquired the beginnings of a musical education by enrolling, after a voice test, in the choir school of a local Benedictine monastery. Sunday by Sunday he sang at high mass and plainly was impressed by the elaborate ritual. For a moment he thought of becoming a monk himself—an idea his father would vehemently have discouraged—but he fell so far from grace as to be caught smoking a cigarette in the monastery garden. For the rest of his life he was fond of praising the propagandist skill of the Roman Catholics and their use of ritual. As a political organiser he used colour and ceremony on an unprecedented scale as a means of persuasion and this must, in the last resort, have gone back to his memories of the Lambach monastic church.

After two years at Lambach the family moved to Leonding, a suburb of Linz, provincial capital of Upper Austria and Adolf entered yet a third primary school, where he continued to do well. Linz, where he lived between the ages of ten and eighteen, he was always to regard as his home town and plans for rebuilding it on a more splendid scale were one of his lifelong interests. Although it was the provincial capital and had a garrison, an opera house and a new cathedral being built, it was in European terms only a backwater, existing mainly as a bureaucratic and marketing centre. Here, just before Adolf's eleventh birthday, the younger brother Edmund died of measles and this must have been a shock.

It was with his entry into early adolescence that Hitler began, according to every evident sign, to be a failure. From being one of the brightest boys at primary school he became plainly backward at secondary school, and that with no valid external reason. There was no need for him to go to secondary school at all. The majority of Austrian boys of his age continued at primary school until the age of fifteen and then left to start work. However Hitler belonged to the lower middle class and his father certainly wanted him to have a proper secondary education. According to Hitler's own recollections, his father insisted that he should prepare himself for the civil service, a career with the highest professional status in Hapsburg Austria and one in which he himself had done well. He even took young Adolf to see the customs office at Linz but Adolf was repelled. Many years later he recalled that it was 'a real bureaucratic cage—in which the old men squatted like monkeys'. Adolf resisted the idea of himself entering such a cage and began to conceive the idea of becoming an artist. In all probability quite a conflict developed between father and son, with their attitudes to life and to Adolf's future diverging. On his primary school record, Adolf was well qualified to enter secondary school and Alois could afford the small fees. The choice was whether he should enter the classical secondary school or the modern secondary school. The classical school had somewhat higher status and was the ordinary preparation for someone intending to enter the real higher bureaucracy, as opposed to the merely clerical grades in which Alois had made his way. The modern secondary school had a bias towards science and modern languages and prepared boys for a more commercial type of career; it led only exceptionally to the civil service. Alois chose the modern school for Adolf and the supposition must be that rather than ram Latin and Greek down his son he was being tolerant and trying to provide Adolf with an education best suited to him. For a boy who wanted to become an artist, the modern school was a better preparation than the classical.

Standards in Austrian secondary education, both classical and modern, were rigorous. Every year each pupil had to reach a satisfactory level in all subjects before being allowed to proceed up to the next form. If he failed, he had to 'sit back' an extra year in the same form and this, although quite common, was something of a social disgrace. It was called 'falling through'. If he did badly over a period of time, he might be required to leave school altogether. The normal boy, who survived the course until the age of eighteen, received the *Abitur,* the document which opened the way for most further education and white collar careers.

Hitler entered the modern secondary school at Linz in September 1900, and embarked on a course which included German, French, mathematics, science, history, geography and drawing. From the start he was unhappy and a misfit, resenting the authoritarian teaching methods. He retreated into what already must have been an exceptionally powerful imagination and well into his teens preferred leading boys younger than himself in games of cowboys and Indians, and Boers versus British, to making friends of his own age. At school he was a failure, but among the suburban youngsters in Leonding a leader and perhaps something of a hero. At the end of his first year Hitler received the dreaded mark 'unsatisfactory' in mathematics and science and so had to 'sit back' a further year in the same form. The following year he managed to scrape through in all subjects and so was promoted to Form II among boys mostly a year his junior. At the end of his year in Form II he was marked 'unsatisfactory' in mathematics and had to sit a special examination in the subject before being allowed up into Form III.

By now Hitler must have been making his first acquaintance with politics and with German nationalism, the more so because the modern school at Linz had a reputation for instilling a German nationalist outlook. It was a crucial question in the Austria-Hungary of the time and there seemed to be no viable answer to it. Austria-Hungary was a medley of nationalities held together as the family dominions of the Hapsburg dynasty. In 1918 it was

25

to break up altogether and today its component territories are Austria, Hungary and Czechoslovakia, plus parts of what are now Italy, Yugoslavia, Rumania, the Soviet Union and Poland. While it delighted people of cosmopolitan taste, it existed in outright and growing contradiction to one of the principal forces of the nineteenth and twentieth centuries, that of nationalism. For centuries the Hapsburgs had, in a shadowy way, been overlords of all Germany but in 1871, the Prussian Bismarck had shut them and their dominions out of Germany altogether and set up a new German Empire under the Hohenzollern dynasty and in Hitler's childhood this was developing rapidly as a modern nation-state. It had less inherent unity than contemporary Britain or France but a genuine German nationalist spirit was a force tending all the time to override local loyalties to its component states, Prussia, Bavaria, Saxony and so on.

In Austria-Hungary the nationalist spirit was tending not towards unity but towards disintegration. The Hungarian section of the empire had a wide degree of autonomy but was being resented by non-Hungarian nationalities in its area, including Rumanians and Slovaks. The Austrian section had yet greater problems, centring particularly on the Czechs of Bohemia. Traditionally the Bohemian cities, especially Prague, had been regarded as centres of German life and culture, while the Czechs were peasants. Any Czech who wanted to get on would Germanise himself and many, in the past, had done so. It is possible, in fact, that the Hitler-Hiedler name had had some Czech origin in the remote past. During the nineteenth century, however, the Czechs, rather like the Irish in the British Isles, acquired a growing sense of national identity. A Czech urban population and middle class grew up and Prague itself came to acquire a Czech majority. Many Czechs took places in the imperial bureaucracy; one of Alois Hitler's best friends and a pall-bearer at his funeral was a Czech. In 1895, when Adolf Hitler was six, the imperial government issued a language decree which was intended to conciliate the Czechs; it announced that the local administration in Bohemia would in future be bi-lingual, German and Czech. This caused a vast uproar which certainly must have penetrated the Alois Hitler household and have come to the attention of little Adolf. The point was that whereas every educated Czech could speak German, almost no Germans spoke Czech. Thus in future, Germans would be excluded from the Bohemian bureaucracy; also what was regarded as the peasant Czech patois was being promoted to a level with German, a language of world standing. Alois would undoubtedly have been deeply interested and the supposition must be that like nearly all German bureaucrats he would have regarded it as an outrage. There arose a vast German nationalist protest, with middle-class people demonstrating in the streets, and eventually the decree was withdrawn. On both sides, German and Czech, nationalism was still a mainly middle-class phenomenon.

The problem for the German nationalist in Austria was what he should aim for. The traditional idea had been that German culture would gradually spread among the minority peoples and, indeed, that the Germans had a 'civilising' mission. This, against rising Czech nationalism, was becoming less and less of a tenable policy. At the same time the Hohenzollern German nation-state to the north, with its vigour and success, could do no other than arouse educated German-Austrians to a growing sense of their own national consciousness. By Hitler's childhood it was becoming the implied policy of extreme Austrian-German nationalists that Austria-Hungary should break up altogether and that the German part of it should join up with Hohenzollern Germany. Even this begged the problem of Bohemia with its mixed Czech-German population and the Czech nationalists wanting their own national community; while the Germans were a minority in Bohemia, they were a long-entrenched one—Prague University had been German since the Middle Ages. However the break-up of the empire was only an implied possibility and would certainly not have been directly advocated by Hitler's schoolmasters. They concentrated on teaching pride in German culture and achievement.

Mixed in with some, but by no means all, German nationalism in Austria was a degree of anti-semitism. Germans of Jewish family background had been prominent in the early nationalist movement of the 1880s but by the 1890s and 1900s, under such Vienna radicals as Georg Schönerer and Karl Lueger, there existed a clear tendency to blame 'the Jews' for much that was going wrong. In this Austria was more akin to contemporary Russia or France, both of which contained virulent anti-Semitism, than to Hohenzollern Germany or to Britain, where anti-Semitism was social prejudice rather than a substantial political force. How soon in his life Adolf Hitler encountered the virulent form of anti-Semitism is not clear. He could have come across it in youth because an extremist nationalist group in Linz published a regular flysheet *Die Linzer Fliegenden Blätter* which certainly attacked 'the Jews'. He is unlikely to have come across it at secondary school, where he had a few Jews among his fellow pupils. The school, of course, was entirely German in-language and character.

27

The pupils were classified according to national origin and to religion. At one point while Hitler was there, the breakdown on nationality was 323 Germans, four Czechs, one Serb and one Italian; the religious breakdown was 299 Roman Catholics, fifteen Jews, fourteen Protestants and one Greek Orthodox. All the fifteen Jews were classified nationally as German. According to his own recollection, Hitler did not regard his Jewish schoolfellows as alien; it was only when in Vienna he came across non-German Jews that his anti-semitism arose.

Also according to his own recollection in *My Struggle*, Hitler was enthralled at the Linz secondary school by the history master, Professor Dr. Leopold Pötsch, who took Germanism back to the old Teutonic tribes. But his actual marks in history were un-distinguished and in *My Struggle* he spelled Pötsch's name in-correctly. Pötsch wrote to him in 1929, when he was becoming famous, to point out the incorrect spelling and to ask for an autographed copy of the book to be handed down as a treasured possession in the Pötsch family. Hitler replied in fulsome terms. A few years later, however, Pötsch was refusing to supply a picture of himself for a National Socialist commemorative album.

In all probability, however, Hitler's real life in early adolescence was not at school but in organising gang games among younger boys back at Leonding. He was an enthralled reader of Karl May, a skilled writer of boys' thrillers on cowboys and Indians. May's books, although frowned on by most schoolmasters, had a vast popularity and Hitler was addicted to them. The actual picture of the United States was false—May had never been there—but the stories were full of adventure and violence. Hitler used May as a source for his gang games and far into his adult life used to return to him for light reading; as Chancellor of Germany he was still, on occasion, relaxing with a Karl May book. A further scenario for the games came from the South African War of 1889–1901 in which Great Britain conquered the Boer republics of the Transvaal and the Orange Free State in conditions akin to the American wild west. Most Germans sympathised with the Boers, seeing them as a gallant little Teutonic people resisting the greedy English, and Hitler at twelve and thirteen obviously followed the progress of the war and the exploits of the Boer commandos. In the closing stages, the British coined the term 'concentration camp' for the camps into which they penned the Boer rural population in order to subdue it. There was a high death rate in the camps, through disease, and stories of British atrocities spread across the world. The leader of the opposition in the British House of Commons referred to the camps as 'methods of

28

barbarism'. In setting up his own detention centres, Hitler was deliberately to copy the British term 'concentration camp' and he always got impatient when the British tried to lecture him about moral principles; he saw the British Empire as a perfect example of how the ruthless use of power could achieve success. Interestingly, although he was leading younger boys in war games, there exists no evidence that the adolescent Hitler was a bully or ever committed a deliberately cruel act. He got boys to follow him because he fascinated them with his inventive ideas.

His father, old Alois, must have been disappointed with his poor showing at school and so the tension at home increased. To every complaint, Hitler replied that he was going to be an artist and he began to retreat into a fantasy world. Then, very suddenly, Alois at the age of sixty-six dropped dead from a pleural haemorrhage. This happened just after Christmas 1903 when Hitler was thirteen and when he saw his father's body he burst into uncontrolled weeping. Evidence of Alois's standing comes from a 300-word obituary of him published in the *Linz Daily Post,* which had the largest newspaper circulation in Upper Austria. It began 'Today we have buried a good man' and went on to describe Alois as 'a progressively minded man through and through', with a 'cheerfulness amounting to positive good humour'. He had been 'universally well-informed' and 'able to pronounce authoritatively on any matter that came to his notice'. The obituary concluded: 'All in all, Hitler's passing has left a great gap.'

There seem to have been some similarities between father and son. Both were restless, clever and ambitious. Alois had the greater self-discipline, Adolf the greater imagination. But in later years Adolf Hitler came to look back on his father with some embarrassment. This was not just because of the Jewish story but also because of the probably incestuous nature of his parentage. Hitler quite often reminisced, fondly, about his mother but rarely mentioned his father and then without affection. On at least one occasion he implied that his father had been a drunkard. This was untrue; Alois liked his glass of wine, and to read a newspaper or hold a conversation over it, but he could not have risen as high as he did had he habitually taken too much alcohol. In 1921, in an autobiographical note, Hitler said his father had been a 'postal official'. This pointless untruth must have reflected the tensions he felt. The age-gap was big. Adolf saw relatively little of his father before the latter's retirement and thereafter, probably, rather too much of him. Alois must have been disappointed over his son's later school performance and would have voiced this, probably in such terms as to provoke such a personality as Adolf into further rebellion rather than conformity. It is worth noting that Adolf's elder half-brother, Alois (junior) had definitely quarrelled with Alois (senior), left home and become a drifting semi-criminal failure, serving prison sentences for theft and bigamy. Alois (senior) would obviously have felt anxiety lest Adolf went the same way.

Alois left his family in a secure financial condition. They owned their own house at Leonding and Klara Hitler received a lump sum gratuity from the civil service, plus a continued pension at half the rate her husband had been receiving, plus extra allowances for her children Adolf and Paula. Thus the family was able to continue with the same lower middle-class standard of living as before and there was no question of poverty. However the disappearance of the authoritative Alois obviously altered the balance of the household. On occasion, when she wanted to emphasise a point, Klara would point to her dead husband's pipes, still there on the shelf, as if they exuded authority. But for practical purposes the wilful young Adolf was more effective than a dead man's pipes and he had little difficulty in getting his way with his mother. He dominated her as his father had done before him.

At school he continued to do badly. At the end of his third year he failed again in mathematics and had to sit an extra examination before being allowed up into the next form. The following year, 1903–4, he failed in French and again had to sit a special examination. Having passed it, he left the Linz school.

Exactly why Hitler left is not clear. A legend, spread twenty years later by his political opponents, is that he was expelled for the blasphemy of removing a consecrated wafer from his mouth at a school communion service and putting it into his pocket. There is no satisfactory evidence for this and so it must be regarded as an improbability. Hitler's attitude to religion at this time seems to have become one of bored indifference; his mother insisted on him being confirmed at Linz cathedral at the age of fifteen and he was sulky about it, rushing off immediately afterwards to play with his gang. A rather better explanation is that he was required to leave the school because of the generally low standard of his work but even this is not conclusive; while his standard was low, he had managed to scrape through in all subjects except French and even in French he had passed the special examination. Possibly the young Adolf, well able to persuade his mother to agree to what he wanted, simply felt like a change of scene. One of his teachers at Linz, Professor Dr. Theodor Gissinger, who taught science, later recalled: 'He was slender and erect, his face pallid and very thin, almost like that of a consumptive, his gaze unusually open, his eyes brilliant.' Another, Professor Dr. Eduard Huemer, who had taught him German and French for three years, gave a more detailed recollection. 'Hitler was certainly gifted, although unevenly, but he had little self-control and, to say the least, he was reckoned to be intractable, arbitrary, dogmatic and hot-tempered and he certainly found it difficult to fit into the framework of a school. Nor was he industrious for else his in-contestable abilities could have achieved much better results.'

Hitler felt that at the Linz secondary school his abilities had not been appreciated and one of his favourite themes in later years was the incompetence of schoolmasters. 'Their one object,' he remarked in 1942, 'was to stuff our brains and turn us into erudite apes like themselves. If any pupil showed the slightest sign of originality, they persecuted him relentlessly.' Such a critique of the Austrian educational system of the time was not im-possibly wild of the mark. Had Hitler in his early teens enjoyed the fortune of meeting a sympathetic schoolmaster who had taken an interest in him and unlocked his talents, his career might have developed wholly differently. He was far from unique among prominent men in having done badly at school—Winston Churchill's record at Harrow was as dismal as Hitler's at Linz. Joseph Stalin and Benito Mussolini, however, performed well as schoolboys.

The fifteen-year-old Hitler transferred to another modern secondary school at Steyr, fifteen miles away, where he lived in lodgings. The change of scene was no good at all and, indeed, was probably an additional handicap. He dropped French al-together and at the end of the year he failed in mathematics and German. His best subjects were gymnastics, in which he was marked 'excellent' and drawing, in which he was marked 'good'. In physics he was 'very satisfactory' and in geography, history and chemistry 'adequate'. For diligence he was marked 'irregular'. His failure in the basic subjects of German and mathematics meant at best his taking a recapitulation examination and at worst his having to sit back another year in the same form. Rather than go through this, Hitler, aged sixteen, decided to leave school altogether with no secondary education qualification. Un-doubtedly there would have been a row about this with Alois, had he still been living, but Adolf was able to persuade his mother that it was best for him to study at home, preparatory to entering the art academy at Vienna at eighteen. By his own account, probably embellished to make an amusing anecdote, the end of his stay at Steyr was a humiliating one. He got drunk

31

with some of his fellow pupils on the last day and used his examination certificate for toilet paper. In the morning, with a hang-over, he regretted what had happened and decided to apply to the principal for a duplicate certificate. But somebody had picked up the ruined original and returned it to the school. On arriving in the principal's room, Hitler received a lecture which crushed and humiliated him. Never in his life again, by his own account, was he drunk and by his thirties he had become a teetotaller.

2

At sixteen, on leaving school, Adolf Hitler entered a further period
of failure which absorbed most of his youth and lasted until his
enlistment in the German army at the age of twenty-five on the
outbreak of World War I. He had no sense of direction, no
outside guidance and no conception of how to apply usefully his
undoubted talents of imagination and retentive memory. In his
early twenties he became a positively unhappy man; perhaps it
was evidence of his will-power that he kept going at all. He was,
by his own choice and taste, a social outsider.

Certainly at sixteen he was an odd young man. He lived with
and on his widowed mother at Linz, neither earning a living nor
receiving any regular form of education. He may for a period
have gone to a private art school over the German border at
Munich but this is not certain and could not have been for long.
There was some suggestion that his health was poor and he was
suffering from a lung ailment and he was certainly a thin youth,
with a pinched look about his face. On the other hand he had
been marked 'excellent' at gymnastics at school—it had been his
best subject. Perhaps the illness was hypochondria. He was a
temperamental, artistic young man, filled with compulsions and
drives. He was now more determined than ever to become an
artist and his excuse for staying apparently idly at home was that
he was studying to enter the Academy of Art at Vienna.

From having been a gang leader in his early teens he had
changed quite abruptly to being a reserved intellectual. He dressed
carefully, even fussily, and carried a walking stick with an ivory
knob on it. He brushed his brown hair carefully. People were
just beginning to notice his smouldering blue eyes which were
the most impressive thing about him. He made a fetish of good
manners but mixed very little with other people. He was living in

a fantasy world as his extraordinary imagination tried to find its outlet. His immediate family circle consisted now only of his mother and his younger sister Paula. His half-brother Alois, seven years his senior, had left home nine years earlier. Alois eventually married an Irish girl and produced a son, William Patrick Hitler, who was to be something of an embarrassment in the 1930s for his aspersions on the ancestry of 'my uncle Adolf'. (Alois himself turned up in the 1930s as manager of a Berlin restaurant and attracted a lot of customers who wanted to see the Leader's half-brother. Hitler then forbade Alois's name even to be mentioned in his presence.) His half-sister Angela had married in 1904 a customs official called Raubal, whom Adolf Hitler disliked and for no obvious reason denounced as a drunkard. They had a daughter, Geli, who was to become eventually a great love of Hitler's life.

As the undisputed man of the household, Hitler at sixteen and seventeen rose late in the morning. He spent his day sketching and designing buildings—his room looked like an architect's office. Apparently he also wrote poetry, none of which now survives, and designed the cover for a book, which he never wrote, which was to be *The Germanic Revolution* by 'A. Hitler'; the cover bore the swastika emblem. Surviving letters and postcards written by him at this time show him to have been quite extraordinarily weak at grammar and spelling, far below the standard to be expected of a boy who had spent five years at secondary school; in later life Hitler wrote very little, preferring to dictate to a secretary. His passions were buildings and music; equipped with his sketching block and his black poetry notebook, he wandered around Linz, dreaming how it might be rebuilt. While he was certainly never anything approaching a trained architect, he did acquire, with practice, a genuine dexterity in drawing buildings. His powerful memory enabled him to sketch in accurate detail dozens of famous buildings he had seen only in pictures. By the 1920s it was his parlour trick to dash out a pencil drawing of, say, the British Houses of Parliament, while sitting with his friends at a café table. But he rarely attempted the human figure and almost all his work was painstaking copies.

His first acquaintanceship with his other passion, music, must have started with his days as a choirboy at the Lambach monastery. By his teens he was attending the Linz Opera House and becoming fanatically attached to the music of Wagner, which fed and stimulated his dreams. He also came to love Beethoven and Bruckner and, on the lighter side, Franz Lehar. Music for Hitler was far more than a relaxation or an amusement; it was like a drug or a quasi-religious experience, driving him into an ecstatic state. As Leader of Germany he sometimes made his big decisions while listening to music. He had a good musical memory and could whistle, in tune, long passages from his favourite works. At the age of about seventeen he took piano lessons but never mastered that or any other instrument.

It was at the Linz Opera that Hitler first met the only intimate friend of his youth, an upholsterer's son called August Kubizek. They got into conversation at the end of the performance and took to each other. Kubizek was a year older than Hitler but Hitler was the dominating partner and laid down exactly what they should do. He captivated Kubizek and treated him as his audience. Kubizek was fascinated. For three years he knew Hitler better than anyone else did and ultimately, when Hitler had become famous, he wrote his memoirs of the friendship. Unfortunately he is probably incorrect on a number of facts, some of them substantial. However his accounts, as a whole, remain inherently convincing in outline and explain much in the young Hitler that would otherwise be a mystery.

Kubizek found that to have young Hitler for a friend was like having a dozen friends at once. To the world at large, Hitler appeared distant and silent. With Kubizek he was a voluble talker, never at a loss for words on almost any subject. His favourite theme was the grand plan to rebuild Linz but he also laid down the law on music, on social conditions and even on literature. He turned hostile at any suggestion of contradiction but at the same time Kubizek felt that Hitler took a deep personal interest in him and knew exactly what he was thinking. When, eventually, Hitler disappeared from Kubizek's ken, Kubizek felt in a sense relieved and liberated; but looking back in old age, he also felt that his whole subsequent life had been pallid in comparison.

Hitler arranged Kubizek's career. Kubizek was apprenticed in his family's upholstery business but he was keen on music and Hitler insisted that he should become a professional musician. Hitler, with his power of persuasion, eventually got Kubizek's family who had formerly been hostile to the idea to agree to send him to study music in Vienna. Meanwhile the two young men went on endless walks around Linz and into the surrounding countryside, Hitler reciting his own poetry, dashing off a quick drawing in his sketchbook, or going on about one of his hobby horses. He had a contempt for dancing. He hated the sight of army officers, whom he regarded as idle and effeminate. Any mention of the word 'civil servant' set him off on a tirade of abuse, although at the same time he was insistent on the fact that he came from a respectable family and that his father had been a man of standing. He was highly strung and never made a joke, beyond occasionally mimicking Kubizek. He already had some anti-Semitic prejudice and remarked, when they passed the small Linz synagogue: 'That does not belong here.'

Two of Kubizek's anecdotes throw important light on Hitler's thought-processes. They have little to do with how he managed to win political power but they vividly illustrate how his mind worked.

The first is the episode of the lottery ticket which happened in 1906, when Hitler was seventeen. It came to Hitler that he and Kubizek were destined to win a big prize in the state lottery. He chose the number of the ticket with care and reckoned that for the scheme to work he and Kubizek must pay exactly half each for it. The ticket bought, he put it inside his poetry note-book and constructed a dream world in which they were to live when the prize came. By Kubizek's account, this dreaming went beyond normal hopes of a gambling win. Hitler took it completely for granted that they would win and made detailed plans. He selected a house in Linz, overlooking the Danube, in which he and Kubizek were to live. At one end of the house Kubizek would have his music room and at the other Hitler would have his studio; in the middle would be a reception room where they would hold elegant soirées. They would make a point of dressing exactly alike. They would have a mature woman as a housekeeper to look after them. Several months every year they would travel around Germany to see famous buildings and pictures and to attend operas and concerts: the idea of travelling any further afield, say to France or Italy, did not form part of the scheme. The dream was shattered when no prize turned up for them in the lottery result and Hitler collapsed in savage rage.

An equally striking fantasy was Hitler's love for a local girl called Stefanie. He and Kubizek had an all-embracing relationship in the sense that neither had any other friends, but there was no homosexual flavour to it and Kubizek found Hitler on the prim side in sexual matters. According to the Russian autopsy on his corpse, Hitler was monorchic, that is he had only one testicle. This is a relatively common defect in a man and has no necessary connection with virility; but anyone who possesses it is, naturally, likely to feel embarrassed and this may have contributed towards Hitler's primness, if he was monorchic.* According to Kubizek, Hitler did not even masturbate. Hitler turned his enormous

---

* Reports survive of detailed medical examinations of Hitler and these make no mention of monorchism. Probably the Russians had the wrong body.

imagination on to Stefanie, a bourgeois girl two years older than himself and of somewhat higher social standing. He and Kubizek used to watch her out walking and Hitler described how he loved her and could see into the depths of her personality. He never spoke to her and Stefanie was unaware of his existence. But, Hitler explained to Kubizek, the moment would come, when he had made his way, at which he would speak to Stefanie and look into her eyes. She would instantly understand him and know that she was to be his wife. He designed a house in renaissance style in which they were to live. When he went off to Vienna, aged eighteen, Hitler wrote Stefanie a letter in which he said he was going away to study and to become a great success; she must wait for his return and then they would be married. It took over half a century before Stefanie, by then the widow of an army officer, first learned from an historian that the author of a crazy, almost forgotten letter she had once received must have been Adolf Hitler.

At eighteen, Hitler came into his inheritance from his father, which was 652 crowns, or about twenty-seven pounds in the exchange value of the time. It would be the equivalent of about two hundred pounds in modern purchasing power, or even more since it would have been ample to keep many a student of those times for a year. (A postman's wage at the time was 60 crowns a month.) His mother, apart from her pension, had capital acquired from the sale in 1905 of the Leonding house and the family had moved to a small flat in Humboldstrasse 31, Linz. It consisted of a kitchen, a living room in which Klara Hitler and Paula slept and a separate bedroom for Adolf. While, of course, there was no question of the family being rich, there was also no question of poverty —Humboldstrasse was in a decent part of Linz. There was just enough money for Adolf, with careful living, to fulfil his ambition of becoming an art student. At the beginning of 1907, Klara underwent an operation for breast cancer and this would have cost about 100 crowns, a heavy expense for her but within her means. Soon afterwards she moved flats to Blütengasse 9 in the Linz suburb of Urfahr; this also was a decent district and Adolf continued to have a room of his own, this time with a view over a garden.

Klara was mortally ill with cancer and her spinster sister Johanna, a retired domestic servant and a hunchback, moved in to look after her until her death on December 21st, the same year. There is some suggestion that Klara had a capital of 3,000 crowns which before her death she divided between Adolf and Paula (Angela Raubal being the latter's trustee) so as to avoid estate duty, but no records exist to confirm this.

On Hitler's attitude to his mother's illness there is a flat contradiction of evidence which cannot be resolved. In September 1907, three months before her death, he set off to Vienna to become an art student and this could be taken as being callous; yet obviously the possibility exists of a fond mother not wishing to spoil a son's career and her minimising her illness and urging him to stick to his plans. On Kubizek's version, Hitler was devoted to his mother, carried her picture always with him and returned home from Vienna to look after her the moment he realised she was dying. Kubizek is graphic on the point and describes how he personally saw Hitler nursing his dying mother and going down on his hands and knees to scrub the floor. But according to evidence gathered from neighbours long after the event, Hitler did not return home from Vienna until the day after his mother died and it was Johanna who had done any necessary floor-scrubbing. The contradiction is complete and it is an historically unfortunate one because either version would be useful evidence on the eighteen-year-old Hitler's character. If one has to plump for one version or the other, possibly Kubizek's is the sounder.

Hitler certainly now acquired a pension as a civil servant's orphan. He and Paula between them, were entitled to half the rate their mother had been receiving so long as they were being educated, up to a maximum age of twenty-four. The rate worked out at 300 crowns a year each, equivalent to twelve pounds, or in modern purchasing power at least one hundred pounds. This was scarcely enough in itself to live on, except possibly in the most straitened conditions, but Hitler certainly also had his patrimony and, probably, also something of his mother's capital.

Thus Hitler was equipped, financially, for an education at the Vienna Academy of Art. This was something to which he had looked forward for years and for which he had prepared himself mainly by self-tuition. The great day of the start of the entrance examination came in September 1907, and Hitler seems to have taken it for granted that he would pass. Standards, however, were rigorous. Hitler was one of 113 candidates for entry. The first stage of the examination consisted of two sessions of three hours each in which the candidates had to make pictures from various alternative subjects put to them—the subjects included such things as 'Spring', 'Cain kills Abel', and 'The Fairy Tale Teller'. Of the 113 candidates, thirty-three failed this stage of the examination, and so received no further consideration. Hitler was one of the successful ones who was allowed into the second stage, which consisted of him submitting his own portfolio of pictures for examination. Here, like most of the candidates, he failed. The reason given, in his case, was that he did not have enough human heads in his portfolio. Only twenty-eight of the original 113 actually passed into the Academy. Among Hitler's fellow-failures was at least one who went on to become a successful artist.

Hitler seems to have been given, at the Academy, the kindly advice that he should try instead for the School of Architecture. But for this he was not qualified because he lacked a certificate of secondary education—the *Abitur*. To have obtained this, he would have had to have crawled back to the schoolmasters, who he so despised, and submit to their instruction, and this to Hitler was inconceivable. He reacted for a while by pretending that he *had* passed for the art academy—it is unlikely that his mother ever knew he had failed. The situation approached or actually reached his defrauding the pension authorities. His orphan's pension only applied if he were a student and he did not become a student in any regular sense of the term, although he did continue to educate himself. When, at the beginning of 1908 Kubizek came to Vienna as a music student and shared a room with Hitler, it took him months before he realised that Hitler was attending no classes or lectures.

Thus at eighteen, without parents, without job, without school but with a little cash, Hitler launched himself from provincial Linz into cosmopolitan Vienna. He was almost completely isolated—nobody ever wrote to him—and he was under no form of discipline nor had access to any form of advice or guidance. It would be a heady experience for any eighteen-year-old and for a boy of Hitler's intelligence, imagination and self-centredness it could well have been a disaster, and perhaps was. His failure to get into the art academy was probably not too significant in that, given his temperament, he would probably have quarrelled with his teachers and failed to stay the course. He 'studied' on his own, with no system and no consistent idea of what he wanted to achieve. It was to be a further twelve years before he fully realised that his exceptional powers were as a political orator.

Kubizek joined Hitler in Vienna in about February 1908 and they shared a bed-sitting room at Stumpfergasse 9, which was in an unfashionable area near the West Railway Station through which they had arrived from Linz. Hitler, although tied to no course of study, was far from idle. He slept late every morning, long after Kubizek had departed for the music academy. In the afternoons, he strode around Vienna studying the buildings, visiting museums, galleries, libraries, the imperial parliament and scribbling out drawings, plans and various literary projects, including poetry and plays.

Many evenings, with Kubizek in tow, he indulged his passion for the opera, especially Wagner. He would live for days just on bread and milk in order to afford the cheapest standing room at the opera. The great Gustav Mahler, was then conducting, but, according to Kubizek, Mahler's Jewishism made no difference to Hitler's enthusiasm. They saw *Lohengrin* ten times in seven months, plus the *Meistersinger* and *Tristan* several times over. Hitler preferred indifferent Wagner at the subsidiary People's Opera to first-class Verdi at the main Court Opera; of Verdi's works, only *Aida* attracted him. On their return home late in the evening, Hitler, fired by the music, would walk up and down the little bed-sitter and talk away for hours. Kubizek, in bed and hoping to get to sleep ready for his early start in the morning, was not expected to contribute anything to the discussion but just to listen and agree; if he dropped off to sleep, Hitler furiously woke him up again.

At one point, Hitler decided to write an opera of his own, based on the theme of Wieland the Smith on which Wagner had been working at the time of his death. He sketched out a libretto and composed tunes which he got Kubizek to write down and harmonise. Sometimes he woke up Kubizek in the middle of the night with a new piece of the opera and Kubizek had to pick it out on the piano while Hitler sang it. He made charcoal sketches of costumes for it and a grand stage setting. For days he worked furiously at it, scarcely sleeping, as if it had to be ready for imminent production. Then suddenly he dropped the project altogether.

Hitler also had a grand plan for building a new town for the Vienna working class, served by an intricate network of railways. In place of the slum apartment blocks he proposed that every family should have its own house, complete with bathroom. Since he despised drunkenness he could not make up his mind whether or not to include taverns. But he sketched out the whole design on paper and also tried to work out the economics of it; there were to be no landlords and the residents were to run the place as a co-operative. In a way it was a prevision of the great working-class dwelling blocks which were the achievement of the Vienna Social Democrats in the 1920s.

In this fantasy, conceived at the age of eighteen and nineteen, Hitler was crossing the border between architecture and politics, realising that the former depended much on the latter. He was primly bourgeois in his outlook in that he had an inbred aversion to anything, which in English lower middle-class terms of the time would have been called 'common'. He was presumably the more sensitive on the point because his family, after all, had been none

too distant from the dividing line with the 'common' people. Like
his father before him, Hitler made something of a point of using
loan-words from other languages in his speech. This gave him a
superficial air of sophistication, but a forced one that could grate
on the truly-educated. Hitler in power was to order that foreign
words brought into the language should be spelled in German as
they were pronounced. Perhaps this reflected some embarrassment
he had suffered himself. Hitler took pains to keep himself clean
and to look after his clothes, pressing his trousers under his
mattress every night. But the glaring discrepancies in Vienna, as in
every other European capital of the time, between extreme wealth
and extreme poverty obviously aroused a form of social conscience
in him, the more especially as his own income was a narrow one.
From his standing place in the opera, he could see the rich and the
nobility with their evening dress, jewels and comfortable seats. In
his walks through the city he saw the slums and the destitute. It,
however, scarcely occurred to him to become a left-wing revolutionary or to think, in Marxist terms, of a future belonging to the
working class to the exclusion of his own. From the beginning he
took the view that the Social Democratic Party, which was growing
into the major working-class force in Vienna, was led by 'agitators',
many of them 'aliens'. He grew into the view that it was the task
of German nationalism to abolish social evils, both in order to win
the support of the masses and to build a viable national spirit;
patriotism alone was not enough.

According to Kubizek, Hitler in these first Vienna days was an
eager visitor to the public gallery of the imperial Parliament,
which from 1908 onwards was elected on universal adult male
suffrage. It was an ineffective body in that the government was
not responsible to it and so the party leaders never felt the
responsibility of office. Hitler's bias was probably already anti-
democratic and the sight of the deputies shouting at each other
and banging their desks increased his contempt. But, according to
Kubizek, he mastered the technicalities of parliamentary procedure
and sat through speeches in Czech, making Kubizek do the same,
although both understood scarcely a word. According to Hitler in
My Struggle, the sound of Czech being spoken in Parliament, in
the German Hapsburg capital, aroused his utmost disgust against
the regime. He had a habit of spitting out the word 'Czech' as if it
were an obscenity and his eagerness to believe anything bad about
the Czechs was a significant factor in his policies of 1938.

At the end of his first year in Vienna, when he was aged
nineteen, Hitler apparently began to run short of money. He still
had his orphan's pension, of course, and this meant he had no

need actually to starve; half of it would have been enough to pay for a bed for a year in a cheap hostel and the other half would have sufficed to buy him a meal a day in a charitable soup kitchen. But when Kubizek returned to Vienna in September 1908, ready to continue sharing lodgings, he found that Hitler had vanished. The best explanation must be that Hitler was ashamed of his poverty. Kubizek went on to become a working professional musician and later a civil servant but found that his life, compared with his days with Hitler, became 'so ordinary, so boring'. There was no further contact between the two men until 1933 when Kubizek wrote to Hitler to congratulate him on becoming Chancellor of Germany. Hitler wrote him a friendly note back, saying he well recalled their friendship and this is a useful underpinning of the basic truth behind Kubizek's narrative, whatever its defects in detail. Kubizek neither asked nor received any special favour from Hitler as Leader of Germany; Hitler did, however, out of the blue once send Kubizek's mother a food parcel during World War II.

Between the ages of nineteen and twenty, Hitler underwent a degree of hardship in Vienna. He moved rapidly from lodging to lodging and sank for a moment to a doss-house, his pension keeping him from total destitution but not being enough to dress him in the bourgeois manner he liked or to run much to visits to the opera. By his own account he was still 'studying'. In 1909, in registering himself at a lodging, he gave his occupation as 'writer'. With this straitened income it would have been natural for him to take a job, although he was qualified for little beyond unskilled labour. (He would, though, have made an excellent tourist guide due to his detailed knowledge of Vienna public buildings.) By his own account he did for a while take a job on a building site but quit rather than join the trade union. By the 1930s he was, on occasion, harking back to his experiences in 'the building trade' as proof that he understood the lives and problems of the manual workers. He was never, as was often stated in his lifetime, a house-painter. But he was certainly a frustrated young man with no idea of how to harness the exceptional abilities he possessed, and quick to feel every slight to his dignity caused by his shortage of cash.

Before his twenty-first birthday, however, Hitler had managed to establish himself in a respectable men's hostel in the Meldemannstrasse. It was a form of cheap hotel, restricted to single men with an income below 1,500 crowns a year—about sixty pounds in the exchange value of the time. A cubicle with four square metres of floor space and an iron bedstead cost 2·50 crowns a week—about 12p (30 cents) in the values of the time, with meals and baths extra. It had room for 544 men and they were a mixed lot, ranging from army officers, clerks, shop assistants and salesmen to a quota of small-time crooks. Hitler lived here for over three years, his life regulated by the house rules which included no spitting, except into the spittoons provided, no standing on beds, no more than one man in a bath at a time and no spirits to be brought on to the premises. There was a games room, with chess, draughts and dominoes, a reading room, where Hitler painted, and kitchens in which the men could prepare their meals. Obviously it was quite an austere place, and it had been erected by public subscription, but for a 'student' aged twenty it was an adequate home. During his years in the hostel, Hitler would have met a wide cross-section of men and it would seem safe to assume that he encountered more Kubizeks whom he could fascinate with his conversation.

Hitler received at this time some financial help from his Aunt Johanna, who dipped into her savings for him. When she died in 1911 she left 3,800 crowns—about one hundred and fifty pounds in the exchange value of the time—and most of this went to Hitler. But she had also assisted her nephew during or before 1910. Apart from such gifts, Hitler at twenty or twenty-one was beginning to scratch an income by producing pictures, in water colour and charcoal, of Vienna public buildings and selling them for a few crowns each. He also drew advertising posters for such products as shoes, bodices and 'Teddy' deodorant. According to *My Struggle* he found that such activity left him plenty of energy to get on with his studies and his ambition was still to become an architect; actually, given his personality, it is unlikely that anything so clear cut could have been in his mind and, anyway, he could never have qualified as an architect in this manner.

Certainly Hitler's earlier ambition to be a great artist had faded— he must have recognised his lack of true talent. His pictures, although correct in perspectives, should have been no more than a hobby for him. He painted them simply to make a living. In later life, when he had the means to use painting as a hobby, he never put brush to canvas and confined his draughtsmanship to sketching outline plans for buildings and fortifications. The only hint that he ever thought of returning to art came once or twice during World War II when, in exhausted musings, he went on about how when he had won the war he would retire to Linz and devote himself to painting pictures.

In Vienna, Hitler used an agent to hawk his work around cafés and taverns, the proceeds being divided fifty-fifty between them. The first such agent, a Hungarian named Hanisch, was probably the man who had put Hitler on to making such a living in the first place, but Hitler soon quarrelled with him, claiming that Hanisch was swindling him. There must have been some justification for Hitler's accusation because he was able to prosecute Hanisch and get him a week's imprisonment. Later Hanisch was to muddy the biographical waters with fictional anecdotes about the young Hitler, mostly showing him in an unfavourable or ridiculous light. Hanisch was unwise enough to stay on in Vienna after the 1938 union with Germany and this time Hitler really got him—he died of 'inflammation of the lungs' shortly after being arrested.

But Hitler was himself on the run from the authorities. Under the conscription law he should have registered for military service in the autumn of 1909, when he was twenty, and reported for training the following spring. There was some check on him at Linz and the police there put against his name: 'Failed to report. Address not known.' However they seem to have been slow moving because it was years before they caught up with him, in spite of the fact that Hitler's various addresses in Vienna were, in the customary way, registered with the police there. Every account of Hitler suggests that he was weak and undernourished at this time, grudging every penny he had to spend on food. Accordingly he could have hoped to get out of military service on purely medical grounds—had he been rejected medically for three successive years, he would have been freed from all liability to serve. Obviously, though, he was so determined not to serve and would not risk the danger of being passed medically. For a man who was to become a fine soldier, serving four years in the front line, winning the Iron Cross first class and being promoted to corporal, this was strange conduct. His motives were, perhaps, in part related to his idiosyncratic way of life which he did not want to give up. He did not want to be disciplined. Also, however, it seems clear that he was motivated politically. Kubizek recalls Hitler raging against the Hapsburg monarchy for betraying German interests and urging him, Kubizek, to evade the draft. (Kubizek ignored Hitler on this and reported for training in the usual manner.) Had, however, the facts about Hitler's evasion of service become publicly known in the Germany of the 1920s they would undoubtedly have been a political handicap to him and might have made all the difference in his squeezing into the chancellorship in 1933. Even though it was only from the Austrian and not from the German army, Hitler had still been a deserter, which was a thing many of his supporters would have instinctively condemned, despite his subsequent war record.

Whatever his resentments against the regime, Hitler continued to draw his orphan's pension for as long as he could, although strictly not entitled to it at all. The rate was fifty per cent of a widow's pension to be divided among the children who qualified. In 1911, when Hitler was twenty-two, his half-sister Angela Raubal, now a widow and with charge of the younger sister Paula, now aged fifteen, apparently applied to the court at Linz for the whole orphan's pension to be allocated to Paula. The court found that Hitler was 'able to maintain himself' and that 'inquiries have revealed that Adolf has received considerable sums of money for the purpose of his training as an artist from his aunt, Johanna Pölzl'. Hitler did not contest this—he would have been on shaky ground had he done so, for he certainly was not in any regular sense a student—and so Paula was awarded the whole pension.

Although by his early twenties Hitler had more or less found his feet in Vienna, he had certainly not achieved success on the sort of scale his personality hungered for and for which he felt himself fitted. He grew actually to hate Vienna, with its mixed population of many nationalities and may well have rationalised his own poor showing by reckoning that he had been done down by 'aliens'. As a white man, especially a poor white man, tends to be much more consciously white in, for example, South Africa than if he were in Paris, so did Hitler feel much more consciously 'German' in Vienna than he would have done back in Linz or in Germany itself. He was a man to build enormous hypotheses on a most limited selection of facts; indeed this lifelong habit was part of his skill as a political populariser. In 1913, when he was twenty-five, he decided to renounce mongrel Austria–Hungary altogether and to seek success in his true spiritual homeland, Germany. It is not clear whether or not any specific incident crystallised his decision but there is little reason to doubt that, as he put it in *My Struggle*, his motives were primarily political. At the same time, he seems temporarily to have changed the spelling of his name to 'Hittler': was this just for effect, or did it have something to do with evading the police over the draft? On May 24th, 1913, he caught the train to Munich at Vienna West Station: he was next to see Vienna twenty-five years later when he arrived to a hero's welcome as its political master.

In Munich, Hitler falsely gave his nationality as 'stateless'. This was probably a piece of over-romanticising on his part to stress his renunciation of Austria–Hungary or it could have had something to do with avoiding the Austrian military service for which he was still liable until thirty-six. Indeed by leaving Austria with his military service obligations unfulfilled, he had incurred a possible penalty of a year's imprisonment. At Munich he quickly secured good lodgings at the family home of a tailor called Popp

45

at Schleissheimerstrasse 34. This was quite a good district and Hitler apparently got on well with the Popps and returned to them after his military service in World War I. As in Vienna he made his living by selling architectural paintings. He dashed them off as quickly as he could, solely as potboilers, and this left him plenty of time for reading. It was possibly during this period that he acquired some command of English. There is indirect evidence that Hitler had enough English to be able to read a book. He also improved his school French, but this would have been during his war service. (Hitler stated in later life that he had no 'gift' for languages and he kept to himself what knowledge he had of them.) Of an evening Hitler would discuss politics, the arts and music with the Popps and their friends, to whom he appeared as an emancipated, interesting figure. There was a certain pathos to him which could readily arouse sympathy. He himself, according to *My Struggle*, felt for the first time in his life truly at home in the beautiful and truly 'German' city of Munich; indeed he went so far as to antedate his arrival by a year.

But only seven months after his arrival in Munich, there came a shock from the past. On January 18th, 1914, the Munich police, acting at the behest of the Austrian authorities, called at the Popp household with a summons for him to report for military service at Linz two days later. Under German-Austrian treaty arrangements, this was an extraditable matter and it put Hitler really into trouble. He must have taken too little account of slow-moving bureaucracy and assumed that by now he would be safe. However he managed to arouse the sympathy of the Austrian Consul-General in Munich and with his help dashed off a letter asking for the reporting date to be delayed and for the place to be Salzburg rather than Linz because it was nearer. The Consul-General, obviously impressed, forwarded the letter with a covering note referring to 'the man's poverty' and stating that 'Hietler [*sic*] seems very deserving of considerate treatment.'

Hitler's letter on this occasion ran to three and a half sides of foolscap and is one of the few surviving documents that he ever wrote. (Most writings under his name were dictated.) It is worth quoting from at some length as an indication of his character under crisis at the age of twenty-five. One point that clearly emerges is that whatever his political motivation may have been over refusing military service, he was not going to make a point of it. At a later stage, when he had become politically active, he might well have claimed martyrdom. Now, however, he just sought to excuse himself. The style is eloquent and dramatic with some of the flavour of his later speeches; the phrase 'oh no!' which occurs in it was to be one of his trade marks in his early public speaking days and occurs also in *My*

Struggle. But the grammar of the letter is bad and it contains several misspellings.

... I earn my keep as a free-lance artist, being completely without private means (my father was a civil servant), I do so merely to be able to continue my studies. I can devote only a fraction of my time to earning a living as I am not yet past the training stage as an architectural painter. So then [misspelled] my income is only very small, just large enough for me to make both ends meet.

He goes on to say that he was making about 100 marks a month, about five pounds in the exchange value of the time.

This must not be taken to mean that exactly 100 marks are earned every month. Oh no. The monthly income is very fluctuating and is certain to be very poor just now as art dealing in Munich has its winter sleep at about this time and nearly 3 thousand [misspelled] artists live or at least try to live here.

Hitler goes on to claim that he in fact had registered in February 1910 [this is almost certainly untrue], had paid a fee of one crown and since had heard nothing more. 'It could never occur to me to evade the call-up.' Excusing his negligence for not having registered on the due date in 1909, the letter explains:

For two years I had no other friend but care and want, no other companion but everlasting insatiable hunger. I never learned [misspelled] the meaning of that fine word Youth. Today [misspelled] after five years the tokens are still with me in the form of chilblains on fingers, hands and feet. And yet, now I am over the worst, I cannot [misspelled] recall those days without a certain feeling of satisfaction. Despite the most utter penury, in the midst of often more than dubious surroundings, I have always preserved my good name, am untainted before the law and clean before my own conscience except for that one omission over the military service report, which at the time was not even known to me.

The Austrian authorities treated him leniently. No penalty was imposed and he was allowed to report, as he had asked, at Salzburg. There a medical examination pronounced him: 'Unfit for combatant and auxiliary duties, too weak. Unable to bear arms.'

Hitler returned to Munich and began to settle down as an interesting local intellectual with a talent for he knew not what.

3

Adolf Hitler was fortunate to survive World War I, in which he fought almost from beginning to end as an ordinary soldier on the Western Front. He was twice wounded and won the Iron Cross first class, an exceptional distinction for someone of his rank and enough in itself to make him a minor war hero. The List Regiment, in which he served, had an establishment of 3,500 men at any one time; during 1914–18 it lost 3,754 killed. Hitler's survival in such conditions must have strengthened his sense of destiny and it was also to have propaganda value in his later political career. He was to appear as 'the unknown soldier' who in some mystical sense represented Germany's two million war dead. Hitler as a political leader was the direct creation of World War I, both in the effect the war had upon his own personality and in it being part of the cause of social conditions which suited his type of policy and leadership.

Hitler, an Austrian citizen, specifically volunteered to fight for Germany. He had evaded Austrian conscription and at the beginning of 1914 had been pronounced by an Austrian medical board to be a weakling, incapable of bearing arms. His motivation can only have been political—he had embraced Imperial Germany with a convert's love. World War I aroused enormous public enthusiasm in most of the combatant states, particularly Germany and Britain, and millions of men were happy to fight and willing to risk death. Being a man of exceptionally strong imagination, Hitler rallied even more fiercely than most to the cry that the Fatherland was in danger. In *My Struggle* he describes how he went down on his knees in tears of thanksgiving when he received a letter giving him permission, as an alien, to join the Bavarian army; perhaps he over-romanticised the incident but there can be no doubt that it accurately represented his general attitude.

Further, his career up to that point had far from fulfilled his ambitions; for such a man, war and the possibility of death or glory can come as an apparently providential new opportunity. He appears to have had no medical difficulty in being accepted, which is somewhat surprising in view of the Austrian verdict of his incapacity previously. The improvement would seem to show he must have found a degree of prosperity in Munich, with good meals from his landlords the Popps, who liked him and to whom he wrote from the front. But given Hitler's unusual personality, there was probably also some psychosomatic side to it. The Austrian doctor had found nothing organically wrong with him, only general weakness; with his will-power and ability as an actor, Hitler could well have appeared either weak or strong according to his motivation.

The Bavarian army, in which Hitler enlisted on August 10th, 1914, was part of the Imperial German army under the supreme command of the emperor. He joined the 16th Reserve Infantry Regiment, a volunteer unit often called the List Regiment after the name of its first commander. Many of its recruits were academics and intellectuals and Hitler, noted from the start for his energetic manner, fitted in well. After two months' training, the regiment went to the front in Flanders, Hitler, by his own account, carrying a pocket edition of Schopenhauer in his knapsack. Hitler became a despatch-runner, noted for his reliability and courage in carrying messages, often under fire. Already in December 1914 he was awarded the Iron Cross second class. He threw himself passionately into his work, welcoming the framework of discipline. 'The only period,' he remarked in 1941, 'when I had no worries was the six years of my life as a soldier.' He explicitly related war to sex. 'The revelation that her encounter with her first man is for a young woman, can be compared with the revelation that a soldier knows when he faces war for the first time. In a few days, a youth becomes a man.' At last young Hitler had found something real and useful to do and it is easy to imagine him quivering to attention, eyes shining, as he received some word of commendation from an officer. He had no patience with the routine grumbles of the ordinary soldier and reproved malcontents with speeches about the glory of coming victories. He kept a close eye on the way the regiment was being run—by his own account he induced his commanding officer to issue orders that only urgent messages should be carried by daylight in the front line and that non-urgent ones should wait until darkness, thus reducing casualties among the despatch runners. Nearly twenty years later he and the British Anthony Eden discovered in dinner conversation that at one point in the war they had fought directly opposite each other at La Fere on the river Oise. Eden had then been a staff officer. He was astonished to discover that the ex-corporal Hitler's recollection of troop dispositions and the terrain was as good as his own. In the only occasion on which he was ever a house-painter he designed and executed a decor for the officers' mess. There is an account of him sleeping in a trench, awakening suddenly with a nightmare that he was being buried alive and scrambling out; seconds later a shell hit where he had been lying.

Unlike most ordinary soldiers, Hitler drew strongly political lessons from the war. He saw it as an opportunity to 'purify' his adopted country. As early as February 1915, he was writing to a Munich acquaintance:

I think often of Munich, and every one of us here has only one wish, that it may come to a settling of accounts with the rabble . . . that by the sacrifices and agonies which hundreds of thousands of us endure every day, that by the river of blood that flows here daily against the international world of enemies, not only Germany's external enemies will be smashed, but our domestic internationalism be broken up. That would be more than any territorial gains. In the case of Austria, things will happen as I have always said they would.

(Presumably, here Hitler was predicting the break-up of the Hapsburg monarchy and the union of German Austria with Germany.) Other letters by Hitler from the front, at around this time, give a vivid, although in some cases exaggerated account of the fighting—he gave casualty figures far in excess of the real ones. Perhaps he was anxious to drive home to the civilians the lesson that the war was a terrible one and that he had been frequently near to death. Or, more simply, he might have lacked correct information and relied upon rumour. Describing a moment while his unit waited in a forest before going into action for the first time, Hitler wrote:

Before us, four big guns are dug in. Behind these, in great dug-outs, we take up our position and wait. Now the first shrapnel comes storming over us and bursts at the edge of the forest and rips trees as if they were wisps of straws. We watch inquisitively. We have so far no real apprehension of the danger. Not one of us is afraid. Each man waits . . .

Of course it is a seeming paradox that whereas in World War II

Hitler was to be supreme commander, with for a moment such success that he seemed to be a second Napoleon, in World War I he rose only to lance-corporal. However the qualities required of a general are by no means identical with those required of a junior commander. Also Hitler achieved command by solely political means and skill at popular political leadership is different from the skills that bring military promotion. Then, too, in World War I Hitler was an alien of undistinguished social background and with no educational qualification; even in the relaxed social standards of wartime, he was a far from obvious candidate for a commission. (He grumbled much that school teachers were automatically commissioned whereas he was not.) Given his long service, his ability and his excellent record he might have been expected to get up to sergeant, as Benito Mussolini did, and the reason he failed to do so is not entirely clear. He was a bit of an oddity:—he did not join in the ordinary soldier's off-duty relaxations of drinking and womanising, he seemed to get no letters or parcels from home, he never applied for leave—and perhaps it seemed best just to keep him in the despatch-runner's job which he carried out so well. However, he made some friends. To a fellow artist in the ranks he confided that he was undecided whether he would return to painting, if he survived the war, or make an attempt at politics. He became friendly with his company sergeant-major, Max Amann, who later became business manager of the National Socialist Party and through this, ultimately, the head of Germany's biggest newspaper and book publishing enterprise. His company commander, Captain Fritz Wiedemann, was to become, in a strange reversal of roles, Hitler's personal adjutant at the Reich Chancellery in 1933. Rudolf Hess, the later Deputy Leader of the National Socialist Party, served for a while as an officer in the List Regiment but he and Hitler did not then actually meet each other. By his own account, Hitler's principal companion in the trenches was his sheep dog, Foxl, which he claimed to have taken over from the British when it strayed from their lines. Hitler and Foxl were inseparable until the introduction of gas warfare made it impossible to take it into the front line.

After his initial Iron Cross second class, Hitler went on to gain the Military Merit Cross, a regimental citation for outstanding gallantry and the Service Medal. On October 5th, 1916, he was wounded in the leg and for the first time left the front and returned to Germany for medical treatment. In *My Struggle*, he describes his emotion as the train crossed the frontier and he saw the first German-style houses with gabled roofs. But it was not on the whole a happy homecoming. Like many soldiers returning

from the Western Front—the feeling was common among both sides—he felt that civilians did not really understand what war was like and knew nothing of the agony of prolonged trench warfare. The Western Front was a world of its own and civilians did not understand what the soldiers were suffering on their behalf. Hitler spotted malingerers and profiteers everywhere and among them kept detecting 'Jews', a term he used loosely. 'The offices were occupied by Jews. Almost every clerk a Jew and every Jew a clerk', he writes in *My Struggle*. The German economy itself was under Jewish domination—'The spiders began slowly to suck the people's blood from the pores.' Actually every available statistic suggest that the German Jewish community was indistinguishable from any other religious or cultural group in the quality of its war service: the Jewish Walther Rathenau, in charge of supplies at the War Ministry, mobilised the German economy for war with unparalleled efficiency. A Jew had been the writer of the popular, propagandist war hymn: 'God punish England.'

After hospital treatment at Berlin—his first visit to the imperial capital—Hitler was posted to Munich with the replacement unit for his regiment. Not surprisingly, he, a veteran from the front, found the quasi-peacetime soldiering here uncongenial. He also, according to *My Struggle*, found a separatist spirit in the barracks, with some soldiers urging that Bavaria should break away from Prussian-dominated northern Germany. This, he saw as a trick of Jewish propaganda—while Prussians and Bavarians struggled against each other, the Jews would steal all Germany. It was with some sense of relief and homecoming that in March 1917 he returned to the front.

Back with the List Regiment, Hitler was promoted lance-corporal and continued his work as the reliable despatch-runner. He took part in the Ludendorff offensive of the summer of 1918, which came near to breaking the stalemate on the Western Front and thus bringing victory for Germany before the fresh forces from the United States had made their full impact. In August 1918, a mix-up in intelligence caused German artillery to bombard the List Regiment and Hitler, under heavy fire, managed to struggle through to them with a message that they were firing against their own side. For this he won his Iron Cross first class, which he wore proudly for the rest of his life. Two months later he was involved in a British gas attack in the Ypres salient and was temporarily blinded. For some weeks his eyes felt like 'burning coals' and he was in doubt over the extent to which he would get his vision back and this, for an artist, must have been especially agonising. Although by the 1930s he was wearing spectacles, in private, for reading, it does seem that for all practical purposes the gas attack left no permanent injury to his eyes. It did, however, affect his throat, giving his voice a not unattractive hoarseness, which stayed with him for life.

While Hitler was in pain in hospital and in doubt about his future eyesight there came what was to him and most German fighting soldiers the amazing and catastrophic news that Germany had capitulated, and that the political structure of the state had dissolved with the abdication of the emperor and the other German royal houses. Like most people who engage in war, the Germans had expected to win. They had already beaten Russia and their lines stood on enemy soil throughout. Now it suddenly appeared that the years of hardship and sacrifice were wasted; so far from Germany vanquishing her enemies, she suddenly stood at their mercy. Hitler, by his own account, on hearing the news buried his head in his pillow and wept. He had given his all but had been let down by incompetent political leadership, by 'criminals' who had betrayed the fighting men in the field. At this moment, he decided to become a politician.

Hitler was posted back with his regiment to Munich which, in the same winter of 1918–19 passed under a revolutionary, socialist regime led by Kurt Eisner, a journalist from Berlin and of Jewish descent. In its final stages it became Communist and, in Moscow, Lenin hailed it as 'Soviet Bavaria'. Exactly what Corporal Hitler did in this period is not clear—he certainly did not desert the city to join the anti-revolutionary forces as many soldiers did. Some of his more extragavant opponents in the 1920s were to allege that he had actually become a Communist in this period and some evidence* does, in fact, exist to suggest that he applied, unsuccessfully, to join both the Communists and their allies the Left Socialists. In *My Struggle* he devotes surprisingly little space to the episode of a Communist regime in his own adopted city and this could be indicative of embarrassment. For part of the time he was out of Munich as a guard at a nearby camp for Russian prisoners of war but he was back in the city by the spring of 1919. Eisner had now been assassinated but the Soviet regime had continued in existence, had formed a 'Red Army' for its own defence, and had embarked on wholesale executions of its opponents. Hitler must be presumed to have been a member of this 'Red Army' and to have worn its red armband. (*My Struggle* has an inherently improbable story of the Communists coming to arrest him, but giving up and making no further attempt after he

* Written and verbal statements by two witnesses cited in Werner Maser, *Die Frühgeschichte der N.S.D.A.P.* (Frankfurt-a-M., 1965).

had pointed a gun at them.) In May 1919, regular troops and free corps units, acting with the authority of the Social Democratic republican government in Berlin, entered Munich and, against little resistance, liquidated the revolutionary regime. The 'Red Army' melted away. There followed mass arrests and shootings of Communists and Hitler himself was picked up on a charge of having fired from the barracks at the incoming troops. He might easily have been shot out of hand as yet another 'Bolshevik' had not some officers from his regiment recognised him and testified to his character and war record.

Any flirtation Hitler had had with Communism was now over. The episode, in fact, gave him his first political opportunity. As one who had remained in Munich during the Soviet period, he had first-hand information about what had happened and because of this he was posted to the staff of the military investigation commission into the events of the revolution. It would be reasonable to suppose that he would have been particularly useful in identifying N.C.O.s and soldiers who had sided with the Soviet. After a month he was sent on an army political training course, during which his abilities as a public speaker first began to show themselves.

It was while Hitler was on this course that the new German republic signed the Treaty of Versailles, a hasty document composed in hot blood which, among other humiliations, stripped Germany of thirteen per cent of her territory plus all her colonies, cut down her army to 100,000 men who were to have no tanks or aircraft, and required her to pay staggering war reparations equivalent to thirty-eight per cent of her national wealth. The Versailles system also set up new European states, largely out of the territories of old Germany and Austria-Hungary and Russia-Poland, Czechoslovakia, Yugoslavia. These represented genuine nationalist aspirations but contained tensions from the minorities within them. Versailles was to be the basis of Hitler's political career. The Germans, not unnaturally, hated it, they having not the least disposition to feel that they had been solely responsible for the war and therefore deserving of what amounted to everlasting punishment. When Hitler said that Germany had lost the war only because she had been betrayed by a criminal clique of traitors, and that Germany must restore her self-respect in the world, he was saying things that Germans wanted to believe. (He never, however, preached in favour of a new world war to win everything back.) Undoubtedly while on his political training course, Hitler eagerly and almost masochistically studied the Versailles Treaty and its attendant humiliations. His analysis that

Germany had lacked sound political leadership was correct; Germany had had no Lloyd George or Clemenceau.

At the end of the course, Hitler, still a lance-corporal and still living in barracks, was posted to an 'information commando' which was intended to pick up political intelligence and to propagate patriotic, anti-Communist ideas among the troops. By August 1919, his commanding officer was mentioning in the course of a report: 'Mr. Hitler, I make bold to say, is a born popular orator, who through his fanaticism and his attractive style compels attention and agreement from an audience.' But he was still a junior figure. It was still: 'Hey you, Hitler, come here' when an officer wanted to talk to him.

On September 12th, 1919, on orders from his unit, Hitler attended a meeting in the Sterneckerbräu tavern, Munich, of a group called the German Workers' Party, his mission being to report back on what it was saying and whether it was subversive. The German Workers' Party was one of forty-nine different political groups and parties which existed in Munich at this hothouse time and few knew of its existence. It had been founded nine months earlier by a thirty-five-year-old railway locksmith, Anton Drexler, and the members were mostly his mates from the railway workshops. Its programme was radical, anti-semitic and nationalist. Hitler, in civilian clothes, was one of about fifty people who attended the meeting and, by his own account, he went purely as an observer, with no intention of speaking. However in the course of it, according to *My Struggle*, a professor named Baumann made a speech advocating the separation of Bavaria from the German Reich and its linking up with rump-Austria to form a new south German state. This was the kind of talk which stung Hitler and on the spur of the moment he got up and made a passionate, impromptu speech contradicting Baumann and advocating the unity of all Germans.

The party chairman, Drexler, recognised Hitler's obvious talent and gave him a forty-page pamphlet, *My Political Awakening*, which he had written. Hitler took it back to his barrack room and read it while at the same time feeding crumbs to mice—he said he had so often suffered hunger himself that he could not bear to see hungry mice. While the pamphlet was pedestrian in style and unlikely to have been capable of converting Hitler to anything, it did chime in with his own ideas. In the morning came a postcard from Drexler saying that Hitler had been made a member of the German Workers' Party. By his own account, Hitler was amused at having been elected to membership without even having applied but decided to give them a try. Numbers on the party membership cards ran from 501 upwards and Hitler was allocated 555. Almost immediately Drexler brought him on to the committee and made him the party's propaganda manager.

Although he remained in the army for another seven months—until March 1920—Hitler, aged thirty, became virtually a full-time politician. In these first stages he must, inevitably, have received a degree of army endorsement. The motivation, obviously, was that with his skill at oratory and his apparently proletarian background, he could be more successful than any member of the officer class in swaying the masses against Communism. Of course he was not at this stage in any way a prominent figure and he was acting primarily on his own volition: National Socialism was not invented by the army and Hitler's career in the long run did not depend on the army. His main contact with the Munich army command was the chief of staff, Captain Ernst Röhm, a relatively junior officer who was quick to recognise Hitler's ability and himself joined the German Workers' Party to keep in touch with him.

Hitler's genius transformed the German Workers' Party from an amateur, directionless group into a genuine political force. It was unlikely (though one cannot be really sure) that at this stage he saw himself as the prospective dictator of Germany. However his imagination was already obsessed with the idea of a Germanic 'revolution' to sweep away the democrats, Communists and Jews who, he believed, had betrayed the nation. He proclaimed himself as the 'drummer' of this revolution and believed it was certain to come. The key to it was that nationalism and patriotism were to be no longer merely bourgeois concepts, with the working masses regarded as objects of fear because of their Marxist, internationalist political organisations. The masses were as capable of being as patriotic as anyone else—Hitler was fond of citing how the appeal of patriotism had been overwhelming in the 1914 mass support for the war. Even the Social Democratic faction in the Reichstag, like the Labour Party in the British House of Commons, had voted for the war credits. Hitler would drum up similar mass patriotism in peacetime. The workers must feel that they were an organic part of the national community and this meant they must be allowed social justice. Drexler claimed that as early as 1919 he was already using the term 'National Socialism' to express this and certainly from the beginning Hitler was making an appeal that was simultaneously patriotic and radical. (The actual term 'National Socialist' had been bobbing up in various fringe groups since at least 1896.)

Hitler practised and developed his natural gift for oratory. Traditional nationalist meetings had tended to be dull and academic. Hitler deliberately made them exciting and provocative. He deliberately made himself into a demagogue and exercised his imagination so that he understood what an audience was thinking and what it wanted. The earliest surviving notice of a Hitler meeting runs as follows:

German Workers' Party
Munich Group

Munich, 2 December, 1919

We hereby request you to be sure to attend a meeting
to take place on Wednesday 10 December 1919 at 7 p.m. in the German Reich Tavern, 143 Dachauer Street (tram stop 24 Lori street).
Speaker: Mr. Hittler [*sic*] on 'Germany in her deepest humiliation'.
This invitation serves as a ticket. The hall is heated.
The Committee
A. Josef Mayer
First Secretary 10/3 Andräs St.

Hitler always had an air of sincerity, and at these early meetings, in particular, there was also an air of innocence to him, almost of naivety. It brought out paternal and maternal feelings to see this young war veteran, with the Iron Cross, expressing himself so passionately and with such a love for his country. He was the voice from the trenches. He marched into the meeting room as if stamping on to parade; although he wore civilian clothes he was, with his stiff bearing, his cropped hair and his narrow, trimmed-back moustache, the epitome of an N.C.O. He began his speech standing stiffly to attention, his chin up. When his throaty, deep voice had caught the attention of his audience, he began to relax and to use gestures; he liked to spread out his hands and rock gently from side to side. He used rough humour, often in the form of an imaginary dialogue in which he stated an opponent's case and then answered it. With variations in pace and style, he could hold an audience for an hour or even two hours. He planted questioners in his audience to 'feed' him. It was, really, a form of dramatic performance; both from instinct and experience he learned to get at an audience's emotions rather than to persuade it by a logical chain of argument. Finally he worked himself up into a peroration, his hoarse voice breaking in passion, his arms moving in sweeping gestures; he finished with a command like a whip-lash: 'Germany awake!' The veins on his face stood out, his

57

eyes bulged and he was drenched in sweat. Then he would take a swig of beer (he was not yet a complete teetotaller) and leave the hall as soon as he could. Apart from the fact that he was emotionally drained, he came to believe that it was tactically an anti-climax for a speaker to hang around chatting normally. He cultivated an air of mystery about himself and refused to be photographed.

In about February 1920, presumably on Hitler's initiative, the German Workers' Party expanded its name to Nationalist Socialist German Workers' Party. This was a mouthful and in practice it was generally abbreviated to just National-Socialist or N.S.D.A.P. (Short for *National Sozialistische Deutsche Arbeiter Partei*.) Later it acquired a popular nickname of 'Nazi', just as the Social Democratic Party was called 'Sozi' but this was rarely or never used officially. In its internal structure the party was still democratic, with Drexler as chairman and Hitler working under the committee as propaganda manager. Drexler, a straightforward fanatic of limited ability, was delighted with Hitler as a speaker and was pleased to sponsor his early career.

The party programme, adopted in December 1919 and declared 'unalterable' in 1926, was drafted by Drexler and Hitler, and had twenty-five points. On the domestic side it was very radical and little of it was ever to be implemented in any literal sense— abolition of unearned incomes, nationalisation of trusts, abolition of land rents, communalisation of department stores. It did, however, demand a unified central state to replace the federal Reich and this Hitler was to carry out among his very first actions in power. On the foreign side—union of all Germans in a single Reich and the abrogation of the Versailles Treaty—Hitler was to fulfil it and go far beyond it. In anti-semitism he was also to go far beyond it. The twenty-five point programme proposed to deprive Jews of citizenship and to expel all who had entered Germany since 1914; even the Nuremberg laws of 1935 went beyond this, not to mention the mass extermination policy of 1942–4.

On leaving the army in March 1920, Hitler began again, on occasion, to give his occupation as 'artist' but really he was a full-time politician. His tastes were simple and he was able to live on gifts and free meals from party supporters and on fees charged to hear him speak; he explained that he never charged the National Socialists anything for a speech but felt free to charge fees to other organisations which wanted his oratorical services. The only luxury he yearned for was a motor car, which then, of course, was a considerable item. He loved riding in cars and examining

58

them and built up quite a technical knowledge. He never learned to drive—he came to say that he would like to do so but could not afford, for political reasons, to be involved in an accident—but a second-hand car for Hitler was one of the National Socialist Party's first purchases when it began to prosper: he habitually sat in the front beside his driver and for years insisted on maximum speeds.

Hitler spoke two or three times a week and this in itself, in view of his style, must have been an immense physical and emotional strain. During the day, he often slept late. Then he busied himself with party administration; in the early days he typed out announcements and duplicated them himself. He read quite a lot, picking up material for speeches. Of an evening, he liked to sit in a café with his party friends to whom he was an object of genuine human affection. There was a poignancy to him and sometime an air of unhappiness. Also he could set them off into uncontrollable laughter with his mimicry: one of his set-piece jokes was to recite a poem about himself by an admirer who had used a rhyming dictionary to find as many words as he could ending in 'itler'. For fear of assassination by his opponents, he carried a heavy revolver which distorted the shape of his cheap clothes. He took also to carrying a heavy dog whip, with which, when aroused, he would emphasise his words by striking it on the table. The original reason for the whip was self-defence and he did use it at least once in this way when a group of opponents went for him in a café. Later it became just a personal trade mark, well suited to his political style; he even continued to carry it during his early months as chancellor of Germany.

Nobody as soon as this saw Hitler as a potential chancellor. He was the 'drummer' from the trenches. But by May 1923 he was beginning to drop hints.

In the end the fire of German youth will conquer . . . What can save Germany is the dictatorship of the national will and of the national resolution. And if it be asked: 'Is there a fitting personality to act as leader?'—it is not our task to look for such a person. He is either given by heaven or he is not given. Our task is to sharpen the sword for his use when he appears. Our task is to give the dictator when he comes a people that is ripe for him.

German people, awake! It draws near today!

4

There were two distinct phases in Adolf Hitler's rise to power. In the first, which lasted from 1919–23, he was naive and almost intoxicated with his new-found gift for oratory and political organisation. Conditions around him were chaotic as the new Weimar republic struggled, with no certainty of success, to maintain German unity against separatist movements in Bavaria and the Rhineland, and to build a liberal democratic state against violent challenges from the left, which wanted to 'complete' the revolution by establishing a Soviet Germany and from the right, which wanted to do down the Marxists completely. Not even the frontiers were safe—the Poles in the east and the French in the west both seemed to have territorial ambitions against disarmed Germany. On top of all this was economic chaos which culminated in 1923 with a grotesque monetary inflation which wiped out the savings of the middle class. In such conditions, Hitler hoped for rapid success and he had before him the examples of Benito Mussolini, who won power in Italy only fifteen months after the foundation of his Fascist Party and V.I. Lenin who won control of the Petrograd Soviet only eight months after his return from exile.

The inexperienced, euphoric Hitler found a ground for hope that he, or the type of movement he represented, might sweep quickly to power in a *coup d'état*. In practice, however, he turned out to be no more than a minor nuisance to the regime. This first phase ended with Hitler in gaol, his party in ruins and the Weimar republic rapidly gaining in authority as the Germans, generally, tired of civil disorder. In the second phase, from 1924 to 1933, Hitler, having had the intelligence to learn from experience, rebuilt the National Socialists, as a 'constitutional' party, designed to win power through the republic's electoral system.

At the start of the first phase. Hitler's preliminary task was to convert himself from being merely propaganda manager of the little National Socialist Party into its absolute leader. Although this took him nearly two years, it presented no fundamental problem to him as he was solely responsible for the party's growth and the only leader to give his whole time to it. In September 1919 he had been the fifty-fifth member to join. Five months later, in January 1920, the membership reached 190. Then, as Hitler really got going, it shot up to 3,000 by January 1921. Of course it was still mainly a local Munich group—as late as 1922, for example, Benito Mussolini had never heard of it—but its rate of growth was indicative of vigour and potential and Hitler himself was convinced that he had hit upon a winning formula. Besides the support of Captain Röhm of the Munich army command, it had acquired the sympathetic interest of the Munich police chief, Dr. Ernst Pöhner, and the head of the police political department, Dr. Wilhelm Frick.

While it would be incorrect in any way to characterise the National Socialist Party as the creation of the Bavarian state authorities, its firmly patriotic and anti-Communist stance obviously made the orthodox right-wing regard it as being sound at heart. In December 1920 it bought, possibly with help from army funds, its own weekly newspaper the *Völkischer Beobachter*. This title is translatable into English approximately as the *People's Observer* but the German *'völkisch'* means 'people's' in the sense of a 'folk' or definite national community. From the beginning it was one of the National Socialist catchwords and the noun *'Volk'* was used to signify the whole German people, irrespective of class, religion or political boundaries. Although to begin with the *Völkischer Beobachter* was a small, entirely local sheet—it did not become a daily newspaper until 1923—Hitler's control over it as propaganda manager obviously added further to his authority within the party.

Moreover as already a full-time politician, living frugally on small gifts and from speaking fees, Hitler was always available for party work. He was free to travel to represent the party at conferences of right-wing groups. In August 1920 he represented the Munich National Socialists at a conference in Salzburg of various akin groups from Germany, Austria and Czechoslovakia. He went on a speaking tour in Austria. In a bizarre episode, he went as an emissary of the Munich nationalists to Berlin during the Kapp *putsch*, in which a right-wing group momentarily seized control of the capital and drove out the republican ministers. This episode gave Hitler his first air journey and he wore a false beard lest he should be recognised by Communist or Social Democratic workers on the way. He pretended to be a bookseller. In Berlin, to his disgust, he found himself greeted by the extraordinary

Jewish-Hungarian Trebistch Lincoln, who had once been a British member of parliament and was now acting as a sort of public relations officer for the Kapp conspirators. The *putsch* collapsed quickly as a result of a general strike by the trade unions and Hitler returned to Munich with nothing gained.

A crisis between the increasingly autocratic Hitler and the original party leadership came to a head during the summer of 1921. In its internal organisation, the National Socialist Party was then democratic, its officials and committee being elected by the membership and its policy decided by party congresses. Decisions were taken by vote after debate. Hitler, reasonably, regarded it as an absurdity for a party which denounced democracy as a way of running the country should yet use the despised system in its own organisation. In July 1921, when the leadership defied him over a proposed merger with a group with aims closely similar to those of the National Socialists, Hitler simply resigned from membership. The committee, or some members of it, hit back with an abusive pamphlet, accusing Hitler of wishing to further 'Jewish' interests. 'How does he carry on this campaign? Like a Jew. He twists every fact . . .' But this was mere wind because the National Socialists without Hitler were nothing; at a pinch he could easily have dropped them altogether and started his own party. The party founder, the locksmith Anton Drexler, recognised this clearly. At first he had been opposed to Hitler's dictatorial ambitions but now, decisively, he swung over to Hitler's side, and took the committee with him. Hitler's terms for rejoining the party were that he should become 'first chairman' with almost dictatorial powers. In the last democratic vote in the National Socialist Party this was confirmed on July 29th, 1921, at a special party congress by 553 votes to one. Drexler became the party's honorary president but never subsequently played any substantial role or attracted much attention. Hitler remarked of him, slightingly, that he had been the kind of person who saw a seat in Parliament as his highest ambition in life. He died in 1942.

Besides being 'first chairman', Hitler from the autumn of 1921 onwards began also to be described as 'the Leader' and this soon came to be the standard usage. In German the word was 'Führer' which has rather wider connotations than the English. Besides being a 'leader' a 'Führer' can, alternatively, be a guide or the driver of a vehicle—every tram driver was a Führer; there was thus a dynamism to it, suggesting that Hitler was not just the Leader but also the man who propelled the movement and found the correct paths for it. So far as can be ascertained, no other party in Germany has ever had a dictatorial leader with the authority Hitler was allowed by the National Socialists.

Hitler, now aged thirty-two, had emerged quite suddenly from obscurity into becoming a definite, although minor, political factor in Bavaria, with absolute control of his own, growing party. It is evidence of this early success that for the first time in his life he was now picking up an entourage of friends and admirers, most of whom were to stay with him for the rest of his life. To them he was to be extremely loyal and one of his overriding principles was to try never to let down an old party comrade. He expected loyalty back, uncritical loyalty; the big exception to his rule of looking after old friends was the Röhm purge of 1934, but this caused him agonising hesitation and he was propelled into action only because he believed that Röhm had been plotting against him. Even when Hitler had reached his most remote and most powerful as Leader of Germany, there existed a network of old party members who felt a sense of personal relationship with him and this was one of the props of his regime.

At the beginning, Ernst Röhm was a very central figure. A short, bulky man, part of whose nose had been shot away in the war, Röhm combined a jovial, laughing manner with considerable skill as both an organiser and a politician. He was two years older than Hitler and as a regular army officer had reached the rank of captain. He was a homosexual. After 1918 he had become an important contact man between the Bavarian army command and the various 'free corps' of discharged soldiers, who had fought against the left-wing revolutionaries; he had joined the National Socialists shortly after Hitler, presumably with a view to keeping in touch with what they were doing, and may well have been the channel through which came the army funds to purchase the *Völkischer Beobachter*. He saw Hitler as an excellent speaker and propagandist for the nationalist cause but he never accepted the more mystical view that Hitler was the German messiah, sent especially from heaven. He was more than just an army officer dabbling in politics; he believed in the necessity for a German revolution in which the masses would be won for patriotism through a social concern for their needs. He was quite a good public speaker and might well have made a political career on his own.

While at this stage Röhm was a useful ally rather than a personal friend, others came in more definitely as Hitler's disciples and sponsors. The odd ex-corporal with his awkward charm, apparent innocence and gift for oratory, gathered a very varied bunch of friends, ranging from people of some cultivation and intelligence to outright cranks.

There was Gottfried Feder, six years older than Hitler, who was a qualified engineer and an amateur economist. He had worked out a theory of 'interest slavery' by which, he reckoned, international capitalism held Germany in thrall. Feder believed, apparently quite sincerely, that all Jews in Germany received instructions from abroad on how they could best wreck the German economy. Hitler first met Feder while on his army political course back in 1919 and instantly took to his ideas. As late as 1924 he was still going out of his way to pay tribute to Feder in *My Struggle* and in the early days Feder undoubtedly provided him with material for his speeches. But the pseudo-academic Feder was too cranky a figure to be prominent in the later growth of the party. With the advent of National Socialism to power he got only a minor government job. He bobbed briefly back into prominence in 1940 when he designed quite a good 'war crocodile', a concrete barge to be used for the invasion of the British Isles. He died in 1941.

A crank of rather a different kind was Julius Streicher, a primary schoolteacher in Nuremberg. Streicher, four years Hitler's senior, had founded his own 'German Socialist Party' and it was an important little accession of strength when in the autumn of 1922 he amalgamated it with Hitler's National Socialists and accepted Hitler's leadership. Ugly and bald-headed, Streicher was completely obsessed with Jews. Often violent in his manner, he could on occasion be unexpectedly appealing and charming—one aristocratic English woman visitor of the 1930s characterised him as 'sweet'. He did not care much about the economic side of things but worried endlessly and beyond the point of obscenity about Jewish 'pollution' of the German race. To him this did not mean simply the production of children of mixed parentage, Jewish and Gentile. He believed, apparently sincerely, that the mere act of intercourse between a Gentile woman and a Jewish man would 'poison' the woman's blood. 'With the alien sperm she has also taken the alien soul into her. Even if she marries an Aryan man she can no longer beget pure Aryan children.' His paper, *The Stormer*, which he ran as his own private enterprise, carried week by week lascivious stories, with illustrations, about Jewish men raping 'Aryan' women and Jewish employers ·violating their 'Aryan' secretaries and maidservants. It was a profitable undertaking and Hitler enjoyed reading it; while with the growth of the party Streicher was too silly to be part of the top leadership, Hitler, partly for old times' sake and partly because he had a genuine regard for him, continued to support him despite scandals. Streicher was eventually executed in his own Nuremberg in 1946; he was adjudged a major war criminal on the ground that although his propaganda had never directly advocated the mass-killing of Jews, it had contributed towards a climate of opinion which made it possible.

A quieter figure from the early days was Rudolf Hess, who had been born of German parents in Alexandria and partly because of this and partly because of his looks was sometimes nicknamed 'the Egyptian'. Five years younger than Hitler, he had served in the List Regiment in the war and then qualified as a pilot in the Imperial Flying Corps. After the war he went to Munich University to read history and economics and quickly became embroiled in politics. He joined the National Socialists in 1920 and became one of the first really to accept the idea of Hitler's messianic mission—whenever he mentioned Hitler's name his voice dropped a tone out of respect. While there was a definitely cranky side to Hess—at one period he slept with magnetics over and under his bed to draw off unhealthy emanations—he was a competent, reliable organiser, always loyal. He rose with Hitler and at times they seemed to be so close that he was ridiculed as 'Frau Hess', with the untrue implication that he was Hitler's homosexual lover. Hess outlived nearly all his fellow pioneers of National Socialism but from the age of forty-seven onwards he was continually a prisoner, at first in England, to which he had flown on an eccentric peace mission, and later in Spandau, Berlin, where a quarter of a century and more after the end of World War II he lingered on as the only surviving symbol of wartime four-power co-operation.

Somewhat akin to Hess, but a thinker rather than an organiser, was the dreamy Alfred Rosenberg, four years Hitler's junior. Rosenberg was a Baltic German from Estonia and had qualified as an architect at Moscow University, where he was studying during the revolution. From a distance, he had decided that German nationalism was all-important and he had deliberately migrated to Germany, from which his family had been separated probably for many generations. He went first to Berlin but found the atmosphere there displeasing and in the winter of 1918–19 turned up in Munich where he linked up with the right-wing 'völkisch' group, the Thule Fellowship. Under the sponsorship of the playwright and journalist, Dietrich Eckart, young Rosenberg wrote an anti-Semitic pamphlet, *Immorality in the Talmud,* of which 100,000 copies were circulated. He was an odd young man, whose grasp of spoken German was at first so poor that he was almost incomprehensible, but he had an air of seeming to know everything. One story about him, in this period, is that he worked it out that laundry bills were so high that it was cheaper to wear the same shirt for weeks on end and throw it away when its condition had become impossible, than to keep having it washed. He was still, technically, a Russian citizen. He met Hitler and joined the infant National Socialist Party at the end of 1919 and at once became one of the party's leading ideologists, especially on 'foreign affairs' which, to Rosenberg, meant relations with the east. He had ideas about the German 'racial community', believing that nationalism should be a form of religion ('Soul means race') and more definite ones that the world's troubles in general and the Russian revolution in particular were due to an 'international Jewish conspiracy'. He whistled tunelessly through his teeth as he wrote. His qualification as an architect must have impressed Hitler and his relatively articulate beliefs certainly helped Hitler to form his own ideas.

Like Hitler, Rosenberg enjoyed sitting around at café tables; he was a poor organiser and his idea of action was to write a rousing article in the *Völkischer Beobachter*—'. . . We are the fore-runners of a new age and even if many or all of us should not survive, we will still at our end be able to say: "We have lived, and it was beautiful to live and to fight."' He saw Hitler as a new Luther, although with no Christianity. Rosenberg was executed as a major war criminal at Nuremberg in 1946; he was the only one of the condemned to refuse the services of a chaplain and also the only one to make no final statement on the gallows.

While Rosenberg was to hold nominally high offices under National Socialism in power and was always to retain Hitler's personal friendship, he was not forceful enough to be part of the inner decision-making circle, so far as any such thing existed at all. It was not until 1923 that two of the really major figures of the future came into the party, Hermann Göring and Heinrich Himmler.

Captain Hermann Wilhelm Göring, four years younger than Hitler, stemmed from a Bavarian family high in the upper bureaucracy of imperial Germany; his father had been governor of South-West Africa, then a German colony. He had become a regular soldier, passing through military academy with high distinctions, and had become a major public hero in World War I through his exploits as a fighter pilot. It had been routine war propaganda to build up the fame of the fighter 'aces' with the German public, and photographs of him were widely sold. Besides being an outstanding pilot—he was the first German to take a machine gun into the air and he scored twenty-two victories—he was also an effective leader, capable of raising the morale and performance of the squadrons he commanded. He gained

Germany's highest military decoration, the *Pour la Mérite*, and ended the war in command of the fabulous Richthofen Squadron, internationally the best known unit in the history of aerial warfare. Under the Versailles Treaty Germany was forbidden to have any air force at all and, apart from that, there was no room for Göring in the shrunken army. He was turned into civilian life with no money and he was humiliated when a revolutionary crowd tore off his rank badges and decorations. He became a private pilot, carrying passengers and giving displays. He married a well-to-do Swedish wife called Carin, falling genuinely in love with her. Carin's income came from her wealthy first husband, who in divorcing her to enable her to marry Göring, settled a good allowance on her.

The young Görings arrived in Munich, installed themselves in a comfortable flat, and, in a more or less desultory manner, Hermann began studying at the university with a view to a business career. He was a nationalist and he hated 'Bolshies' but he was not really an ideological kind of man; he dismissed opponents as 'rascals' without bothering about details of the 'international Jewish conspiracy' or 'race pollution'. He was highly intelligent, a natural leader and greedy; when crossed, he could be very rough, but he was more of a normal human being than most of the National Socialist leadership. Had he, rather than Adolf Hitler, become the Leader of Germany, there would have been no World War II, at least in the form in which it took place. He had the peculiarity that his weight and physical appearance varied considerably from time to time. His British prosecutor at Nuremberg was to describe him as 'the most formidable witness I have ever cross-examined'.

Göring joined the National Socialists after hearing a speech by Hitler and was immediately put in charge of organising the party's uniformed stormtroopers. He was an important new asset not only because of his wartime prestige but also because of his abilities. There was a childish side to him but he could be a hard worker and, probably as a result of his experience as a fighter pilot, he was always at his best in a crisis; he never lost his head but came to cool, quick decisions. Whenever anything went wrong, Hitler liked to call in Göring and hear his views; he reckoned that in a moment of crisis Göring's brain seemed to be 'packed with ice'. On his side Göring accepted and propagated the view of Hitler as a miraculous leader; he was capable of standing up to Hitler to the extent of stating disagreement but in the end always accepted Hitler's decision as conclusive.

That such a man could subordinate himself to an ex-corporal is important evidence of Hitler's early ability to win loyalty. Of course the fact that he was a former fighting soldier, with the Iron Cross, was essential in his getting the support of such figures as Göring and Röhm—they would be unlikely to have been much impressed by the drifting pre-war Hitler, the petty artist, or still less Hitler, the evader of military service. But this was only incidental to Hitler's hypnotic appeal. The elderly Englishman, Houston Stewart Chamberlain, who had taken German nationality and devoted his life to dreamy writings about German racial destiny and attempts to prove that Jesus of Nazareth could not have been a Jew, met Hitler at Bayreuth in 1923, at about the same time as Göring joined the National Socialists. Chamberlain, who died four years later, had nothing to hope to gain for himself from Hitler but after the meeting he wrote to him:

You are not as you were described to me; you are not a fanatic. I could almost say the opposite. A fanatic wants to persuade people. You want to convince them, just to convince them—and that is why you succeed . . . Your eyes have hands, they capture people and hold them in their grip . . . Such a man can administer peace to a poor tortured soul. My belief in Germany never wavered, but I confess that my hopes were at a low ebb. You have transformed my state of mind with one stroke. That Germany should give birth to Hitler in her hour of need proves that she is still alive.

It was in this kind of spirit that Hitler could win the allegiance of a Göring; later Göring did well for himself materially out of National Socialism but that cannot have been his original motivation.

But of all Hitler's friends in the early Munich period, the most decisive was that of Dietrich Eckart, twenty-one years his senior. Eckart was quite well known for his plays, poetry and dramatic criticism and his nationalist, patriotic drama *Henry VI* had been a success in Berlin back in 1906. He regarded himself as a disciple of Schopenhauer and Ibsen. He had a tendency to go to extremes in what he did and for a time had been in a mental hospital. He was a gregarious fellow with a walrus moustache, who liked to drink enormous quantities of beer and also to pose as the most typical of Bavarians. With the end of the war in 1918 he became gravely worried about the future of the German 'soul' and started a periodical *In Good German* in which he propagated extreme nationalism and anti-semitism. The point about Eckart was that he was a man of established social position and that he deliberately furthered the careers of young men in whom he believed. Both Hitler and Rosenberg profited from his sponsorship. In particular Hitler, through Eckart, began to become something of a pet in part of the bourgeois society in Munich. People liked to meet this strange orator from the trenches.

Hitler appeared in fashionable houses, looking shy, stiff and charming. It was something quite new to him and he had the over-punctilious manners of a well brought up child, bowing gallantly to ladies and kissing their hands, taking exaggerated care to use the correct formal modes of address—'Herr Doktor Professor', 'Herr Diplomingenieur' and so on. Confronted with an artichoke, he confessed with engaging humility that he had never seen such a thing before and asked how he should eat it. He was noted for his appetite for sweet things; he sugared his wine. With time his manners loosened up somewhat but on social occasions he always had an air of gallantry towards women. He also came to relax his mode of dress; he had assumed that it was correct for him to wear a stiff collar when speaking in public and on social occasions but friends persuaded him that a soft collar was becoming acceptable. Hitler could bring out women's mothering instincts and he was a particular success, among others, with the middle-aged Mrs. Helene Bechstein of the wealthy piano manufacturing family: on occasion Hitler sat with his head in Mrs. Bechstein's lap, while she stroked his soft brown hair. The Bechsteins contributed to party funds, looked after Hitler himself and, above all, introduced him to Berchtesgaden, the alpine mountain resort on the frontier with Austria, where they had a villa. Hitler fell in love with the mountains and so far as ever in his adult life he had a home, it was here.

All this Hitler owed to Eckart's sponsorship. Ever since his adolescence he had been imprisoned in a private dream world but now he was breaking out into reality, commanding acceptance for his ideas, broadening his knowledge. To get material for his speeches he read widely but unsystematically; he took some pride in the fact that rather than read a book as a whole he was capable of extracting from it only the passages that interested him. That a man of Eckart's standing should have faith in him and take a quasi-paternal interest in him was something new for Hitler.

A friend of a somewhat similar type, but of his own age, was Ernst Hanfstaengl, who was six feet four inches tall and ironically nicknamed Putzi, which in Bavarian dialect means 'little fellow'. Hanfstaengl belonged to a cosmopolitan family of Munich art dealers with a branch in New York; he had been educated at Harvard, in the class of 1909, and was married to an American wife. He used to claim that the crashing shouts of 'Sieg Heil! Sieg Heil!' (Victory, hail!') at National Socialist rallies were his invention and that he had based them on the Harvard 'Rah, rah, rah!' at football games. Two years older than Hitler, Hanfstaengl had spent World War I in New York and then returned home to Munich to find Germany in what he regarded as an appalling condition. He was a blatant snob and thought Hitler looked like 'a suburban hairdresser on his day off'. But he was captivated by Hitler's oratory and decided that with a little *savoir faire*, to be provided by Putzi, he might go far. In fact Hanfstaengl, although useful, became little more than Hitler's court jester; he had a boisterous sense of humour and also could delight Hitler by hammering out Wagner on the piano with his huge hands. Hanfstaengl, with some reason, regarded himself as well informed on foreign affairs and he was irritated at Rosenberg going on about the east, and holding Hitler's attention, while his own first-hand knowledge of the United States was treated by Hitler as being of little importance. He was to spend part of World War II in Washington, D.C., as a special White House adviser on German affairs; this was partly because he thought Göring had tried to murder him and partly because he came to disapprove of National Socialism itself.

Hitler's obsessive interest, however, was not making personal friends but building up his party and trying to use it to sway public opinion. The masses were more important to him than individuals. Aided by some suggestions from a dentist member, he personally designed the party's emblems. He chose the colours of black, white and red, those of old Imperial Germany, in preference to the black, gold and red of the Weimar republic and of German traditional liberalism. He placed particular stress on the red; right back from his Vienna days he had recognised the effectiveness of red as a revolutionary colour, capable of heightening people's emotions. The National Socialists, too, should have their red banners. The main party symbol, the swastika, had existed for many centuries with varying significance. There had been a swastika in the coat of arms of the Benedictine monastery at Lambach, where Hitler had been at school, and the British writer Rudyard Kipling was using a swastika as his personal symbol on the title pages of his books. (Hitler's success in identifying the swastika with German National Socialism forced Kipling, to his annoyance, to drop it.) Hitler took it over from the old-style German bourgeois nationalists and went to much trouble to get the balance of it right in his party flag, which he designed with a red background, and a white circle in the middle containing a black swastika. He designed standards with eagles and, under them, the slogan 'Germany awake!'

One of the essentials for any movement of the National Socialist type was a capacity both to defend itself and to take offensive action to break up the meetings of its opponents. Hitler did not invent violence in the German politics of the time; murder and armed conflict were part of the country's ordinary political life in the tumult that followed the 1918 collapse, and both left and right extremists advocated it: the question of which side was the more to blame depends largely on the standpoint of the observer. One computation, made in 1923, is that from 1919 to 1922 the left committed twenty-two political murders and the right 354; the left certainly suffered more in terms of prominent personalities, including the Communists Rosa Luxemburg and Karl Liebknecht and the Weimar ministers Matthias Erzberger and Walter Rathenau. The main atrocity against the right had been the mass shooting of members of the right-wing Munich 'Thule Fellowship' during the soviet regime of 1919.

Hitler plunged himself with zest into this almost civil war situation. He believed as a dogma that nothing short of complete hardness and ruthlessness could win political success; pacifism or tolerance were human weaknesses which ought to be overcome. His four years on the Western Front must have had something to do with this and he developed a form of neo-Darwinism in which he saw all life as a merciless struggle which only the fittest could survive. He also realised, or perhaps came to realise, the sheer propaganda value of a fight in binding his own members together in a common loyalty and of a victory in impressing mass public opinion.

From almost the beginning Hitler began to build up his own private army, at first in dozens, then in hundreds and by 1923 in thousands. They were the Sturmabteilung (Storm Detachment), abbreviated to S.A. The term 'stormtrooper' was that used for the especially selected and trained assault troops who in the Ludendorff offensive of 1918 had managed to break through the allied lines of the Western Front and momentarily had looked like winning the war for Germany. The significance was something like that of the term 'commandos' in Britain during and after World War II. The S.A. uniform, the brown shirt, was more accidental than most of Hitler's design decisions; it originated in a job lot of ex-army shirts, designed for Africa, which the party had been able to pick up cheaply. Of course the S.A. was in the tradition of the free corps of ex-servicemen which in the years after 1918 had banded themselves together to put down Marxist revolution and man the frontiers with Poland and Lithuania. But whereas the free corps were vague in their political objectives, beyond a dislike for republicans and revolutionaries, the S.A. had skilful and definite political leadership from Hitler. Its opponents characterised the S.A. members as thugs and its supporters as idealists; in fact it was a mixture, bound together in part by sheer camaraderie and a nostalgia for the comradeship of the trenches. The S.A. seemed, in this early phase to be particularly successful at attracting men in the seventeen to twenty age-group, who had been too young for the war.

The early successes of the S.A. were defensive. Beer mugs often flew at Hitler meetings—Hess was scarred in the face by one— and the S.A. moved in to throw out and beat up interrupters. Their weapons were mainly fists and truncheons but some units trained privately with firearms against the day when the real conflict would begin. Then the S.A., Hitler often leading them personally, moved on to attacking their opponents' meetings. In August 1921 he personally led a raiding party which rushed the platform of a Bavarian separatist speaker, Otto Ballerstedt, and beat him up. The police arrived and Hitler beamed at them with the words: 'Fine, fine, our objective has already been achieved. Ballerstedt is not speaking.' For this he was sentenced to three months in gaol, of which he served just over a month before being let out.

The first great outing for the young S.A. came in October 1922, when Hitler was invited to speak at a 'German day' in the former princely capital of Coburg in northern Bavaria. It was organised by various 'völkisch' societies, of the kind which put forward an academic and somewhat precious form of German traditionalism, and the main speaker was to be the Duke of Coburg himself, who had been sovereign until 1918 and was a cousin of the King of England. Hitler had few or no National Socialist members in Coburg, but he decided to make a huge splash. He chartered a special train to take 700 S.A. men with him from Munich, complete with band and swastika banners. During the 170 mile journey, Hitler, wrapped in the tattered old blanket he had used during the war, sat with his immediate and adoring entourage on the bare wooden seats of a third class compartment. At Coburg the police refused permission for the National Socialists to march but Hitler ignored this and the 700 set off through the town, being greeted with hails of cobblestones from the 'Bolsheviks'. In pitched battle, the S.A. won. The impression of strength won recruits for the National Socialist cause—including the Duke of Coburg himself, who was deeply impressed. The 'Battle of Coburg' took its place in the heroic mythology of the National Socialist Party and after he

72

came to power Hitler awarded a medal to all serving party members who had taken part in it. It established a pattern of street fighting which was to be of high significance in the party's growth.

While Hitler lacked any talent for or interest in regular, detailed administration, he recognised from the start that it was important that the party should have an efficient headquarters. He liked to have an organisational machine at his disposal to which he could give such instructions as his mood or intuition of the moment suggested. In 1920 he happened to meet in the street in Munich Max Amann, who had been his company sergeant-major during the war. Amann, two years Hitler's junior, was not particularly interested in politics but at his ex-corporal's prompting he attended a National Socialist meeting and then became a party member. He was a former law student and, after five years' wartime army service, had obtained a good job in a Munich mortgage bank. In August 1921, Hitler, having gained full control of the party, proposed to Amann that he should throw up his job and become the full-time National Socialist 'business manager'.

Amann's first instinct was to reject the offer—at the bank he had security, career prospects and a pension to look forward to, while employment by the little National Socialist Party could only be a gamble. Hitler worked on him for two hours. 'What good will your pension rights be if some day the Bolsheviks string you up from a lamp post?' Amann thought over the proposition for three days and then accepted it. Obviously he must have been impressed by Hitler's capabilities which he knew both from the war and from the new political movement. Hitler, on his side, was making a good choice in Amann. Parsimonious, efficient, incorruptible and jovial, and at the same time lacking in direct political ambition, Amann was exactly the right man for the job. He combined a loud voice—it was said that when he spoke normally in his office he could be heard outside in the street—with a brusque common-sense and sympathetic manner; he was the kind of man that people went to for advice. Through the party he was eventually to become the biggest newspaper, magazine and book publisher in Germany, with a millionaire's income and one of his functions, as the movement grew, came to be to look after Hitler's personal finances. He was one of the very few who used the intimate *'du'*, the German for 'you' within families and between close friends, in conversing with Hitler.

With Amann in charge of the office, Hitler could concentrate all the more on the purely political and propagandist side of the movement. His intimates on this side were Eckart, Rosenberg, Feder, and, to some extent, a wild young journalist in his early

73

twenties, Hermann Esser. After Hitler, Esser was the best speaker the young National Socialist movement possessed but the straighter members disliked his personal morality; he made something of a point of boasting that he lived on gifts from his mistresses. He burned himself out early and with the later growth of the party was overtaken by newer members, notably Josef Goebbels. Although he was sometimes capable of listening to others, Hitler really made his policy decisions himself and it is extremely difficult to pin down, in exact terms, what they were.

Underlying everything was a deep-rooted anti-semitism. How and when it grew up in him is not clear, although probably it originated in his Vienna period. When he became a public speaker he suddenly had to start explaining it. Some of the National Socialist anti-semites, notably Rosenberg, Streicher and, later, Adolf Eichmann, knew quite a lot about their subject in the sense that they had studied Jewish history and Jewish customs; they took an masochistic pleasure in leafing through the Talmud. Hitler, however, was blatantly ignorant of such things and in his speeches and conversation made important factual errors of a type which were of no particular advantage to his cause; his anti-semitism came largely out of his imagination. He was capable, for example, of stating that the Jews had fought no war since the Maccabees, whereas the most cursory reading of Jewish history would inform him of the Jewish wars in Palestine in the first and second centuries A.D. The really dedicated kind of cranky anti-semite could never make such an error. Hitler was also fond of using the word 'Jew' as a generalised term of abuse rather than as an exact statement. For example in a speech on April 13th, 1923, at Munich he discussed wartime allied propaganda against Germany and came up with the mis-statements that the British press magnate, Lord Northcliffe, had been 'a Jew', that '99 per cent of the press of England is in Jewish hands' and that the Hearst press in the United States was 'a Jewish concern'. A few days later he was claiming, incorrectly, that Theobald von Bethmann-Hollweg, Chancellor of Germany at the outbreak of World War I, had been 'the descendant of a Jewish family'. Such statements implied either lack of information on Hitler's part or else a deliberate attempt to mislead. In all probability, it was a mixture of the two—in Hitler's intuitive way of thinking tactical convenience and principle were inextricably muddled together, and it is rarely possible to assert whether in any given statement he was being sincere or merely seeking political advantage.

With the ending of World War I there was a good deal of anti-semitism in all the combatant countries, extremist groups trying to prove that everything that had gone wrong in the world was the result of a secret Jewish plot. Even the London *Times* momentarily took quite seriously *The Protocols of the Learned Elders of Zion* published in both English and German in 1920; so, in the United States, did Henry Ford I. This is a curious concoction, which originated in France at the time of the Dreyfus case and was fostered by the Tsarist secret police in Russia; it purports to contain the methods and aims of a secret Jewish government which, through the ages, had sought to dominate the world. The 'Jewish conspiracy', according to the book, had its first break-through with the French revolution and during the nineteenth century further advanced its power by using democracy, capitalism, socialism, freemasonry and the like as its tools. It is unlikely that *The Protocols* ever converted many people to anti-semitism but it provided a superficially rational case for many who were already prejudiced against the Jews before reading it. In particular, the Russian revolution was regarded as being a part of the 'Jewish conspiracy' and in Germany there was a clear tendency among extreme nationalist groups to argue that the loss of the war had the same cause.

Thus it was of some advantage to Hitler in gaining an early hearing among the nationalists to express extreme anti-semitic views and, indeed, it has been held that his whole anti-semitic policy was basically a propaganda exercise, that he believed it psychologically necessary to give the people something to hate. As Sir Oswald Mosley, the British Fascist leader of the 1930s was reported by his sister-in-law as putting it: 'a dynamic creed such as Fascism cannot flourish unless it has a scapegoat to hit out at, such as Jewry.' In fact it is unlikely that Hitler was quite so cynical or that, on balance, his anti-semitism was a propaganda advantage to him. It helped him get support at the beginning but by the early 1930s, when he for the first time was attracting a mass vote, he deliberately muted it and made whole speeches without mentioning the word 'Jew'. Most observers then regarded anti-semitism as a temporary excrescence on the National Socialist movement rather than as fundamental to it, and this was exactly the impression Hitler wanted to give.

Hitler endorsed *The Protocols* and its associated line of argu-ment in his book *My Struggle* and later they were to be a convenient explanation of why capitalist America and Communist Russia were in alliance against him. But at root he was not an anti-semite of the *The Protocols* type. According to the 'secret conspiracy' line of argument, the victory of the 'elders of Zion' would mean Jewish domination of the world, with the rest of the human race subject to Jewish authority. Hitler, however, stated in *My Struggle* that Jewish victory would lead to the world becoming unpopulated and that is not at all the same thing. The root of his thinking lay not in a 'conspiracy' but in an idiosyncratic view of human biology which he had worked out more or less on his own. He believed that Jewish 'blood' was a corrupting and weakening influence, that the Jews were a 'bacillus' which poisoned the human race and imperilled its future. In particular, Jewish 'blood' was poisoning Germany. The Jew 'is and remains the eternal parasite, a sponger, who like a damaging bacillus spreads himself ever wider if he gets into favourable territory. The effect of his existence is exactly that of a parasite; where he enters, the host nation sooner or later dies.' The only safe working assumption can be that Hitler really believed this but even here certainty is not possible; he may only have been trying to create prejudice.

The anti-semitism was the thread that connected his other policies. Thus both Marxism and unchecked capitalism he described as Jewish inventions, but 'socialism' was a purely 'Aryan' idea. 'The Jew', he said in 1922, 'will always be the born champion of private capital in its worst form, that of unchecked exploitation.' This applied not only to Jewish business itself but to the upper classes generally, whom the Jews had contaminated. Simultaneously the Jews were infiltrating the lower classes with ideas of robbing the rich. 'The Jews are a nation of robbers.' Exactly what he meant by 'socialism' was none too clear beyond his obvious advocacy of economics being subordinated to politics. In general he avoided any detailed constructive plan but contented himself with such generalities as: 'It is not an economic question which now faces the German people; it is a political question: how shall the nation's resolution be recovered?' (May 1923) and '"National" and "social" are two identical conceptions. It is only the Jew who succeeded, through falsifying the social idea and turning it into Marxism, not only in divorcing the social idea from the national, but in actually representing them as utterly contradictory ... To be "national" means above everything to act with a boundless and all-embracing love for the people, and if necessary even to die for it. And similarly to be "social" means so to build up the state and the community of the people that every individual acts in the interest of the community of the people.' (April 1922.)

Another Jewish invention was internationalism. 'Whatever in human civilisation has real value, it arose not out of internationalism; it sprang from the soul of a single people. When peoples have lost their creative vigour, then they become international.' (May 1923.) More specifically, the League of Nations, the child of the Versailles Treaty, was a Jewish instrument. The treaty should be abrogated but even over this cardinal point Hitler was vague as to how disarmed Germany could bring this about. 'If 60 million men had only one will—to be fanatically nationalist in their outlook—the arms would spring out of men's fists.' (May 1923.)

Rather than put forward a specific programme, Hitler was consciously trying to create a general political mood. It was to be one of nationalism taken to the furthest conceivable extreme.

'We should have too much faith and love: we need an excess of national fanaticism. Ours shall be no state where tolerance reigns. No, we would be intolerant against all who do not wish to be German.' (August 1923.) Above all, Hitler had to exert his will-power to persuade his followers and stormtroopers that National Socialism was not just a minority party in Munich but a force capable of seizing control of all Germany.

'Power', he said in April 1922, 'in the last resort is possessed only where there is strength, and that strength lies not in the dead weight of numbers but solely in energy. Even the smallest minority can achieve a mighty result if it is inspired by the most fiery, most passionate will to act. World history has always been made by minorities.'

5

By the start of 1923, after less than four years' political activity, Hitler had become a considerable figure in Munich. Now, instead of speaking just in beer halls, he was able to draw an audience of thousands to the city's permanent circus arena. National Socialist membership passed 50,000. People were beginning to describe him as the most effective German orator since the socialist pioneer Ferdinand Lassalle of sixty years earlier. Foreigners were noticing him and his movement attracted the more attention because of its apparent similarity to Mussolini and the Fascists in Italy, who had gained power in October 1922; the National Socialists were often nicknamed 'the Munich *fascisti*'. Swastika badges, worn by party members, were a normal sight on the Munich streets and there were occasional incidents of bands of excited stormtrooper youths bursting into smart restaurants to shout abuse at 'Jews' they found eating in them. Outsiders, unanimously, regarded the movement as just a froth on the prevalent right-wing nationalism of Bavaria and so unlikely to be a lasting influence. Hitler had been banned from speaking in most of the German states, including the great state of Prussia which comprised two-thirds of the Reich, but in Bavaria the authorities, who disliked Berlin, regarded him as a normal, if extravagant, part of the political scene.

Conditions both in Germany generally and in Bavaria in particular could scarcely have been more favourable for an extremist movement. In January 1923, on the pretext that the Germans were 100,000 telegraph poles short in reparations deliveries, the French army occupied the Ruhr. Disarmed Germany was incapable of defending itself militarily so the Reich government, under the businessman Wilhelm Cuno, embarked on a campaign of 'passive resistance'. This entailed not only the shutting down of the Ruhr industries but also an economic boycott of France which hurt Germany more than it hurt the intended victim. During a dispute at the Krupp works at Essen, the French opened fire on the workers with machine guns, killing thirteen; later a French court martial sentenced the owner of the firm, Gustav Krupp von Bohlen, to fifteen years' imprisonment. Some resisters went beyond purely 'passive' activities and there were attacks on French units approaching a state of guerilla warfare, with the French retaliating. Almost all Germans, including the Communists, were against the French; the exceptions were Rhineland separatists, who could see advantage in an independent Rhineland republic, and, surprisingly, Adolf Hitler. Although individual National Socialists co-operated with 'passive resistance', Hitler himself came out with a speech, reported across the world, in which he said the real villains were not the French but the 'November criminals', or in other words the Weimar regime, which he said, had betrayed Germany and left her helpless. This was a sound tactical move in that he attracted attention to himself and made himself the more distinctive; it also exemplified his method of defining patriotism in his own terms, and then claiming that anyone who disagreed with him could not be patriotic. In the long run, the latter formula, successfully applied, was to be one of the factors in his power.

Side by side with the French occupation of the Ruhr, and largely as a result of it, went a total collapse of the German currency. In 1914 the mark had been worth 4·2 to the United States dollar. The war and its immediate aftermath brought an inflation which by itself seemed catastrophic—by 1922 the mark was down to 500 to the dollar—but this was nothing to the final decline. On the occupation of the Ruhr, the mark fell to 10,000 to the dollar and then to 50,000. It rallied briefly back to 20,000 and then, from the spring of 1923 onwards, plunged down ever more sharply. By July it cost one million marks to buy one dollar. Prices rose daily, sometimes twice or thrice daily. Every foreigner in Germany, with hard currency, could live like a prince. Industry and industrial workers did not do too badly and, at the peak, workers were being paid twice a day and they hurried off to convert their cash into goods before prices doubled again. Middle-class incomes tended to rise rather more slowly and, devastatingly, the value of middle-class savings was wiped out. 'The state itself', said Hitler at Munich, 'has become the biggest swindler and crook. A robbers' state!' The inflation was something that no German, no matter how non-political, could escape and even those who did well out of it—for example anyone who owed money—were not disposed to advocate it publicly as a desirable system. Even after the apparent bottom of July 1923, Hitler's denunciation of the 'robbers' state' seemed to take on yet further point as the inflation speeded up to the complete extinction of the currency. By the autumn, a ten dollar bill could buy enough marks to have financed, at former prices, the whole cost to Germany of World War I. With the introduction of a new currency, the rentenmark, in November, 1923, it cost a billion old marks to buy one new rentenmark.

For a man so euphoric and intuitive as Hitler, such a situation seemed to be proof of his destiny. His denunciations of the new German state appeared to have been proved right; he was clearly thinking of himself as now possibly not being just the 'drummer' of a 'Germanic revolution' but also as being destined to seize power. In a directive to his members, he instructed them not to be content with propaganda but 'to bring political power into the fist of our movement'.

The special situation of Bavarian politics further stimulated his hopes. Germany was a federation of states of widely differing sizes. In the United States of America of the time, for example, no single state could be predominant; the most populous, New York, contained under ten per cent of the electorate. But in Germany, the state of Prussia, swollen by its nineteenth century annexations, contained two-thirds of the whole population. Such states as Schaumburg-Lippe, with a population of under 50,000 or even Hamburg with well over a million, could not hope to compete with Prussian predominance. However, Bavaria was the second biggest state of the Reich, after Prussia, and with a seven million population was well ahead of the third biggest, Saxony, which had under five million. The Bavarian Wittsbach dynasty dethroned in 1918, dated back to the twelfth century, and the state had had a long independent history; even under the Bismarckian Reich it had retained a degree of control over its own foreign policy and army. Prussia, or at least its northern heartlands, was traditionally Protestant whereas Bavaria was Roman Catholic. To many Bavarians, the German Reich appeared to be not so much a federation, as an alliance between Prussia and Bavaria in which Bavaria got the worst of it. In particular, the Prussians were blamed for starting World War I or for losing it, or for both. After the initial troubles of 1918–19, with the Bavarian 'soviet republic' overthrown in civil war, Bavaria had settled down into apparent stability; at any rate Communism had been virtually eliminated. Increasingly the Bavarian government acted independently of 'red' Berlin and by 1923 even the army in Bavaria was showing a disposition to prefer Munich to the Reich high command.

Side by side with the development of this special form of nationalism came the growth of various 'right-radical' militarist groups of which Hitler's National Socialist S.A. was politically the most articulate. The motives of the groups were muddled and, indeed, contradictory. Some wanted an independent Bavaria, perhaps linked up with German rump-Austria. There was a powerful movement in favour of a restoration of the Wittelsbach monarchy and this, almost inevitably, would have led to secession from the republican Reich. Against this, some saw Bavaria as potentially a 'purifying force' for the whole of Germany. The unifying force was a hatred of Berlin, which Hitler at this time liked to describe as 'Babylon'. Hitler had absolutely no sympathy with Bavarian separatism but he would play along with the monarchists even to the extent of referring, in their company, to the dethroned Ludwig III as 'His Majesty the King'. The various groups—besides the S.A., they included the Oberland, Bavaria and Reich, and the Reich Fighting Flag corps—joined together in March 1923 with Hitler as 'Political Leader' and Colonel Hermann Kriebel as military commander. Hitler's 'leadership' was far from absolute—he was scarcely more than orator and public relations officer—and to obtain it he had given up authority over his own S.A. Furthermore, despite his unusual talents for political organisation, he was still short of actual experience and so in any combination was liable to find himself out-manoeuvred by the more seasoned Bavarian politicians. As the correspondent of the London *Times* put it on May 22nd, 1923, Hitler was regarded by the established right-wing as 'a useful tool to be discarded in case of success and disowned in case of failure'.

The true hero of the far right was not Hitler but General Erich Ludendorff, the brilliant German chief of staff from the war. Ludendorff had won major victories on both the Eastern and Western Fronts and after the 1918 surrender had become one of the leading proponents of the 'stab in the back' explanation. Ludendorff was a curious mixture. As a military organiser and, even, in some respects as a politician, he was clear-headed, rational and possessed of a sound sense of realities. At the same time there was a streak of eccentricity, even barminess in him. His mind became clouded with ideas of Jews, Jesuits and Freemasons having plotted together to bring about Germany's downfall; he dabbled in the occult and sought out mystical numbers. His second wife, who liked to wear Wagnerian-style flowing robes, encouraged him in this and she developed a cult of the old Nordic gods. In 1918 the Ludendorffs had withdrawn for a while to Sweden but then they took a house, surrounded by high walls, on the outskirts of Munich. The Prussian Ludendorff was suspicious of Bavarians and fearful that they might be being run by their Roman Catholic priests, but by 1922 or the beginning of 1923 he had become impressed by Hitler.

Ludendorff was clear-headed enough to realise that mere patriotic or nationalist slogans were no longer enough to keep the masses away from Marxism and internationalism; there had to be a social concern for their welfare in order to bind them into a national state. In Hitler he saw an orator who could put over such a message more effectively than any member of the officer class. Thus from the spring of 1923 onwards there grew up a bizarre alliance between the Prussian general and the ex-corporal from a Bavarian reserve regiment. At any time previously, it would have been wholly inconceivable for such a thing to have existed but both Hitler and Ludendorff were exceptional men and the situation around them was without precedent. There was no personal warmth between them and Ludendorff did not join the National Socialists. But each, for the moment, regarded the other as useful.

Probably through Ludendorff, Hitler in March 1923 met General Hans von Seeckt, the fastidious, clever commander-in-chief of the truncated German army. Seeckt was a monarchist at heart but had accepted the Weimar republic as the least available evil. His overriding aim was to avoid a German civil war and to keep 'politics' out of the army; he wanted to bind such paramilitary formations as the S.A. into the reserve defences of the country. Hitler in his more mature days—by the early 1930s—would have been capable of putting on an act to impress Seeckt but the impression he in fact left was one of simple fanaticism, which Seeckt found disturbing. Seeckt did get Hitler to promise that in the event of the Ruhr occupation leading to outright war between Germany and France, the S.A. would be at the service of the army. But almost immediately after the meeting, Hitler came out more strongly than ever against the 'passive resistance' campaign to a point at which it was seriously, and possibly accurately, being alleged against him that the National Socialists were being subsidised by the French secret service. Such was Hitler's tactical flexibility, that it is difficult to see any reason why he should have refused such aid, if offered, but the evidence that it existed is weak.

During the 1923 summer of crazy inflation and 'passive resistance' on the Ruhr, politics both in Germany generally and in Bavaria were continually on the boil. By August, Hitler was able to join with Ludendorff in taking the salute at a parade in Nuremberg of 70,000 members of the League of Nationalist Associations, which included the S.A. The London *Times* commented: 'With a population, many of whom are on the verge of starvation, and tired of the unfulfilled promises of successive politicians, it is little wonder that his movement gains new adherents.' At the same time, revolution from the left, in a Marxist, Soviet direction, appeared to be an even greater threat to the liberal republican system. In Saxony and Thuringia there were radical leftist governments, backed by 'workers' councils' in the factories, which were more and more defiant of Berlin; in October 1923 they took Communists into their membership to help in what they regarded as a struggle against 'the danger of plutocratic military dictatorship'.

On August 13th, Gustav Stresemann, who was to become the greatest figure of the republic, took office for the first time as Reich Chancellor. Stresemann, who was forty-five in 1923, represented above all else the liberal business community. His doctoral thesis as a young man had been entitled 'The development of the bottled beer trade in Berlin' and he had first become prominent when, as manager of the Association of German Chocolate Manufacturers, he had battled against the German Sugar Cartel for keeping its prices too high. In pre-war politics he had risen in the National Liberal Party which had represented businessmen as against the landowning aristocracy around the Kaiser. He had supported World War I with vigorous speeches in the Reichstag in which he had argued that it had been due to the aggressiveness of France and the commercialism of Great Britain; the allies had been out for conquest, while Germany had been acting merely defensively. The Versailles Treaty he had seen both as proof of his wartime statements and as the ruin of Germany. He had opposed signing it. 'We are crying for a sword', he said, 'but no god can give it back to us. We once possessed it, and it was one of the choicest ever given to a nation. But we broke it wantonly in the shameful days of the Revolution and, as a nation and an empire, we are therefore entering on a future beginning in misery and shame.' This was not so different from the attitude of young Corporal Hitler in Bavaria. But Stresemann, who in 1920 founded his own party, the German People's Party, drew different conclusions; he came around to the view that the only atmosphere in which Germany could solve her legitimate grievances was one of conciliation and European co-operation. This led, ultimately, to the Locarno treaties of 1925 with their mutual guarantees of frontiers and provisions for disputes to go to arbitration.

Stresemann's 1923 administration lasted only twelve weeks (he was to return later as Foreign Minister) but it was the turning point of the Weimar republic. It was a grand coalition of all the democratic parties and was firmly backed by the Social Democratic President of the Reich, Friedrich Ebert. In Munich, Hitler described it as 'the Jew government' although, in fact, it contained no Jewish member. Stresemann started on the path to Locarno by calling off 'passive resistance' on the Ruhr; he brought in the banker Hjalmar Schacht to reform the currency, and he used the army to overthrow the left-radical governments in Saxony and Thuringia—many thought that he thereby prevented a Communist revolution. He took little action against the equally unconstitutional right-radicals of Bavaria—in his eyes they were a lesser danger than the Communists if only because they seemed to be so hopelessly divided about their objectives. Stresemann was well aware, at this time, of Hitler and the National Socialists but he had much else to think about.

On the eve of the proclamation calling off 'passive resistance', the Bavarian government of Eugen von Knilling proclaimed a state of emergency and appointed the conservative, monarchist Gustav von Kahr, a former Bavarian premier, to be general state commissioner with virtually dictatorial powers. Stresemann retaliated by proclaiming a state of emergency for the whole Reich. Kahr, a bumbling forty-six-year-old, in a frock coat, was at heart a Bavarian separatist. However he and the Bavarian army commander, General Otto von Lossow, were in communication with the ultra-rightist groups and were playing with the idea of a march on Berlin to throw out the 'Marxists'. Meanwhile they defied the Stresemann administration, notably by refusing to suppress the *Völkischer Beobachter*, and to arrest leaders of the paramilitary bands. Seeckt dismissed Lossow but Kahr said he refused to recognise the dismissal. Hitler, eagerly, prepared for the rising. 'Today we know what will happen,' he orated. 'In a few weeks the dice will roll. Victory must be ours.'

However Kahr, while willing to be truculent towards Berlin was not, in the last resort, willing to march against Stresemann, particularly after the 'red' governments of Saxony and Thuringia had been overthrown and the Social Democrats had quit the Berlin coalition in protest. It became extremely difficult to characterise the Stresemann coalition as a 'Marxist' one in the circumstances. Moreover although Kahr had been willing to negotiate with the ultra-rightists as a possible useful tool, he recognised that public opinion was moving towards moderation. One of his political bases was to appeal to devout Roman Catholics and on November 6th, the Archbishop of Munich, Cardinal Michael Faulhaber, issued a pastoral letter calling for moderation and conciliation.

How [he wrote] can we hope to master the economic crisis that already is so great and the miseries of the coming winter, which widespread unemployment will incur, unless all decent men work together, regardless of faith, position, or party? How else can we eradicate the blind, raging hatred for our Jewish fellow-citizens and other ethnic groups, a hatred that rages throughout the land screaming 'Guilty!' but never asking proof? And how else can we avoid a civil war, which would wreak new, untold desolation and seal the ruin of our poor nation?

The Germans were beginning to come together and already, on November 2nd, Hitler had realised that Kahr was not going to rise. He called him and his associates 'thunderstruck geese' and decided to go ahead on his own. Looking back, twelve years later, he said it had been 'The most desperately daring decision of my life. When I now look back on it in thought, I grow dizzy.' It was certainly a futile enterprise. A Bavarian coup supported by government, army and police could easily have started civil war in Germany and might even have won power. A coup by the recently-emerged orator, Hitler, on his own, would need an out-right miracle to get anywhere. Later Hitler justified the attempted coup, tactically, as having been worthwhile solely for propagandist reasons and it certainly made him better known and the memory of it became part of the mystique of the National Socialist movement. At the time however, he was being driven on by an over-powering sense of destiny and believed that he had a chance of winning; his attitude was comparable with that in which he was to take gambler's decisions in World War II. Blind faith and will-power, already justified by early success, made him tackle impossible odds. He would die rather than give up. Every account of the coup agrees that he was tense and agitated, acting by intuition rather than calculation.

For his coup, Hitler chose a public meeting to be addressed on November 8th by Kahr in the Bürgerbräu tavern, at which, at the request of the Munich business community, he was to outline his future programme. Most of the notabilities of the Bavarian political scene were to be present, including Lossow and the police chief Hans von Seisser. Under Hitler's orders, the National Socialists prepared placards to be stuck up in Munich and across Germany announcing that the revolution had taken place and that a new Reich government had been formed with Hitler as Chancellor. At the last moment Ludendorff, who had not been involved in the planning, was brought in. Exactly why Ludendorff allowed himself to join so impossible an enterprise is not clear; probably he made a snap decision under the impression that the conspiracy ranged wider than it did. He certainly never forgave Hitler.

The Bürgerbräu beer cellar, on the outskirts of Munich, was a vast, highly-respectable place and on the night of Kahr's speech there was an audience of 3,000, drinking their beer at a billion marks a mug. The cloakroom was piled with top hats and officers' swords. Several hundred S.A. men, many of them armed with carbines and revolvers, surrounded the hall from the outside after the meeting had begun: they erected a machine gun at the entrance. Meanwhile Röhm, at the head of the Oberland free corps, set out to occupy the War Ministry.

Inside the hall sat Hitler, in a scruffy trench coat, and accompanied by Hess and Göring and by his personal bodyguard Ulrich Graf, a noted amateur wrestler. Kahr, a small man with his head deep between his shoulders, began his speech in a dull, droning voice. Exactly what he had been intending to announce is unknown; some thought he might be going to declare Bavarian independence but, more probably, he was going to make conciliatory remarks towards Berlin. After half an hour he was still only on his preamble and then came the prearranged moment for the revolution.

Hitler stood up and took off his trench coat, revealing that he wore underneath what he regarded as his proper costume as the new Chancellor of Germany—an ill-cut black tailcoat, with the Iron Cross pinned to the breast and a swastika badge in the buttonhole. 'Putzi' Hanfstaengl thought he looked like a rural bridegroom. Hitler produced a revolver, climbed on to a table and silenced Kahr by firing a shot at the ceiling. 'The national revolution', yelled Hitler in his hoarse voice, 'has begun . . . The Bavarian and Reich governments have been removed and a provisional national government formed . . . The army and the police are marching on the city under the swastika banner.'

His aim, obviously, was to force and bluff Kahr and the other notables into joining the 'revolution' before they realised that so far it existed only in Hitler's imagination. Then, from a power base in Bavaria, he could march on Berlin. For a moment it seemed to work. Armed stormtroopers swarmed into the hall, outnumbering the police on duty, and nobody could know exactly what was happening or how extensive the conspiracy was. Waving his revolver, Hitler marched Kahr, Lossow and Seisser off to a side room and 'appointed' Kahr to be Regent of Bavaria, Lossow to be Reich Defence Minister and Seisser to be Reich Police Minister. Back in the hall there was some murmuring of complaint and Göring jumped on to the platform to calm things down:

'. . . There is nothing to fear. We have the friendliest intentions. You've no cause to grumble. You have your beer . . .' The police talked to their headquarters by telephone and the head of the police political department, the lawyer Wilhelm Frick, instructed them to prepare a report on what was happening but not to start shooting against superior numbers. Frick joined the National Socialists two years later; he was a solid family man, well educated and with an air of professional respectability and although never in the inner leadership he was a useful 'front' man.

In the side room, the euphoric Hitler obviously hoped that by sheer power of personality and argument, coupled with threats, he could get Khar, Lossow and Seisser to join him. But he was over-excited and far from his best. At one point, apparently, he shouted: 'I have four shots in my pistol. Three for my collaborators, if they abandon me. The last bullet for myself. If I am not victorious by tomorrow afternoon, I shall be a dead man.' Melodramatically he pressed the muzzle against his forehead. Kahr and the other two appear to have been worried, dignified and unforthcoming. The innocent fanatic was being confoundedly awkward.

Hitler tried a new tack. He rushed back into the main hall and announced that Kahr, Lossow and Seisser had agreed to join him. Presumably he hoped that they would accept a *fait accompli* and certainly the announcement produced a burst of applause, which impressed the trio in the side room. There was, said Hitler, to be a march on the 'sinful Babel', Berlin. The Reich government had been 'removed' and he, Hitler, was forming a 'provisional government' to 'save the German people'.

Then Ludendorff turned up, under the impression that he was to be offered the post of Chancellor of Germany. He was badly put out to learn that Hitler was reserving this for himself and that he, Ludendorff, was only to be commander-in-chief of the army. Presumably he felt, however, that this could be rearranged later and he joined in pressing Kahr, Lossow and Seisser to join 'the National cause'. Overawed by Ludendorff, the trio now agreed to collaborate although the extent to which they did so is not certain. Hitler, behaving like a delighted child, rushed them to the platform where they made short speeches confirming their stand. Hitler promised that in place of 'the wretched Germany of today' he would erect 'a Germany of power and greatness, of freedom and splendour'. He then gave a sort of press conference; the London *Times* correspondent reported of him: 'He scarcely seemed to fill the part—this little man in an old waterproof coat, a revolver at his hip, unshaven, and with disordered hair, and so hoarse that he could hardly speak.'

But Kahr had scarcely left the tavern before he repudiated his agreement to work with Hitler. He issued a proclamation saying 'The declaration extorted from myself, General von Lossow and Colonel von Seisser at the point of the revolver is null and void.' He declared the National Socialist Party to be dissolved. Army units surrounded the War Ministry, occupied by Röhm and his men. The only bit of the Reich that Hitler's 'provisional government' controlled was that and the Bürgerbräu beer cellar. Hitler thought of retreating to the countryside and raising 'a force of peasants' but Ludendorff put his own personality into the scales. He suggested a public march through Munich, with himself at the head of it; the police and army, rather than fire at him, would rally behind him. Although this was foolhardy and meant that Ludendorff rather than Hitler would be the effective leader, Hitler's options had so narrowed that, short of surrendering altogether, he had no real alternative but to agree.

The march took place the following morning, November 9th, at about eleven o'clock. It started from the Bürgerbräu tavern and was intended to reach the War Ministry and link up with Röhm's besieged group there. In terms of a challenge to public order, it was quite a formidable demonstration; some 3,000 S.A. men and free corps members, many of them armed, took part and there was a lorry containing machine guns. But as a means of taking over the state it was comically inadequate. The front rank included Hitler, Ludendorff, Göring, Hess, and Rosenberg; on the way Streicher joined in and marched immediately behind Hitler.

The column managed to pass one police cordon without a fight but in the centre of the city, near the War Ministry, it encountered a further police road-block, shutting off the entrance to the Odeonsplatz. The police, armed, were only about a hundred strong but the narrowness of the street gave them a sound defensive position. There was some shouting at them from the column, Hitler calling 'surrender!', but almost immediately firing broke out—which side started it is not clear. Within a minute sixteen of the marchers and three of the police were dead and Hitler was lying on the ground with a shoulder dislocated in his fall. To what extent Hitler behaved in a cowardly manner was subsequently much disputed. It could be held that he merely behaved like an old soldier in dropping to the ground at the sound of gunfire. He himself explained that he was pulled down by the mortally-wounded man next to him. On the other hand, Ludendorff, lacking the reactions of a front line soldier and trusting in his inviolability as a war hero kept marching and passed unscathed right through the police and into the open square beyond, where he was arrested. Had the whole demonstration followed Ludendorff the out-numbered police would have been swept aside; however, the ultimate result could only have been the same, and perhaps with further bloodshed. As it was, the one burst of fire at the entrance to the Odeonsplatz was itself enough to finish off Hitler's coup. Had a bullet gone a little differently and killed Hitler rather than his immediate neighbour, Hitler would have been remembered only as an historical footnote, a quaint young orator from the trenches who had been innocent enough to believe his own words.

In pain from his shoulder, Hitler climbed into a supporter's car and was driven off to the country home of the Hanfstaengls; he showed no regard for his wounded followers. Göring, severely wounded in the groin, received emergency treatment from a Jewish doctor and fled to Austria. Hess, also, went to Austria. Röhm was arrested at the War Ministry which, on the afternoon of the shooting, he surrendered peacefully.

Hitler's initial reaction was one of apparent suicidal despair, which was probably partly real and partly an hysterical show. When after two days the police arrived to arrest him at the Hanfstaengl home, he waved his revolver and said he would shoot himself rather than be taken; Mrs. Hanfstaengl, an American, managed to wrest the gun from him, his dislocated shoulder making this easier for her. In custody, he embarked on a hunger strike. As in 1945, the collapse of over-inflated hopes made him think of killing himself. In 1923, however, there was still scope for a revived optimism and Hitler's powerful mind obviously began to take stock of the tactical situation: despite his basically intuitive method of thinking, Hitler could be tactically rational. The coup had failed ludicrously but it was capable of being turned to propaganda advantage. It had made him better known outside Bavaria than he had been before and he had staked a definite claim for power. As he himself put it twelve years later: 'While our opponents thought that they had destroyed us, in fact the seed of the movement at a single blow was cast over the whole of Germany.' To the world at large, Hitler now appeared to be the chosen colleague of the famous Ludendorff. Then there was the sheer value of martyrdom. Of the contemporaries he noted most closely, both Lenin and Mussolini had suffered imprisonment during their early political careers.

By the time that, with nine others, Hitler appeared on trial for treason, in February 1924, he was back at the height of his powers. With the world press listening, Hitler was able to use the trial for his own advantage. During the twenty-four days of hearings, his speeches were eloquent and he asked skilful questions which embarrassed the prosecution witnesses.

Ingeniously, Hitler managed to do two things at once at the trial. The first was that, like any orthodox defendant, he sought to minimise his own culpability, as charged, and to secure if not an acquittal at least the lightest possible sentence. He did this by asserting, without serious contradiction, that until the last moment the actual Bavarian government of Kahr had been with him in planning to seize the Reich. 'If our enterprise was high treason,' he said, 'then during the whole period Lossow, Kahr and Seisser must have been committing high treason along with us, for during all these weeks we talked of nothing but the aims of which we now stand accused.' He portrayed himself—and to some extent accurately—as a simple, innocent patriot who had been led astray by the politicians.

Secondly, Hitler used the court as a political platform, on which, with eloquence, he could advance his own reputation and appeal to the whole of German nationalism. 'If today,' he said, 'I stand here as a revolutionary, it is as a revolutionary against the revolution. There is no such thing as high treason against the traitors of 1918.' He pitched his own claims at the highest possible level. 'Believe me,' he said, 'I do not regard the acquisition of a minister's portfolio as a thing worth striving for. I do not hold it worthy of a great man to endeavour to go down in history just by becoming a minister. One might be in danger of being buried with other ministers. My aim from the first was a thousand times higher than becoming a minister. I wanted to become the destroyer of Marxism. I am going to achieve this task.' He explained his philosophy of power. 'The man who is born to be a dictator is not compelled. He wills it. He is not driven forward, but drives himself . . . The man who feels called upon to govern a people has no right to say, "If you want me or summon me, I will co-operate." No! It is his duty to step forward.'

Said by the wrong type of person, this kind of thing could have sounded absurd. In fact Hitler, with his burning eyes and air of passionate sincerity actually made converts in court; even those whom he did not convert could see him with sympathy as an innocent patriot who had allowed himself to be carried away in his love for Germany. Interestingly, on this as on subsequent occasions when Hitler was really trying to convert people, he made relatively little mention of the Jews.

Hitler undoubtedly had the sympathy of the Bavarian Justice Minister, Franz Gürtner, who later became a National Socialist and ended up as the Reich Justice Minister under Hitler. (But the Bavarian Interior Ministry definitely was against him.) Of more immediate importance was the impression he made on the lay assessors who sat as a form of jury with the judge, with the power to vote on sentence as well as on the verdict. For no very clear reason, beyond the fact that he was a national hero, the court acquitted Ludendorff altogether. Hitler was liable to life imprisonment but, through the votes of the assessors, received a sentence of only five years, to be served in 'fortress confinement' as a political prisoner rather than a criminal one.

In all the circumstances, his oratorical skill had got him off lightly. But Hitler did not forget Kahr. In 1934 he had him killed.

6

Hitler served only nine months of his five-year sentence and he did so in relatively comfortable conditions. However he had no certainty that he would be out so soon and on the face of it his political career had ended. The petit-bourgeois element in his complicated character must have revolted against his being locked up as a convict but against this he could take pleasure from his own followers regarding him as a martyr. Hitler showed resilience in prison and came out a cooler and more effective politician than when he had gone in. At thirty-three, after his first four years' political activity, he had been forced into a breathing space, a chance to take stock. At the time of the 1923 attempted coup, Hitler had still, in the main, been the euphoric ex-corporal from the trenches, brimming with naive hatreds, loves and enthusiasms. He came out a sophisticated party leader, willing to calculate the movements of public opinion and to act with patience and tactical skill. Whether, while in prison, he still believed that he could become dictator of Germany is not clear. In 1938, referring back to his prison days, he remarked: 'I always saw myself as a party leader, or at most as private counsellor to a head of state.' Probably his moods on this varied and it is certainly true that office for its own sake never particularly interested Hitler; what mattered to him was to get his ideas carried out.

The fortress at Landsberg, overlooking the river Lech, where Hitler and about forty of his followers served their sentences following the attempted coup, lay a convenient twenty miles from Munich. Hitler had a room rather than a cell (sometimes, apparently, two rooms), furnished with a bedstead, table, two chairs, a cupboard and a bedside table. It was usually filled with gifts of food, books and flowers from his admirers outside. The prisoners lived a communal life, with the prison authorities accepting Hitler as their leader, and ate the same food as the warders, with an entitlement to a half bottle of wine or a pint of beer a day. A good deal of extra drink was smuggled in; one prisoner later recalled: 'The warders' mouths watered whenever they got a glimpse inside our drink cupboards.' One prisoner, a law student, busied himself with writing his doctoral thesis; in a letter to a friend he wrote:

So far everything is all right with me. Life goes on like this: get up at 7.30 a.m., have a bath and breakfast, go for a walk. At 10 a.m. there is normally an hour's discussion with the Chief or better still an address by the Chief. At mid-day we all have lunch together and then one kills time until 4.30 p.m. when we are allowed out in the courtyard once more; physical training, games and dinner bring one to 8.30 p.m. and then once more we can do as we please.

The very tone of the law student's letter suggests the love his prison companions felt for Hitler. They cheerfully cleaned his room for him and they listened when he addressed them on politics. They maintained silence around his room when he was reading or working on his book, *My Struggle*. Hitler's capacity in many personal relationships to draw out affection and protectiveness was a fact. He did this partly instinctively but, also, he took conscious care to maintain his position as Leader; for instance, he refrained from joining the other prisoners in their games and athletics for the reason that he considered it would be unsuitable for the Leader to be defeated. One prisoner later recalled the atmosphere in the recreation room when, with warders as well as prisoners listening, Hitler gave one of his addresses:

Seldom can the concepts of race and people, blood and soil have been brought so vividly to life as by the passion and oratory of the Leader at that time. Two apparently incompatible points of view, two concepts, the national and the social, were so exalted in our minds that there seemed to be only one path to tread, only one goal for which to strive.

Officially Hitler was allowed to receive visitors from outside for six hours a week, subject to them being vetted by the prison authorities and the conversation not being directed against the government or the prison conditions. In practice, however, Hitler seems to have been allowed latitude and he saw whomever he wanted for as long as he wanted. Even his Alsatian dog was allowed to visit him, brought on a leash by a supporter. He was particularly a magnet for nationalist-minded women, who loved him as a

93

martyr and brought gifts. He also received politicians, journalists, businessmen, clergy and academics, usually doing most of the talking himself.

While, through his visitors, keeping in touch with outside conditions, Hitler was not able to control the National Socialist movement which, anyway, had officially been banned. He appointed Rosenberg, who was still free, to be his deputy but this was scarcely more than a joke and the party split up into rival factions. The inevitable conclusion must be that it suited Hitler well for the party to be ineffective in his absence and that no alternative leader arose. Apparently, however, he was able to smuggle some directives out of prison. An anonymous directive at this time to party organisations in northern Germany bears all the marks of his style:

A large number of learned professors have plunged enthusiastically into researching on the Jewish problem. A flood of literature has been let loose on our people, but one thing has been neglected— propagation of the basic truth that all this so-called educated circle's knowledge is worthless and purposeless so long as: 1, They are not in a position to transmit it to the broad mass of the people. 2, They do not possess ruthless, dictatorial determination to translate their knowledge into practice without regard for parliamentary majorities, inspired solely by the sacred conviction that the truth justifies the use of force to compel men's acceptance when necessary.

Hitler read quite a lot while at Landsberg and, indeed, later looked back on his stay there as 'free education at the state's expense'. But, as always, his reading was a means of gaining ammunition for his own ideas rather than for actual instruction. His major activity, however, was not reading but writing the first volume of his own book, *My Struggle*.

The original motivation for writing *My Struggle* was not political at all. Hitler had no burning desire to set down his ideas systematically on paper. Nor was he particularly eager to write his autobiography. Especially at this period of his life he specifically mistrusted the printed word as a political weapon. He believed that German nationalists, by devoting their energies to books and pamphlets, had lost ground to the Marxists, who were willing to go out into the streets and workshops to convince the masses by verbal argument and speeches.

The knights of the pen [he wrote in *My Struggle*] and the literary snobs of today should be made to realise that the great transformations which have taken place in this world were never conducted by a goose quill. No. The task of the pen must always be that of presenting the theoretical concepts which motivate such changes. The force which has ever and always set in motion great historical avalanches of religious and political movements is the magic power of the spoken word.

His own success as a speaker gave him practical confirmation of this view.

Hitler wrote *My Struggle* on the suggestion of his business manager, Max Amman, as a means of raising some ready cash to pay the expenses involved in his trial. It is partly autobiographical, partly ideological and partly, and most interestingly a treatise on the techniques of propaganda. Some of it, apparently, he typed out with two fingers but the bulk of it bears evidence of having been dictated. The story, which seems to have had backing from Hitler himself, was always that Rudolf Hess (who had returned from Austria, been arrested and sentenced) had taken it down at Hitler's dictation but this was later specifically denied by his wife Ilse Hess. Whatever the truth of the matter, Hess was certainly Hitler's close companion at Landsberg and helped him on *My Struggle*. Also the book, rather than being a considered treatise, must be taken as a living specimen of Hitler's style of speaking and speechifying as a young politician. It had to be much edited and cut down to eliminate the worst of the repetitions and incorrect grammar. Hitler was conscious, however, that he was writing a book and attempted a veneer of sophistication by using involved clauses and many parentheses. The result is a few passages of eloquence and power but they have to be quarried out of page after page of boring material. Only a minority of Hitler's followers ever read the whole book and it is doubtful whether anyone at all was ever converted by it.

For propaganda purposes, Hitler needed his personality as well as his words—his charm, his pathos, his scornful humour, his changes of pace, his mimicry, his passion, his brilliant eyes could, when he was on form, have made even the railway timetable sound interesting. The writings which really best express Hitler are not *My Struggle* but his table-talk of 1941–4, taken down by a stenographer, when he was at the height of his powers and success; like *My Struggle*, the table-talk is not particularly persuasive but unlike *My Struggle*, it is rarely boring and this must be because it was straight material from Hitler's mouth, rather than him struggling in a medium he disliked. Although he believed himself in some fields to be a genius, Hitler never claimed talent as a writer. He remarked in 1938: 'I am no author. What beautiful Italian Mussolini speaks and writes. *My Struggle* is simply a collection of leading articles for the *People's Observer* and from the stylistic point of view I don't think they would have been accepted with any great enthusiasm.'

The autobiographical section of *My Struggle* was how Hitler wanted to present his life in 1924 rather than an exact record. For political reasons, and probably also through carelessness, it is incorrect on very many details. He describes his father as a civil servant who 'looked up to the dignity of a state office as the highest of all' and that when young Hitler had said he wanted to be an artist, the father had replied: 'Artist! Not as long as I live, never.' He described how as a boy he had learned how 'the poison of foreign races was eating into the body of our people' and how his secondary school performances had been at the extremes of good and bad. He had early been a Pan-German and an opponent of the Hapsburg regime: 'There arose in me a feeling of intense love for my German-Austrian home and a profound hatred for the Austrian state.'

His failure to get into the academy at Vienna came 'like a bolt from the skies' but he goes on, 'Obstacles are placed across our path in life not to be boggled at but to be surmounted.' He had been 'firmly convinced that one day I should make a name for myself as an architect'. He alleges he suffered poverty in Vienna and that his eyes were opened to 'Marxism and Judaism'. But he had still been the student: 'Every book I bought meant renewed hunger.' He sums up Vienna as 'that mammoth city which greedily attracts men to its bosom in order to break them mercilessly'. But he had drawn political conclusions. 'The aim of all social activity must never be merely charitable relief, which is ridiculous and useless, but it must rather be a means to find a way of eliminating the fundamental deficiencies in our economic and cultural life.' Working people should be given pride in the Fatherland, and be weaned away from the habit of 'reviling all authority'. This could be done by 'nationalising' them, giving them a sense of patriotism. But 'the question of "nationalising" a people is first and foremost one of establishing healthy social conditions'. He had at first been attracted by the Social Democrats but then repelled on learning their 'inner nature'. 'Knowledge of the Jews is the only key whereby one may understand the inner nature and real aims of the Social Democrats.'

It had taken him two years in Vienna really to become anti-semitic. He had found the Jews 'dirty'—'that they were water-shy was obvious from looking at them'. They ran prostitution in

Vienna and of Jewish writers he writes: 'One of these fellows, acting like a sewage pump, would shoot his filth directly in the face of other members of the human race.' Democracy, he had come to realise, was 'the breeding ground in which the Marxist world pest can grow and spread'; it was wrong if only because 'a hundred blockheads do not equal one man of wisdom'.

Hitler describes how with joy he migrated from Vienna to Munich but gets the date of the move a whole year wrong; this may well have been an attempt to fog up things against the eventuality of the facts on his avoidance of Austrian military service coming out. He describes how enthusiastic he and his fellow soldiers had been at the beginning of the war. 'At one stroke, in the August of 1914, all the empty nonsense about international solidarity was knocked out of the heads of the German working classes.' He saw the Rhine for the first time when approaching the Western Front with his unit. 'The whole troop train broke into "The Watch on the Rhine". I then felt as if my heart could not contain its spirit.' Interestingly, Hitler makes no attempt to glamourise his war service, or even to describe how he won his decorations; he simply makes it clear that he had been in the front line almost throughout and that the experience had been profound. Then comes his sense of horror at the surrender of 1918 and his joining the National Socialists. His original title for the book had been *Four and a Half Years' Struggle Against Falsehood, Folly and Cowardice* and presumably he had intended the main weight of it to be his meteoric political career which had taken him from being 'the unknown soldier' to the position of an important state prisoner. In fact, however, his narrative is thin and in places inaccurate; his ideas keep bursting in and swamping the story.

Ideologically the book, so far as it is systematic at all, bases itself on the twin pillars of race and of struggle. 'The ultimate and most profound reason for German downfall is to be found in the fact that the racial problem was ignored.' Nature hated mixed breeding. 'No cat exists which has a friendly disposition towards mice.' 'All the great civilisations of the past became decadent because the originally creative race died out.' 'Every manifestation of human culture, every product of art, science and technical skill, which we see before our eyes today, is almost exclusively the product of Aryan creative power.' 'The Aryan alone ... founded a superior type of humanity.' 'He is the Prometheus of mankind, from whose shining brow the divine spark of genius has at all times flashed forth ... Should he be forced to disappear, within a few thousand years human culture will vanish and the world will become a desert.' 'The first forms of civilisation arose where the Aryan race came into contact with inferior races, subjugated them and forced them to obey his command.' 'In this world everything that is not of sound racial stock is like chaff.'

Of course mixed up with such racial passages is continual abuse of the 'Jewish bacillus'. Whereas 'the greatness of the Aryan is not based on his intellectual powers; but rather on his willingness to devote all his faculties to the service of the community', the Jews behaved like a pack of wolves which would act together only in face of common danger. 'If the Jews were the only people in the world they would be wallowing in filth and mire and would exploit one another and try to exterminate each other.' There had never been any creative Jewish musicians or architects and apparent Jewish success in drama was due solely to a Jewish gift for mimicry. Even the Jewish religion was a fake: 'Here also everything is copied, or rather stolen; for the Jew could not possess any religious institution which had developed out of his own consciousness, seeing that he lacks every kind of idealism.' Baptised Jews were even worse than unbaptised ones because they could the more easily infiltrate the Aryan race. 'The black-haired Jewish youth lies in wait for hours on end, satanically glaring at and spying on the unsuspicious girl whom he plans to seduce.' Hitler remarks that the gassing of a few hundred Jews in 1914 would have been sufficient to prevent World War I but does not directly advocate mass extermination.

Struggle and the survival of the fittest were part of the law of nature. Man had no power to control nature: 'All he can do is to discover something.' 'Man must realise that a fundamental law of necessity reigns throughout the whole realm of nature and that his existence is subject to the law of struggle and strife . . . Man must submit to the eternal principles of this supreme wisdom. He may try to understand them but he can never free himself from their sway.' Applied practically, this law meant that nobody owed the Germans a living and that they had to fight to exist. Losing the war had almost been a good thing in that it had brought home this truth. 'To depend on the mercy of the enemy was a precept which only fools or criminal liars could recommend.' It was necessary to 'acquire soil for the German plough by means of the German sword.' He considered the British Empire, which then covered a quarter of the world, as being a supreme proof of this. 'No nation more prepared the way for its commercial conquests than England did with the sword and no other nation has defended its conquests so ruthlessly . . . It is not possible to build up such a mighty organisation as the British Empire by mere swindle and fraud.'

On practical points of policy, Hitler keeps neutral on the monarchy question, advocates friendship with England and warns of the implacable enmity of France against Germany. The pre-war Kaiser's government had been disastrously ill-advised by incompetent professional diplomats. Agriculture rather than industry should be the dominating social force. The army and its traditions should be jealously preserved.

Only the fact that Hitler became dictator of Germany and actually tried to carry out his ideas makes the bulk of *My Struggle* have any lasting interest. His dull style, his blatant prejudices and the serious gaps in his knowledge mean that most of the book is inherently worthless as a political treatise. The ideas within it had been drifting around Germany, and around Europe generally, for the previous fifty years or more and Hitler, by taking them up and pressing them to extreme conclusions, was in the long run to discredit them rather than advance them. However, the exception to this is the passages on propaganda and political organisation. In insight and force they are comparable with Machiavelli's *The Prince* and could well be of lasting interest. To his intuitive skill at propaganda, Hitler had added four years practical experience in Munich and when he describes his methods he does so as a master.

His starting point is that British propaganda had been a decisive factor in the war. How closely, if at all, Hitler had been acquainted with the work of such British propaganda geniuses as Northcliffe and Horatio Bottomley is not clear but he was convinced that the British had realised the propaganda advantage of sheer repetition. 'The success of any advertisement, whether of a business or political nature, depends on the consistency and perseverance with which it is employed.' This the British had done with their use of such terms as 'barbarians' and 'Huns' to describe the Germans. 'At first all of it appeared to be idiotic in its impudent assertiveness. Later on it was looked upon as disturbing, but finally it was believed.' The point was that 'the broad masses of the people are . . . but a vacillating crowd of human children who are constantly wavering between one idea and another'. Propaganda directed at them must be directed by 'the most skilled brains that can be found' and should ignore any question of objectivity. It must be 'systematically one-sided towards every problem that has to be dealt with . . . What should we say of a poster which purported to advertise some new brand of soap by insisting on the excellent qualities of the competitive brands?' Propaganda 'must present only that aspect of the truth which is favourable to its own side'.

Sometimes, however, it was necessary to ignore the truth

altogether but this had to be done carefully. Paradoxically, the big lie was more effective than the small lie.

In the big lie there is always a certain force of credibility; because the broad masses of a nation are always more easily corrupted in the deeper strata of their emotional nature than consciously or voluntarily, and thus in the primitive simplicity of their minds they more readily fall victims to the big lie than the small lie, since they themselves often tell small lies in little matters but would be ashamed to resort to large-scale falsehood. It would never come into their heads to fabricate colossal untruths, and they would not believe that others could have the impudence to distort the truth so infamously . . . The grossly impudent lie always leaves traces behind it, even after it has been nailed down, a fact which is known to all expert liars.

In this passage Hitler, formally, is describing only 'Marxist' and 'Jewish' methods but it is difficult to doubt that he was also exposing his own thought processes.

Hitler, naturally, had had no experience of radio or television and insists that the only really effective method of changing people's opinions is that of a skilled orator meeting them face to face. From the reactions of his audience he can tell whether or not his points are getting home and adjust his words accordingly. The essential thing was to get at people's emotions.

It is a case of overcoming ingrained prejudices which are mostly unconscious and are supported by sentiment rather than reason. It is a thousand times more difficult to overcome this barrier of instinctive aversion, emotional hatred and preventive dissent than to correct opinions which are founded on defective or erroneous knowledge. False ideas and ignorance may be set aside by means of instruction, but emotional resistance never can. Nothing but an appeal to these hidden forces will be effective here.

It was essential to have political meetings in the evening, when an audience was at its most receptive. There had to be the right kind of room. 'There are rooms which leave one cold for reasons that are difficult to explain. There are rooms which steadfastly refuse to allow any favourable atmosphere to be created in them.' It did not matter if a speech read badly afterwards, provided, like those of the British orator David Lloyd George, it had got at 'the soul of the people'. 'One must never judge the speech of a statesman to his people by the impression which it leaves on the

100

mind of a university professor but by the effect it produces on the people. And this is the sole criterion of the orator's genius.' People must be encouraged, gripped by the force of mass suggestion so that they no longer felt isolated or afraid. 'Mass demonstrations must burn into the little man's soul the proud conviction that, though a little worm, he is nevertheless part of a great dragon.'

The first volume of *My Struggle*, as dictated in prison, was scarcely more than a draft and required months of further work before it was fit for publication. By then Hitler was free. There was some dissention among the Bavarian authorities about his release. The police opposed it and so did the Interior Ministry. If he were to come out, the police wanted to put him over the border to Austria, as an undesirable alien; this, however, was thwarted through the Austrians ruling that Hitler had forfeited his citizenship in enlisting in the German army. Hitler had, however, a powerful sympathiser in the Bavarian Justice Minister, Franz Gürtner, who ended up as Reich Justice Minister on Hitler coming to power. It is unlikely that Gürtner, in 1924, foresaw such a future for Hitler and himself; his motivation was more probably that he saw Hitler as a sincere patriotic orator who had been carried away by over-enthusiasm, had already been taught a sufficient lesson and in the quietened political scene could do more good than harm.

The prison governor, Otto Leybold, had obviously taken a liking to Hitler and warmly recommended his release.

Hitler [he reported] has shown himself to be an orderly, disciplined prisoner, not only personally but also in his relations with his fellow prisoners . . . He makes no exceptional demands, is calm and sensible, serious, in no way aggressive and scrupulously anxious to comply with the restrictions imposed on him by his sentence. He is without personal vanity, is content with the prison diet, neither smokes nor drinks and when in the company of his fellow-prisoners is capable of exerting a certain authority over them . . . He is busy many hours a day with the draft of his book which is due to appear in the next few weeks; it will consist of his autobiography together with thoughts on the burgeoisie, Jewry and Marxism, German revolution and Bolshevism, the National Socialist movement and the events leading up to 8th November, 1923 . . . Hitler will undoubtedly try to revive enthusiasm for the national movement as he sees it; he will not, however, employ his previous violent methods . . . During his ten months under detention while awaiting trial and under sentence, he has undoubtedly become more mature and calmer than he was . . . He emphasises how completely convinced he is that a state cannot exist without solid law and order at home and without firm government. Hitler undoubtedly has a versatile and politically original brain, combined with extraordinary will-power and sensible ideas. In the light of the above considerations, I have no hesitation in saying that Hitler's general behaviour while under detention merits the grant of a probationary period of release.

The Munich police, in a report to the Interior Ministry, took a different line.

Numerous acts of violence committed by his followers . . . must be ascribed entirely to his influence. With his energy, he will undoubtedly be the instigator of serious fresh disturbances and constitute a permanent danger to the security of the state. The moment he is released . . . Hitler will resume his ruthless struggle against the government and will not be afraid to break the law.

In fact Leybold, the governor, was nearer to the immediate truth than were the police. Hitler really could be safely released, on licence, without immediately plunging back into illegal insurrection. He had calmed down. His destiny, he now considered, was not to win power in a single swift stroke. It was to use his skills and his will-power to construct a mass movement, covering all Germany, which would use the democratic machinery of the Weimar republic in order to destroy it.

7

A fair measure of Hitler's standing, when, after his release from prison, he re-embarked into politics on a 'legal' basis, is the early sales of the first volume of *My Struggle*. The first edition, of 10,000 copies, was published by Amann at twelve marks on July 18th, 1925. This, apparently, sold out and a second impression of 18,000 copies was issued at the end of the same year: but this was in excess of demand and as late as 1930 there were still 5,000 unsold copies. Since *My Struggle* would have been unsaleable in its own right and attracted buyers simply on the name of its author, these early figures indicate that Hitler was attracting some measure of interest and sympathy. At the same time however, he was remote from winning power and not a factor at all in mainstream German politics.

After the excitements and struggles of the 1919–23 period, the Weimar republic now appeared to be stabilising itself. The currency was sound and industry was flourishing. The psychological damage done by the war and the Versailles Treaty was still there but it was easy to suppose that the passage of time would heal it. With the fading of the bitter enmities of 1914–18, there was even a prospect that in the long run Germany would be able to get the worst of her legitimate grievances rectified peacefully. Certainly nobody wanted a war and even so extremist a politician as Hitler never publicly advocated one.

The new stability was epitomised by the election, in 1925, of the seventy-eight-year-old Field Marshal Paul Ludwig Hans von Beneckdorf und von Hindenburg for a seven-year term as President of the Reich, on the death of the first President, the socialist ex-saddlemaker Friedrich Ebert. Hindenburg belonged to the austere, relatively impoverished east Prussian aristocracy which dominated the German officer corps. His long military career had been successful but for most of it not outstandingly distinguished—apart from anything else, the Emperor Wilhelm II had disliked him. He had retired in 1911 after commanding an army corps and but for World War I would never have been prominent. In 1914, however, he had been brought out of retirement to command the army in East Prussia against the invading Russians. This was not because he was selected as an especially brilliant general but because it was felt that the temperamental, brilliant, domineering Ludendorff, who had already been selected as the army's chief of staff, needed a solid, experienced superior to keep him in check. Ludendorff did the work and Hindenburg oiled the machine by reconciling the disputes and hurt feelings that arose from Ludendorff's methods. Between them, they smashed the Russians at Tannenberg and then in 1916 moved to Berlin, with Hindenburg as nominal chief of staff of the whole army and Ludendorff, again, doing the real work with the title of first quartermaster general. Despite the loss of the war, Hindenburg became a genuine national hero. But he was badly troubled in his conscience because in November 1918 he had advised the Emperor to cross the frontier to the Netherlands and so played a part in the downfall of a monarchy to which he had owed allegiance.

Hindenburg was a Protestant Christian, fanatical on questions of honour and of keeping his word, but the fact that he had been born so long ago as 1847 and had lived his whole life in a restricted circle made the Germany of the 1920s and 1930s a puzzling place for him. He was a huge, impassive old man, consciously self-disciplined, and his air of calm authority made many people nervous in his presence. He had no belief at all in the Weimar republic or in democracy; he disliked politics and considered that the restoration of the monarchy, plus the power of the rural aristocracy, was the answer for Germany. Before running for President of the Reich he sought and obtained the consent of his exiled Emperor. However he took seriously his inauguration oath as President and was prepared to carry it out to the letter; if the monarchy were ever to be restored, it would, in his view, have to be through the constitutional Weimar processes.

Hindenburg's acceptance of the presidency represented a considerable accession to the strength of the Weimar system; with Hindenburg at the head, it was the more difficult for traditionalists to regard it as just a socialist and liberal trick. In particular, the support of the army was now absolutely assured. He was the embodiment of old Germany in general and of old Prussia in particular and made the ideal figurehead for healing the state. Things only began to go wrong when this puzzled old man, from

1930 onwards, was forced by events to be not just a figurehead but an actual maker of decisions.

Beyond the fact that he was now determined to act 'legally', Hitler had no cut and dried plan for achieving power. One essential, towards which he felt his way and which had begun to take shape by 1926 or 1927, was to build up the National Socialist movement into a form of 'state within the state', with its own inner life. This was quite different from most of the German political parties, which did not aim for mass membership and really consisted of committees formed to fight particular election campaigns. The outstanding exception to this was the great Social Democratic Party, which was both Hitler's leading opponent and, in many organisational matters, his model.

The history of the Social Democratic Party dated back to the 1860s and had been one of almost continual progress. Already by 1912, although in total opposition to the imperial regime, it was the largest single party in Germany and commanded a third of the electorate. The Weimar constitution, ultra-democratic in tone and with specific provision for the future transformation of the German state into a socialist one, was above all else the work of the Social Democrats. In 1919 they had a party membership of a million and thirty-eight per cent of the vote. The first president, Ebert, was a Social Democrat and so was the first Chancellor, Philipp Scheidemann. Later, during the 1920s, the party provided two further Chancellors, Gustav Bauer and Hermann Müller. In the great state of Prussia, Social Democratic administrations under Otto Braun and Karl Severing were almost continuously in office from 1920 to 1932.

The Social Democrats were above all the party of the urban working class and they were closely linked with trade unions. There was also a substantial middle-class and professional membership, with special organisations for such groups as Social Democratic lawyers and Social Democratic teachers. A child could join its most junior section, the Nest Falcons, at six, then progress to the Young Falcons at ten, the Red Falcons at twelve, the Socialist Workers' Youth at fourteen and the Young Socialists at eighteen before reaching the main party at twenty-five. It ran (in 1927) 188 daily newspapers, headed by the internationally famous *Forward,* plus hundreds of magazines. It made its own films. It even had its associated private army, the Reichsbanner Black-Red-Gold, formed in the aftermath of Hitler's Munich coup with the specific purpose of defending the republic; the Reichsbanner enrolled three and a half million members. Other party organisations proliferated off into completely non-political fields; there were Social Democratic choirs, Social Democratic cycling clubs, Social Democratic photographic clubs and so on almost limitlessly. The party formed a state within the state in that it was possible to live almost one's complete life within it and its ancillaries. At birth one could be put into Proletarian Nursery Care and, after passing through all the stages of party membership, end up in the hands of the Free Thinkers' Cremation Club. However, unlike the National Socialists, or for that matter the Communists, there was little attempt at thought-control, or interference in private life; although the party was nominally Marxist and had an anti-clerical bias, there was no official line on religion.

The failing of the Social Democrats was that they never succeeded in winning much more than a third of the popular vote. Hitler never did so either in a normal election but he had the will to translate a third of the votes into power whereas the Social Democrats waited hopelessly for a majority. They were hamstrung because whether or not they happened to be in office, in a coalition, at any given moment, they felt a continuing need to defend the Weimar system, the first step towards socialism. The British Labour Party, in contrast, although in many ways similar to the German Social Democrats, had no fear that its principal opponents would subvert the constitution and so could fight elections all out. Unlike the Social Democrats, the Labour Party felt no particular responsibility for the existing political system, and was not on the defensive about it. The Social Democrats also lacked leadership. So far as there was a leader at all, it was the former paper-hanger Otto Wels, aged fifty-two in 1925, but he was more the manager of the enormous party bureaucracy—there were nearly 50,000 full-time employees of the Social Democrats and their ancillaries—than a candidate for the leadership of Germany. The party was controlled by its elderly bureaucrats who considered personal leadership, on the Hitler model, an absurdity; but they underestimated its popular appeal.

While the Social Democratic organisation was obviously a model for Hitler to try to copy—the Communists, who had also gone on to a 'legality' tack were trying to copy it too—there is no evidence that Hitler fully foresaw or planned in advance how he would use it. The characteristic dictatorships of the early twentieth century were unlike any previous autocracies. They were based primarily neither upon brute force nor upon tradition. They were based on the fanatical support of a section of the population— the 'party'—and this group was able to permeate all social institutions. The party, with millions of members, controlled the country and the dictator controlled the party. In 1925, however, this development had still not really taken place. In the Soviet Union, Lenin was dead and had no apparent successor; Hitler, like many others, believed that the Soviet system was on the verge of crumbling into chaos. In Italy, Benito Mussolini was head of the government but he had not yet constructed a totalitarian state and rival political parties were still permitted. To Hitler it was always the ends that counted and he used whatever means he considered tactically profitable at any given moment. By about 1930, when both Stalin and Mussolini had established their systems, Hitler had obvious models to work from. Although many a National Socialist member was to take the party extremely seriously, Hitler, in the last analysis did not do so. The party was a tactical device to be used in whatever way seemed promising according to circumstances.

While he was now moderately well-known inside Germany and able to command over 10,000 buyers for a dull book, probably nobody at all, with the possible exception of Hitler himself, thought that Hitler would become dictator of Germany within eight years. He had lost some of his abler supporters. Göring was abroad and did not come back into party affairs until 1928. Röhm took a job in the Bolivian army. Old Eckart was dead of a heart attack— the story was that he had died of fright in Landsberg when the guards opened fire in a rehearsal of their procedure if the prisoners were trying to escape. Hitler mourned Eckart and spoke of him affectionately for the rest of his life and Eckart had certainly helped Hitler get launched in the early 1920s. But, politically, the loss of Eckart was something of a gain for Hitler. It forced him back on to his own judgment which, politically, was sounder than Eckart's and freed him from Eckart's alcoholic over-optimism.

Hitler's first task was to regain control of the National Socialist movement itself and it was far from certain that he would be able to do so. In the presidential campaign of 1925, Ludendorff (who now had no faith in Hitler at all) ran against Hindenberg as an extreme nationalist candidate and so attracted support from National Socialists: but he failed so miserably that the net result was to eliminate him as a serious rival. While Hitler had been in prison, a potential rival to him had emerged in Gregor Strasser, a pharmacist from Landshut in Lower Bavaria. Strasser, who was aged thirty-three in 1925, had worked with immense energy to build up a National Socialist organisation in northern Germany: the groups he founded were very small—the Hamburg branch, for example, had only two or three dozen members—but they had their own, special flavour, significantly different from the parent organisation in Munich. Most of Strasser's recruits were, like

Strasser himself, ex-servicemen from the trenches who believed that wartime comradeship should be translated into civilian terms as the basis of the state. On economics they were more radical than Hitler.

Strasser drafted a constitution for a National Socialist Germany, which would be run by a dictator-president, elected for a seven-year term. Under it, the state would take a fifty-one per cent share in major industrial enterprises, encourage craftsmen and small businessmen to form themselves into guilds on a medieval model and, quaintly, weaken the power of 'money' by getting wages paid, whenever possible, in kind. Strasser was always more an ally of Hitler than a disciple. Their common anti-semitism made their ideas sound more alike than they really were; Hitler, fundamentally, was obsessed by foreign policy whereas Strasser's interests were primarily domestic.

Hitler went from prison to the Bechstein villa at Berchtesgaden and then, after a fortnight, called on the Bavarian Minister-President, Heinrich Held. Using his charm and his persuasive powers, he convinced Held that in future he was going to act entirely within the law. Held, thereupon, lifted the bans on the National Socialist Party and on Hitler speaking in public. Legalising the National Socialists was not particularly significant because the party members had been able to keep going by calling themselves by different names but, obviously, it was central to Hitler to be allowed to make speeches. But he followed up this success with a tactical blunder which was uncharacteristic of his methods and difficult to explain. To build it up into a great public occasion, he delayed his first speech for nearly three months. He wanted people to be curious and excited. For the scene of it he chose the great Bürgerbraü cellar, at which he had proclaimed his seizure of power in the 1923 attempted coup.

The speech was due to begin at eight p.m. and such was public curiosity that people began to line up to enter the hall in mid-afternoon. By six p.m. the hall was full, with 3,000 people, and the police turned away a further 2,000 who arrived later. Infected by the excitement, Hitler seemed to lose control of himself. Parts of the speech, and those which tactically were most important to him, were intelligent enough. He asked for absolute control of the National Socialists for one year. 'I am not willing to accept any conditions. Once again I take the responsibility for everything that happens in this movement.' The audience accepted this by acclamation. Then, he went on to identify the republic with 'Marxists' and 'Jews' and to threaten violence against it. 'To this struggle of ours there are only two possible issues: either the enemy passes over our bodies or we pass over theirs.' It sounded as if he did not intend to be 'legal' after all, and Held immediately reimposed the ban on his speaking in public in Bavaria. Most of the other German states followed suit, including Prussia, and so Hitler lost his main political weapon, his oratory. Until 1928, over most of Germany he could speak only to closed party meetings.

Hitler's main managerial device for keeping the whole party under his control, and reducing the independence of the north, was to succeed in insisting that every member should have a membership card, issued from Munich and signed by Hitler himself. The legal corporation, which controlled the party's assets, was the Munich membership. The local branches had no real rights at all and were governed by area managers (*Gauleiter*) who were the personal delegates of Hitler. It took, of course, three or four years to build up even a skeleton organisation on this basis. That Strasser agreed to become an area manager, rather than leader of the northern National Socialists in his own right, helped to get the system started; however when Strasser started founding news-papers—the first was the *Berlin Workers' News* in 1925, under the editorship of his younger brother Otto—he kept them in his own private ownership.

Part of Hitler's skill as a political leader was an unusual ability to spot and enlist talent. Some of his choices were surprising to the orthodox. He took on people who had criminal records or were scandalous homosexuals. To every complaint, he replied that the only thing that interested him was whether a person could be of service to the party; but it was often reckoned that he liked to have a hold over his subordinates and went out of his way to favour those who could be blackmailed. By his own account, he built up his machine on the basis of the personalities available rather than on any cut and dried organisational plan. 'Discontinuing the form-ation of a local group is better than the disaster of organising one when a capable and progressive leader-personality is lacking.'

Although not capable himself of systematic administration, Hitler recognised the importance of efficiency. At the heart of the party apparatus, besides the capable Amann in charge of pub-lishing, he had two rigidly efficient bureaucrats in Philip Bouhler, a clerk who became party secretary, and Franz Schwarz brought in from the Munich municipal accountancy office to be party treasurer. Bouhler delighted in issuing ever more complex rules for the party's administrative procedure; whenever he spoke to Hitler, he made a slight bow before saying anything. Schwarz had a frugal nature and his hatred of financial waste helped to make the most of the party's narrow income. Hitler himself took no salary but the party ran his Mercedes car for him and, besides royalties from *My Struggle*, he could still attract personal gifts from admirers. His simple private life required no considerable income to support it, although in 1925 he acquired his own small villa, House Wachenfeld, at Berchtesgaden and this for the rest of his life—although eventually rebuilt on a more substantial scale—became his retreat and his only real home. In Munich he continued to lodge in two rooms in a private house until in 1929 he took a substantial, middle-class flat of his own.

The crucial meeting which established Hitler's full control of the whole party came on February 4th, 1926, at Bamberg in northern Bavaria. Up to this point, Strasser and the other northern leaders had been acting semi-independently with their 'radical' programme. Strasser's private secretary, Josef Goebbels, had actually called for the expulsion from the party of 'the petit bourgeois Adolf Hitler'. The northerners wanted to expropriate all major capitalists, not just Jewish ones, and in foreign policy they called for an alliance with the Soviet Union. The actual breaking point, or near breaking point, between them and Hitler was that they wanted the party to campaign against the compensation allowances paid by the state to the displaced German royal families. Hitler, who wanted no outright breach with the monarchists, opposed this. He invited about twenty of the northern leaders to a conference at Bamberg ostensibly on the ground that it was a convenient place, in the middle of Germany, for all to travel to. Actually he chose Bamberg because it was one of the most successful centres of the Bavarian party. The northerners, accustomed to branches of only twenty or thirty members in the Ruhr, Berlin and Hamburg, could hardly avoid being impressed by their being welcomed by hundreds of local enthusiasts and the town being garlanded with posters and placards.

Hitler spoke for five hours but avoided ideological argument. The original 1920 programme should be retained simply because it was 'the foundation of our religion' and for it the 'martyrs' of 1923 had died. He was not prepared to negotiate at all. The northerners had the choice of rejecting him altogether or falling into line, although Hitler put this tactfully. He was at his most masterly and the northerners surrendered. Moreover Hitler had noticed Goebbels.

Josef Goebbels, aged twenty-nine in 1926, was the son of a factory foreman in the Rhineland and at the age of four suffered from poliomyelitis which left his right leg permanently twisted and two inches shorter than the other one. He was a brilliant but unpopular boy at school, with an unusually strong memory and a

110

love of reading. In August 1914 he tried to join the army but the doctor rejected him without even bothering to examine him; he spent, by his own recollection, the following forty-eight hours locked in his room, sobbing hysterically. Financed by scholarships and loans, he went to university and his parents, Roman Catholics, hoped that he would become a priest; Goebbels himself first accepted this but while at university lost his religious faith. He ended up with a doctorate at Heidelberg in 1921, his thesis being on the romantic playwright Wilhelm von Schütz. He was a waif of a man, scarcely five feet tall, but he busied himself with writing plays, novels and poetry in the hope of becoming a famous literary figure. Publishers turned all his work down and he came to the view that this was because they were Jewish. He entered politics in 1923 by becoming secretary to a right-wing Reichstag deputy and two years later became secretary to Otto Strasser. He was already an accomplished public speaker.

Hitler met Goebbels first in 1925 and was instantly impressed by his ability. He set out to win him over. Extracts from Goebbels's diary of the time indicate, very frankly, how Goebbels was wooed from being suspicious of Hitler into becoming an adoring disciple. He was impressed by *My Struggle* and in October 1925 wrote: 'I am finishing Hitler's book. Thrilled to bits. Who is this man? Half plebian, half God! Really Christ, or only John?' At the same time, however, he was criticising the Munich leadership—'those schlerotic bosses in Munich' . . . 'the movement in Munich is a bear garden' . . . 'Strasser is to be our battering ram against the Munich bosses.' Criticising the right-wing, he wrote: 'Germany's sons will bleed to death on the battlefields of Europe as mercenaries of capitalism. Perhaps, probably in a "holy war against Moscow"' . . . 'Better to go down with Bolshevism than live in eternal capitalist servitude.' But in November 1925 he met Hitler in Hanover and Hitler obviously exerted his charm. 'He is having his meal. He jumps to his feet, there he is. Shakes my hand. Like an old friend. And those big blue eyes. Like stars. He is glad to see me. I am in heaven . . . That man has got everything to be king.'

A few weeks later Goebbels met Hitler again. 'What a fellow. And he tells stories the whole evening. I could go on listening for ever . . . I want Hitler to be my friend. His photograph is on my desk. I could not bear it if I had to despair of this man.' But at the Bamberg conference, Goebbels was disillusioned. In rejecting the socialistic side of National Socialism, Hitler was being 'horrible'. 'I can no longer believe in Hitler absolutely. That is terrible: I have lost my inner support.' But two months later Hitler,

111

who must have sensed what was going on in Goebbels's mind, invited him to Munich and Berchtesgaden. They went on a motoring trip together to celebrate Hitler's birthday. It was a happy time with Hitler at his best as a companion. 'Pouring rain. Breakdown. Hitler like a boy. Riotous, singing, laughing, whistling . . . I believe he has taken me to his heart like no one else . . . Adolf Hitler, I love you, because you are both great and simple.' After further meetings in July, Goebbels caved in completely.

The chief talks about race questions. It is impossible to reproduce what he said. It must be experienced. He is a genius. The natural, creative instrument of a fate determined by God . . . He is like a child: kind, good, merciful. Like a cat: cunning, clever, agile. Like a lion: roaring and great and gigantic . . . A star shines leading me from deep misery! I am his to the end. My last doubts have disappeared. Germany will live! Hail Hitler!

Goebbels had been worth taking trouble over. One of the major propaganda geniuses of the early twentieth century, he was, at the same time, completely loyal to Hitler personally. Despite his abilities and his undoubted personal courage, he was the kind of person who needed to subordinate himself to a kind of father figure. He would cheerfully tell lies for the sake of the cause but he had a sense of humour and could be kind-hearted. He remained the most left-wing of the leading National Socialists. In the late 1920s he had some fellow-feeling with the Communists; he regarded them more as rivals than as enemies. His weakness was vanity and this presumably was a reaction from his weak physical figure: it was the means through which Hitler caught him and held him.

While Goebbels was the big catch in the aftermath of Hitler's release from prison, there were hundreds of lesser adherents within the party won in the same kind of way to acceptance of Hitler's Messianic mission. During 1926, almost every National Socialist in Munich met Hitler personally, receiving a handshake, a glance from the appealing blue eyes and a warm word. For the moment, indeed, from Hitler's point of view, this kind of thing was immediately more important than winning fresh recruits from outside. The energy he would otherwise have used in making speeches, he devoted to writing a second volume of *My Struggle*.

According to the announced plan, the first volume was supposed to cover Hitler's biography and the early history of the National Socialists. The second volume was supposed to be about policy. In fact, characteristically, the arrangement is not so clear cut as that.

Hitler had already dealt with some policy in the first volume and in the second volume he adds further narrative material. There is, however, a clear difference in tone between the two volumes. The first, written in prison after an attempt to overthrow the government and with Germany in turmoil, is a fighting document, dealing with current realities, or what Hitler regarded as current realities. The second, dictated to Max Amann in the peace of Berchtesgaden and with German politics quietened down, is reflective, dreamy and fantastic. The core of it is a lengthy consideration of German foreign policy. Nobody who was expecting soon to be in power could possibly have written it and, as it was, it was to cause Hitler some embarrassment when he did become the German leader. Volume two is the day-dreams of a political thinker, not the action programme of a political leader.

Hitler lays it down that Germany's potential allies were Britain and Italy. It was useless to try to come to any understanding with France. He quotes Clausewitz; 'French policy may make a thousand detours on the march towards its fixed goal, but the destruction of Germany is the end which it always has in view as the fulfilment of the most profound yearning and ultimate intention of the French.' Germans in the past had too often fought for myths. 'In the case of a people like the Germans, whose history has so often shown them capable of fighting for phantoms to the point of complete exhaustion, every war-cry is a mortal danger. By these slogans our people have often been drawn away from the real problems of their existence.'

The leading diplomatic errors of the pre-war imperial government had been to expect Italy ever to fight in alliance with Austria-Hungary and to have aroused British rivalry by building a navy and acquiring overseas colonies. The true model for Germany should be the methods of the British, which were 'brilliant opportunism'. By keeping Europe in turmoil and allowing no single power to become dominant, they had freed themselves to conquer a world empire. The British were still as ruthless as ever. It would be 'puerile to suppose that . . . England could lose India without having first put forth the last ounce of her strength in the struggle to hold it . . . Indian risings will never bring this about.'

The British were now worried at French dominance in Europe and so, in accordance with their historic principles, would be glad to turn to Germany, provided it were a strong Germany. Sentiment did not come into it. An alliance must offer 'the prospect of a common success, of common gain and conquest.' Whatever the value of Hitler's historical analysis, he was plainly short on contemporary information. Stanley Baldwin and James Ramsay

MacDonald, who for most of the period between the wars dominated British politics, had already plainly emerged by 1926 and they were not the kind of men to fit Hitler's ideas at all. Had he known about them, he would have considered them hopelessly wet and this would have been a factor to take into account. That he did not do so must have been a shortcoming.

Hitler dismisses any idea of simply trying to restore the frontiers of 1914. Racially and militarily they had been 'illogical'. Germany should turn her attention away from the south and west and look for new territories for colonialisation in the east. It was simply a matter of power. 'Only an imbecile could look on the physical geography of the globe as fixed and unchangeable . . . State frontiers are established by human beings and may be changed by human beings.' 'When we speak of new territory in the east today we must principally think of Russia and the border states subject to her . . . This colossal empire in the east is ripe for dissolution.' Russia was now fundamentally weak because, in the Bolshevik revolution, it had lost its aristocracy which, because of the 'German strain' in its blood had been able to hold it together. Hitler is vague over exactly what parts of Russia should become German but is clear that the occupation would have to be by force. 'The soil on which we now live is not a gift bestowed by heaven on our forefathers. But they had to conquer it by risking their lives.' 'The territory on which one day our German peasants will be able to bring forth and nourish their sturdy sons will justify the blood of the sons of peasants that has to be shed today.'

In fact Hitler did not carry out the policy outlined in this volume. His presuppositions were a Britain and an Italy friendly to Germany and thus neutralising France, plus a Russia falling into anarchy. When he did actually invade the Soviet Union such conditions did not exist and he was motivated by an over-confidence bred from two years of military victories. It would therefore be incorrect to argue that *My Struggle* set out a systematic programme, which Hitler systematically implemented, and so everyone ought to have known exactly what he was up to. Hitler was not a systematic man and volume two of *My Struggle* is the day-dreams of a relatively inexperienced politician. It represents his mood in 1926 and is a set of speeches turned into a book, rather than a considered treatise written to guide him in later years. The most it proves is that Hitler yearned for German expansion eastwards, and, reasonably enough, regarded force as the only method of achieving this. It is a set of ideas, not a programme.

Some German nationalists of the time, including the Strasser wing of the National Socialists in the north, were advocating that Germany and the Soviet Union, as the defeated powers, should band together against the victorious west. Indeed at the military level in the 1920s a good deal of actual co-operation did exist; the Germans provided instructors for the Red Army and, in return, were allowed to practise on Russian soil with weapons that had been banned to them under the Versailles Treaty. Hitler explicitly rejects this line of policy. No alliance with Russia was necessary because it would be possible to get alliances with Britain, or Italy or both. It would be a disaster to link up with the Bolshevik government which consisted of 'blood-stained criminals' who were 'the dregs of humanity'. 'The fact of forming an alliance with Russia would be the signal for a new war. And the result of that would be the end of Germany.'

There is no plan at all for world conquest. In the epilogue, in a rhetorical flourish, Hitler does remark: 'A state which, in an epoch of racial adulteration, devotes itself to the duty of preserving the best elements of its racial stock must one day become the ruler of the earth.' But this, if it means anything at all, is obviously aimed only at a remote future. Earlier in the book, in any case, Hitler has already remarked that the United States 'could become mistress of the world' if she chose to use her power intelligently. While the Germans were 'members of the highest species of humanity on this earth', and thus biologically entitled to expand, they were not yet a master race. That was something which had not yet come. 'In the distant future man may be faced with problems which can be solved only by a superior race of human beings, a race destined to become master of all other peoples.'

Naturally Hitler goes on about the Jews 'the hereditary enemies of our people' but with a rather different twist than in the first volume. The book says 'France is becoming racially more and more negroid, so much so that now one can actually speak of the creation of an African state on European soil.' Thus the French occupation of the Rhineland had caused 'an influx of negroid blood' into Germany itself. This was part of the 'Jewish' plot for doing down the Germans. 'Systematically these negroid parasites in our national body corrupt our innocent fair-haired girls.' Germany was the 'chief pivot' of the Jewish struggle to capture the world.

This volume was published at the end of 1926 in an edition of 18,000 copies at a retail price of twelve marks. Sales at first were slow—the first volume had been sufficient to satisfy the merely curious; up to the end of 1927 the sales were under 6,000 and they dropped to 3,000 in 1928. In 1930, when Hitler had really begun to spring into national prominence, Amann combined the two volumes into a single book in a bible-like binding and put down the price to eight marks: it was then that the sales began to soar.

It is an interesting sidelight on Hitler's character that in future years he always looked back on this period, from 1926 to 1930, as the happiest in his life. Particularly during World War II, his table conversation kept harking back to how much he had enjoyed himself in the late 1920s. Many a politician, in his circumstances of the time, would not have been happy at all, but rather would have felt a sense of frustration. For example, Winston Churchill found no enjoyment at all in being out of office; he fulfilled himself as war leader and had no nostalgia for his periods of failure. Hitler, however, was in a worse position than simply being out of office. He was stateless; he had lost his Austrian citizenship in 1925 and the Weimar authorities refused to grant him German citizenship. While he did make private requests to the Bavarian government for citizenship, he refused to make a public issue of the matter, taking the view that his wartime military service should have been enough to qualify him without his asking. But his lack of citizenship made him liable at any moment to expulsion as an undesirable alien. Moreover he was out of prison only on licence and in the event of being caught out in misbehaviour was liable to be hauled back to complete his five-year sentence. His ambition was not just to get office—indeed he genuinely was not interested in this. He wanted to become dictator of Germany and felt himself uniquely fitted for the post. Yet his National Socialist Party was a splinter group which attracted little outside attention; before 1930 there was no case of any outsider being perceptive enough to recognise its potential.

So far as nationalism was a force in Germany, it was represented by the conservative National People's Party, which had at least four times the strength of the N.S.D.A.P. and much more money.

Yet Hitler pottered around happily. He spent weeks on end in Berchtesgaden. In Munich he liked to talk for hours to his cronies in an artists' café, the Osteria Bavaria, with much laughter coming from his table. It was in the Osteria Bavaria that in 1927 he more or less commanded one of his young women members, Ilse Prohl, to marry Rudolf Hess. In the autumn he attended the Wagner festival at Bayreuth, staying with the composer's son Siegfried, with whose wife, Winifred, he had one of his gallant, sexless friendships. Such was the power of his imagination that his ideas were almost as real to him in thought as if they were actually being applied: Hitler's thinking was always a unique mixture of tactical shrewd-

116

ness with sheer fantasy. Moreover, the party, although small, was definitely going forwards rather than backwards.

The exact membership figures are impossible to establish, for this period; apart from actual falsification to make the party seem bigger than it really was, there was also a habit of counting as a member anyone who had ever enrolled, without taking account of deaths, resignations, drop-outs and expulsions. In 1926, the party probably had about 35,000 members, about 0·08 per cent of the adult German population. This may have doubled by 1929 to 70,000 or 0·16 per cent of the adult population. But Hitler was using his skill to build a sound organisation with such people as Goebbels within it.

If the current rate of progress were maintained, without setbacks, then Hitler had a fair chance of becoming a considerable political figure by about 1940. Meanwhile he had the joys of being a party leader with little or none of the strain involved in taking difficult decisions. His immediate entourage consisted of people who loved him and considered him to be a kind of saint. Now in his late thirties, Hitler had found a sense of direction. He had progressed far from his obscure life in the men's hostel in pre-war Vienna. He had even found a measure of calm; he was no longer the agitated ex-corporal, fresh from the army, and filled with passionate anguish about the loss of the war, but a calm man with freedom to live how he pleased.

His life would have been the happier had this been the limit of his success.

8

Hitler and the National Socialists appeared for the first time as a nation-wide movement in the Reichstag elections of May 1928. They were short of money and members, but they had a high proportion of militants and they planned their campaign carefully. They contested all thirty-five of the election districts into which Germany was divided under the complex proportional representation system of the republic. Hitler himself, as a non-citizen, was not able to be a candidate and the party's list was headed by General Franz von Epp, the man who had overthrown the Communist regime in Munich in 1920. Epp was chosen more for his name than for his services to the party. Other candidates included Goebbels, Gregor Strasser, Feder, the bureaucrat Wilhelm Frick and Göring, who had recently returned from abroad and who was chosen for his glamour as a war hero. The others of the thirty-six candidates were mostly paid party officials.

Putting up thirty-six candidates for a Reichstag which had 489 seats was not an attempt to win power. Undoubtedly, however, Hitler hoped to use the campaign to get over his message to the electorate as a whole and to win his first power base in the Reichstag. Also—and this was an indication of the party's financial problems—it was a serious factor that Reichstag members received salaries and free railway passes and so getting party officials into the Reichstag would be a relief to party funds. There was also the point that Reichstag members were immune from arrest. Goebbels, on his election, went so far as to state: 'I am not a member of the Reichstag. I am a possessor of parliamentary immunity and a possessor of a free railway pass.' He reckoned that the election of sixty or seventy National Socialists would 'equip and pay for our fighting machine'. While the latter,

118

obviously, was an exaggeration it does give an indication of the scale of National Socialist resources at that moment.

The election, as a whole, was a placid one with only the National Socialists being fanatical about it. They started their planning a year ahead and had their first posters up by the spring of 1928. They hoped, in particular, to do well in Bavaria, the Ruhr and industrial Saxony and in these areas Hitler, Strasser and the movement's other leading speakers concentrated their efforts. Over the whole Reich, the party claimed to have organised 10,000 election rallies and to have used 118 speakers. The result of this effort had no effect on the broad movement of public opinion, which was a swing in favour of the Social Democrats and the Communists, but nevertheless the National Socialists did not go down into total defeat. They secured 810,000 votes, which was just under three per cent of the poll. This gave them twelve seats in the Reichstag. On the face of it, this was a weaker performance than in the previous election of 1924, when National Socialist candidates had won fourteen seats. But in 1924 Hitler had been in prison and had been exercising no control; of the fourteen no more than seven had really recognised his leadership—the others had mostly been followers of Ludendorff. Now he had a disciplined group in the Reichstag, with Frick as its leader and Frick was ready to take orders from the party headquarters in Munich. Moreover Hitler had won his twelve seats at a moment when the nationalist movement, generally, was losing ground disastrously. The main nationalist party, the German National People's Party had its representation cut from one hundred and three to seventy-three.

In fact this election was the last really normal one of the Weimar republic. Fantastic as it would have seemed to any observer of the time, Hitler in less than five years of it was to become absolute dictator of Germany. Even Hitler himself, in his most vivid fantasies, is unlikely to have expected this to happen so soon. But the particular balance of the parties in the 1928 Reichstag was to turn out to be a significant contributory factor in this happening.

The Social Democrats, who had pushed up their representation from 131 to 153, were by far the largest single party. But it required a minimum of 245 seats to control the Reichstag and so they could not govern without allies. Even if they had enlisted their fellow-Marxists, the Communists, they would still have been short of a majority. The Communists had increased their vote by twenty per cent and now held fifty-four seats. But in practice Communists and Social Democrats were violently hostile towards each other. The Communists, like Hitler's little National Socialist group, had no interest in making the Weimar system work—

they wanted and expected a revolution. They called the Social Democrats 'the auxiliary police of Fascism', 'agents of big business' and so on.

Since neither in terms of ideology nor in the numbers of votes available were the Communists viable allies, the Social Democrats had to look to the bourgeois parties. Of these the most apparently solid was the Centre Party which, with its ally the Bavarian People's Party, had secured seventy-eight seats. But the trouble with the Centre was that it was not only a political party but also an interest group. Founded in the days of Bismarck's cultural struggle with the Roman Catholics, it was the political voice of the Roman Catholic thirty-two per cent of the German population. It had some working-class support, especially in the Rhineland and Bavaria, and it was not lacking in social conscience; its leaders included such considerable figures as Heinrich Brüning and Konrad Adenauer. However its fundamental motive as a party was not so much to govern Germany as to preserve the interests of the Roman Catholic Church, especially in such matters as education. Because it was based upon a firm interest group, its support fluctuated remarkably little; the Centre and the Bavarian People's Party were always there in the Reichstag with eighty or so seats.

Between them the Social Democrats and the Centre commanded 231 seats but even this was short of the minimum controlling majority of 245. So allies had to be found yet further to the right. Here the main forces were Stresemann's German People's Party, with forty-four seats, and the Democratic Party with twenty-five seats; these were right-wing parties of a character somewhat similar to the British Conservatives or Liberals, or the American Democrats and Republicans; that is they were liberal on constitutional matters and supported the Weimar system, but at the same time were anti-socialist. While the Centre's principles were primarily religious, and so it could bargain quite easily on political matters, the parties of what can be termed the 'democratic right' had definite economic and political principles which, especially in a moment of economic crisis, made it difficult for them to collaborate with the Social Democrats. Both these parties did badly in the 1928 leftward swing, each losing seven seats.

The 1928 Reichstag was completed by the Economic Party, which stood for shopkeepers and the like and won twenty-three seats, the Christian National Peasants' Party with thirteen seats, the Land Union with three seats, and the People's Rights Party, a curious group which wanted to revalorise pre-inflation securities, with 2 seats.

As a whole, the result was an overwhelming vote of confidence

120

in the parliamentary system. Many members of the Centre and the 'democratic right' had monarchist inclinations but they nevertheless accepted bourgeois democracy and envisaged a restored monarchy as largely a figure-head on the British model. Only the National Socialists, with their twelve seats, the Nationalists with their seventy-three and the Communists with their fifty-four, were in outright opposition to the parliamentary system and it could be reckoned that they were extremists who more or less cancelled each other out; the voting had been more than three to one against them. Commenting on the results, the London *Times* said in a leading article 'Republican Germany has become a reality'.

In this political kaleidoscope, the National Socialists commanded little attention. Many summaries of the composition of the Reichstag ignored them altogether by name and lumped them into the category of 'minor parties'. The London *Times* referred to them as the 'Hitler-Fascists' and gave them only ten words in a 500-word report on the election. The big question was how to form a viable government, with a majority in the Reichstag. Hindenburg appointed a Social Democrat, Hermann Müller, as Chancellor but he failed in trying to negotiate an agreement with the Centre. So instead of a formal coalition, Müller ended up after some weeks with what he called 'a cabinet of personalities' recruited across the whole moderate spectrum, from Social Democrats to the 'democratic right'; he avoided seeking any vote of confidence. This was a sound, indeed inevitable, procedure but it could work only on a caretaking basis. The cabinet was divided on fundamental matters of economic policy and so was liable to break up when decisions were needed in crisis conditions.

One side-effect of the election was of advantage to Hitler. Whereas he had improved, or at least held his parliamentary position, the Nationalist Party, with its fall from one hundred and three to seventy-three seats, had lost ground badly. The Nationalists were super-patriotic, monarchist, often possessed of anti-Jewish prejudices and dedicated to the proposition that Germany should assert herself to get rid of the Versailles Treaty. Their leader, effectively, was the industrialist and newspaper magnate Alfred Hugenberg who had made his fortune during the inflation period. Hugenberg was a shrewd administrator, reactionary in his political views and in close touch with the east Prussian aristocracy. However he could not match Hitler as a public personality—he was a short, tubby man who wore old-fashioned clothes and was only an indifferent public speaker. Also the Nationalists, in comparison with the National Socialists, were sterile in their views. They looked back to the past whereas Hitler wanted to construct a new type of Germany. Although, in 1928, they had nearly five times the voting strength of the National Socialists, the election result still increased Hitler's standing in nationalist circles generally. He was no longer just an odd Bavarian with a comic coup behind him, but a man clearly capable of winning votes for the broadly nationalist cause. In particular he seemed to have a little success in attracting the young, whereas the Nationalist Party tended to have a middle-aged membership.

Another side-effect of the election, to Hitler's advantage, was the twenty per cent rise in the Communist vote. If the bourgeois parties were unable to stem the tide of Communism among the ordinary working people, then an orator of Hitler's genius might be able to do so; it was from the 1928 election onwards that some industrialists began to look upon Hitler with interest and to consider how he might be used to defend their property. The steelmaster Fritz Thyssen, who had previously considered Hitler a mere agitator, added the National Socialists to the list of parties benefitting from his donations, and in 1928 he contributed to the funds for building the National Socialist headquarters in Munich, the Brown House. He was finding that Hitler had 'miraculous political intuition, devoid of all moral sense, but extraordinarily precise'.

In fact analysis of the 1928 election results—and Hitler made it at the time—shows that he was hardly appealing to the proletariat at all. In the industrial Ruhr and Saxony, where the National Socialists had made so much effort, their results were well below their average—only 1·3 per cent in the Ruhr. Where they had done better than their average was in the countryside and the small towns, especially in Schleswig-Holstein and Weser-Ems. In the latter, where their party membership was weak and they had conducted only a local campaign, they won 5·2 per cent of the vote. They were getting the support of small craftsmen, of independent shopkeepers, of peasants who felt their interests were being neglected by the right-wing bourgeois parties and threatened by the Marxists. The main vote of such people did not, at this stage, go to the National Socialists but to such groups as the Economic Party, which put up its representation from eighteen to twenty-three and the various new Peasant Parties which had not been at all in the previous Reichstag but now won twenty-three seats. Nevertheless the National Socialists, almost by accident, had stumbled upon what in the future was to be the backbone of their mass support.

Hitler, of course, was at home among the small town and rural lower middle class because it was the world of his own youth.

His intuition and understanding were powerful in dealing with almost anyone, but he knew the fears and aspirations of his own people best of all. It has been held, possibly exaggeratedly, that the National Socialists were not a political party at all but merely a conspiracy for seizing power. The best supporting evidence for this was the sharp change in emphasis and content in National Socialist propaganda following the 1928 election. The party's rural and small town voters had known little or nothing of National Socialist ideology and they had supported it because of the military glamour of Epp and Göring and partly as a protest against the bourgeois parties. As the London *Times* correspondent put it, perceptively, there was an element in the German electorate which would vote for anything, provided it were new. Systematically Hitler set out to exploit lower middle class discontent and harness it for his own purposes. One joke of the time, and a not inapt one, was of a National Socialist orator proclaiming: 'We don't want higher bread prices. We don't want lower bread prices. We want National Socialist bread prices.'

Thus agriculture had not previously been a leading National Socialist interest. But by the end of 1928, it seemed, in rural areas, as if the party thought of little else. The party then had twenty-two national speakers, recognised by headquarters as 'specialists' in particular fields. Of these ten, or nearly a half, were agricultural specialists; civil servants' affairs had two speakers, railway affairs three speakers, the war disabled two speakers, the economy had four speakers and 'Freemasons and Bolshevism' only one. There was no specialist speaker at all on the Jews. From now until he was in power, Hitler more and more muted his anti-semitism; nobody who wanted to do down the Jews could have any doubt of where he stood on the question and it was important not to alienate people who were uninterested in them.

Since Hitler intended to come to power as a dictator or not at all, he was free from the democratic discipline of having to make at least a show of carrying out campaign promises; winning power was a separate matter from what he intended to do with it. Thus the National Socialists were free to woo votes from any quarter, to swing rightwards or leftwards as any tactical situation demanded; while Goebbels, as area manager for Berlin, tried to stir up the proletariat with arguments closely similar to those of the Communists, the speakers in the countryside represented the National Socialists as ultra-patriotic conservatives, devoted to the interests of the small proprietor. In the towns, especially the small towns, the party made a particular point of campaigning in favour of small shopkeepers and against the chain stores which, in Germany as elsewhere were extending their share of the retail trade. Chain stores were characterised as 'Jewish'. There was an additional advantage that the small shopkeepers provided advertising revenue for the struggling National Socialist newspapers. For purposes of appealing to the mass electorate, the true National Socialist doctrines were hidden in a form of code or sometimes ignored altogether. Göring, in a frank moment in 1930, commented on a law which prohibited attacks on the republic: 'Before we had the law . . . we said we hated this state; under this law we say we love it—and still everyone knows what we mean.'

Besides the concentration of propaganda effort on the countryside and in the small towns, the National Socialists also had to make a showing in the great cities, especially the Reich capital of Berlin—'red Berlin', or 'Babylon' as Hitler had called it in his early days. By his own account, probably accurate, Hitler had delayed making any major campaign in Berlin until he had found exactly the right man to conduct it. The man he had eventually found had been the twenty-eight-year-old Josef Goebbels, who after he had been wooed into a fanatical adherent of Hitler personally, was appointed the Berlin area manager at the end of 1926.

Goebbels found an apathetic party membership of, by his own account, about a thousand. He immediately purged it down to 600 by getting rid of ineffectives. Then in five years he built it up into a major force in Berlin politics, using violence, humour and sheer gimickry. While he had obviously read with care the propaganda sections of *My Struggle* and learned from them, he also had his own gifts as a propagandist. Apart from Hitler himself, Goebbels was the best orator in Germany. Unlike Hitler who spoke out of his deepest sub-consciousness in the effort to carry conviction, Goebbels's performances were studied in advance and carefully rehearsed; Goebbels spoke from his brain. On occasion he 'debated' with his opponents at his meetings by playing recordings of extracts from their speeches and then 'replying' to them. His mockery could get an audience helpless with laughter and then he would suddenly turn serious and explain about the coming saviour, Adolf Hitler. He made a point of provoking physical violence with the Communists and held meetings in Communist districts; the Communists were only too easy to provoke and, indeed, welcomed battles as evidence of imminence of a revolutionary situation. Goebbels paraded wounded stormtroopers, with crutches, wheel chairs and stretchers, on to his platforms and orated about their sufferings—on occasion, the 'wounds' were completely fake. He especially liked a good funeral of a stormtrooper who had died in some street battle; his members paraded with their banners to the cemetery and Goebbels spoke movingly over the open grave. Underlying all the tricks was a passionate faith in the product he was selling and this carried its own conviction. Goebbels was so successful that in 1929 Hitler, while keeping him as Berlin area manager, appointed him as propaganda director for the whole party. In fact, though, Goebbels never really won Berlin; so long as there were free elections, it remained 'red'.

Hitler's real thoughts in the aftermath of the 1928 election were not farmers or small shopkeepers. He was obsessed with foreign policy and in the summer of 1928 settled down at Berchtesgaden to write another book, or rather to dictate it, mostly to Amann. Presumably he had some intention of publishing it at the time but in fact its existence was long kept a secret and it was first published as late as 1961 under the title *Hitler's Secret Book*. Like *My Struggle,* it has a few perceptive passages but much of it consists of enormous hypotheses erected upon inadequate or incorrect facts. The overriding theme is that Germany would have to fight a war but should choose her ground for doing so with skill and care and with the right allies.

War had its unpleasant aspects, as he himself knew. 'I did not learn about the war at a restaurant table reserved for regular customers' *(Stammtisch)*. It was racially dangerous in that it tended to kill off the best elements in the people. But, on the other hand, too long a peace could cause the best elements to emigrate. The United States, which he describes as 'racially selective', had been 'bleeding Europe of its best people'. She was thus likely to become the greatest power in the world and a strong Germany was needed to counterbalance her. The fault of World War I was that it had been an 'aimless squandering of the most precious German blood' with no real objective. The Germans should learn from the British who would, with 'iron determination', shed the whole blood of their nation, if necessary, to maintain their world empire. 'A world empire of the size of ancient Rome, or of present-day Great Britain, is always the result of a marriage between the highest race value and the clearest political aim.'

Germany needed new territory, both for counterbalancing the United States and for living space for her own population. There was no use in being soft about this.

Every healthy, vigorous people sees nothing sinful in territorial acquisition, but something quite in keeping with nature. The

125

modern pacifist who denies this holy right must first be reproached for the fact that he himself at least is being nourished on the injustices of former times . . . The present distribution of possessions on the earth has not been designed by a higher power but by man himself.

He is indefinite about what territory, exactly, Germany should conquer but it should certainly be in the east. France must be taught 'a decisive lesson' but 'We will also never sacrifice the blood of our people in order to bring about some small border rectifications, but only for territory in order to win a further expansion and sustenance for our people. This aim drives us eastwards'.

Hitler rejects from first principles any solution of Germany's 'overcrowding' by methods of population control. This would only weaken the race. He praises the Spartans for having put out their weaker children to die. This 'was more decent and in truth a thousand times more humane than the wretched insanity of our own day which preserves the most pathological subject, and indeed at any price, and yet which takes the life of a hundred thousand healthy children in consequence of birth control or through abortions'. Contraception was wrong if only because of the many great Germans who had not been elder sons in their families. But the German race had its defects. The English kept up a better average quality of people than the Germans, although they lacked the German capacity for producing extremes of genius and 'lowness'. Thus the English were a steady nation. 'In contrast, German life in everything is infinitely unstable and restless and acquires its importance only by its extraordinarily high achievements, through which we make amends for the disquieting aspects of our nation.' Hitler's belief in German instability, as expressed here, must have been one of the key factors in his planning. He could use the instability as a means of overthrowing the existing regime. When in power, one of his leading ideas was that a disciplined, totalitarian regime would eliminate the instability but enable 'the extraordinarily high achievements' to continue. In any event, the Germans were clearly superior to the Slav races, notably the Russians. Old Russia had really been run by Baltic Germans who had adopted Russian names; the Bolshevik revolution meant that she was now controlled by Jewish capitalism, and this lacked 'constructive forces'. There is no analysis of the actual course of events in the Soviet Union—the new economic policy, the first five-year plan, the emergence of Joseph Stalin, the fall of Trotsky.

In *My Struggle,* Hitler had stressed the value of an alliance between Germany and Britain. In the new book he makes rather less of this but goes on at great length about the importance of getting an alliance with Italy. Although he does not specifically say so, it is clear that he was motivated, in part, by sheer admiration of Mussolini and the Facist system. What he does argue is that Germany and Italy faced similar problems of having done badly out of the war and of over-population. Italy had to behave like imperial Rome 'not out of any presumption to power but out of deep internal necessities'. Other potential allies for Germany were Spain and Hungary.

Over both Russia and Italy, Hitler was running counter to much orthodox German nationalism, including the Strasser wing of the National Socialist Party itself, and the conservative officer class. In particular, the army was concerned at Germany's weak position against France; not only was France, with her numerically vastly superior forces, able to enter Germany from the west at will, her allies in the east, Poland and Czechoslovakia, formed almost an encirclement. In view of Poland's clear territorial ambitions against Germany, which were in fact to be realised in 1945, the threat was more than an academic one. The obvious answer was to form an understanding with Poland's traditional enemy, Russia, as in fact the army was already doing. In calling for an attack on Russia, Hitler, on this line of reasoning, was imperilling rather than strengthening Germany's security. However this was all capable of argument and Hitler could always bring out straight anti-Communism in his support.

Italy was a much trickier question. Orthodox German nationalism was much excited over the 250,000 German-speaking population of the South Tyrol which had been annexed to Italy from Austria under the Versailles Treaty. Under the rigorous Fascist government, they were being forcibly Italianised in language, culture and education. In some ways their plight was similar to that of the Germans in the Sudeten areas of Czechoslovakia but most observers regarded it as being a good deal worse; in the late 1920s it was the grievances of the South Tyroleans rather than of the Sudetens which aroused German nationalist ire. Yet Hitler was urging an alliance with the Fascist oppressors and modelling his movement upon them. Because of his public refusal to take up their grievances, he was even being accused of taking money from Mussolini. In the book he argues that the Tyrolean agitation was caused by 'Jewish internationalists' who were not interested in the question as such but only in using it as a stick to beat Mussolini. Italy had a fair claim to the South Tyrol in that it gave her a natural geographical frontier; her friendship could only be won at the price of recognising this. What mattered was the future destiny of the whole German people, rather than the problems of one minority who had unfortunately got cut off. When new territory had been won in the east, the colonisers could include South Tyroleans. Meanwhile the South Tyroleans should form a bridge between Germany and Italy rather than a cause of division. However such a line of argument was difficult to put in public without seeming to advocate a war and Hitler rarely or never used it in speeches. The book does state: 'The National Socialist movement as such must educate the German people to the effect that it must not shrink from staking its blood for the sake of shaping its life.' But in practice the National Socialist movement never put things like that in election propaganda. It merely stressed the need for individuals to make sacrifices for Germany, without being specific.

This book was written by Hitler in his final phase as a dreamer rather than a practical politician. It was the last flash of the naive orator from the trenches. While, undoubtedly, it represented his true thoughts, it was not the kind of thing with which he could win power. The principal reason it was not published at the time seems to have been the purely business judgment of Max Amann that *My Struggle* was selling very slowly and it would be a mistake, at that particular moment, to overload the market with another dull Hitler book. Later, when a sale would have been very easy on the basis of Hitler's fame and power, it would have been politically unwise, or even disastrous, for it to have been published. When, in the great struggle for power, Hitler was appealing to millions of German voters, it would scarcely have been politic to put out a book telling them that they must stake their blood. Later, when Leader of Germany, Hitler was trying, with only moderate success, to get the rest of the world to think he was a lover of peace; a book stating exactly the opposite would have ruined his pre-1939 diplomacy. *My Struggle* was a definite embarrassment internationally to him in the 1933–9 period but at least it could be represented as the work of his immaturity; in fact he made something of a point of refusing to alter *My Struggle* but said he would 'make his corrections in the pages of history'. A new book from him, such as the 'secret book', would have been impossible to explain away; world politicians and journalists would have got on to it at once.

Their weak showing in the elections and their stress on 'legality' helped the National Socialists to secure full freedom to organise and hold public meetings. The last restrictions on them, those in Berlin, were removed actually the day after the elections. It was an interesting conundrum, which attracted discussion at the time, whether or not a liberal, democratic state should tolerate the existence of political parties which proposed to abolish it. This, of course, was just as much a problem over the Communists as it was over the National Socialists. The prevailing liberal view of the time, both in Europe generally and in the United States, was that such parties should be allowed to exist, and all the democratic countries permitted them. In Germany in 1928, the fact that the National Socialists were apparently quite weak was an obvious reason for not bothering too much about them. Hitler, himself, justified his line of wanting to abolish the constitution by constitutional means with solid argument: 'The German nation does not live for a constitution, but it gives itself that constitution which serves its life . . . We National Socialists hope that we may be able to give the German people a new and better consitution.' Paradoxically, despite the pre-1933 anti-constitutional campaigning, the National Socialists never did give Germany a new constitution but acted merely through special powers voted under the Weimar system.

Less obviously constitutional was Hitler's private army, the S.A., and there was always some confusion about the exact purpose of it. Many S.A. members themselves, despite Hitler's talk of 'legality', regarded themselves as a potentially revolutionary movement, preparing to take over the state by force. At this period—the late 1920s—the S.A., with a membership of a few tens of thousands, was youthful and middle-class; it was a significant source of funds for the party that the quartermaster department in Munich provided the brown shirt uniform for them at a profit. Hitler declared that through them he was trying to build a force of young men free from traditional German beer-swilling. 'We like to see the young man who can stand all weathers, the strong young man. It does not matter how many glasses of beer he can drink, but how many blows he can stand; not how many nights he can spend on the spree, but how many kilometers he can march.' This kind of Baden-Powell approach was less than wholly successful and there was a club-like atmosphere to many S.A. units, with much beer consumed. The S.A. men were of a type who actually enjoyed drilling and weapon training for their own sake; had the size of the army not been restricted to 100,000 men under the Versailles Treaty, many of them would have been happy to volunteer as soldiers. Descriptions of them, as always, varied according to the viewpoint of the observer. To any opponent of Hitler they appeared mere 'rowdies' and, beyond doubt, there was a definite hooligan element in the membership, and this was not something Hitler did anything to discourage, beyond insisting, formally, on 'legality'. Hitler supporters, of course, and even many detached onlookers saw them as serious patriots. Thus the London *Observer* described them as 'honest and earnest' and consisting of 'splendid young people of the German middle classes'.

In terms of numbers of course, the S.A. was far outstripped by the Steel Helmet organisation which had a million members; the Steel Helmet were the army veterans from the war, nationalistic and conservative, distrustful of the new age; it was equivalent to the American Legion or the British Legion. The Steel Helmet had little regard for the Weimar system but it idolised Reich President Hindenburg; its members tended to be middle-aged, unlike the youthful S.A., and it was more a social and charitable organisation than an effective political force.

Hitler long had difficulty in controlling the S.A. It was a useful instrument for conducting propaganda parades and marches, for providing physical protection for National Socialist speakers, for collecting money and for taking part in well-publicised fights with 'reds'. But the S.A. itself tended to resent being used as a mere tool of the 'civilian leadership'; Goebbels managed to win its loyalty in Berlin but on the whole it had its own separate life, and Hitler himself was spoken of derisively in some of the late-night carousing.

There was no particular qualification for membership of the S.A. apart from being male, non-Jewish, in the right age-group and willing to accept the broad aims of the party. On the 'divide and rule' tactics, which were one of the secrets of his administrative success, Hitler decided to form a select, inner group of the S.A. which would be personally loyal to himself. From the beginning he had used, and needed to use, personal bodyguards. In 1925 they were organised into a definite unit, the Defence Squad, which was abbreviated to S.S. *(Schutzstaffel)*. The first commander was Hitler's driver, Julius Schreck. Later Hitler objected to Schreck making up to his niece and girl-friend, Geli Raubal, and dismissed him. But the S.S. remained in existence as a specialised detachment of the S.A., concerned with Hitler's personal protection. The full development did not begin, as always, until Hitler had discovered whom he regarded as the right man to command it.

This was Heinrich Himmler, who was easily the most cranky of what became the top National Socialist executive leadership. (Rosenberg and Streicher were about as odd but they had little real power.) Himmler had been born in 1900 of a bourgeois family, with snobbish tendencies. He had been just too young to get into World War I, a fact he bitterly regretted, and had gone on to read agriculture at university at Munich. He had at first been a devout Catholic but student activities, including duelling in which he got scarred, had by his early twenties turned his fervour to nationalism, flavoured with paganism and superstition. (He believed in astrology and reincarnation.) He had been the more eager to prove his manhood because his stomach had been too weak to take the beer which virile students were expected to consume by the litre. He had entered politics via Röhm and during the 1923 attempted coup had marched with the rank and file, bearing the imperial war flag. He had then obtained work with a chemical company but continued his National Socialist activities, acting as an assistant for Gregor Strasser. He had acquired some reputation for enthusiasm and diligence, being willing to rush off on party errands on his motor cycle. Long before he knew Hitler personally he had become haunted by him—he would talk to Hitler's picture hanging on his wall. He joined a curious group called the Artamans, which shared some common membership with the National Socialist Party. The Artamans were obsessed with the dangers of Polish infiltration and they volunteered to work on German farms in the east to replace Polish hired workers; the scheme collapsed when it became clear that these young enthusiasts were merely providing cheap labour for the farmers and landowners. Himmler had some idea of emigrating to Russia itself as a farmer and began to learn the Russian language.

In 1928 Himmler chose his wife, at first sight. She was called Margarete Boden and was big, blonde, blue-eyed and eight years older than himself. In view of her obvious 'racial' merits, the fact that she was Protestant, divorced, probably too old and certainly unknown to him did not count with Himmler. With her, Himmler started a chicken farm but the whole enterprise was disastrous. The chicken farm did not pay properly and he and Margarete found they could not get on; after the birth of a daughter, Gudrun, they separated.

It was in the aftermath of this fiasco that Hitler first got to know Himmler and to recognise his qualities. Although in many ways absurd, Himmler was honest, loyal and (although previously he had given only slight evidence of this) an efficient organiser. He was an emotional man, but so much so that he learned to hide his emotions and to appear calm. He was an excellent listener. Once he had an idea, he would no more than flinch from carrying it through to its ultimate, logical conclusion, in the meantime being happy, at a superficial level, to appear to be a jolly fellow and to crack affable jokes. He came to believe that he was a reincarnation of Henry the Fowler, the medieval Saxon king, who had conquered the Slavs. (He is a character in Wagner's *Lohengrin*.)

On January 6th, 1929, Hitler appointed the twenty-eight-year-old Himmler to be head of the S.S., which then had a membership of

131

280. It is unlikely that either of them foresaw the future implications at all except that Hitler, intuitively, must have realised that Himmler was possibly capable of being creative. But Himmler was not an important catch, at the time. There had been no need to flatter him into submission, as with Goebbels, or to give him a Reichstag seat, as with Göring. He was just a functionary who, through Hitler, was to become a distinct force in the European history of the early twentieth century. Himmler at once got going, extending the S.S. on a selective basis. He scrutinised the photograph of every prospective member through a magnifying glass and stipulated a minimum height of five feet eight inches. 'I knew that men of a certain height must somewhere possess the blood I desired', he later recalled. Until 1930, the S.S. remained a specialised branch of the S.A. but its membership grew to nearly 3,000. Then Himmler was given a degree of organisational independence and by 1932 the membership was some 30,000. Up to this point the S.S. had worn the ordinary brown shirt of the S.A. but with black cap and tie to indicate special status; from 1932 onwards, however, a new all-black uniform was gradually introduced. Hitler himself frequently wore S.A. uniform but he was not a member of the S.S. and did not use its uniform. However, the S.S. was consciously an élite; intelligently, Himmler and Hitler harnessed the obvious pride that came from this to try to make it entirely devoted to Hitler personally. In 1931 it received its motto: 'My honour is loyalty.' *(Meine Ehre heisst treu.)* The retention of the word 'squad' *(Staffel)* for what was growing into an army-sized organisation helped to keep a sense of intimacy and elitism among the members, at least until about 1941. The swollen S.S. of the later war years, containing many non-Germans and conscripts, was a different proposition and included anti-Hitler elements in its top leadership.

Sheer concentration of forces and marching in the streets was one of Hitler's basis propaganda techniques. He liked always to give an impression of strength. This had started, really, with the 'Battle of Coburg' back in 1922 and by the late 1920s had developed into the pageantry of the annual party rallies at Nuremberg. The annual party congress had originally been a genuine meeting for discussion of policy and tactics but this quickly withered and it became a pure demonstration planned on obviously theatrical principles, plus speeches from the leadership to inspire and instruct the rank and file. Hitler chose Nuremberg, the city of Dürer and the seventeenth-century *Meistersinger*, because there was a sense in which it was easily the most 'German' place in Germany, the classical period of the eighteenth century having passed it by. In National Socialist terms it was the fief of Julius Streicher, who although disliked and even despised by many in the movement for his crudity, was quite a capable organiser. The first Nuremberg rally, in 1927, was a relatively small affair but still the concentration of party members and S.A. from all parts of Germany gave an impression of strength: some 30,000 attended in forty-seven special trains. There was no rally in 1928 but in August 1929, when Hitler was aged just over forty, the series began really to get off the ground. Hitler had the willpower to keep his right arm outstretched in salute for hours at a time. In reviewing a parade he concentrated his personality on the marchers, trying to scan each man's face.

The spectacular high spot of the 1929 rally was a vast firework display, which culminated in the swastika flaming across the Nuremberg sky, with an eagle above it. The sentimental heart of the occasion was the 'consecration' of new party banners by Hitler; he did this by touching each new banner with the 'blood flag', the standard that had been carried in the 1923 attempted coup. There were some 60,000 men on parade, plus spectators (many of whom, naturally, were not party members) estimated at 150,000. As was to become his annual custom at Nuremberg, until the last rally in 1938, Hitler devoted much of his main speech to a recital of the history of the movement; he was attempting to create, and succeeding in doing so, a distinctive National Socialist mythology.

9

Hitler's private life was a restricted affair. He lived mainly for politics and secondarily for art, architecture and music. He never put himself before the German people as a super-efficient administrator, better suited than anyone else on brain-power to run the country, but as a mystical man of destiny. Indeed the idea that Hitler was a new Christ, or Messiah, a 'man sent by God' to save Germany was a part of National Socialist small-talk and many of those close to him believed in it. Part of the mysticism lay in Hitler's bachelorhood. In the ordinary course of politics it can be a handicap for a candidate to be unmarried and it was part of Hitler's exceptional skill that he made his bachelorhood an asset. He went so far as to represent himself as 'married to the German people', rather as a Catholic nun may be described as a 'bride of Christ'. While in the ordinary course of events, women voters, in particular, tend to be suspicious of an unmarried political candidate and to feel that he cannot really understand ordinary life, in Hitler's case his bachelorhood actually attracted women. This must have had something to do with the World War I casualties which had left many women single who would otherwise have been married. Hitler's passionate avowals of his love for the German people, and the fact that he had no wife, could make many single women feel that here was someone who really cared about them. It was nothing out of the way, as Hitler's career progressed, for women to write to him and ask to make love to him. Something of the same kind of thing happened to Benito Mussolini, although he was not a bachelor, and Mussolini cheerfully took advantage of it. Hitler, however, preserved intact his celibate public image.

In fact Hitler was not chaste. Relations with women were far from being his top priority and he was unusually careful and secretive. But he did have a sex life and there have been many attempts to guess at its exact nature. He has, variously, been defined as a voyeur, a sado-masochist, impotent, an habitual masturbator and a reader of pornography. There was a rumour that he experienced orgasms at the climaxes of his speeches. Obviously, it is a likelihood that so unusual a person as Hitler may well also have been unusual in his sexual tastes, but the evidence for any particular version is tenuous. All that can be stated with certainty is that in superficial relations with women he was gallant and charming and that his deeper relationships could have an incestuous tone. He believed, deeply, that a woman's place was in the home and could never bear to discuss politics with a woman. He hated syphilis with exceptional animosity and could well have caught it during his Vienna period. One of his jokes, when in relaxed mood, was that he had never had any luck with women. He would defend his apparent celibacy on the ground that he could never dare to have children for the reason that they would be sure to be a disappointment; they would never match his own genius. More lightly, he compared women to flowers: he loved flowers but that did not mean he had to be a gardener.

It was in 1928 and 1929, when he had established his party in the Reichstag and had become a recognised, although still minor, figure on the German political scene that Hitler began what was probably the only deep love affair of his life. This was with his niece, Angela 'Geli' Raubal, who was twenty years younger than him. Geli was not his full niece, her mother, also called Angela, being only Hitler's half-sister, but the incestuous implications are inescapable. It could be relevant that his own mother had been in the habit, on occasion, of addressing her husband as 'uncle' and this could have stuck in young Adolf's mind.

In 1929 Hitler was affluent enough—he returned his income for that year as a 'writer' to the income tax authorities at 15,448 marks—to leave his backroom lodgings and rent a solid middle-class apartment in Prince Regent Street, Munich. It had nine rooms and was the kind of place that might have been occupied by a lawyer or bank manager. Hitler's return of his income was probably on the low side, omitting gifts from admirers and fees as a public speaker, and, in addition to the Munich apartment, he was also renting House Wachenfeld at Berchtesgaden. But, while living in a comfortably bourgeois style, he was far from rich and showed no ambition to become so. He installed his half-sister, Angela, as housekeeper, and she brought the blonde young Geli with her.

Hitler dominated Geli. Nobody else saw very much to her— she was a normal type of twenty-year-old, without any special looks, brains or charm—but Hitler spent every moment he could in her company. To him she was a sort of daughter, as well as girl-friend. Exactly what went on between them is, of course, unknowable; but a fair assumption would be that they were physical lovers. One account is that Hitler sketched her in the nude, but it was not his normal habit to attempt the human figure. Another account is that she was seen to flinch when Hitler tapped his leg with the dog-whip, which he still habitually carried Certainly there are indications that Geli did not entirely reciprocate her uncle's devotion. They went together to theatres, on long mountain walks and to cafés, Hitler making no secret of their closeness. Some party leaders expected that they would marry and it would be difficult for such an idea not to have entered Hitler's own mind. Had he married Geli, and made a lasting match of it, the consequences to his career could have been considerable. He would have lost his 'celibate' appeal and gained no compensating political advantage. Geli was not a sophisticated kind of woman suitable to be the wife of a public man. Indeed in Berlin, Magda Goebbels, the well-to-do, sophisticated bride of Josef Goebbels made a point of introducing Hitler to women of a type who could have helped him on the social side. It was said, even, that Magda had wanted to marry Hitler herself and accepted Goebbels only as second best. (Hitler was best man at their wedding in 1929.) But no other women could compare with Geli for Hitler. The fact of her being his niece, could by itself, have been enough to weaken him politically; opposition papers loved making political capital out of National Socialist amatory scandals—Röhm's homo-sexuality, Streicher's love of pornography and the escapades of some lesser figures—and they were already feeling their way towards 'exposing' the Geli affair. On the other hand, at least, Hitler was happy with Geli.

It was while Hitler was causing almost open scandal with Geli that his political career suddenly started to race ahead. It did so for reasons beyond his control. In the world depression, unemploy-ment in Germany, as in every other industrial country, began to rise catastrophically. The middle classes had mistrusted the Weimar system ever since the collapse of the currency in the 1923 inflation. Now the working classes, too, were suffering. The constitution collapsed under the strain. The 'grand coalition' led by the Social Democrat Hermann Müller was an alliance of Socialists with the Catholic Centre and the democratic right-wing parties and so long as it held together it could control the Reichstag; the anti-constitutional parties—that is the Nationalists, the National Socialists and the Communists—were in a minority of less than a third. But the unemployment imposed an impossible tension on the coalition.

The Socialists, with their concern for the working class, wanted the state to alleviate the hardship of unemployment, whereas the Centre and right, in the economic orthodoxy of the time, thought in terms of coping with depression by reductions in state expenditure. The latter was closely similar to the philosophy of the Hoover administration in the United States and the MacDonald-Snowden line in Britain.

The Müller cabinet fell on March 27th, 1930, through the Socialists resisting cuts in unemployment benefit and never again was there to be a normal parliamentary government under the Weimar system. The puzzled old Hindenburg appointed Heinrich Brüning, a deputy from the Centre, to be the new Chancellor but he, with the Social Democrats in opposition, could not command a majority in the Reichstag and relied upon emergency decrees signed by Hindenburg. Brüning, a coldly-honest intellectual with little understanding of how to sway public opinion, embarked on an austerity programme with cuts in unemployment benefit and official salaries and state expenditure generally. It was an inherently unpopular course of action and he made no attempt to sell it, beyond delivering dissertations which were scarcely more than academic lectures. Unlike Philip Snowden, the British Chancellor of the Exchequer, who was a skilled enough propagandist to get old age pensioners sending in their pension books and children emptying their money boxes to help the government, Brüning could bring no sense of national drama to his austerity. Moreover the austerity blatantly failed to produce results; unemployment continued to rise. In January 1930, the official total of unemployed was 3,218,000; a year later it was 4,887,000. Both figures showed less than the full truth as they took no account of short-time working and people out of work who were not qualified for benefit.

In Germany, as in other industrial countries, the depression, to the ordinary unemployed worker, was a puzzling phenomenon. Was it for this he had fought in the war? The Communists, and to some extent the Socialists, could explain it in terms of a capitalist plot to do down the workers, or at least in terms of an inherent weakness in the international capitalist system. In Germany, however, Hitler and the National Socialists had a concrete answer. They blamed it on the lost war, on the 'enslavement' of Germany by the winning side and the exaction of reparations. Successive Weimar governments, by caving in to the demands of the French and the British, had betrayed the German people with results that were now plain to see.

It was convenient for Hitler that the rise in unemployment

coincided with the Young Plan of November 1930. This was supposed to be a final settlement of the reparations question. By it, Germany was supposed to pay about one hundred million pounds a year for fifty-nine years. Compared with the entirely absurd Versailles claims, it was a realistic scheme, within Germany's capacity. It was geared, largely, to the war debts which the former allied countries owed to the United States and they could claim they were not really getting anything out of it. The signing of the agreement—it was in many ways the posthumous culmination of the career of Gustav Stresemann, who died in October 1929—brought Germany fully back into the comity of Europe; it involved the abolition of the last rights of the allies to intervene in German affairs and the evacuation of the Rhineland by allied troops.

But the German nationalists, with Hitler in the van, had plain grounds for denouncing it. This was not a *Diktat* forced upon a recently defeated nation in the heat of warlike emotion but a calmly negotiated agreement signed in conditions of peace. The only justification for Germany paying reparations at all was that she had been guilty of starting the war. This was an incorrect view of history, and it was a scandal that Germany's leaders should accept it. This line of arguments was not just an eccentricity of Hitler's but commanded wide support, in Germany and outside. Even as early as 1929 there was no consensus among outside historians that Germany had been solely guilty for the war and it was certainly psychologically impossible to expect the German people themselves to accept such a proposition. By throwing himself into the campaign against the Young Plan, Hitler won money and support from such 'respectable' figures as the nationalist newspaper magnate, Hugenberg, the industrialist Fritz Thyssen and the economist, Hjalmar Schacht, who had resigned the presidency of the Reichsbank in protest against it. Schacht met Hitler and, as he later recalled, was impressed by his 'energy' and also by the fact that he appeared 'simple and restrained'. Thyssen, chairman of the United Steel Works, Essen, had already contributed in a small way towards building the new National Socialist headquarters at Munich, the Brown House, and acted as a link between Hitler and some other industrialists. By his own later account he respected Hitler's 'intuition' and expected National Socialist success to lead to a restoration of the monarchy. While the big money from industry did not reach Hitler until 1932, the campaign against the Young Plan was the start of his political respectability.

Formally, the campaign was only a moderate success. The Young Plan was ratified by the Reichstag and a petition against it and the 'enslavement of the German people', attracted only about four million signatures, or only ten per cent of the electorate. Moreover reparations really had nothing to do with unemployment. If anything, indeed, the need to raise one hundred million pounds a year in foreign exhange should have stimulated rather than depressed German production. In the period after World War II, West Germany was able to pay out one hundred million pounds a year in voluntary reparations to Israel, and to German Jews and former German Jews in general, with no crippling effect on her economy. Nevertheless, it came to seem to many a plain German that the miseries of unemployment and depression were due to Germany having lost the war, being mulcted by her greedy former enemies and being betrayed by politicians who would not stand up for her rights. A somewhat similar process was at work, in reverse, in Britain where it was widely believed among the unsophisticated that having been on the winning side in the war should somehow guarantee prosperity and social justice. David Lloyd George, who in oratorical prowess was the British equivalent of Hitler, had specifically promised to create 'a land fit for heroes'.

Hitler worked with sporadic bursts of great energy but he was also dallying with Geli. He gave little sign of realising that his destiny was just around the corner. In his conversation he did, of course, take it for granted that one day he would be in power and he had already drawn up architectural plans for a new Berlin; but the time for it had not yet come. Local elections in December 1929 provided a flash of hope, with the party polling well but still only as a fringe group; in Berlin Goebbels got the National Socialist vote up to 5·7 per cent, compared with the 1·5 per cent in the 1928 Reichstag election. The party was acquiring its own momentum of growth, irrespective of Hitler's activities, and, spasmodically, he had to intervene sharply to ensure that it remained under his control. While passionate on the platform, Hitler appeared 'moderate' and 'reasonable' to important outsiders he met privately. Mass unemployment stimulated recruitment to the S.A. From being a mainly middle-class body it changed rapidly to a rough, proletarian image, inflamed by the radical ideas of the Strassers and Goebbels. Hitler kept the 'radicalism' in check. In May 1930, he had a stand-up row in Berlin with Otto Strasser, emphasising his words by striking the table with his whip. By Otto Strasser's account, Hitler insisted that 'socialism' meant taking over only concerns which were acting against the interest of the state. Indiscriminate socialisation would be 'simply a crime' because it would 'destroy the economy'. Strasser thereupon quit the National Socialists and set up his own 'Black Front' which, however, was never to be more than a minor nuisance to Hitler.

139

The elder brother, Gregor Strasser, was not so fanatical about socialism and he continued as the party's organisation manager.

Few real Socialists joined the S.A.; when articulate working men despaired of Social Democracy and the Weimar system they generally went over to the Communists, who were expanding nearly as quickly as the National Socialists. The S.A. was a club for men who were just bored and disgusted. The striking thing about it—and few outsiders liked to recognise it at the time—was that the Hitler formula was genuinely capable of breaking through the class barriers which were such a rigid feature of German society. Whereas the Communists insisted that class conflict was the key to everything, the National Socialists, successfully, propagated the idea that national identity was more significant than class. What mattered above all else was to be 'German'. Membership of the S.A. fluctuated from month to month—it seems to have been between 60,000 and 100,000 strong in 1930—and, particularly in Berlin, some units were gangs which owed more loyalty to their immediate leaders than to the party as a whole. Some of the Berlin leaders adopted half-jocular nicknames, such as 'King of the Boozers', and there were units which nicknamed themselves 'The Robbers' and 'The Pimps' Brigade'. In cases of dispute with the central leadership they were occasionally known to go on 'strike' and refuse to defend meetings.

In 1930 Hitler offered the command of the S.A. to Ernst Röhm, his army befriender in the very early days in Munich. Röhm in 1925 had emigrated to Bolivia to become a training officer in the army there. This was a good job, in its way, and he hesitated before accepting Hitler's offer. Hitler's handling of the 1923 attempted coup had not impressed him. But Röhm was an ambitious man and recognised the possibility of a considerable career for himself in what was now a rapidly growing force in German politics. Moreover he had been personally unhappy in Bolivia through loneliness and wrote naive, unobscene letters about the lack of homosexuality there. 'They know nothing of this kind of love', he wrote in a letter which fell into anti-Nazi hands and was published. Röhm made no attempt to disguise his tastes and would boldly declare: 'I have never pretended to be a goody-goody.' Although the Berlin of the time was world-notorious for its homosexual and transvestite night-clubs, homosexuality was far from socially respectable and the National Socialists were much attacked for including 'perverts' among their leaders. Hitler, however, tolerated Röhm's inclinations, and even justified them by remarking that Wagner himself had been a pederast. At the same time, the fact that Röhm had lovers among his young men of the

140

S.A. was always a useful potential weapon against him, and one that Hitler eventually used.

Röhm was an efficient organiser and leader. He came to see himself, at the head of the S.A., as a second Scharnhorst who would create a new German army: old Prussian-style discipline would have to disappear and its place would appear the self-discipline of dedicated men. It would be a 'people's army'. While Röhm went a long way towards creating such a spirit in the S.A., he made the fundamental miscalculation that the real German army was in the hands of blimpish conservatives. He failed to realise that the generals were as eager as himself to learn from past errors and would be easily intelligent enough to be able to repulse any attempt by the retired Captain Röhm to usurp their functions. However Röhm did build up an understanding with General Kurt von Schleicher, who acted as the main link between the army and the politicians.

One aspect of the S.A.-National Socialist phenomenon from 1930 onwards was a cult of youth. It could be claimed, not without justification, that the middle-aged and elderly in Germany had made a mess of things and that it was time to give in-experience a chance. Almost all the National Socialist leaders were young men—Hitler himself in 1930 was forty-one and most of his chief associates were in their thirties. There had been a rapid expansion in university education—between 1925 and 1931 the numbers of students in Germany rose by seventy-five per cent—but this was not matched by an availability of suitable jobs. Instead of a degree meaning automatic middle-class security for life, students found themselves confronted with mass unemployment. Although Hitler himself had little interest in students, the National Socialist movement swept through the universities. By 1932 the American H. R. Knickerbocker was reporting that sixty to seventy per cent of the students at Heidelberg were National Socialist and the remainder were mostly politically uninterested. Their search was for what the British Fascist leader of the time, Sir Oswald Mosley, was calling 'a new movement for a new age'. The leading idea that got through to the students was a need for tough, efficient government, equipped with power to act decisively against blatant social evils. It was wet and old-fashioned to hold to the nineteenth-century liberal dream. What was needed was what Hitler called 'an élite of leaders', who should rise by merit rather than because of birth. Goebbels tried to put over a similar idea to the Berlin proletariat: 'Arise, young aristocrats of a new working class. You are the aristocracy of the third Reich, and the seed you have sown with your blood will bring forth a glorious harvest.'

In September 1930, in an unwise attempt to strengthen his position in the Reichstag, Chancellor Brüning persuaded President Hindenburg to call fresh elections. The existing Reichstag, which was less than two years old, would normally have continued until 1932, but Brüning's aim was to weaken the Social Democrats, who although out of office, were by far the biggest single party within it. Much of the election campaign consisted of the democratic, bourgeois parties attacking the 'Marxism' of the Social Democrats; they saw this as the main issue. But in fact Hitler and the National Socialists had tapped a deeper vein of public opinion, that of distrust of the whole republican system. With their usual energy, the National Socialists conducted a vivid campaign with a claimed total of over 40,000 public meetings. Because of the practical propagandist skills of Hitler, Strasser and Goebbels, and their flair for and study of mass psychology, the National Socialists were easily the best party in Germany at electioneering. But they really had very little to say; their only concrete commitment was to reduce taxes on farmers. Their main platform, as defined by Hitler was 'the preservation and securing of the bases of our Christian-German culture, the nationalisation of the people and the defence of federalism'. The latter, federalistic point, was aimed to scoop in the votes of local patriots and had nothing to do with inner National Socialist policy, which was to establish a unitary state. There was little mention of the Jews and there are indications that the party was even attracting a few Jewish votes. The aim was to stir up public opinion on a vague, patriotic basis and, in particular, to attract the attention of people who had previously been uninterested in politics. There was no programme to cure unemployment beyond the assertion that if people would only be 'German' enough, all problems would be solved. Brüning, and bourgeois politicians generally, were accused of being out of touch with ordinary people and there was just enough truth in this to make the accusation stick.

We must [said Hitler in his speeches of this time] learn once more to think generously, we must once again become selfless, and the German people must learn to live again without envy . . . A new spirit will come alive in the German people and will take up the struggle against the decay of the world . . . The road a people must travel if it wishes to scale greater heights is not the road of comfort and ease but the road of relentless struggle. Everything on this earth is strife and struggle. Work and struggle are two concepts which are in reality one and the same.

There was no need for the National Socialists to attack the Social Democrats—that was already being done for them by the bourgeois parties—and so they could concentrate their whole fire on the bourgeois parties. The Social Democrats were also under attack from the Communists. Almost nobody bothered to reply to the National Socialist campaign—the established politicians failed to realise its significance.

Backing up the oratory and rallies—Hitler delivered twenty major speeches during the campaign—was the efficient National Socialist organisation, the fruit of six years' work of Hitler's political genius. While not himself a good routine organiser, Hitler's capacity for finding and attracting the right men and fitting them to the right jobs had made the National Socialist machine thoroughly professional, although still relatively small. Apart from such leading 'politicals' as Strasser, Göring, Goebbels and Frick, there was now a framework of thirty-seven salaried area managers, who were mostly men of a sergeant-major type, uninterested in policy but efficient executives. The area managers organised thousands of unpaid 'cell foremen' who took the party down to the grassroots.

But nobody foresaw the extent of National Socialist success in the September 1930 elections. Plainly the party had made some progress since 1928 and the more optimistic members discussed the possibility that, with luck, they might gain as many as fifty seats in the new Reichstag. Hitler himself, despite his imagination and will-power, showed in his conduct in the summer of 1930 that he had no expectation of a quick break-through; his relaxed attitude, including his affair with Geli, was that of man willing to wait another decade until he had got his message across. In fact the election was one of the decisive turning points of twentieth-century European history.

The voting, on September 14th, produced the staggering new political fact of the National Socialists polling nineteen per cent of the electorate—six and a half million votes—and gaining 107 seats in the Reichstag, as against their twelve in the 1928 election. They had suddenly become Germany's second strongest political party, with only the Social Democrats ahead of them. Power for the National Socialists, instead of being a remote dream, had abruptly become an imminent possibility. A further two years' progress, at the 1928–30 rate, would sweep them into power by an overwhelming popular vote.

The losers were primarily the Social Democrats. The new Reichstag had a total of 577 seats, compared with 489 in the previous one, and the Social Democratic representation fell from

152 seats to 143. Thus they commanded only a quarter of the Reichstag, instead of a third. The bourgeois parties of the 'democratic right' also did badly, losing about twenty seats. The Catholic Centre, allied with the Bavarian People's Party, stolidly maintained its position; it now had eighty-seven seats, compared with seventy-eight. The old conservative Nationalists were in almost total decline; their strength went down from seventy-three to forty-one and obviously their lost voters had gone over to the National Socialists. Hitler was now, unambiguously, the leader of German nationalism.

The victors in the election, apart from the National Socialists, were the Communists, whose strength went up from fifty-four seats to seventy-seven. This was actually convenient to Hitler. The Communists got their support by eroding the Social Democrats and it was the Social Democrats who had to be destroyed if Hitler were to take over Germany. Also a thriving Communist Party was a useful bogey; increasingly, Hitler presented himself as the only person capable of preventing the 'bolshevisation' of Germany. Yet in strict statistical terms, Communist advance had not been swift enough to rival Hitler in scooping the extremist vote.

The 1930 election made Hitler overnight a major figure in Europe. Few foreigners knew anything about him and there was some doubt of his exact standing among the National Socialists. As late as 1931, the *New Statesman,* London, was able to remark: 'German Fascism still awaits its Mussolini'; this was matched by some observers in Germany—for example the philosopher Oswald Spengler was declaring at about the same time that the National Socialists were a 'party without leaders and without a programme.' *The Observer,* London, commenting on the 1930 election result, considered Hitler to be 'dramatic, violent and shallow' but went on to say that he had 'rallied honest and earnest elements especially among the splendid young people of the German middle classes.' The London *Daily Telegraph* took an almost contrary view and reported that Hitler himself tended to be moderate but that 'it is always possible that his hands may be forced by the hotheads among his followers'. There was frank mystery about Hitler's origins, with widely differing versions being given: foreign newspapers described him, variously, as a former paperhanger, an architects assistant, and a house painter: there was equal confusion about his war record—the London *Times* thought, for a moment, he had been a former commanding officer of a company, while the London *Sunday Express* was describing him as having refused a commission in favour of 'a sergeant's stripes'.

On September 28th, 1930, that is a fortnight after the election, an article under Hitler's name appeared on the leader page of the *Sunday Express*. Although it bears every mark of having been ghosted and shows nothing of Hitler's customary literary style, the article is significant as Hitler's first attempt to appeal to a substantial readership outside Germany. He begins with a flat assertion that without him Germany would go 'Bolshevist'. He goes on to claim that the German political leaders in Berlin were out of touch with the feelings of the ordinary German people; he, Hitler, through his frequent public meetings knew more about the people than any of the parliamentarians. He insists that the Germans felt 'enslaved' and needed a sense of self-respect; for this it was essential to revise the Versailles Treaty, to end reparations and to abolish the 'Polish corridor'. (The latter was the strip of Polish territory which, under the Versailles system, gave Poland access to the sea but also cut off East Prussia from the rest of Germany.) There is no mention of Czechoslovakia, of the Jews or of German rearmament, nor any threat of Germany going to war. The nub of his argument is, simply, that short of his demands being fulfilled, Germany, to the inconvenience of Europe in general, would go Communist. 'You cannot ruin and bolshevise Germany and think the rest of Europe will remain immune. That is blindness.' Commenting on the article in a leader (which bears clear marks of the style of the paper's proprietor Lord Beaverbrook), the *Sunday Express* remarks that the unknown factor was not Hitler himself but the 107 National Socialist Reichstag deputies.

In fact the 107 deputies had very little idea of their function, in parliamentary terms. They were nearly all paid party officials and, apart from Frick, Göring and Goebbels, had little knowledge of how to debate. (Hitler himself, of course, still a non-citizen, again was not a deputy.) On the first day of the new Reichstag, the National Socialists, in brown shirts, stamped in, as if in a drill movement, gave Roman salutes and shouted 'Hail Hitler!' The Communists, from their augmented ranks, replied with 'Hail the Revolution!' Ingeniously, the bourgeois parties and the Social Democrats brought in a new procedural rule by which any proposal for increasing government expenditure would also have to cite exactly where the money would come from to pay for it. This was effective in hindering the National Socialists from introducing purely demagogic proposals and they reacted by stamping out, in a body, in protest; such tactics were scarcely skilled parliamentarianism and the National Socialists called off the boycott of their own accord. The net result was an exceptionally disorderly Reichstag, with much banging of desks, books being hurled and occasional physical fights between the deputies; this, of course, suited Hitler by making the republican system appear the more ridiculous. With Brüning continuing as a purely presidential Chancellor, it was difficult for Reichstag deputies of any party to feel responsible for government. In particular the Social Democrats, the largest single party, were torn between the desire to go all out in opposition against the 'capitalism' which, in their view, had caused the economic slump and a desire to protect the Weimar constitution, which had largely been of their making.

While there was a genuinely classless element to the National Socialists in that the party was capable of recruiting anyone from royalty to unemployed manual workers and there was much stress in National Socialist teaching on power of 'leadership' being more significant than the outdated concept of class, the actual appeal of the party was mainly to the middle classes and to small farmers, especially in the Protestant parts of Germany. In the election in Berlin, for example, Goebbels's efforts produced a 25·5 per cent National Socialist poll in the petty bourgeois Steglitz district but only 17·7 per cent in the socially more fashionable Zehlendorf district. In the workers' Wedding district, a stronghold of Communism, the National Socialists polled almost 9 per cent; this left them a long way behind the 'reds' but it did, at least, show a capacity, well beyond that of the bourgeois parties, to attract some proletarian support.

The quiet Brüning was appalled at the election result. Far from getting a more manageable Reichstag, he now faced one in which it was almost impossible to form a working majority. One possibility, of course, would have been for him to attempt to 'tame' the National Socialists by giving them office in a coalition and some tentative moves were made towards this. But Hitler insisted that his representatives in such a coalition should be allowed the key posts of Interior Minister and Defence Minister. This was obviously out of the question and, in any event, old Hindenburg found Hitler, at this stage, personally distasteful. He referred to him as 'the Bohemian corporal' and could not understand what the world was coming to when such a fellow could achieve political prominence. He refused even to meet Röhm. Another possibility would have been an alliance between Brüning and the Social Democrats but Hindenburg disliked this, too, and there was also the solidly political point that the Social Democrats were opposed to Brüning's austerity programme. In the end, however, there was a working arrangement by which the Social Democrats gave Brüning a measure of day-by-day support in the Reichstag without formally joining the government. Some, at least, of the Social Democrats were aware of what could happen if the whole republican system collapsed: a memorandum circulated among their Reichstag fraction after the 1930 elections warned with some accuracy: 'A Hitler government would follow the Italian example. This would mean the destruction of all labour organisations, a permanent state of military emergency, suspension of freedom of Press and assembly and other political rights, constant danger of civil war at home and of a war of revenge abroad.'

Brüning, in a sad new year message at the start of 1931, announced: 'Politics can do much for us but it cannot make people happy.'

Hitler was intent on trying to prove the exact opposite. His election triumph had fired him with the reasonable belief that through continued agitation he could win power. As always in a political party, the prospect of imminent power was a unifying factor; Hitler could now be as dictatorial as he wanted within the party with few willing to rock the boat by challenging him. Hitler identified German national interests with those of himself and his party. The last significant revolt within the party centred on Hitler banning the S.A. from joining in military training in eastern Germany against possible Polish invasion. Hitler, blatantly, argued that a Polish incursion was rather to be welcomed than otherwise, on the ground that it would increase popular dissatisfaction against the Weimar system and so win votes for National Socialism. The east German S.A. Commander, Walter Stennes, arose in open revolt in the spring of 1931 and tried to take over the Berlin organisation. He failed because only his immediate staff supported him—the ordinary S.A. men remained loyal to Hitler. It is probable evidence of Hitler's power of imagination that he came seriously to believe that Stennes had been a paid police spy. For what other reason could Stennes have opposed him? Whatever difficulties some outsiders had in detecting who was the National Socialist leader, most actual party members were already agreeing with Göring: 'We love Adolf Hitler because we believe deeply and unanswerably that God has sent him to us to save Germany.'

The new strength of the party was symbolised by the opening at the end of 1930 of the first permanent headquarters, the Brown House in Munich. The subsequent growth of the party was, of course to be too much for the Brown House and it was to be dwarfed in area by supplementary party offices in Munich. At the time, however, its acquisition was significant. It was a substantial, three-storey mansion in a fashionable quarter, opposite the residence of the Papal Nuncio. Hitler himself planned the conversion of the building into offices, in collaboration with the Munich architect Paul Ludwig Troost. He made the most of it. Some of the reception salons had to be partitioned off to make offices but Hitler planned this so as to preserve an air of grandeur. Troost, much of whose reputation lay in designing the interiors of ocean liners, believed in rigorously plain and functional architecture, with a minimum of ornament. Hitler, humbly and pupil-like, accepted the Troost maxims and modified his own, previously ornate ideas. While Hitler was not fool enough to fall for blatant flattery, nothing could give him more pleasure than for a visitor to compliment him on the Brown House. For the first time, since as a teenager in Linz he had first designed public buildings, his plans were real and not imaginary. Hitler had no illusions about his lack of training and knew he was only an architectural amateur: he loved talking to real architects, and treated them respectfully. Even after he had become Chancellor of Germany, he still visited Troost's offices rather than demand that Troost came to him.

The Brown House included a grand study for Hitler at a corner of the building. It was ornamented with a picture of Frederick the Great and a bronze bust of Mussolini. Hitler himself was not much of a desk man and used it mainly for receiving visitors. The *New York Times* man, H. R. Knickerbocker, interviewed him there in 1931 and thought he looked like 'a rising young district attorney in one of the southern states with his eye on the governorship'. There was also a 'senate chamber', hung with party banners. The idea was that the National Socialists were to have a 'senate' of senior members, either as their supreme authority or as advisers to Hitler. The model, obviously, was the Fascist Grand Council in Italy. As it turned out, however, Hitler never created such a body; in constitutional matters it was never his custom to start any organ which could have been a check on his own intuition. The basement contained a beer cellar and restaurant, the haunt of party veterans, run by the enormously fat and joking Arthur Kannenberg, a man whom Hitler greatly liked and later put in charge of catering at the Reich Chancellery; Kannenberg loved cracking boisterous jokes as he served food and drink. In Munich, however, Hitler rarely used the Brown House beer cellar and preferred the Osteria Bavaria, an artists' restaurant where he enjoyed the ravioli and the atmosphere.

The Geli idyll began to fade during 1931 but the details are tantalisingly vague. In particular it is impossible, reliably, to get at Geli's own feelings. There was some suggestion that she was jealous of the other women Hitler met, especially smart ones in Berlin. Also Hitler may well, at the start of 1931, have begun to acquire a new girl-friend, Eva Braun, in addition to Geli. While exactly what was going on is not clear, Eva, unlike Geli, is a clear historical character with much known about her. She was born in 1912, and was thus twenty-three years younger than Hitler, and was daughter of a schoolmaster. She was a superficial, kind-hearted person. After a convent education she took a job, as a general assistant, in the studio of the Munich photographer Heinrich Hoffmann, who had had a close acquaintanceship with Hitler since the early 1920s. She was aged only seventeen when in 1929 she first met Hitler—she was standing on a ladder in the studio when he entered it and looked up her legs. He became, in a cheerful hand-kissing way, her friend, bringing her small presents of sweets and flowers, as he did for other girls at Hoffmann's. Eva for the rest of her life kept the first orchid he ever gave her. There was nothing political about Eva but, gradually, she became obsessed about Hitler personally. Hitler, on his side, was attracted by her but probably without any grand passion. She was a pretty little thing, with a heart-shaped face and blonde hair. By the winter of 1930–1, when she was nineteen, she was occasionally going out with Hitler on drives and to the cinema, usually or invariably chaperoned. She was then still addressing him as 'Mr. Hitler'. (Geli called him, at least publicly, 'Uncle Adi'.)

The existence of a superficial relationship between Hitler and Eva Braun may have helped to upset Geli and certainly by the autumn of 1931 things were going wrong. One version is that Geli, who had a good singing voice which Hitler enjoyed, wanted to go to Vienna to train professionally and her tyrannical uncle forbade her. An embroidered form of this is that she had a boy-friend in Vienna and wanted to be with him. A contrary version is that Hitler was trying to force Geli to take singing lessons but she was refusing. It has been conjectured that Hitler had made Geli pregnant.

Whatever the truth about the details, the hard fact was that on the evening of September 17th, 1931, Geli was found dead of a gunshot wound in the Prince Regent Street apartment. The only satisfactory explanation is that Geli committed suicide and police reports at the time on the nature of the wound indicate that it was probably self-inflicted. Of course many of Hitler's opponents and even some of his supporters suspected murder. That Hitler himself killed Geli would appear highly improbable. He could have had no motive for creating a scandal and his shock and grief on hearing of what had happened are well witnessed and even in a man of his acting ability, could scarcely have been faked. Some supporters of the murder theory have, ingeniously, planted the crime on Himmler; he shot Geli, it is claimed, because she was about to betray scandalous details about her uncle. But the evidence for this is only speculative. Suicide is the best explanation. And it is a fair guess that Geli had gone neurotic and hysterical, to the extent of killing herself, from the pressures of her relationship with her extraordinary uncle.

Hitler nearly went out of his mind with grief and may well have actually considered killing himself. He went to stay with Gregor Strasser and, by Strasser's account, did not eat for a fortnight. He kept the furniture in Geli's room unchanged and had fresh flowers continually put in it. He had a portrait of her painted from a photograph and hung in the Reich Chancellery; he burst into tears the first time he saw it. He had lost someone who had filled an odd double role of daughter and lover and lost her in the most disturbing way possible. It was an emotional crisis which could only have further hardened him.

It was when he was still in the first stage of recovery from the loss of Geli that Hitler and Eva Braun became lovers, at about the beginning of 1932. Hitler at first took it lightly and it would appear to be improbable that he went out of his way to seduce her. Eva, on her side, had become really fond of Hitler and must have wanted to comfort him. She was discreet and she was un-demanding; if Hitler sent her a present, she sent one back in return. Due to political pressures, he was much away in Berlin and rather neglected her. Then, probably artlessly, she did something which above all else would upset Hitler and make him think about her. She attempted to commit suicide by shooting herself, first posting a letter to Hitler to tell him of her intention. That it was more than a demonstration is shown by the apparent facts that she made the attempt before Hitler could have received her letter and that the bullet lodged in her neck, just missing the artery. Hitler hurried around, with flowers, to see her the moment he got her letter the following morning. (He happened to be in Munich at the time.) From then on the relationship became permanent and Hitler accepted Eva as a part of his life. There were times, especially when he first became Chancellor, when he almost ignored her existence and they were never close partners. (But they did have it in common that their thoughts turned readily to suicide as soon as things were going wrong.) They spent thirteen years as lover and mistress and they died together as man and wife.

10

It was while Hitler was still shaken by the suicide of Geli Raubal, that he began plainly to emerge as prospective ruler of Germany. By nature he was a spasmodic worker who liked to alternate between periods of idle dreaming and short bursts of intense activity. But in the sixteen months between the death of Geli and his accession to the Chancellorship, he worked flat-out in an atmosphere of continual crisis. It could well be that Geli's death contributed towards this systematic harnessing of his skills and energies to politics, that is he may have worked hard in an effort to forget her. More substantially, German politics of the period were plainly unstable and full of opportunities for him. An octogenarian President stood at the head of a parliamentary system in which he did not believe and which was proving unworkable. The economy seemed to be breaking down in mass unemployment. Capitalists feared Communist revolution and patriots were disturbed by the international nature of the Communist Party, which was a mere section of the internation Comintern at Moscow; the German Communist headquarters, Karl Liebknecht House, Berlin, was decorated with an enormous poster of a foreigner, Lenin. The Communists themselves saw the break-down of the republican system as being the first stages of the 'revolutionary situation' in which they would seize power. 'There is only one way the German worker can win bread, work and freedom—by fighting for a Soviet Germany,' said Walter Ulbricht, the Communist leader in Berlin, to the Reichstag in February 1931. Against this was an extraordinary mushrooming of the National Socialist Party, using propaganda methods that were suited only to a mood of national hysteria.

Following the 1930 election success, which had put it on the map, the party, by vigorous agitation attracted a tidal wave of new members: at the end of 1930 the claimed membership was

389,000 and by the end of 1931 it had swollen to 806,000—in the same period, unemployment rose from 4,887,000 to 6,128,000.

Hitler flashed up and down Germany, with his entourage, in a cavalcade of open Mercedes cars. His personal bodyguard, dressed in black, with helmets and goggles, and armed with revolvers and sjambok whips according to one account looked like 'men from Mars'. Hitler himself, wrapped in heavy motoring gear with goggles, customarily sat in the front, beside the driver, a map on his knees; especially in such areas as 'red' Saxony he planned the route so as to try to avoid Communist areas. He was particularly suspicious of ambush in a strange town and ordered last-minute changes of route to confuse the enemy. He loved speed and, on the open road, ordered his driver to overtake everything. (Later, though, he became converted to road safety and imposed a twenty-five mile an hour speed limit on himself.) In relaxed moments, he chatted about the countryside to his companions; one recalled that he seemed to know every inch of the road between Munich and Berlin. His entourage included, often, his young press relations chief, Otto Dietrich from Essen, the photographer Hoffman, and perhaps Hess or Goebbels. At wayside restaurants, the whole party, including bodyguards, would gather around a single table like a family, with Hitler leading the conversation. Few political leaders in Europe at the time were as 'democratic' as that but there remained a degree of formality in that Hitler, however closely he mixed with his staff, regarded himself as definitely the boss. He was always 'Mr. Hitler' or 'My Leader' and never Adolf. Among the very few who used the familiar '*du*' with him were Röhm, Amann and, presumably, Eva. Many of his inner staff, and also Eva, referred to him as 'the Chief'.

In Berlin, Hitler stayed in a suite at the Kaiserhof Hotel, customarily descending in mid-afternoon to take tea and rich pastries in public. But he only felt really at home in Berlin in the apartment of Magda and Josef Goebbels, where he liked to spend his evenings. His homes were still Munich and Berchtesgaden; he was proudly a provincial. While the National Socialist Reichstag fraction acted under his instructions—he vetoed a measure they introduced for nationalisation of the banks—their day-by-day activities were controlled by Frick, Göring and Goebbels. It was indicative of Hitler's methods of dividing authority that whereas Frick was leader of the Reichstag fraction and Goebbels was the head of the Berlin party organisation, Göring, although having no rank in the party hierarchy, acted as Hitler's personal ambassador.

The speech which finally established Hitler as a serious contender

152

for power was to the Industrial Club, Düsseldorf, on January 27th, 1932. The audience were top industrialists and managers; while they were by no means expert on politics, they were not easy to impress. Many of them had hitherto regarded Hitler as just a mob-orator and his initial reception was cool. But Hitler made the speech of his life, held their attention and ended it to their tumultous applause. It was more of a lecture than his usual emotional appeal; or, at any rate, he knew he had to appeal to the sophisticated emotions of men accustomed to authority. His primary aim was to win their support for purely financial reasons, to attract funds for the party. Secondarily, he wanted them to take him seriously as a politician; it was his aim to use the German industrial ruling class for his own purposes, not to overthrow it. He gave an impression of reason and moderation, of quiet sincerity. The word 'Jew' occurs nowhere in the speech, there is no proposal to start a war and only the briefest of allusions to a German need for 'living space', that is new territory. The overriding argument was that if the businessmen wanted to overthrow Communism, they had to enlist the support of the masses and that this could be achieved only through National Socialism. Hitler presented himself modestly as having begun as 'only a nameless German soldier, with a very small zinc identification number on my breast'. He called the National Socialists 'young Germany'. He was glad that the movement was intolerant. 'When people cast into our teeth our intolerance, we proudly acknowledge it—yes, we have formed the inexorable decision to destroy Marxism in Germany down to the very last root.'

Of course Marxism was one of the chief fears of his audience. Hitler spoke about it at length, and with an air of reason. It was no use dismissing Communism as a mere aberration of misguided manual workers

Bolshevism today is not merely a mob storming about in some of our streets in Germany, but is a conception of the world which is in the act of subjugating to itself the entire Asiatic continent, and which today in the form of a state stretches almost from our eastern frontier to Vladivostock. With us the situation is represented as if here it was merely a question of a few purely intellectual problems, of views held by a few visionaries or evil-disposed individuals. No! A philosophy has won to itself a state, and starting from this state it will gradually shatter the whole world and bring it down in ruins. Bolshevism, if its advance is not interrupted, will transform the world as completely as in times past did Christianity. In 300 years people will no longer say that

153

it is a question of a new idea in production. In 300 years perhaps people will already realise that it is a question almost of a new religion, though its basis is not that of Christianity. In 300 years, if this movement develops further, people will see in Lenin not merely a revolutionary of the year 1917 but the founder of a new world-doctrine, honoured as is the Buddha. It is not as if this phenomenon could be simply thought away from this modern world. It is a reality and must of necessity overthrow one of the conditions for our existence as a white race.

Hitler argued that liberal democracy and Communism were really the same thing, and the one inevitably led to the other. It was an absurdity to say that men should be economically unequal but politically equal.

I am bound to say that private property can be morally and ethically justified only if I admit that men's achievements are different . . . It must be admitted in the economic sphere, from the start, in all branches men are not of equal value or equal importance. And once this is admitted it is madness to say: in the economic sphere there are undoubtedly differences in value, but that is not true in the political sphere . . . In the economic sphere Communism is analogous to democracy in the political sphere.

There was an inevitable struggle between the principle of democracy and the principal of authority. 'It cannot be supposed that this struggle should suddenly cease; no! on the contrary: this struggle will continue until a nation is finally engulfed in internationalism and democracy and thereby falls into complete disintegration, or else creates for itself once more a new logical form for its internal life,' Pacifism was another aspect of democracy and internationalism and led inevitably to 'the destruction of competitive spirit and thus to destruction of outstanding achievement'. He drew animation from his audience and some cries of 'very true' as he continued: 'For fifty years you can build up the best economic system on the basis of the principle of achievement, for fifty years you may go on building factories, for 50 years you may amass wealth, and then in three years of mistaken political decisions you can destroy all the results of the work of these fifty years.'
Hitler hammered in the ideas of struggle and competition, and that a sound governmental framework was a prerequisite for business success. The 'white race' had a privileged position in the world not through the law of nature but through struggle.

Take any single area you like, take for example India. England did not conquer India by way of justice and law; she conquered India without regard to the wishes, the views of the natives, or to their formulations of justice, and, when necessary, she has upheld this supremacy with the most brutal ruthlessness. Just in the same way Cortez or Pizarro annexed Central America and the northern states of South America, not on the basis of any claim of right in any democratic or international sense . . . it was the exercise of an extraordinarily brutal right to dominate others.

Hitherto Germany had failed to realise this. When she had founded overseas colonies before the war she had done so with a romantic notion of spreading German culture and civilisation, and without the 'cool, sober English conception' of force and ruthlessness; the colonies had therefore been a disappointment.

When a people takes the path which we have taken—actually for the last thirty or thirty-five years, officially for the last thirteen years—then it can arrive nowhere else than where Germany finds herself today . . . The position that faces you today is not the consequence of a revelation of God's will, but the result of human weakness, of human mistakes, of men's false judgments.

But bad government could only distort, not destroy, a nation: only a fundamental change in 'blood' could be totally destructive. Democracy had caused German decline but this could be put right if Germany allowed itself 'to be governed and led by its most capable individuals'. Democracy was 'not the rule of the people, but in reality the rule of stupidity, of mediocrity, of half-heartedness, of cowardice, of weakness, and of inadequacy'. Anything could be put right through will-power. 'I am of the opinion that there is nothing which has been produced by the will of man which cannot in its turn be altered by the human will.'
An essential area where fundamental change was required was that of mass unemployment.

Always people see only six or seven million men who take no part in the process of production: they regard these men only from an economic standpoint and regret the decline in production which this unemployment causes. But, gentlemen, people fail to see the mental, moral and psychological results of this fact. Do they really believe that such a percentage of the nation's strength can be idle, if it be only for ten, twenty or thirty years, without

155

exercising any mental effect; must it not have as its consequence a complete change of spirit?

Such conditions would make Bolshevism inevitable. But by radical treatment they could be cured.

One thing, however, is certain, every distress has some root or other. It is therefore not enough—it matters not, gentlemen, how many emergency regulations the government issues—that I doctor around on the circumference of the distress and try from time to time to lance the cancerous ulcer; I must penetrate to the seat of the inflammation—to the cause.

Beyond, however, such essentially abstract talk, Hitler put forward no concrete proposals for dealing with unemployment. In Britain, at about the same time, his equivalent, Sir Oswald Mosley, was issuing detailed manifestos with specific proposals for public works, control of investment, control of imports, a higher school-leaving age and so on; Mosley could be argued with but could not be called vague. That Hitler, in addressing businessmen, could get away with sheer abstraction, is an interesting side-light on his ability as an orator, and also on the psychology of his crisis-haunted audience.

Hitler swept straight on to the problem of how Bolshevism could be defeated. The industrialists should look at many of their own workers who as members of the N.S.D.A.P. were struggling against Bolshevism.

Remember that it means sacrifice when today many hundreds of thousands of S.A. and S.S. men of the National Socialist Movement every day have to mount on their lorries, protect meetings, undertake marches, sacrifice themselves night after night and then come back in the grey dawn either to workshop and factory or as unemployed to take the pittance of the dole: it means sacrifice when from the little which they possess they have further to buy their uniforms, their shirts, their badges, yes, and even to pay their own fares. Believe me, there is already in this the force of an ideal—a great ideal.

The stormtroopers should not be regarded as louts but as defenders of the bourgeois against Communism.

I know quite well, gentlemen, that when National Socialists march through the streets and suddenly in the evening there arise a tumult and commotion, then the bourgeois draws back the window curtain looks out, and says: 'Once more my night's rest disturbed: no more sleep for me. Why must the Nazis always be so provocative and run about the place at night?' Gentlemen, if everyone thought like that, then no one man's sleep at nights would be disturbed, it is true, but then the bourgeois today could not venture into the streets.

. . . I cast my mind back to the time when with six other unknown men I founded this association . . . The bourgeois parties have had seventy years to work in; where, I ask you, is the organisation which could be compared with ours? Where is the organisation which can boast, as ours can, that, at need, it can summon 400,000 men into the street, men who are schooled to blind obedience and are ready to execute any order—provided that it does not violate the law?

National Socialism eliminated the ideas of 'bourgeois' and 'proletarian' and substituted patriotism. It had the spirit of 1914 when the overwhelming majority of the working class had abandoned Marxism and thrown itself into the national struggle. The nation again had to be united.

It is quite conceivable to turn Germany into a Bolshevik state—it would be a catastrophe, but it is conceivable. It is also conceivable to build up Germany as a national state. But it is inconceivable that one should create a sound and strong Germany if 50 per cent of its citizens are Bolshevist and 50 per cent nationally minded. From the solution of this problem we cannot escape.

Germany, at the moment, was not even capable of defending itself against outside invasion. 'If you were to summon the German people to a levée *en masse* and for this purpose supply it with arms, tomorrow the result would be civil war, not an attack on the foreign foe.' To get over this, everyone had to play his part.

It is no good to say that the proletarians are alone responsible. No. believe me, our whole German people of all ranks has a full measure of responsibility for our collapse—a measure pressed down and running over—some because they willed it and have consciously sought to bring it about, the others because they looked on and were too weak to stop our downfall . . . Today no one can escape the obligation to complete the regeneration of the German body-politic; everyone must show his personal sympathy, must take his place in the common effort.

Hitler talked a little of his own qualifications for power. They rested on his having created from nothing the National Socialist movement. Instead he could have joined the Social Democrats and become an ordinary government minister.

But for me it was a greater decision to choose a way on which I was guided by nothing but my own faith, my indestructible confidence in the natural forces—still assuredly present—of our people, and in its importance which with good leadership would one day necessarily reappear . . . People say to me so often: 'You are only the drummer of national Germany.' And supposing I were only the drummer? It would today be a far more statesman-like achievement to drum once more into these German people a new faith, than gradually to squander the only faith they have. Take the case of a fortress, imagine that it is reduced to extreme privations: as long as the garrison sees a possible salvation, believes in it, hopes it, so long can they bear the reduced ration. But take from the hearts of men their last belief in the possibility of salvation, in a better future—take that completely from them, and you will see how these men suddenly regard their rations as the most important thing in life . . . the more will they concentrate their thoughts on purely material interests. On the other hand, the more you bring back a people into the sphere of faith, of ideals, the more it will cease to regard material distress as the one and only thing that counts.

This speech was of decisive importance in unlocking industrial funds for the National Socialists. Although by the end of 1932 the party had reached the verge of bankruptcy, it had in the meantime fought four major election campaigns on a lavish scale. Without industrial money this would not have been possible, and Hitler got on to the political subscription lists by promising the industrialists that he could wean the masses away from Marxism. The year 1932 was one of almost constant electioneering in Germany, with both Communists and National Socialists bounding ahead; in terms of strict election results, the conclusion was one of deadlock. Undoubtedly, however, the incessant barrage of political propaganda from rival parties contributed to a public weariness with the democratic process.

The first election was for the presidency, on the expiry in the spring of 1932 of Hindenburg's six-year term. In ordinary conditions it could be accounted an absurdity that Hindenburg should be President. He was in his eighty-fifth year and his mental powers were flagging. He did have periods of lucidity, especially in the mornings, but he liked to get business over quickly and then fall to reminiscing about the remote past. He had more or less forgotten the details of World War I but his memory was still fresh over the wars of 1866 and 1870; he would sit reciting lists of the names of the non-commissioned officers and men who had then served under him. Sometimes his conscience troubled him and he spent hours drafting memoranda, which he never sent, justifying his conduct. 'How is history going to judge me? I lost the greatest war. I was unable to help my people which called me to the most responsible post in its gift.' Then he would comfort himself. 'I believe the most important thing is to try to do your duty as best you can.' Hindenburg would have been capable, barely, of acting as a purely ceremonial head of state; he still cut a massive figure on a parade ground, towering a head above his staff. But in the crisis conditions of no majority existing in the Reichstag, he had in large measure to act as executive head of state: he chose the Chancellor and he had to back up the Chancellor by signing emergency decrees. For Hindenburg this was a perplexing process. He was already a monarchist acting as head of state of a republic. Now it seemed to be impossible to operate the constitution he had sworn to maintain, and Hindenburg was keenly conscious of his oath.

Hindenburg wanted to retire on the expiry of his term but the Chancellor, Brüning, saw him, with his still enormous public reputation, as a barrier against extremism. Brüning was busy with savage deflationary decrees and believed Hindenburg's personality would make them more palatable to the public. It was not easy to persuade Hindenburg to stand and there was much manoeuvring; Hindenburg gave in, eventually, on the ground that it was his duty. One of his favourite remarks was: 'In Prussia we know only obedience when the fatherland calls.' Hitler, too, hesitated for several weeks, and tried, unsuccessfully, to work out a deal by which he would have supported Hindenburg in return for the dismissal of Brüning and his own appointment as Chancellor. This Hindenburg indignantly refused. He still saw Hitler as 'the Bohemian corporal'; when some National Socialists shouted slogans at him at his country estate, he turned on them furiously with the words: 'We have men governing today, not rowdies.'

A preliminary difficulty for Hitler was that he was still not a German citizen and so was disqualified from running for the presidency. Certainly he could expect no favours from the Reich government of Brüning in getting naturalised. However the federal nature of the republic came to his assistance. Anybody appointed to public office in any of the states could automatically claim citizenship. Frick had become Minister of the Interior in the small state of Thuringia, (in a coalition), and he planned to appoint Hitler chief of police in the village of Hildburghausen. This leaked out prematurely and there were many jokes about Hitler becoming a village policeman. The scene moved to an even smaller state, Brunswick, where the National Socialists were also part of a coalition government. There the first idea was to appoint Hitler 'Professor of Organic Sociology and Politics' at the Brunswick School of Technology. This aroused much protest from local academics and it, too, was dropped. Ultimately, Hitler was appointed counsellor in the Brunswick legation in Berlin, a post which carried neither duties nor salary but enabled him to take the oath of allegiance to the republic and become a citizen. While his lack of German nationality was on occasion used against him, especially in jokes, it was never a serious electoral handicap; Hitler could always answer that he had fought for Germany in the war.

Deciding whether or not to stand for the presidency was a more substantial problem. With his party organisation to back him up, Hitler could easily have converted the presidency into dictatorship. But at the same time it was an obvious risk to put his claims to a direct vote of the German people; to lose badly would be bad for prestige. There was also a question of how much money was going to come in from industry. It was not until February 22nd, 1932, barely three weeks before election day, that Goebbels, at a mass meeting in the Berlin sports palace, announced Hitler's candidature. Also in the field were the Communist, Ernst Thälmann, and Theodor Duesterberg, the candidate of the orthodox Nationalists. (There were also some splinter candidates of no weight at all.) There was no Social Democratic candidate, the reasoning being that Socialists should support Hindenburg as the best available defender of the constitution. So the puzzled old man found himself in the extraordinary position of being the candidate of the moderate left which, politically, he detested.

Hindenburg conducted no campaign beyond a single radio broadcast in which he called for a return to the spirit of 1914 and made the curious remark: 'I ask for no votes from those who do not wish to vote for me.' His election manifesto stated: 'Around his name shines the glory of Tannenberg . . . Hindenburg—this means the defeat of the party spirit, the symbol of the national community, the road to freedom.' Brüning campaigned vigorously on his behalf, describing him as the man sent by God to the German people. Otto Braun, the Social Democratic minister-president of Prussia, called him 'a man of noble intentions and mature judgement'.

Hitler spoke in twenty cities in three weeks, transporting himself and his staff by air. This in itself was a novelty and made Hitler seem a modern man, using the latest technology. It was a none too comfortable method of travel. The airplane, with its unpressurised cabin and roaring engines, bucketed up and down in the air currents and the National Socialists chewed tablets to prevent air-sickness. A legend of Hitler's intuition grew out of one such trip. The machine got lost in fog off North Germany and found itself over the North Sea with fuel running low and the pilot having no idea of his position. Hitler, who could not swim, glared down at the waves. Then Hitler went to the cockpit and, miraculously, told the pilot in which direction to fly, with the result that the machine eventually landed at Bremen with only two minutes' fuel to spare. The official National Socialist slogan was 'Adolf Hitler is our last hope'. Whereas on such occasions as the Industry Club speech in Düsseldorf, Hitler had avoided anti-semitism, it did appear in a crude form during the presidential campaign. One of Goebbels's posters showed some villainous-looking 'Jews' saying: 'We are voting for Hindenburg' and some upright-looking 'Germans' saying: 'We are voting for Hitler.' And the National Socialists were delighted to discover and publicise the fact that one of Duesterberg's great grandparents had had the fore-name Abraham. The National Socialists were excluded from the radio and had almost the whole press against them but they drenched Germany with propaganda, holding election meetings at a rate of 3,000 a day. It is doubtful whether Hitler himself expected to win but some of his associates, notably Goebbels and Himmler were so swept away by enthusiasm that they were certain of victory. Himmler issued special regulations to forbid the S.S. to drink too much on victory night. But when the results came in, Goebbels wept with frustration:

> Hindenburg: 18,651,497 (49·6 per cent).
> Hitler: 11,339,446 (30·1 per cent).
> Thälmann: 4,983,341 (13·2 per cent).
> Duesterberg: 2,557,876 (6·8 per cent).

The only comfort for Hitler was that Hindenberg had failed, by about 170,000 votes to win an absolute majority and that there therefore had to be a run-off election four weeks later. The result of the run-off could scarcely be in any doubt at all and there would have been a good case for Hitler withdrawing from it.

Hindenburg, on publication of the result, had issued a statement: 'Forget your quarrels and close ranks . . . We must concentrate our strength if we are to cope with the misery and confusion of the times . . . Forward therefore in unity and with God!' Hitler, who believed that Hindenburg was liable to die at any moment, could have responded to this appeal with some show of dignity. But in fact, without hesitation, Hitler jumped straight into a renewed campaign: he revived the spirits of Goebbels who vowed that it should be 'a masterpiece of propaganda'. It was partly an intuitive desire to keep the pot boiling, partly his dislike of ever retreating and partly because a renewed presidential campaign would get off to a good start the local state diet elections due on April 24th.

One notable recruit came over to Hitler in the second presidential campaign. This was the Crown Prince Wilhelm, heir to the exiled Kaiser Wilhelm II. The Crown Prince, a lightweight who enjoyed horses, girls and night-clubs, was eager in a futile way to get back the throne. His father, after all, had officially abdicated. Hindenburg and the Crown Prince were on bad personal terms and Hindenburg had vetoed a scheme of Brüning's by which the Crown Prince should accede to the throne with Hindenburg as regent; on Hindenburg's death, the Crown Prince would assume full powers. In the first presidential election, the Crown Prince had voted for Duesterberg but now he announced he was switching to Hitler. 'Since,' he announced, 'I regard it as absolutely essential for the national front to close its ranks, I shall vote for Adolf Hitler.' What he meant was that he hoped that Hitler in power would restore the monarchy; Hitler, at this stage, was careful to make occasional encouraging noises to the monarchists but without committing himself. Hitler worked himself to a standstill, with his voice reduced to a croak, in a passionate appeal to the Germans. He spoke at four or five meetings a day and became personally known to the people to an extent never before known in German politics. It worked to the extent of increasing his vote but he was still far from victory:

Hindenburg: 19,367,688 (53 per cent).
Hitler: 13,419,603 (36·6 per cent).
Thälmann: 3,705,898 (10·1 per cent).
spoiled papers: 94,951 (0·3 per cent).

Hitler, obviously, had scooped up the bulk of Duesterberg's support and thus made himself more definitively than ever the leader of German nationalism. Moreover his opponent, Hindenburg, had been the only person evidently capable of uniting the whole anti-Hitler vote, with its various components of left, right and Catholic Centre; Hindenburg was unlikely to live out his six-year term and did, indeed, die just over two years later. However in only one of the thirty-five electoral districts into which Germany was divided had Hitler, in the second ballot, won an absolute majority; this was Pomerania, on the Baltic coast of East Prussia, where he polled 52·6 per cent of the vote. In the Cologne-Aachen district, in the Catholic Rhineland, his poll was as low as 20·5 per cent. In 'red' Berlin, the most volatile and extreme district, he and the Communist Thälmann polled almost equally. In the first ballot Hitler scored only 19·4 per cent while Thälmann had an enormous 29·4 per cent, the best Communist result in Germany. In the second ballot, however, Hitler went up to 27·4 per cent while Thälmann dropped to 26 per cent. There were indications that some Berlin Communists actually voted for Hitler, rather than for their own Thälmann, on the reasoning that Hitler's accession to power would advance rather than retard the day of revolution; this, however, was never the official party line.

In the state diet elections, on April 24th, the National Socialist impetus kept on. In every state except Bavaria, they now became the largest single party, although with an absolute majority nowhere.

The aim of the orthodox politicians was now somehow to 'tame' Hitler and the National Socialists. On the day after the second presidential election, Hindenburg signed a decree of Brüning's to ban the S.A. and S.S. This the National Socialists accepted quite peacefully, although they re-formed many of their units into 'sports clubs' and 'anti-Communist leagues' and on occasion paraded in white shirts. Hitler was insistent on 'legality' to the point at which the more extreme National Socialists bitterly mocked at him as 'Adolf légalité'. But Hitler knew that to come to power by legal means would give him unchallengeable control of the machinery of government and would make it difficult for the army to interfere; civil servants who were opposed to National Socialism in their private opinions would still accept orders from a legal National Socialist government. Moreover there was a genuine fear, especially among the army and the bourgeoisie, of Germany breaking up into civil war. While fomenting this fear in his speeches, Hitler had to argue that civil war would come from the Communists and that he and the National Socialists stood for 'law and order'. Hitler's insistence on 'legality', and particularly his peaceful acceptance of the suppression of his private armies, undoubtedly impressed Hindenburg and was the first step towards breaking down the enormous prejudice of the old field-marshal against the ex-corporal.

However there was a clear tendency towards violence among the National Socialists, no matter how carefully it was justified as 'self defence'. In the battles against the Communists anything was fair; it was a condition of neo-civil war with both sides happy to fight it. The physical combat spread to the Prussian diet itself. On May 25th, 1932, a Communist deputy rushed up to the tribune and slapped the face of a National Socialist speaker. Immediately the 167 National Socialist deputies went for the fifty-seven Communist ones and a battle broke out in the chamber, with ink-pots and water bottles hurled as weapons. Neutral deputies withdrew to the gallery, where they could watch in safety. The outnumbered Communists tried to defend themselves by breaking up the chairs used by members of the cabinet and wielding the legs as clubs but, after about fifteen minutes' fighting, they were all thrown out of the chamber and the National Socialists, alone among the debris, sang the Horst Wessel song:

> Raise high the flags!
> Stand steady on rank together,
> Stormtroopers march with steady quiet tread.

Horst Wessel was a pastor's son and an S.A. man who, aged nineteen, had fallen in battle with the Communists in Berlin in circumstances that were not entirely clear. His opponents described him as a 'pimp' but the National Socialists considered him a hero and representative of the best of German youth. The truth was probably somewhere between these two extremes. Goebbels organised a spectacular funeral for him and produced words which, he said, Horst Wessel had written. Put to what had been the music of a minor cabaret ditty of the early 1900s, they became the principal National Socialist anthem. Massed male voices rendering the Horst Wessel Song, to an accompaniment of marching jackboots, was one of the most characteristic sounds of Europe of the 1930s and early 1940s. It was undoubtedly a stirring and cheerful song but at least one line in it caused misunderstanding. The true English of it is 'For today Germany hears us, tomorrow the world'. Because *'hören'* the German for 'hear' is similar to *'gehören'*, meaning to 'belong to', the line was widely and often maliciously translated as: 'For today Germany belongs to us, tomorrow the world.' In view of later circumstances, the misunderstanding was not entirely surprising, but it would be a fallacy to suppose that S.A. and S.S. were thinking of world conquest in the early 1930s; it would not have suited Hitler at all for them to have done so.

But there were some National Socialist songs which were definitely sinister compared with the innocent heroics of the Horst Wessel Song. One ran:

> So stand the storm battalions
> Ready for racial fight,
> Only when Jews lie bleeding
> Can we be really free.

Whatever the facts of mutual provocation between Communists and National Socialists, there could be no question of the German Jews, as a community, challenging the National Socialists to physical combat. Aggression here came entirely from the National Socialist side and, at this stage, it was sporadic rather than systematic. Thus on the Jewish New Year's Day, in September 1931, a gang of S.A. men assaulted Jews in the smart shopping street, the Kurfürstendamm, Berlin, and smashed the windows of Jewish-owned stores. They shouted the slogans: 'Germany awake!' and 'Rot Judah'. (*'Juda verrecke!'*) The police made fifty arrests. Commenting on the incident, the London *Times* said it was 'a display of organised hooliganism almost incredible in a city like Berlin'. Among the German population as a whole, the degree of social prejudice against the Jews is unlikely to have been much, if any, more prevalent than in England or, more particularly, France in the same period. Of course such a statement is un-measurable and unprovable but it is certainly clear that in the crucial stages of his final rise to power, Hitler did not regard anti-semitism as a major vote winner. Even so relatively mild a measure as the Nuremberg laws of 1935, forbidding intermarriage between 'Germans' and 'Jews', was not previsaged in his election speeches of 1932; still less did he put forward any programme for genocide. Inside the National Socialist movement itself, the anti-semitism varied from the fanatically doctrinaire type of Hitler, Goebbels and Himmler to the formless, almost jocular type of Göring, Röhm and Strasser. One National Socialist fanatic, Count Ernst zu Reventlow, put forward the view: 'The Jew is the tape worm in the human organism and it is our duty to exterminate him' and, more prominently, Streicher in Nuremberg, rambled on in *The Stormer* about Jewish sexual iniquities. Some S.A. men in Berlin took to distributing among 'German' girls, supposed to be associating with 'Jews', cards reading: 'Your name will be put down in the register of those women who possessed no pride of race and threw themselves away on a Jew. In a new Germany, a visible sign will be etched or branded on the face of such persons.'

This kind of thing, although presumably it gave some satisfaction to the individuals involved, and thus made them keener National Socialists, tended towards the discredit of the movement as a whole. In particular Hindenburg knew and brooded on the fact that 12,000 Jewish Germans had died in action in World War I.

According to the 1925 census, the Jewish population of Germany was 564,379 out of a total population of over sixty-two million: thus Jews accounted for just under one per cent of the German people. In Austria, where of course Hitler had spent his youth, the Jewish proportion was substantially higher, nearly three per cent. Over much of Germany, particularly in the National Socialist strongholds in the rural north, the Jewish population was virtually nil. The major Jewish communities were in the Rhineland and in Berlin. The Rhineland Jews had been settled for centuries, and although exposed to sporadic social anti-semitism. of the type widely prevalent in western Europe, were on the whole well integrated with the general community. They regarded themselves firmly as Germans in nationality and Jewish in religion. The Rhineland was an area where the National Socialists, in free elections, always polled badly.

Berlin, as the cosmopolitan capital, was a melting pot which had attracted immigrants of many types from all parts of Germany. As in the Vienna of Hitler's youth, there were definite strains between the various categories of population and the National Socialists under Goebbels were able to exploit them. In particular it was argued that Jews held an unduly high proportion of posts in the legal profession, in medicine, in entertainment, in publishing and in multiple stores. Middle-class unemployment could thus be attributed to a 'Jewish conspiracy'. Ruthless use was made of the weeks long trial of the three Sklarek brothers, clothing contractors who had bribed government officials to buy civil service uniforms at inflated prices; it was a splendid scandal, resulting in five suicides, and the fact that the Sklareks were Jewish was a godsend to Goebbels. However although virulent, violent anti-semitism was a real factor in Berlin the fact remained that the National Socialist vote there was one of the smallest in Germany.

The muddled Hindenburg had never felt liking for his Chancellor, the ascetic Brüning; and he felt no gratitude to Brüning for having successfully promoted his re-election to the presidency—he had not wanted to carry on and served only from a sense of duty. Brüning, plainly, seemed to be incapable of checking National Socialist growth. Moreover, and this was a matter that deeply interested Hindenburg, Brüning was intent on reforming the scandals of 'eastern aid'. These scandals, which were on a considerably bigger scale than the Sklarek one, resulted from a scheme in 1927 for state grants to relatively impoverished East Prussian landowners to enable them to improve their farming methods. In some cases the money had been blatantly misused, with recipients gambling it away on the Riveria and so on. Brüning proposed to expropriate, with compensation, estates which despite government grants were still unprofitable. The land would be distributed among small peasants and the unemployed. To the Prussian aristocracy, of which Hindenburg was a member and which he regarded as the fount of nearly all virtue, this seemed like 'rural bolshevism'.

Prominently on to the scene came the figure of Major-General Kurt von Schleicher, who had served as a staff officer under Hindenburg in the war. Schleicher, aged fifty in 1932, was a highly 'political' general, and now head of the ministerial office in the Ministry of Defence; this meant, in practice, he was in charge of 'civilian' aspects of army administration and acted as the link between the army and the politicians. Hindenburg, at this stage, trusted him. Schleicher fancied himself as an intriguer behind the scenes and also had political ambitions of his own. In fact he was not a very successful intriguer and understood politics no better than many others. Schleicher, with reason, believed that government of Germany through the Reichstag had become impossible and that the only answer was a strong presidency. He felt that Hitler needed to be kept on 'apron-strings' to keep him in touch with reality. Schleicher had originally backed Brüning as Chancellor but now he believed that Brüning had failed and told Hindenburg so. To replace him, Schleicher made the extraordinary recommendation of Franz von Papen, as somebody who could harness the National Socialists. To prevent Brüning taking steps to safeguard his position, Schleicher assured him of his continued support. The lie was intended to make Brüning's dismissal a complete surprise to him.

While slowly pondering over all this at his East Prussian estate of Neudeck, Hindenburg refused even to meet Brüning. Then, on May 29th, 1932, he sent for Brüning and, without inviting him to sit down, read off from a piece of paper a short speech telling him he was dismissed. Brüning made no public protest on the ground that the presidency had to be supported. 'In spite of all,' he told his cabinet, 'Hindenburg is the only rallying point the country still has.'

Brüning had reason to feel aggrieved. Although Germany was in a calamitous condition with nine million unemployed, agricul-

167

tural production thirty-one per cent lower than in the previous year and industrial production thirty-six per cent lower, the first signs of recovery were in sight. Brüning, legitimately, felt that he had weathered the worst of the storm and that things could now only get better. He had obtained a suspension of reparations and, even, a measure of French and British agreement for German rearmament. The National Socialist tide, which had swept up so suddenly, would recede as rapidly as the economy improved. Now these advantages would go to Papen.

A former officer and diplomat, Papen, aged fifty-three in 1932, belonged to the same Centre Party as Brüning. But unlike Brüning there was nothing monkish about him; he was a debonair aristocrat from Westphalia and Hindenburg took a great personal liking to him. Papen's long-term aim was to restore the monarchy. For the short run he publicly proposed to reform the constitution on conservative lines so as to cut down the scope for National Socialists and Communists. The powers of the presidency would be strengthened, governments would cease to be responsible to the Reichstag, there would be a nominated upper chamber with powers of veto, the voting age would be raised from twenty to twenty-five, with fathers of families and ex-servicemen having double voting rights. There would be a crusade against immorality and materialism so as to restore Germany to 'Christian' standards. Naturally all this sounded pleasing to Hindenburg but it was catastrophically irrelevant to the real situation. Papen was cutting himself off from the Social Democrats, the largest party in the existing Reichstag, and even from some in his own Centre. His only method of getting mass support was to tame the National Socialists and Hitler had no intention of being tamed. To be fair to Papen, Hitler was a new phenomenon; he had, after all, only twenty months earlier been an obscure Bavarian crank. Pending the harnessing of Hitler, Papen formed an upper-class cabinet of a type which had not been seen since the days of the Emperor. In a gesture to conciliate the National Socialists, he lifted the ban on the S.A. and S.S.; during the following month there were ninety-nine deaths in street fights.

Papen dissolved the Reichstag and set new elections for the latest legal date, July 31st, his hope being that in the meantime he would win some popular support. Meanwhile he prepared to remove the Social Democratic government which had ruled Prussia since 1922. He travelled to Neudeck and presented Hindenburg with a decree, the date left blank, superseding the Prussian constitution and appointing himself commissioner to take over: it was of doubtful legality and Hindenburg signed it only grudgingly.

168

Papen's motive in removing the government was to win conservative and nationalist support; his pretext was that the government could not maintain law and order. On July 17th at Altona, near Hamburg, there was a great street battle, with seventeen deaths, resulting from a National Socialist march through a working-class district. Three days later, Papen put his decree into effect and the Social Democratic ministers left their offices without resistance. In fact they would have had a certain capacity to fight back, had they wanted; they still commanded the loyalty of the police. They went quietly partly because they feared that resistance would provide a pretext for a National Socialist rising and partly because they thought public opinion would be so offended at Papen's 'dictatorship' that they would gain heavily in the election. In fact the Social Democrats had lost their only power base.

Now that he was a citizen, Hitler was entitled to stand himself for the Reichstag but in fact he did not become a candidate. Presumably he felt he should keep a certain distance rather than be just another Reichstag deputy. But he threw himself into a new frenzy of work for the election campaign, again travelling around Germany by air. His attacks were mainly on the Social Democrats and the Communists; he on the whole kept off Papen. The sheer pageantry of his campaign was sufficient to get people worked up; to attend a Hitler meeting was an almost religious experience and people paid for seats. The greatest rally was at the Grunwald Stadium, Berlin, with an audience of 120,000 inside and a further 100,000 listening outside from loudspeakers. As was quite customary with National Socialist meetings it started late but with four bands, rich in trombones, to play rousing marches. Then came the procession of party banners, with bronze eagles and swastikas. Warm-up speakers, and a previously rehearsed chorus of hundreds, conducted an antiphon.

> *Versicle:* 'Who is responsible for our misery?'
> *Response:* 'The system.'
> *Versicle:* 'Who is behind the system?'
> *Response:* 'The Jews.'
> *Versicle:* 'What is Adolf Hitler to us?'
> *Response:* 'A faith.'
> *Versicle:* 'What else?'
> *Response:* 'A last hope.'
> *Versicle:* 'What else?'
> *Response:* 'Our LEADER.'
> *Versicle:* 'Germany!'
> *Response:* 'Awake!'

Versicle: 'Germany!'
Response: 'Awake!'
Versicle: 'Germany!'
Response: 'Awake!'

Dusk falling on the July evening, more and more of the audience joined the thundering roar 'Awake!' The bands played the 'Badenweiler' march and, standing in an open car with a spotlight on him, in came Hitler. He himself was as much affected by the atmosphere as anyone else. He climbed to the podium and, in a voice almost sobbing with emotion, began his speech.

The result was Hitler's biggest-ever vote in a free election. Nearly fourteen million Germans voted for him, which gave 37·3 per cent of the total poll, which was marginally more than his 36·8 in the second presidential ballot. He won 230 seats in a Reichstag of 608, and the National Socialists became the largest single party. The Social Democrats held up surprisingly well, their poll being 21·6 per cent compared with 24·5 in the 1930 election. The Communists edged ahead; they had polled 13·2 per cent in the presidential first ballot four months earlier and now polled 14·3, winning seventy-seven seats. The Centre also increased its poll, from 14·8 per cent in 1930 to 15·7 per cent. It was clear, therefore, that Hitler's new strength came from the annihilation of the old nationalists and the bourgeois parties. He had, in particular, the middle classes behind him. To have increased his Reichstag representation from 107 to 230 seats was, of course, a notable triumph. At the same time, however, the fact that his share of the poll had gone up by less than one per cent since the presidential second ballot was clear proof that his hitherto meteoric progress was slowing up. And without an absolute majority in the Reichstag he could not demand the chancellorship as of right.

The new Reichstag was in the extraordinary position of having a majority of its members—that is the 230 National Socialists, the seventy-seven Communists and the surviving thirty-seven Nationalists—being opposed to its own existence. Neither the Chancellor, Papen, nor the leader of the largest party, Hitler, was a member of it. Germany had voted by a decisive majority against a parliamentary system but there was no majority for any alternative. Many National Socialists, especially the S.A., believed that the election results should be a signal for a National Socialist *coup d'état*. In the days following the election result, there was a series of incendiary raids by S.A. units on Social Democratic and Centre party offices in which twenty-five people were killed, including five police. The Berlin police were issued with carbines in expectation of a brownshirt march on Berlin on the lines of Mussolini's 'march on Rome'. Hitler, however, judged that the army, with its loyalty to Hindenburg, would be capable of suppressing a National Socialist rising and that the chaos of it would alienate many of his bourgeois voters. He wanted the supreme prize of becoming Chancellor by legal means. He was tense, nervy but obstinate and, with power just outside his grasp, still gambling on an all-or-nothing demand, and with the danger that his own party would slip out of his control.

Hitler met Schleicher on August 3rd and demanded the chancellorship for himself, plus the minister-presidency of Prussia. There should be an Enabling Act to give his government authoritarian powers; in the event of the Reichstag rejecting it, there should be fresh elections. Schleicher accepted this, subject only to the proviso that the rest of the cabinet should be non-National Socialist as a 'check' on Hitler. But Hindenburg blew up when he heard the terms. He said he was 'unshakable' on refusing the chancellorship to Hitler. Even if Hitler got an alliance with the Centre and thus a majority in the Reichstag, he, Hindenburg, would resign the presidency rather than give Hitler the chancellorship. The fellow was entirely lacking in government experience and could not even control his own party. The most he would allow would be for Hitler, or Hitler's representatives, to take subordinate posts in a continued Papen administration.

Papen followed this up on the morning of August 13th, by meeting Hitler, offering him the vice-chancellorship and promising that, when he had 'proved' himself, he would be promoted to the top job. As Göring was to remark during the Nuremberg trial, this was an impossible proposition if only because it would be impossible to conceive of Hitler being 'vice' anything; his temperament demanded complete authority or none. In conventional terms this would appear to be a disqualification for any office at all, and it is an indication of the neuroticism of German politics of that moment that Hitler was able to behave in that way with any show of conviction. Hitler stuck out for the chancellorship and the same afternoon, accompanied by Röhm and Frick, saw Hindenburg personally. It was only their second meeting and it lasted only twenty minutes, with all standing throughout. That Hitler took along Röhm was of some significance, because to Hindenburg the sight of him was almost that of a red rag to a bull, and so negotiations were likely to be hampered rather than advanced. The point was that Röhm, as head of the S.A., had to be convinced at first hand of the political realities so as to enable him better to control the unruly brownshirts.

Hindenburg opened the discussion by saying he would welcome National Socialist participation in a Papen cabinet. Hitler replied that this was out of the question; the purpose of the National Socialist movement was to take over the whole leadership of the state. Hindenburg, according to the official record, replied 'Before God, his conscience and the Fatherland, he could not take the responsibility of handing over complete power to a single party, especially a party which was intolerant of opposition. There were a number of other reasons which he would not spell out in detail, such as fear of increased public disorder, the effect abroad and so on.' Hitler repeated that he excluded any solution short of full power for himself. Hindenburg made no further attempt at argument, but urged Hitler to act 'chivalrously'. 'I have had,' he said, 'no doubt of your love of the Fatherland . . . Surely we are both old comrades and we want to keep open the possibility of our paths eventually coming together. Accordingly I want to reach out and shake your hand in a comradely fashion.'

To be called an 'old comrade' by Hindenburg was an improvement upon 'Bohemian corporal' but the way to power was obviously still blocked. The party itself was in danger of splitting. On the 'moderate' side, Gregor Strasser, the head of organisation, was in favour of accepting the Hindenburg-Papen terms; Hitler should himself stay out of the government but National Socialist ministers should join and gradually take over the administration from inside. The 'radicals' of the S.A. wanted a straightforward uprising and were in danger of getting out of control altogether. Only a week after Hindenburg's appeal for 'chivalry', four S.A. men were condemned to death for a particularly brutal murder of a Polish 'Communist' miner at Potempa, Silesia. They had broken into his house and, before the eyes of his mother, kicked him, stabbed him, poked out an eye with a billiard cue and trampled on his throat. The body had twenty-four wounds. Probably the cause was a village feud rather than anything directly political but immediately on hearing the death sentence, Hitler telegraphed the condemned men: 'In view of this terrible blood sentence, I feel myself bound to you in unlimited loyalty. From this moment your freedom is a question of our honour. The struggle against a government, under which this was possible, is our duty.' Probably Hitler did not know the full facts when he sent the telegram but his motive must have been at all costs to identify himself with the S.A. and, in launching a campaign for the liberation of the Potempa men, to divert its attention from other issues. The campaign succeeded to the extent that Papen reprieved them (later, when Hitler was in power they were freed altogether) but it damaged Hitler with much moderate public opinion and could have done him no good with Hindenburg. He was performing a balancing act.

The new Reichstag, which met with the Papen government still in office, was a comedy.

By arrangement with the Centre, Göring was to be President of the Reichstag, which gave him the constitutional responsibility not only for presiding over debates but for assisting Hindenburg to form a government which could command a majority. The job also carried an official house. By custom, the preliminary session, at which Göring was to be elected, was presided over by the oldest member and this happened to be the eighty-four-year-old Communist, Klara Zetkin. She was a life-long revolutionary who now was more or less dying in hospital in Moscow. She was determined to come to Berlin to perform her last duty for the cause. One account is that she had to make the thousand mile train journey on a stretcher.

On the opening day of the Reichstag, Klara Zetkin tottered up the steps to the rostrum, supported by the arm of the Communist fraction leader, Ernst Torgler. There she delivered a half hour's revolutionary speech, Torgler prompting her whenever she faltered. The ranks of the uniformed National Socialist deputies sat with faces of stone as, swaying on her stick and gasping for breath, she taunted them. She lashed into Hindenburg and into the Reichstag itself. In her most memorable phrase, she said that to indict Hindenburg before the Reichstag was 'to indict the devil before his grandmother.' She collapsed at the end and the women Communist deputies carried her down from the rostrum and out to an ambulance. (The Communist delegation of eighty-nine included twelve women whereas the National Socialist one of 230 had none.) Göring stamped firmly up the steps to take her place.

At the second sitting of the Reichstag, the Communists proposed a surprise vote of no confidence in Papen which, if carried, would have entailed his automatic dismissal. The National Socialists, caught off guard, successfully proposed a half hour's adjournment so that they could consult Hitler, who was in Göring's official house nearby. Hitler plumped for voting with the Communists to put Papen out: this seems to have been an exercise of sheer intuition. Papen, for his part, sent for a decree, which Hindenburg had signed in advance, for the dissolution of the Reichstag. When the chamber reassembled, Papen rose from his seat and, as he was entitled to, attempted to announce the dissolution. Göring, in the chair, studiously avoided looking in Papen's direction and instead proceeded with the count, which resulted in the grotesque total of

512 votes against Papen and only forty-two in his favour. Papen, furious, marched up to Göring's desk, slapped the dissolution decree in front of him and left the chamber. Göring, blandly, read the decree and announced that it was invalid because it was countersigned by a Chancellor who was now out of office. Of course this was only a charade; there could be no doubt that the Reichstag had been effectively dissolved, although the constitutionality of the action was arguable.

Papen, again, delayed elections for a new Reichstag to the latest legal moment, November 6th.

This was Germany's fourth election campaign in eight months, or the fifth if the state elections are included. Papen had no hope of winning—his only backers in the Reichstag had been the rump Nationalist Party: some of his supporters, to fog up the issue, urged that pro-Papen voters should abstain in the election. Nor did the National Socialists stand much chance of improving their position; indeed the indications were that they had already passed their peak. Money was relatively short, the rate of recruitment to the party was falling (in some districts there was an actual net loss of members) and sales of party newspapers were going down. Gregor Strasser thought it little short of insanity to have forced an election at such a moment; the sensible course would have been for the party to have come to an accommodation with Hindenburg and Papen. To go to the electorate again was merely to bang one's head against the wall. Goebbels, privately, was also pessimistic but Göring, as always, sustained Hitler's will.

It was evidence of Hitler's will-power in a crisis that he went into this difficult campaign with apparent joy and self-confidence. Once again he used an aircraft and he spoke at forty-nine cities in a period of less than four weeks. There was a youth rally at Potsdam of 110,000 girls and boys marching past Hitler. With the human side to him that could often crop up, he fussed with anxiety about their sleeping arrangements; his face glowed like that of a proud parent and tears came to his eyes as he looked at them. The actual tactics for the election were, however, difficult. It was necessary to attack the Papen regime as 'reactionary' but this meant loss of money from the big businessmen, most of whom supported it.

Compared with the relatively conservative nature of Hitler's Düsseldorf speech at the beginning of the year, the National Socialists appeared to be almost red radicals. In particular in Berlin something of an alliance began to form between the Communists and the National Socialists. When the tramworkers there went on unofficial strike, without the support of their union

174

or the Social Democrats, the Communists and the National Socialists competed with each other in supporting them, and brownshirted S.A. men and Communist militants stood side by side with collecting boxes on their behalf. Goebbels, at least, was prepared at this moment to envisage the possibility of the alliance going a good deal further: at least Communists and National Socialists had it in common that they both wanted fundamental changes in 'the system'.

The result of this, the last fully free election of the Weimar republic, was a clear set-back to Hitler. He dropped two million votes. In July he had won 37·3 per cent of the vote and 230 Reichstag seats. Now he won only 33·1 per cent and 196 seats. The gainers were the pro-Papen Nationalists who jumped up from thirty-seven to fifty-one seats, and the Communists who went up from eighty-nine to one hundred seats and became the third largest party in the Reichstag. The Social Democrats (still the second largest) and the Centre more or less maintained their existing position. In Berlin the Communist vote reached 37·7 per cent, as against 22·5 for the National Socialists. In no electoral district did the National Socialists win an absolute majority: their best performance was 43·4 per cent in Chemnitz-Zwickau and their worst was 17·4 per cent in Cologne-Aachen. In their Bavarian homeland the National Socialists were the single biggest party in Munich itself and in Franconia but elsewhere were beaten by the Catholic Centre, in its local form of the Bavarian People's Party.

The new Reichstag consisted of 196 National Socialists, 121 Social Democrats, 100 Communists, seventy Centre, fifty-one Nationalists, and twenty-six representatives of minor parties. Hitler's advantages were that his party was still the biggest and that the Communist advance was frightening to the bourgeoisie. Germany had voted decisively against Papen but in favour of no positive alternative.

The negotiations began again, with Hindenburg showing some signs of mental deterioration and, also, a slightly more cordial attitude towards Hitler. It was still Hindenburg's determination to refuse Hitler power on a 'presidential' basis, that is supported by emergency decrees, but he was now willing to do so if Hitler could knit together some form of working majority in the Reichstag. Above all, however, Hindenburg hoped to keep Papen, whom he liked and trusted.

Papen could not possibly meet the Reichstag and a week after the election resigned, with a view to negotiations taking place to form 'a government of national concentration'. Hitler, who was resting at Berchtesgaden, was summoned to Berlin to meet

Hindenburg. According to the official records, the conversation went as follows:

Hindenburg: 'I can only repeat my request. Help me. I entirely recognise the great ideas which live in you and your movement and therefore salute them, and envisage you and your movement participating in the government. I have no doubt at all of the honesty of your intentions but I cannot accept a party government.'

He went on to ask Hitler to work out a practical programme in collaboration with the other parties.

Hitler: 'I have no intention of making approaches to other parties; I don't want to get involved in party negotiations. The decision is for you, Mr. President. *(liegt beim Herrn Reichspräsidenten)* If you, Mr. President, give me a commission to attempt to form a government, only then would I enter into conversation with the parties and carry out painstaking consultations over a practical programme and personal collaboration. I believe I would find a basis on which I and the new government could obtain an Enabling Act from the Reichstag. Nobody but I could obtain such powers from the Reichstag. In that way the difficulty would be solved.'
Hindenburg: 'I will think over the whole question quietly and think we will be talking about it again. I also plead with you to seek advice; I appeal to your patriotic and soldierly feelings of duty and the old comradeship which has bound us from the battlefield. Meet me halfway in this question and thereby we would be able to work together.'

Hindenburg reappointed Papen but then the army came decisively into the picture. This was not because the army, as such, wanted to be involved in politics or that it was entirely reactionary in its views. Schleicher, who had now definitely come into politics as Minister of Defence under Papen, wanted to harness what he regarded as the best elements of the National Socialists but without giving Hitler power. (Indeed Schleicher regarded Hitler as a dangerous monomaniac.) The army chief of staff, General Baron Kurt von Hammerstein-Equord, although in lineage and manner a Prussian aristocrat, held liberal political views and kept in contact with the Social Democrats: his two daughters were members of the Communist Party. What concerned the army was the preservation of public order. A 'war game' played by staff officers on November 25th and 26th came up with the

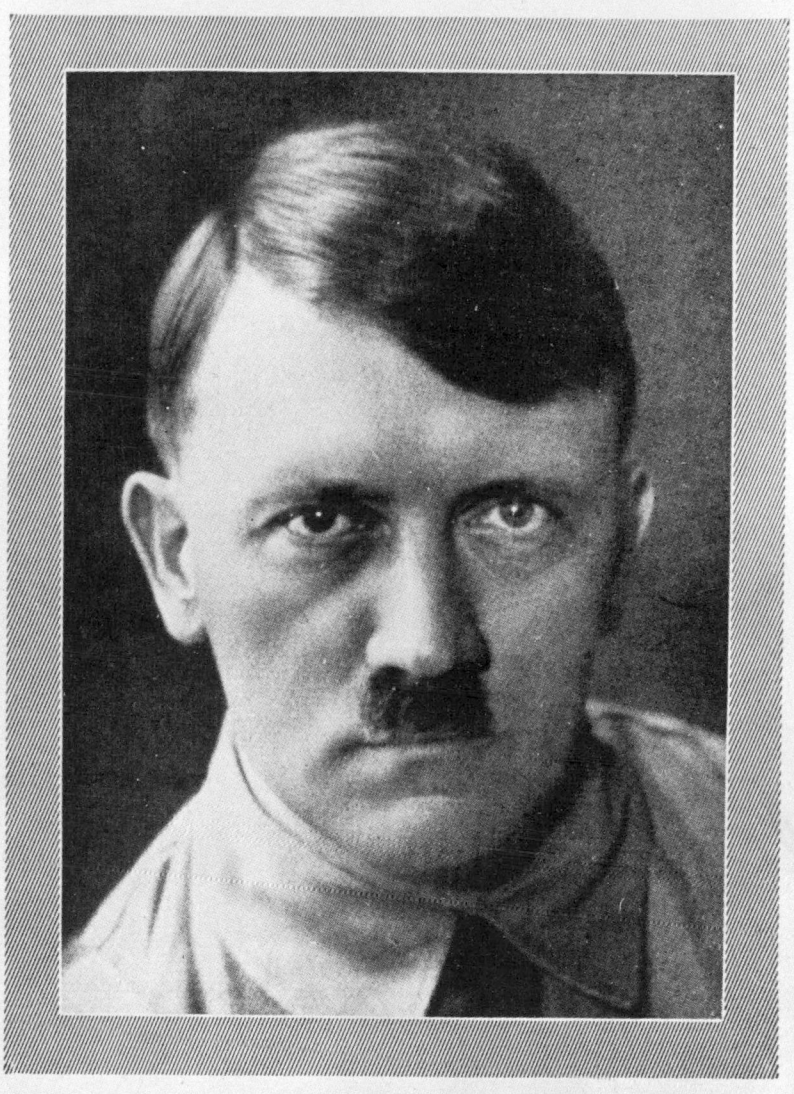

The picture of himself which Adolf Hitler chose as the frontis-
piece for his book *My Struggle*. It was accompanied by a
facsimile of his signature.

Munich street scene executed by Hitler in watercolour in 1914. By
painting and selling such pictures, Hitler could make an adequate living
for himself, with plenty of spare time for reading and political discussion
He regarded them as potboilers rather than works of art.

(*Above*) The orator from the trenches: Hitler speaking in Munich at about the time of the 1923 attempted seizure of power.

(*Below*) Hitler presides at the conference which in 1923 refounded the National Socialist German Workers' Party, subsequent to his release from prison. Also present: Alfred Rosenberg, three places to Hitler's right; Franz Schwarz, immediately to Hitler's right; Gregor Strasser on Hitler's immediate left; and Heinrich Himmler on Strasser's left.

Study of Hitler, 1929, by his official photographer and crony Heinrich Hoffmann. Later, Hitler forbade pictures of himself wearing Bavarian leather shorts on the ground that they detracted from his dignity.

Caricature of Hitler as a
public speaker by Erich
Schilling, 1927.

Chancellor Heinrich
Brüning campaigning
in 1932 against Hitler
and in favour of the
re-election of Paul von
Hindenburg as Presi-
dent of the Reich.

Communist propaganda for the election
of March 5, 1933, after Hitler had
become Chancellor. Translated it reads,
'Fight in unity. Close the ranks against
fascism and reaction. Vote Communist. List 3.'

Social Democratic election poster
much used in the summer and
autumn of 1932.

(*Above*) Hermann Göring on his election as President of the Reichstag, 1932. With him are his deputies Thomas Esser (Centre Party) and Hans Rauch (Bavarian's People's Party).

(*Below*) What the Reichstag became after Hitler had made Germany a one-party state and held single list elections in November 1933.

The 'People's Chancellor' visits a factory, 1935. Hitler's great claim was that he had eliminated mass unemployment in Germany. Many industrial workers, who had formerly voted Social Democrat, were won over to the regime for this reason.

Hitler at the Olympic Games, 1936. To his right is Josef Goebbels and to his left Max Amann.

Hitler welcomes a visitor to his 'Wolf's Lair' head-quarters in East Prussia on July 15, 1944. On the left of the picture is Claus von Stauffenberg, who five days later attempted to assassinate Hitler. On the right is Field-Marshal Wilhelm Keitel.

The last picture of Hitler taken in April 1945, a few days before his suicide.

disturbing result that in the event of a general strike or uprising, with the National Socialists and Communists collaborating, the army would be defeated. Moreover such an event would leave the eastern frontier wide open to Polish invasion. The obvious political conclusion was that it was not a realistic option for Papen to remain in office. There had to be a chancellor who could command wider public support. Schleicher reported this to Hindenburg who, with tears running down his cheeks, dismissed Papen, 'You'll consider me a cad, my dear Papen . . . But I am too old now, at the end of my life, to take responsibility for a civil war. We'll have to let Herr von Schleicher try his luck, in God's name.' The following day he sent Papen a signed photograph of himself, with 'I had a comrade' written on it. Papen carried on as Hindenburg's unofficial but influential adviser.

Schleicher's aim as chancellor was to form an alliance of the Strasser wing of the National Socialists, the trade unions, the Centre and the Social Democrats, the whole thing backed by the army. This regime would set itself against the capitalists, the banks and the landowners and start a practical programme of social reform and public works. He had been in contact with Strasser since August and had made progress, too, with the other potential participants. Frick, the national leader of the National Socialist Reichstag fraction, was also in favour but really it was Strasser that counted. Besides being head of the National Socialist party bureaucracy he was one of the party's chief speakers and public figures. The *Völkischer Beobachter* ranked him in 1932 with Göring and Röhm as one of Hitler's three chief lieutenants. He was certainly dissatisfied with Hitler's tactics and certainly would have been capable of getting some National Socialists to follow his leadership in the event of an open split.

It had not been Schleicher's aim to become chancellor himself. He had thought of some relatively neutral figure, such as the former Reichsbank President Schacht. But Hindenburg insisted upon his doing so, to the point of threatening to resign himself if Schleicher did not accept. So on December 3rd, 1932, Schleicher took office as Germany's last pre-Hitler chancellor.

For a moment Schleicher's prospects appeared good. He attracted support from the Centre and the Nationalists and hoped, in time, to get more from the Social Democrats and some of the National Socialists. But Strasser failed to come up to scratch. Although he was being offered the vice-chancellorship of Germany, Strasser still saw himself as more an intermediary between Schleicher and Hitler than as a power in his own right. And although he believed Hitler was following a disastrously mistaken line, Strasser was not prepared to fight him all out. On December 7th Strasser and Hitler had a quarrel at the Kaiserhof Hotel, Strasser insisting that Hitler should support Schleicher and Hitler refusing. Strasser thereupon resigned all his offices in the party. Hitler was disturbed and spent much of the ensuing night pacing up and down his room and contemplating suicide. 'If the party once falls to pieces', he said, 'I'll put an end to it all in three minutes with a pistol shot.' Strasser, of course, was not operating at such a degree of emotional intensity. Instead of going on to split his own following away from the N.S.D.A.P. and into alliance with Schleicher, he went off on holiday to Italy. By the time he had returned, the following month, Hitler had rallied the party and got the officials to sign fresh declarations of loyalty to him.

Even apart from the Strasser trouble, the National Socialists were in a mess. They had existed as a major party for scarcely over two years and had reached their peak in the July 1932 election. It was probable that they were not going to win power by any popular majority, and so there was the clear possibility of their declining again as rapidly as they had arisen. They were financially almost bankrupt and many of the S.A. men were mutinous; in December 1932 the bulk of the brownshirts in Franconia broke away to form their own independent free corps. In local elections in Thuringia, in December 1932, the National Socialist vote fell by forty per cent. '1932' wrote Goebbels in his diary, 'has brought us eternal bad luck . . . The past was difficult and the future looks dark and gloomy; all prospects and hopes have quite disappeared.'

Hitler, however, hung on. With the same unreasoning faith as that which in 1944 was to cause him to go on fighting a war that was plainly lost and which in 1923 had caused him to launch the Munich coup, he continued to hold out for the chancellorship. He would rather everything fell to pieces, with himself a suicide, than compromise.

This blind faith paid off primarily because of the vanity of Papen, who resented his displacement by Schleicher. Papen had been dismissed because the army believed he could not attract enough public support. But if he could make an alliance with Hitler, this objection would no longer be valid. Papen believed that with his superior experience and education he could harness and master Hitler as a rider masters a difficult horse, a metaphor he used among his friends. Papen knew that it would be a difficult undertaking but he saw it as his mission. Hindenburg, while maintaining Schleicher as chancellor, was still receptive to Papen's advice: so far as Hindenburg was capable of thinking clearly at all, he wanted to keep his options open. Schleicher once said that he

178

was Chancellor of Germany for fifty-seven days and was betrayed fifty-seven times.

Papen's gamble was that it would be possible to make Hitler the nominal head of the government but so to hedge him in with restrictions that he would be almost powerless. Hitler's personality would bring in the National Socialist vote while behind the scenes the orthodox ministers would get on with the real work.

Their talks began on January 4th in the house at Cologne of the banker Kurt von Schröder. Papen at first proposed that they should have a form of dual chancellorship, with him and Hitler equal. Hitler, of course, insisted on a sole chancellorship for himself but agreed that Papen and other non-National Socialists could be in the government, provided they collaborated in removing Social Democrats, Communists and Jews from 'leading positions'. Papen accepted this in principle and the two agreed to meet in Berlin for further discussion.

One result of the meeting was a new flow of money from industry to pay off the National Socialist debts. To keep the ball rolling, the National Socialists mounted a ludicrous campaign for the local elections in the tiny state of Lippe, which had a population of only 164,000. Hitler, Göring, Hess and Goebbels all turned up in person to canvass on rural doorsteps. Hitler addressed eighteen meetings in twelve days. The little state was drenched in propaganda. The aim was to give the impression that the National Socialists were still a growing force. The campaign succeeded to the extent that they won 38,800 votes as against only 33,000 in the November Reichstag election; but, on the other hand, they had won 42,300 back in July.

The preliminary step towards a Hitler-Papen government, naturally, had to be to get Hindenburg to dismiss Schleicher. This was becoming possible because Schleicher was obviously failing in his efforts to split the National Socialists and form a broadly-based government and, also, was irritating Hindenburg by proposing measures against the 'eastern aid' scandal. There also had to be some attempt to make Hitler more acceptable personally to Hindenburg. The latter was accomplished through the President's son and adjutant Oskar von Hindenburg who, although not particularly intelligent, had a strong influence on his father. Hitler was introduced to Oskar at a secret meeting in the home of Joachim von Ribbentrop, a socially-ambitious Berlin wine merchant who had served with Papen during the war and had joined the National Socialists in August 1932. (The 'von' in his name was irregularly acquired.) Hitler led off Oskar to a separate room and the two of them talked, by themselves, for an hour.

It was a contradiction in Hitler that whereas some people found his monologues dull and absurd, others were fascinated and convinced by them. During the hour's conversation Hitler converted Oskar from an opponent into a sympathiser. There seems to have been some element of threats in what Hitler said; he may well have introduced the disturbing idea of the National Socialists in the Reichstag moving the impeachment of old Hindenburg before the constitutional court. But, substantially, Hitler worked by straightforward persuasion and it was effective. An indirect assistant to Hitler in softening Hindenburg was General Werner von Blomberg who commanded the army in East Prussia and was a frequent guest at the President's country estate, Neudeck. Blomberg, one of the few senior army officers to be definitely sympathetic to National Socialism, now advised Hitler's appointment as chancellor; he told the President that the alternative would be a civil war between army and S.A. which the army might not win.

Schleicher was now back in the same position as Papen had been at the start of December. He could not face the Reichstag and he proposed to Hindenburg a dissolution and, in breach of the constitution, an indefinite postponement of fresh elections. This, to Hindenburg, was useless. Why had he ever dismissed Papen? On January 28th, 1933 in face of Hindenburg's refusal to accept his proposals, Schleicher resigned. Hindenburg thereupon commissioned Papen to form a new government, with Hitler a member of it, which would be 'in agreement with the Reichstag'. It seems, therefore, that Papen at this stage was assuring the President that Hitler could obtain a Reichstag majority. Schleicher, who knew perfectly well that this was not the case, was convinced that the attempt would fail and that he would soon be back in office.

Meanwhile Göring was negotiating with the Nationalist leader, Hugenberg, whose main condition for coming into a 'Hitler coalition was that there should be no fresh elections, in which he feared his party would do badly. Göring made some concession to Hugenberg over thus but Hitler, when he heard of it, flew into a rage and talked of quitting the whole scene and returning to Munich. He seems, at the moment, really to have meant this, as he had with his suicide threat, three weeks earlier. But Göring, calmly, went on with the negotiations and then turned to the final allocation of offices with Papen. Hitler was to be Chancellor, Papen Vice-Chancellor and Hugenberg Minister for Economic Affairs. Apart from Hitler, the only National Socialists in a cabinet of eleven were to be Frick as Minister of the Interior and Göring as Minister without Portfolio. The remaining ministers were to be conservative nationalists and non-party figures. A peculiarity of the negotiations was that there was no discussion, of any kind, of what the new government's actual programme should be.

Until the last moment there was a danger of the arrangement breaking up because of Hugenberg's opposition to new elections. The new government was supposed to be appointed at eleven in the morning on January 30th, 1933, but at eleven fifteen there was still a Hitler-Hugenberg argument going on in the ante-room. Hindenburg, furious, threatened to go away. Hugenberg compromised on the weak formula that it would be left for the President to decide whether new elections were necessary. At eleven twenty the new ministers came into Hindenburg's presence and were sworn into office. Hitler made a short speech in which he talked of uniting Germany and finding a Reichstag majority, thus saving Hindenburg from the necessity to sign emergency decrees.

Hindenburg said nothing in reply, but merely closed the meeting with his routine formula: 'And now, gentlemen, forward with God.'

11

In becoming Chancellor of Germany at the age of forty-three, Hitler was the youngest head of government of any major country in the world. Although he had acquired thorough experience of political agitation, he had never before held any kind of public office—he had not even been a member of the Reichstag—and in fact the chancellorship was the first, regular employment he had ever obtained as a civilian. He was a 'man of the people' in the sense that he had grown up outside the traditional ruling class, but this was a part of a general European trend of the time. The British Prime Minister, James Ramsay MacDonald had been born the illegitimate son of a maidservant; Benito Mussolini of Italy was a blacksmith's son; Pierre Laval of France was a butcher's son; Joseph Stalin of the Soviet Union was a shoemaker's son. In the world of 1933, the new United States President, Franklin D. Roosevelt, whose career in power coincided almost exactly with that of Hitler, was almost exceptional in that he sprang from an affluent family with a strong political tradition. That a man such as Hitler could become Chancellor was, ironically, a direct result of the liberal democracy he was determined to destroy.

He came to power constitutionally rather than as a revolutionary leader and his powers, initially were those of a democratic chancellor under the Weimar system; in fact because only a minority of his cabinet were members of his party and because Papen, as the Vice-Chancellor, had a supposedly special position, it could even be reckoned that Hitler's powers were less than those of an ordinary chancellor. The administrative machine depended upon an efficient, established bureaucracy, wedded to traditional forms of procedure and with which, initially, he had little power to interfere. The army leadership, a world of its own, was suspicious of him and had no sense of personal loyalty to him.

The law courts were outside the formal control of the executive. The state governments, especially in Bavaria, had their independent spheres of authority. Hitler commanded no majority in the Reichstag and depended upon the near-senile Hindenburg, who had distrusted him, in order to remain in office. His party had mushroomed up from almost nothing in two years and, according to the most recent national election two months previously, was now on the down-grade. Moreover, sections of the party itself were distrustful of him; he had just parted with Gregor Strasser who had apparently been the number two man in the organisation, and there were potential strains in Röhm's brownshirt movement, for which no real role now remained.

Despite all this, it took Hitler only nineteen months to transform his shaky initial position into an absolute dictatorship. He was aided by luck, by his party organisation and by such individuals as Göring, who worked ruthlessly to take over the great state of Prussia, and Goebbels, who organised masterpieces of propaganda. Hitler himself, to all appearances, had no settled programme of how he was to win absolute power; but he had the objective of doing so and the skill to use the opportunities that happened to arise. He used both legal and illegal methods as best suited him at any particular moment; enough of what he did was legal to give a show of legality to the whole. But so little was he fully in control of events, that, in the two crucial matters of the Reichstag fire and the Röhm blood-purge, he was ignorant of the correct facts. He truly believed that the Reichstag fire was started by the Communists and was the signal for red revolution, and he truly believed that Röhm was about to launch a coup against him. In fact he was mistaken on both matters, but his actual handling of them was effective in increasing his power. Hitler was also efficient in that he knew how to delegate and usually knew well the capabilities of the people to whom he delegated.

Unlike Mussolini, who spent up to sixteen hours a day at his desk and ran Italy in minute detail, Hitler hated office routine and was at his most effective when he could forget administration and intervene in policy only as the mood took him. Decisions regarded by Berlin bureaucrats as urgent could pile up for days at Berchtesgaden until Hitler felt in the mood to make up his mind. At his best, he was meticulous in obtaining information and advice but he never in any ordinary sense of the word made decisions by consultation. Having gathered his raw material, he would make decisions on his own; one of his characteristic remarks as ruler of Germany was: 'I have been thinking during the night, and I have decided . . .' (He suffered from chronic insomnia.) At his worst, (in terms of effectiveness), this could degenerate into fantasy decisions, remote from reality, but Hitler was far from always at his least efficient.

In his very first weeks, Hitler did try to behave like a normal Chancellor and was punctually at his desk by ten every morning. This has been explained, with a measure of spite, on the basis that he was trying to impress Hindenburg. The more rational explanation is that he was feeling his way in a new situation, trying to behave as was expected of him but finding, soon, that it did not matter. He had the wit to realise that he either had to be his own unsystematic self or he was wasting his time and soon gave up regular hours.

But pleasing and impressing Hindenburg was certainly central and Hitler applied himself to it. Carefully he studied the psychology of the President and sought to flatter him, addressing him always in the respectful manner due from a former corporal to a field marshal. The very mention of Hindenburg in private conversation could make Hitler go dreamy. 'Ah yes, the old man, the old man . . .' he would murmur to himself. With apparent affection, tinged with malice, he would, in private, mimic Hindenburg; he hobbled around the room, one hand on his hip, the other holding an imaginary stick, and rumbled 'Brou-ha-ha. Brou-ha-ha-ha.' To his face, Hitler addressed Hindenburg as 'Field Marshal' rather than as 'Mr. President' because the old man preferred it. More substantially, he buried the 'eastern aid' scandal, on which Hindenburg was so sensitive, and accommodated Hindenburg's prejudice in favour of Jews who had served in the war. By the end of the first fortnight, the rule that Hindenburg should receive Hitler only with Papen also present was dropped. Comments or complaints from Hindenburg were treated with high respect, as if from the source of all wisdom.

Although he was puzzled by the world in which he was living, Hindenburg had the dim idea that fundamental changes he could never hope to understand were necessary for Germany. Perhaps this mysterious young chancellor, who was so respectful, really did represent the future. (The forty-three-year-old Hitler was certainly a stripling in Hindenburg's eyes; Hindenburg had been known to address the sixty-seven-year-old Hugenberg as 'young man'.) Hindenburg was impressed by a brownshirt parade, by torchlight, on the evening of Hitler's appointment. Previously the government area of Berlin had been banned to political demonstrators but now the brownshirts were allowed to march into the Wilhelmstrasse itself. Hindenburg, watching them stream past, remarked: 'I never knew there were so many.' A more spiteful version is that he was in such a daze that he said: 'I never knew we had taken so many Russian prisoners.' But the overall impression Hindenburg now gained of the National Socialists was that they represented youth, discipline and strength.

The great prize that Hitler could seem to offer Hindenburg was a fully constitutional government. The original Hitler administration was a coalition of National Socialists, Nationalists and right-wing non-party men. It could count on only 247 seats in a Reichstag of 564 and thus was far short of a working majority; like the preceding Schleicher, Papen and Brüning administrations, it depended upon the emergency powers of the President. Hitler's strategy was that with the added prestige of office, plus the opportunities of harassing the opposition and monopolising the radio, he could call fresh elections and win a majority, if not for the National Socialists, as such, at least for his coalition. He would use the majority to pass an Enabling Act which would authorise the 'cabinet' to legislate by decree. Formally, this was a legal scheme and for Hindenburg it had the supreme advantage of removing from him the unwanted responsibility of having to sign emergency decrees which he barely understood. Hugenberg and his Nationalists opposed fresh elections; they proposed the simpler measure of excluding the 100 Communist deputies from the Reichstag, and this would have been enough to have given the coalition a working majority. Hitler rejected this, apparently in the hope than an election with himself in office would give him an absolute majority, with no need to depend on alliances. He would ban the Communists only when it suited him. For form's sake he went through the motions of negotiating with the Catholic Centre, which had ninety seats, but broke them off the moment that the Centre began demanding pledges of constitutional behaviour in return for its support. Hugenberg, outmanoeuvred by Hitler in all this, had no real option but to agree to the election Hitler demanded. Hindenburg wanted it as the means to obtaining a 'parliamentary' government and Hugenberg had to be satisfied with Hitler's promise that whatever the result of the election the Nationalists would keep their existing representation in the cabinet. Hitler, who was acting ruthlessly and with high tactical skill, was soon to break the promise.

To raise money to fight the election, Hitler promised his industrial backers that it would be 'the last'. Since they coughed up to support Hitler and other parties in four national election campaigns in eight months, this was a pledge they could readily accept with some relief. The National Socialist Party which a month earlier had been near to bankruptcy became more flush with funds than ever.

185

Equally practically, Hitler got Hindenburg on February 4th to sign an emergency decree to prevent 'disorder' during the campaign. By it, the authorities were empowered to ban 'seditious' and 'disorderly' meetings, pamphlets and newspapers. Power was also given to the police to detain people without trial. By later standards these powers were mild. A detainee had to be under reasonable suspicion of having committed a serious crime, he had the right to appeal to a judge and he could not be held for longer than three months.

In this, his final contested election campaign, Hitler's main theme was: 'Give me four years.' He put it, typically, in a speech at Dortmund on February 17th, 'Only four years for us and then others shall form their judgment and pass sentence. I shall not flee abroad, I shall not seek to escape sentence.' Officially he was no longer fighting just for the National Socialist Party but for the 'National Front' as formed by his coalition. To get an absolute majority, he had to increase by at least 16 per cent his 34·7 per cent poll of the November 1932 election. The style of his speeches suggests that he had little hope of getting this from Social Democratic or Communist voters but he hoped that the Catholic, mainly rural voters of the Centre would swing to him. He went out of his way to praise the peasantry and he ridiculed the Centre leadership which, in the campaign, was arguing that it favoured national revival but opposed a one-party state or restrictions on liberty. Hitler tried to ridicule the Centre leadership for having 'tolerated' Marxism and declared that its faith in liberty must be hypocrisy because it had supported suppressive measures against National Socialism; he himself had been in prison. The Centre had been willing to sit in the same government with 'those who deny God'.

Hitler treated Marxism as being self-evidently bad; so far as he argued against it at all, it was in passing references to the widespread famine in the Soviet Union, caused by Stalin's programme of forced collectivisation. What he was doing was to appeal to the Catholics and the peasants to join him in 'rescuing' the industrial workers from their Marxist delusions. He himself stood for the true interests of the German worker. 'I myself was and still am a child of the people. It was not for the capitalists that I undertook this struggle, it was for the German working man that I took my stand.'

Of course 'Give me four years' was not a programme and Hitler avoided making any specific pledges beyond one to build up the German 'national community'. In this he was following his own propaganda methods, as outlined in *My Struggle* and which aimed at influencing the emotions rather than the intellect. This was quite typical of political reactions in several countries to the world slump. In a near-hysterical election in Britain in 1931, the National Government won a record majority with no programme save a demand for 'a doctor's mandate'. In the United States in 1932, Franklin D. Roosevelt carried forty-two of the forty-eight states on a promise of 'a new deal' which he defined only as 'bold, persistent experimentation'. Roosevelt's most memorable words at this time were: 'The only thing we have to fear is fear itself', which was stirring rather than meaningful. Hitler went out of his way to repudiate the necessity for a programme. 'Programmes are of no avail, it is the human purpose which is decisive. The decisive thing is to see aright, to have great honesty and an honourable purpose.'

Hitler's speeches in this campaign made almost no mention of the Jews. He had no proposals for setting up concentration camps. He did not advocate war. He was less than specific, even, on his intention of setting up a personal dictatorship, although he did use cloudy phrases about his intention to 'liberate the German spirit from the fetters of a democratic parliamentary majority.' (His ability to get away with such words as 'liberate' and 'freedom' in such contexts was characteristic of his skill.) His keynote for the campaign, hammered in repetitively, came in such passages as:

We are convinced that the restoration to health of our people must start from the restoration to health of the body-politic itself, and we are persuaded of the truth that the future of our people, as in the past so now, lies first of all in the German peasant. If he perishes, our end has come; if he survives, then Germany will never go under. There lie the strength and source of our people's life, the source of our renewal. The towns would not exist at all, if the peasant did not fill them with his blood. The dweller in our countryside may be primitive, but he is healthy.

While he obviously expected to win the election, Hitler intended to try to stay in power whatever the result of the voting. He made a virtue of this both in appealing privately for funds and in code passages in his public speeches. 'Always my only promise to my followers has been: one day you will determine Germany's future' . . . 'We will not capitulate before any resistance, whatever form it take, for we all know how hard it is to build up any sound construction.'

Backing up such words were the practical activities of Göring, as Minister of the Interior of Prussia, and the actions on the streets of the brownshirts. Nominally Göring was subordinate in Prussia to Papen but, in fact, he took over the real administration of the state, which comprised two-thirds of Germany. He showed energy, leadership and brutality, eating and sleeping in his ministerial office, as he conducted a revolution in the police.

As a relic of the long years of Social Democratic administration, the Prussian police contained a high proportion of senior officers of liberal and socialist inclinations. By his own account, Göring in his first month purged twenty-two of the thirty-two police commanders, replacing them with National Socialists from the S.A. and S.S. In the lower ranks he got rid of 'hundreds' of inspectors and 'thousands' of sergeants. He formed an 'auxiliary police' of 50,000 members of the S.A., S.S. and conservative Steel Helmet organisation. He laid the foundations of what became the political police, the Gestapo.* The aims were partly to build up National Socialist power on a permanent basis, partly to provide spoils for and contain the enthusiasms of National Socialist members and partly to prepare for a Communist uprising, which Göring and Hitler believed to be a serious possibility. In the early weeks, many of the ordinary S.A. men got out of hand. Particularly in Berlin, they made arbitrary and illegal 'arrests' of opponents and 'Jews', dragged them off to party headquarters and beat them and tortured them. Apart from occasional rescue operations, the ordinary police were generally powerless to interfere. The extent to which atrocities of this kind occurred is difficult to establish, if only because they were built up by anti-Nazi propagandists without an invariable strict regard for truth. But Göring, while in the long run successful in suppressing private enterprise atrocities, did lean far on the side of excess, presumably with a view to keeping control of the situation.

Whoever does his duty in the service of the state, who obeys my orders and ruthlessly makes use of his revolver when attacked is assured of my protection. Whoever, on the other hand, plays the coward, will have to reckon on being thrown out by me at the earliest possible moment. A bullet fired from the barrel of a police pistol is my bullet. If you say that is murder, then I am the murderer.

Physical resistance was slight. While the National Socialists acted with energy and roughness, the Communists, Social Demo-

* This was originally the *'Gestapo'* an abbreviation of *Geheimstaatspolizeiamt*—Secret State Police Bureau.

crats and even the Centre submitted to their election meetings being banned and their publications confiscated. Despite such docility, Hitler and Göring believed that Communists insurrection was imminent and that they might soon have a civil war on their hands; their strategy, decided at the first cabinet meeting, was to let the Communists make the first move and then hit back in a vigorous counter-attack. In fact the Communists had no concrete plans for revolution at all and so far as they thought of the immediate future were devising only a scheme for keeping their party in existence in a clandestine, underground form. Many of them were quite cheerful about Hitler's advent to power, their Communist dialectic convincing them that it could only be the final, crazy convulsion of capitalism. When Hitler failed, there would be no alternative but a 'workers' government.

Into this chaotic situation came an eccentric young Dutchman called Marinus van der Lubbe. By trade he was a bricklayer; he suffered from extreme short-sightedness and he was aged twenty-four. In his teens he had been a Young Communist activist in Leyden but had left the party on the ground that its leaders were too dictatorial. He became a sort of free-lance Marxist agitator; he was an eccentric but well-informed and by no means insane. Conceivably he would have been more at home in 'the new left' of the 1960s and 1970s than he was in the politics of his own time. One of his penchants was for walking huge distances across Europe; he even tried to reach China. In various countries he served short prison sentences for vagrancy, illegal entry and petty agitation.

Lubbe, with some prevision, decided that Hitler's accession to power in Germany was not an ordinary political event but one which the left should fight at all costs. He immediately walked and hitch-hiked from Leyden to Berlin, where he made anti-Nazi speeches to the unemployed lining up outside labour exchanges. He appeared to be a wild young man, his Dutch accent was difficult to understand and nobody took any notice of him. So, eccentrically, he decided to arouse the masses by a programme of arson. He bought a supply of matches and firelighters and, successively, started fires in a state welfare office, Berlin town hall and the former imperial palace. All were discovered before they could do serious damage.

On the evening of February 27th, 1933, Lubbe, a quaint, shabby figure in a peaked cap and wearing trousers that were far too short for him, penetrated the Reichstag building. The Reichstag was, of course, not sitting and security precautions seem to have been slight. The principal users of the building were the Communists

189

who, since the National Socialist take-over, had found it a relatively safe base from which to administer their party. (The official Communist headquarters, Karl Liebknecht House, had been raided by the police three days earlier but the Communist offices in the Reichstag still had a degree of parliamentary immunity.) At about nine p.m. Lubbe made his way into the Reichstag debating chamber, which contained much wood in its panelled walls; three tier tribune and deputies' seats. He distributed lighted firelighters around it, which took him only a few minutes. This time his arson really worked and the place began to blaze. The heat broke the circular glass dome overhead and this created a draught with the result that the fire completely gutted the furnishings and fittings of the debating chamber. (The main structure of the building was unaffected.) The fire was first noticed at five past nine and Lubbe, skulking around the building with incendiary material on him, was arrested twenty-two minutes later. He made a full and defiant confession, saying that he had started the fire to encourage the German workers to fight for freedom.

To Hitler, Göring and the others of the National Socialist leadership, the news of the fire was an intense shock. This was not because they or anybody else cared particularly for the Reichstag building, but because it seemed to be the signal for the awaited Communist uprising. Hitler seems momentarily to have lost all self-control. He drove up to witness the blaze and raved: '. . . The German people have been soft too long. All Communist deputies must be hanged this very night. All the friends of the Communists must be locked up. And that goes for the Social Democrats and the Reichsbanner as well . . .' Then he drove off to the *Völkischer Beobachter* office and, in a slightly calmer frame of mind, dictated a leading article calling for vengeance on the Communists.

The following day, February 28th, 1933, still convinced that he was facing a Communist revolution, Hitler got Hindenburg to sign a 'Decree of the Reich's President for the Protection of People and State.' This was the real start of the National Socialist dictatorship; technically the decree was supposed to be only an 'emergency' arrangement but in practice it remained in full operation until the final collapse of the National Socialist regime twelve years later. The decree could scarcely have been more far-reaching in terms of police power, although Hindenburg did veto a scheme of Hitler to hang the 'Communist conspirators' who had fired the Reichstag outside the Reichstag building; Hindenburg regarded public executions as being against German tradition.

The decree suspended the guarantees of individual liberty and gave the police unlimited rights of search, arrest and detention;

they did not even have to state a reason for what they were doing. The death penalty was introduced, with retroactive effect, for offences against public order, including arson and poisoning. It was indicative of the hysteria of the moment that poisoning was included; the National Socialists claimed that the Communists were about to poison the German milk supplies and seem to have been sincere in thinking this. The decree also, crucially, gave power to the central Reich government to take over control of the police in the individual states; this, of course, much reduced the capacity of the state governments to resist Hitler's will. In signing the decree, Hindenburg obviously could not have foreseen Hitler's capacity for making an 'emergency' last indefinitely and he must also have believed that the firing of the Reichstag was a signal for the attempted 'bolshevisation' of Germany. For that matter, Hitler also believed in the Communist conspiracy. He had a capacity for being taken in by his own propaganda; he was at once foaming with near-hysteria and taking intelligent, ruthless action to crush enemies whom he believed to possess infinite guile and infinite infamy.

For all his anger at the fire, Hitler undoubtedly benefited from it. The police powers which he needed as the basis for his dictatorship had now been obtained; without the fire, he would have had to find some other pretext for getting them. Indeed so convenient was the fire to Hitler that it became widely believed, even by some National Socialists, that it was a frame-up from the start. The favourite version was that Göring had used a tunnel which for central heating purposes connected his official house as President of the Reichstag with the main Reichstag building to introduce S.A. men who had started the fire. An embellishment was that he had them shot immediately afterwards so as to silence them. Lubbe, according to this theory, was a lunatic who had been used as a dupe. It is credible that Göring was capable of arranging such a scheme (although less credible that he would have executed his own men) but in fact it did not occur to him to do so. Lubbe was an eccentric, not a lunatic, and his apparent apathy during his trial at Leipzig came from despair that neither the National Socialist prosecution nor the Communist defence believed his confession; also he had been loaded for months with heavy chains.*

The regime was careful to use euphemisms for its new police powers. Thus arbitrary arrests were termed 'protective custody', as if it were necessary to 'protect' the victims from the anger of the

* The authority primarily relied upon for this account of the arson in the Reichstag debating chamber is *The Reichstag Fire* by Fritz Tobias (London, 1963). Although no published evidence exists to controvert the Tobias version there are still some authorities who do not accept it as conclusive.

ordinary German people. The centres to which the prisoners were sent were termed 'concentration camps'—the first was opened at a disused gunpowder factory at Dachau near Munich on March 20th, 1933,—and this came from the camps set up by the British in the Transvaal in the closing stages of the South African War some thirty years earlier. The British concentration camps, which had aroused world-wide humanitarian protest, were correctly named in that they 'concentrated' the normally scattered rural Boer population into camps to prevent it providing basis for guerrilla warfare. The German camps were not intended to 'concentrate' people in this sense but were just detention centres for political prisoners; the word 'concentration' was used solely because of the British precedent.

It is indicative of how little either side understood the potentialities of the Reichstag fire episode that Ernst Torgler leader of the Communist Reichstag fraction surrendered voluntarily to the police the day after. He had been in the Reichstag building until about half an hour before the fire and had then gone off to dine with friends in a restaurant. When he heard that he was wanted for 'treason' and 'arson' he turned up at a police station, accompanied by two lawyers, in the belief that he could prove the accusations groundless and so make the government look absurd. The National Socialists, on their side, were thunderstruck that a supposed revolutionary enemy, whom they had assumed would have to be hunted down in conditions that might amount to civil war, should behave so calmly. In fact during the raid on Karl Liebknecht House, Göring's police had found nothing more damning than propaganda material and some sets of forged S.A. orders which had been intended to be used to cause confusion. Göring, falsely claiming that grossly treasonable material had been found, went ahead energetically to suppress a revolution that did not exist. Thousands of Communist functionaries and members were arrested and also a few Social Democrats. As a 'punishment' for the fire, the Communist press was banned for a month and the Social Democratic press for a fortnight. 'It may be', commented the London *Times* in a leading article on March 1st, 'that Germany is marching towards the abolition of parliamentary government and the establishment of a dictatorship'.

It was seven days after the fire that, on March 5th, 1933, Germany went to the polls in the last contested election of the Weimar republic. Especially in the closing stages, almost the only propaganda that existed was in favour of the National Socialists who organised marches, lit 'liberation bonfires' on hill-tops and along the Rhine valley, and monopolised the radio. In Berlin, loudspeakers were set up in the streets to relay Hitler's speeches and to ensure that 'the last slumberer awakes'. On top of this was outright intimidation of the opposition both by formal bans on their meetings and unofficial violence by stormtroopers.

Yet it was still a free election in that any party was allowed to put up candidates and the voting procedures and secret ballot remained inviolate. The electorate turned out in record numbers; 88·8 per cent of those entitled to vote went to the polls and this was the highest proportion in the history of the Weimar republic.

The result must have been a disappointment to Hitler. On February 28th he had told his cabinet that he expected the Reichstag fire to ensure that he would win at least 51 per cent of the vote; such an absolute majority would have been of supreme moral value to him in legitimising a dictatorship. He wanted victory on the scale of Franklin D. Roosevelt in the United States, who had won 57·4 per cent of the popular vote in the crisis election of 1932, or of the MacDonald-Baldwin coalition who in Britain in comparable circumstances in 1931 had won 67 per cent.

In fact the National Socialists secured only 43·9 per cent of the vote and only 288 seats in a Reichstag of 647. This was a substantial improvement on their performance the previous November, when they had won only 33·1 per cent. The shift in their favour must have been a result not only of intimidation but also a reflection of a genuine popular distrust of the Weimar system and a disposition to try something else. It was reckoned that Hitler had done particularly well among young voters who had just come on the registers. The rise in his vote was fairly uniform across Germany and this suggests the existence of an element in the electorate which was making a choice for him independently of the old regional, confessional and party loyalties. Hitler's best performance was in East Prussia, where he won 56·5 per cent of the vote; in five other of the thirty-five electoral districts he polled over 50 per cent. His lowest vote was 30·4 per cent in Cologne-Aachen but in terms of the Catholic Rhineland this was quite a break-through for him; in the November 1932 election he had won only 17·4 per cent in this district. Hitler also did well in Bavaria, where during campaign speeches he had made much of a claim to be the first 'Bavarian' ever to be Reich Chancellor. In lower Bavaria he shot up from 18·5 per cent to 39·2 and in Upper Bavaria from 24·6 to 40·9.

A majority of Germans had positively voted against National Socialism. But Hitler had the advantage that the opposition to him was fragmented. The Communists, whom he had carefully allowed to participate in the election, held up well; they had 12·3 per cent of the vote and eighty-one seats in the new Reichstag, as against 16·9 per cent and 100 previously. This was actually an asset to Hitler in that the Communist deputies were either arrested or liable to arrest under the February 28th decree and so could not take their seats; this was better than an outright ban on Communist candidates which could only have strengthened the Social Democrats. Even so, though, the Social Democrats held up remarkably well; their vote fell from 20·4 per cent to 18·3 per cent and their seats only from 121 to 120. The Centre and its allied Bavarian People's Party also maintained its position; its poll fell from 15 per cent to 13·9 but it increased its representation from ninety to ninety-two seats.

Between them, the Communists, the Social Democrats and the Centre could outvote the National Socialists in the Reichstag but there was no prospect of them working together and trying to win over Hitler's Nationalist allies. The Communists were intent on 'revolution'. The Social Democrats were in the conservative position of being the chief defenders of the Weimar constitution. The Centre regarded Marxism as being as at least as great an evil as National Socialism. In its character of Catholic pressure group, the Centre was concerned to preserve Church institutions, especially schools, in what looked like being a period of rapid social change. Its Reichstag leader was not ex-Chancellor Brüning, but the prelate Ludwig Kaas who gave priority to religious rather than political matters.

The 'National Government' was an alliance of National Socialists, Nationalists, the German People's Party and various splinter groups and individuals. The component parties had put up rival lists of candidates against each other in the election. Thus it had been possible to vote for the government without supporting the National Socialists directly. Hugenberg's Nationalists, despite their fears of January, held their position well; they dropped only from 8·3 per cent of the vote to 8 and their seats went up from fifty-one to fifty-two. The little German People's Party dropped from 1·9 per cent to 1·1. Between them the three parties and their allies could command 340 seats in the Reichstag of 647 which was enough for a working majority and so Hitler had at least delivered the goods to Hindenburg in that he had at last provided him with a fully 'parliamentary' government.

What the electorate had not done, however, was to provide a mandate for the Enabling Act which would enable Hitler to rule by decree, without reference to the President. Such a law required a three-quarters majority of the Reichstag. The Social Democrats would be bound to oppose it and so Hitler's only chance was to get not only his coalition allies but also the Centre to vote for it.

The burning-out of the Reichstag debating chamber gave Hitler the adventitious advantage of being able to summon the new Reichstag to meet in surroundings which had no connection with democratic tradition. The arrangements were a mixture of an emotional appeal to patriotism and sheer intimidation.

First Hitler called a ceremonial session in the garrison church at Potsdam, the sanctuary of the traditions of the Prussian and imperial monarchy. This was partly to impress Hindenburg and partly to identify himself in public opinion with classical nationalism. The ceremony was dignified but theatrical, with Hindenburg delighted to play his part. The old man lifted his field marshal's baton in salute to an empty chair representing the exiled Emperor; to organ music, he made his way slowly down to the crypt to commune at the tomb of Frederick the Great. Goebbels's propaganda machine extolled the ceremony as the union of 'old' with 'young' Germany. Hitler, in tail coat with top hat, had a youthful air; he was modest in manner but with an air of dedication.

We are determined, [he said,] to create a new community out of the German peoples—a community formed of men of every status and profession and of every so-called class—which shall be able to achieve that community of interests which the welfare of the entire nation demands. All classes must be welded together in a single German nation.

In the afternoon the Reichstag got down to business in the Kroll Opera House which had been especially adapted for the occasion into a passable imitation of a normal Reichstag debating chamber. The deputies sat in the body of the theatre facing a speaker's tribune and seats for the government, and the representatives of the state and the throne of the President of the Reichstag had been erected on the stage. But the dress circle and galleries were packed with National Socialist supporters and 'security guards' from the police, S.A. and S.S. lined the walls. All eighty-one Communist deputies were absent, being either under arrest or in hiding; nine Social Democratic deputies were also absent under arrest. The National Socialists, by far the biggest single delegation, wore uniform and entered in quasi-parade formation. Hitler, for the first time himself a deputy, sat modestly among the National Socialists instead of taking the Chancellor's seat on the platform. The only business of the session was to elect

195

Göring as President, with representatives of the Nationalists and the Centre as his deputies. 'The holy fire of the national revolution has seized the German people,' said Göring in his acceptance speech.

The Reichstag then adjourned for two days for the purpose of Hitler negotiating on the Enabling Bill which would empower the 'cabinet' to make laws by decree during a four-year period. By ordinary standards, no such Bill was necessary. Whatever had been the situation in the previous three years of successive Chancellors being forced to rule by emergency presidential decree, Hitler's coalition now had a working majority in the Reichstag and could have used ordinary constitutional processes. From his own point of view it is easy to understand why he did not want to rule through the Reichstag; it was contrary to what he had preached, it would limit his powers and make him liable to dismissal and, however much he used his police powers to harass the opposition, he would have to have justified his measures in open debate, with opposing views liable to be stated. His coalition partners would have been able to withdraw support at any moment. What is psychologically difficult to understand however—Hjalmar Schacht, writing after World War II, described it as a 'mystery'—is why members of the opposition accepted it. The Enabling Bill required a three-quarters majority in the Reichstag and so could not be carried without opposition support.

The Social Democrats were fundamentally opposed to the Bill and would certainly vote against it. This left only the ninety-two-strong Centre, the Catholic party which since the 1870s had been accustomed to ride the balance of power and to negotiate deals. From hindsight, the Centre would obviously have served its own interest best by denying Hitler the Enabling Bill but at the same time promising not to obstruct in the Reichstag the swift passage of measures necessary for the national economy. Such a scheme would have given Hitler all reasonable power but maintained the right of opposition; it was this that the Centre's politically most experienced member, former Chancellor Brüning, advocated in inner-fraction debates. However not he but Monsignor Kaas was the party leader.

If Hitler were to conduct a 'national revolution' it was important, from the Centre's viewpoint, to safeguard Catholic rights and interests, particularly in education, and it was obviously capable of being argued that the best tactics were not outrightly to defy Hitler but to use the Centre's voting power to do a deal; the Centre would give Hitler the Bill in return for him guaranteeing the Church. Hitler, in his private views, was totally opposed to

Christianity, which he regarded as an emanation of Jewish corruption, and to his own circle he was already, desultorily, talking of a long-term need to eradicate it. But for the short-term he was perfectly willing to give Kaas the guarantees he wanted and did so: in fact a concordat with the Vatican was one of Hitler's first international acts.

The Hitler persuasiveness and charm must have worked on Kaas and there was then almost no way of knowing that a Hitler promise was unreliable. Whatever his faults, he did appear in 1933 to be utterly sincere. More broadly, the Centre had to reflect that Hitler represented Germany's biggest party and that there was reason, in the crisis conditions of 1933, in giving him unhampered power. He was the only political saviour in sight. The power was, after all, only to be for four years and somebody had to make decisions for Germany. The actual use that Hitler was to make of such power was unforeseeable; even his most bitter opponents in 1933 fell far short of what was to be actuality when they predicted what Hitler would do.

Until the last moment there remained some doubt on how the Centre would vote. There was thus high tension when the Reichstag reassembled on March 23rd, this time Hitler sitting on the rostrum, and again an atmosphere of intimidation. The Social Democrats were silent and looking nervous. One of their leaders, Carl Severing, still technically Minister of the Interior of Prussia (in the government which Papen had suspended), had been arrested that morning, although he was let out of custody to attend the Reichstag and vote against the Enabling Bill. The Centre looked puzzled and worried. The National Socialists, massed on their deputies' benches and in the public galleries, were boisterous but disciplined.

Hitler started his speech by talking of a 'moral cleansing of the national life'. There had been false values in the theatre, the cinema, literature, the press and the radio but now 'blood and race will again become the sources of artistic inspiration'. To please the Centre, however, he went out of his way to refer to 'Christianity' as 'the unshakable foundation of the nation's morality'. He blamed the war and the Treaty of Versailles as the principal cause of Germany's troubles; a breed of traitors had grown up, but 'sedition and treason will in future be burned out with barbaric ruthlessness'. He advocated no war but claimed that Germany had 'equal rights' with other nations to arm herself.

The speech contained no mention of the word 'Jew'.

Economically, Hitler was as vague as ever and he did not specify exactly what he wanted to do with the Enabling Bill powers. 'The people' he said 'is not made for the economic system and

197

the economic system does not exist for capital, but capital serves the economic system and the economic system serves the people.'

He specifically pledged that he would not use his powers to interfere with the rights of the German states.

In his closing words, Hitler implied that it would be better to give him the Enabling Bill powers voluntarily, than to oblige him to seize them by force. 'Now gentlemen,' he concluded, 'you may yourselves decide for peace or war.'

The next speaker was the Social Democrat, Otto Wels, who in an atmosphere of hostility, made a weak but not ignoble speech. He took it for granted that the Bill would be passed, stressed his own party's opposition to it and pleaded with Hitler to act in the interests of the German people. This was the only time in his whole career that Hitler heard any kind of debating speech from an opponent. It seemed to sting him to fury. He could well have ignored it but instead he returned to the rostrum and, impromptu, lashed into Wels and the Social Democrats for having betrayed and divided Germany, surrendered the national interests and put the economy into ruins. Hitler had the audience on his side but, even without that, it was in debating terms an effective performance.

Kaas, briefly, announced that the Centre would vote for the Bill and Göring, from the President's chair, called for those in favour to stand. The National Socialists crashed to their feet in a drill-like manoeuvre and the Centre rose in a muddled, civilian manner. Göring declared the Bill carried; a card vote followed which confirmed the decision by 441 votes to ninety-four. The Reichstag had abdicated.

Formally the Enabling Bill gave power to the cabinet rather than to Hitler personally. But it had always been the German political practice for the chancellor to rank as chief of the ministers, rather than first among equals, and it had long been accepted that he had sole responsibility for defining basic policy. The subordinate ministers ran their own departments and acted as the chancellor's assistants rather than colleagues. In fact the system was in some ways closer to that of a United States President and his cabinet, than of a British and French Prime Minister to theirs. At the height of the Weimar system in the 1920s this constitutional practice, although still defined in the legal textbooks, had tended to drift towards the British and French pattern. But the period of 'presidential' government had tended to restore the former system and Hitler made the most of it. In his first months in power his cabinet meetings did have some air of discussing government business and making decisions; Hugenberg, so long as he was

Minister for Economics, was particularly active in keeping this up. But, gradually, the cabinet became merely a forum at which Hitler announced decisions he had already made and then it dwindled away altogether. Hitler's final cabinet meeting was in 1938. From the middle of 1933, the cabinet's task of co-ordinating the departments of state became a paper operation, with all major disputes liable to Hitler's arbitration; Hitler, however, often insisted that ministers should settle technical differences among themselves rather than bother him.

Hitler had made no mention in his Enabling Bill speech of banning all opposition parties. (Although his references to creating a 'national community' could have been taken as code-words for this.) But he now had limitless police power and the right, by 'cabinet decree' to make whatever laws he wanted. He moved in swiftly.

The first to go were the trade unions. May 1st was the traditional day for trade union celebrations and Hitler took it over, claiming it as National Socialist day also. The unions, hopeful of conciliating the government, accepted this and joined in National Socialist rallies. Hitler, addressing a union rally at the Berlin Sports Palace, made an appeal to end class conflict.

The German people, [he said,] must learn to know each other again. The millions who have been split up into professions and kept apart by artificial class distinctions, who, foolishly clinging to profession and status, cannot understand each other any longer, must find once more the way to each other. An enormous and stupendous task—we know it. Nevertheless . . . what has been built up by the hands of man, can also be destroyed by the hands of man; what human madness once invented, can be overcome by human wisdom.

The following day the police moved into the union offices and independent trade unionism was abolished by decree. But some union officials found employment in the new 'Labour Front', under National Socialist control; some others found themselves in concentration camps.

The Social Democrats tried to maintain their existence and even collaborated with the regime to the extent of condemning their members who had fled abroad. But on June 22nd they were dissolved by decree. During the following fortnight the smaller parties 'voluntarily' dissolved themselves, including Hugenberg's Nationalists with Hugenberg himself resigning from the cabinet on the ground he was not being listened to. The last to go was the

Centre, which dissolved itself on July 5th, issuing a final manifesto which ended: 'All for Germany—Germany for Christ!' On July 14th, Hitler issued a law making illegal any party other than the National Socialists.

At the same time, in flat contradiction to his Enabling Bill speech, Hitler was abolishing the independence of the German states. The Bavarian government was thrown out more or less by force and a law on April 7th put all state administrations under the control of governors appointed by Hitler.

These changes, made with the speed of a hot knife cutting butter, aroused surprisingly little resistance. Opposition groups did exist, especially among Communists and Socialists, but they were disconnected and powerless. Hitler, after all, was in the cases of the parties and trade unions abolishing wealthy movements who in the recent past had attracted far more public support than he had. In the case of the states, he was abolishing entities which went deep into German history; even Bismarck had never gone beyond federalism in unifying Germany. There were various reasons he was able to do this.

One obvious point was that something like 60,000 people had gone into exile in the early months of his regime; these included many of his most active opponents, as well as Jews. The loss of such people inevitably weakened opposition. Then there was the point that Hitler was acting 'legally' and to go against him was to encourage anarchy in a Germany already in economic crisis. More practically, Hitler had the police power in his hands, plus the power of a mass party which now penetrated to almost every level of German society.

The crudities and cruelties of the early concentration camps were partly accidental; they were set up in a hurry by untrained, underpaid staff in makeshift quarters. As the system settled down, it became more regular although, as in any prison system, it did give scope to sadists. And it was unmistakeably part of Hitler's policy that the concentration camps should be places of mystery and terror. Prisoners, on release, were specifically forbidden, on pain of reinternment, to tell anyone of their experiences; here, obviously, the psychology was that mystery was more frightening than any explicit threat. Concentration camp staff were occasionally punished for 'excesses' but they tended to get pardoned; thus in 1934, in a public trial, twenty-three camp guards at Hohnstein, Saxony, were found guilty of torturing prisoners. Gürtner, the man who had released Hitler from prison in 1924 and was now Reich Justice Minister, in a memorandum on the case, wrote: 'Such cruelty, reminiscent of oriental sadism, cannot be explained

200

or accused.' On Hitler's direct order, the men were pardoned.

But ruthless use of cruelty and fear was by no means the whole secret of Hitler's success in power. He seemed, to many, to represent for better or worse the destiny of Germany. There was no logical reason why he should be dictator, only mystical ones. In all political systems, and especially in crisis conditions, there is a tendency for leaders to attract an aura of infallibility: this was particularly so in apparently advanced countries in the 1930s and 1940s. It was the era of personal leadership. Ordinary people identified with their leaders and resented any attack on them as an attack on themselves. Sometimes this is purely emotional. The overwhelming majority of Englishmen in 1934 would have bitterly resented any personal criticism of King George V, even although the King had done nothing, which in strictly rational terms was worth special praise. Significantly, however, the King had established personal contact by taking up broadcasting. In the Soviet Union the cult of personality was developing around Joseph Stalin. Italy had Benito Mussolini. In the United States Roosevelt attracted extremes of adulation as well as of distaste but the adulation was to be sufficient to enable him, eventually, to break a taboo reaching back to George Washington and become President for a third and fourth terms. Hitler in Germany followed this trend in its most extreme form. It was a novelty that, through broadcasting, popular newspapers and mass meetings, ordinary people could feel a sense of personal contact with their leader. One of Hitler's characteristics, during the consolidation of his power, was to be frequently on the move and showing himself. He enjoyed himself and his eyes seemed to shine with love for the people who crowded around him; he was young, celibate, classless, had sprung apparently from nowhere and was hailed as a genius. But he was careful to leave his choice of route until the last moment so as to hamper any potential assassin.

Hitler did not abolish the Reichstag altogether, although it was rarely to meet. It was a useful means of providing salaries and status to deserving party members and it was a good forum for his speeches. But it had to be purified from the non-Nazi majority that had been elected in March 1933. So he had yet another dissolution, with fresh elections set for November 12th. He tied in with the election a plebiscite on his foreign policy. As in the Soviet Union, there was psychological value in creating a sense of participation by getting the people out to vote for the ruling party.

A year earlier, in November 1932, the National Socialists had been losing ground. Now, however, they presented a single list of candidates, with no opposition allowed. Even Hindenburg was wheeled on to broadcast in favour of 'firm national unity'. Hitler gloried that his revolution had been 'almost bloodless'.

When has there ever been a revolution so free from excesses as ours? [he said in an election speech.] Even if there were excesses, we could still stand comparison with the excesses of revolutions among other peoples. It is true we have to barricade the streets, but not because the people wants to stone the government, but because the people wants to express to the government its jubilation. I go any day among the people without a cordon of police. People can always know where I am and where I am going. I have not the least fear that the people may attack me: on the contrary my greatest anxiety is that perhaps a small child might be crushed before my motor.

And if I compare the excesses of the French Revolution, I can only say: We at least have established no guillotine, we have not created any Vendée in Germany. Even with the worst elements we have only kept them apart from the nation.

Election procedure was based on the methods used in the Soviet Union. According to the official figures, the party organisation was efficient enough to get 96 per cent of the electorate to the polls, a far higher proportion than had ever done so in the democratic period; even the concentration camp inmates voted. There were many irregularities as local party organisers competed with each other to put on the best show. In some places, National Socialist loyalists spurned the curtained voting booth and marked their ballot papers in full public view; many of the less enthusiastic felt it wise to follow their example. Everywhere, S.A. guards stood with police at the polling stations and anybody who wanted to vote against the government list did so in the reasonable fear that the secret ballot could no longer be regarded as sacrosanct and that retribution might easily follow. There were some claims that the National Socialists recorded votes for dead or absent voters but the evidence suggests that, on the whole, the count was honest.

Each elector could vote for or against the single list of candidates. Of those voting, 92·2 per cent voted in favour and the not totally insignificant number of 7·8 per cent voted against. (This was a higher opposition vote than has ever occurred in the Soviet Union.) The foreign policy plebiscite produced an even better result for Hitler: 95 per cent in favour and 5 per cent against. The difference between the two figures is of some little interest. Hitler's foreign policy of the time—discussed more fully in chapter thirteen—was presented as being one of building up Germany's 'equality' with other European countries. This could undoubtedly appeal very widely. In the Reichstag on May 17th, in its last substantial political act, even the Social Democratic fraction had voted in favour of it. For some two per cent of the German electorate— it must have been a sophisticated and courageous element—it was possible to distinguish between support for a patriotic but ostensibly peaceful foreign policy and support for Hitler generally.

There remained for Hitler the problem of what to do with his private army, the S.A., now that he had achieved almost absolute power and no longer really needed it. The politically more useful elements in the S.A. had already been drained off into paid jobs. There was a limit to the amount of enjoyment which the bulk of the membership could get out of picketing Jewish-owned shops, going out into the streets with collecting boxes for the Winter Relief Fund and beating up opponents. With the return to 'normality' and Hitler claiming that the 'revolution' was over, the scope in the future was to be even less. Hitler had always had difficulty in controlling the S.A. and the feeling undoubtedly grew up among some S.A. units that there should now be a 'second revolution' in which they would take over full control of the state. The jargon was that they would 'liberate' Hitler from the 'reactionaries' that surround him and build up a really socialistic state.

Röhm, the S.A. chief of staff, had a different aim. He wanted his 400,000 S.A. men to become the new 'people's army' of Germany, enrolled as full-time soldiers. Since the regular army only had 100,000 men, it would be eclipsed by Röhm's organisation. Röhm was acting partly, naturally, from personal ambition but he also had a genuine doctrine that the regular army was too tradition-bound and cast-ridden to be effective in the modern age. The 'people's army', with promotion on merit, political indoctrination, informal discipline and a spirit of comradeship between officers and men would be an asset to Germany. 'I am the new army's Scharnhorst,' Röhm remarked.

Hitler's aim, however, was to use German institutions, not overthrow them. The army, and particularly its general staff, had prestige and skills he wanted to employ. Moreover Hindenburg would always support the army. While he played along with Röhm—in January 1934 he appointed him to the cabinet and wrote him a public letter of thanks for his services—he was not going to sacrifice the army to him. Röhm became quite mutinous in attitude and, in private, described Hitler as 'a ridiculous corporal' who ought to 'go on leave'.

The denouncement, like the Reichstag fire, was not a result of any cold planning by Hitler. Rather, he was deceived.

The process began in May 1934 with S.S. Brigade Leader Reinhard Heydrich, a former naval officer who was chief of the Gestapo, assembling a dossier against Röhm and the S.A. leadership. Heydrich was intelligent, cruel and a lover of the violin. He detested Röhm for his crude manners. Partly because he genuinely feared a Röhm attempt at revolution and partly because he wanted to eliminate the S.A. as a power factor, Heydrich fabricated evidence that Röhm was preparing a *coup d'état*. It included such items that Röhm had been paid twelve million marks by the French ambassador to overthrow Hitler. He showed his evidence to Göring and to the S.S. leader, Heinrich Himmler, both of whom had their own reasons for wanting Röhm's elimination. (Himmler wanted more power for his S.S. and Göring saw Röhm as an obstacle to his ambition of becoming commander-in-chief of the armed forces; Göring and Himmler were later rivals but at this stage they had a close, working alliance.)

On the basis of Heydrich's 'evidence', Göring, Himmler and various functionaries of the Gestapo and S.S. drew up lists of people who were to be executed for being associated with Röhm. There were some quite heated arguments on whom should be included—all the participants had prospective victims nominated for reasons of personal feuds—and the gangster side of National Socialism was at its most blatant.

Hitler at this stage was not involved but he was obviously nervy about what he could see. On June 17th, Papen, still Vice-Chancellor, delivered a speech at Marburg University in which he criticised the National Socialists for their 'confusion between vitality and brutality'. He said the 'German revolution' ought to lead to 'a Christian state'. While publication of the speech was suppressed, it did indicate the existence of opposition. (Papen was shortly afterwards sent off to be ambassador to Austria.) Then there was Röhm conducting S.A. parades and calling for 'the second revolution'. Hitler, afraid of an alliance of the Papen-type bourgeoisie with the S.A. hit on a scheme for sending the S.A. on 'leave' for a month from July 1st. Fulsomely, it was announced that they had earned a rest after their valiant work. At the same time the devoted Hess, Hitler's deputy for party affairs, made a broadcast: 'Adolf Hitler is the revolution's great strategist. Woe to him who plants his flat feet among the fine threads of the Leader's strategic plans.'

The decisions to send the S.A. on 'leave' entailed some quick re-thinking for Heydrich. His scenario had been that Röhm and the S.A. were to attempt revolution in July; but this would obviously lack conviction if the S.A. organisation was on holiday.

So Heydrich advanced the date to the end of June. He supplied the Defence Ministry with a list of generals who, he said, Röhm was planning to shoot on seizing power. He sent other fabricated evidence to Hitler who was worried but indecisive about it.

On June 28th Hitler went to Essen to attend the wedding of the local area manager. While he was at the wedding reception at the Kaiserhof Hotel, Himmler telephoned him from Berlin with a tale that the S.A. planned to occupy public buildings on the morrow. Another call, from area manager Adolf Wagner of Munich, who was also in the conspiracy, informed him that the S.A. were parading the streets and shouting anti-Hitler slogans; this was true to the extent that the S.A. really were marching around in Munich, but they had been called out by mysterious leaflets, presumably prepared by the Heydrich group.

On the spot, in the Kaiserhof Hotel, Hitler made the decision to act ruthlessly. He believed he was at a crisis in his career. 'I've had enough,' he said. 'I shall make an example of them.' He flew straight off to Munich, sitting silently in the aircraft as in a trance.

So far from executing a *coup d'état*, Röhm and his staff were relaxing on holiday, with homosexual lovers and much drinking, at the Hanselbauer Pension, Bad Wiessee, near Munich. Hitler, with an S.S. escort, burst in on them at six thirty on the morning of the twenty-ninth and, waving a revolver, personally arrested them and had them driven off to gaol in Munich. It must have been an unpleasant awakening with their hangovers, the more bizarre because Hitler himself was acting as the policeman.

Back in Munich, Hitler assembled the unarrested S.A. leaders in the senate chamber of the Brown House and harangued them furiously about 'treason'; at some points he was incoherent with emotion and he foamed at the mouth. Then he held an impromptu conference, with Hess and Max Amann playing prominent parts, to decide who should be shot. Hess, also very excited, thought he should be the one to rub out Röhm. 'My Leader,' he shouted, 'the duty to shoot Röhm is mine.' But Hitler said he would pardon Röhm because of his past services. He ordered six other S.A. leaders to be shot and then set off to the airport for Berlin.

Meanwhile Göring, with Himmler at his side and Heydrich piling in false information, had been in charge of the purge at Berlin. Among their first victims was Gregor Strasser (a rival whom Hitler might always bring back into favour) and General von Schleicher, Hitler's predecessor as chancellor (shot by mistake—it had been intended only to arrest him). Some of the executed died shouting 'Hail Hitler!' in the belief that the regime, to which they were faithful, was being overthrown. One fraction wanted to do in the

Crown Prince, but Göring vetoed that. Papen was another lucky to escape; as it was, his press secretary was shot.

Hitler, on his arrival in Berlin from Munich, had calmed down. He believed that the 'coup' had already been nipped in the bud and that the time had come for moderation. He was proud that he personally had arrested Röhm but Göring and Himmler were appalled to learn that Röhm was still alive. They feared, quite possibly with accuracy, that Hitler was preserving Röhm for future use as a counterweight to them.

For another day executions continued up and down Germany, mostly in Berlin and Munich, but with Röhm still unshot, although in custody. Göring and Himmler kept on at Hitler about how it would be disastrous to allow Röhm to live. Hitler weakened to the point of saying that Röhm should be allowed to commit suicide. But Röhm refused this option. Eventually on July 1st, Hitler sent orders to Munich for Rohm's death. The execution was carried out in the cell by two S.S. men; Röhm, mortally wounded, sank to the floor gasping: 'My Leader, my Leader.' Hitler had parted from the man who in the early days at Munich had been his most valuable supporter.

The shootings ended on July 2nd. Rumour ran the total into hundreds but the correct figure seems to have been that announced at the time—eighty-three. All were shot without trial and some by total mistake. (Old Kahr, who had let down Hitler in 1923 was killed with a pick-axe.) The army general staff—which thought it had been scheduled for execution by Röhm—was delighted. One general telegraphed delightedly, in English: 'All catched.' The worst mistake was when S.S. men in Munich sought out Dr. Ludwig Schmitt, an associate of Gregor Strasser. They were careless enough to catch instead a music critic called Dr. Wilhelm Schmid who had never had anything to do with politics. His body was delivered to his family with an apologetic note and an injunction not to open the coffin.

This was 'the night of long knives', a phrase taken from a National Socialist marching song. By any ordinary process of law, the killings had been illegal. Even the emergency upon which they had supposedly been based had been fraudulent. While Röhm and the S.A. certainly were troublesome and needed to be watched, they were not plotting anything immediate. Hitler had acted intuitively and ruthlessly, and in Göring, Himmler and Heydrich he had had intelligent aides who would goad him and support him. On his side, he had the advantage that few opponents of the National Socialists would have sympathy for the Röhm group. He had the homosexuality element to use as a smear. The episode was yet another proof to the recalcitrant of how fierce National Socialism could be. Yet it was basically unplanned by Hitler. The nearest equivalent, in the decade, was Joseph Stalin's purges of his opponents and supposed opponents which began five months after Hitler's action and lasted until 1939. Stalin in conducting his vastly greater purges acted with calculation and was at pains to stage 'show trials' at which the accused confessed guilt. Hitler, in contrast, had acted in hot blood. He had the killings retrospectively legalised by an emergency cabinet decree and his justification for them was a two-hour speech to the Reichstag, especially summoned on July 13th.*

Hitler accused the S.A. of having committed 'excesses' against opponents of the regime.

An authoritarian regime is under special obligations [he said]. When one demands of a people that it should put blind confidence in its leaders, then for their part these leaders must deserve this confidence through their achievement and through specially good behaviour. Mistakes and errors may in individual cases slip in, but they are to be eradicated. Bad behaviour, drunken excesses, the molestation of peaceful decent folk—these are unworthy of a leader, they are not National Socialist, and they are in the highest degree detestable.

On this, said Hitler, he had originally differed from Röhm. He had felt 'unswerving loyalty and comradeship' towards Röhm but by May, he had begun to feel suspicious. Hess had been of particular value in drawing his attention to Röhm's shortcomings.

Then in May came promotions in S.A. districts and with them 'the horrible realisation' that they had been based upon member-ship of a 'circle' of people possessed of a 'special disposition'. [Hitler was implying homosexuality.]

Röhm had conspired with Schleicher to form a new government with Röhm as Minister of Defence. This would have been a betrayal of Hitler's oath to Hindenburg. 'The promise which I gave him that I would preserve the army as the non-political instrument of the Reich is for me binding, both from my inmost conviction and also from the word I have given.' Hitler went out of his way to praise the existing Defence Minister, Blomberg, as 'a man of honour from the crown of his head to the soles of his feet'. He made the assertion for which the army had been longing: 'In the state there is only one bearer of arms, and that is the army; there

* The authority primarily relied upon for this account of the blood purge is Heinz Höhne, *The Order of the Death's Head* (London, 1969).

207

is only one bearer of the political will, and that is the National Socialist Party.'

Finally, by the beginning of June, said Hitler, he had begun to get evidence that Röhm was plotting a 'national bolshevist' uprising. He saw Röhm and 'implored him for the last time to oppose this madness'. But Röhm ignored the plea and went on with plans that would entail 'the blood of ten thousand innocent folk'. By June 29th, Röhm was ready to rise the next day.

If disaster was to be prevented at all, [said Hitler,] action must be taken with lightning speed. Only a ruthless and bloody intervention might still perhaps stifle the spread of the revolt. And then there could be no question that it was better that a hundred mutineers, plotters and conspirators should be destroyed than that 10,000 innocent S.A. men should be allowed to shed their blood . . .

Mutinies are suppressed in accordance with laws of iron which are eternally the same. If anyone reproaches me and asks why I did not resort to the regular courts of justice for the conviction of the offenders, then all that I can say to him is this: in this hour I was the supreme lord justice [oberster Gerichtsherr] of the German people . . .

It is not my duty to inquire whether it was too hard a lot which was inflicted on those conspirators, these agitators and destroyers, these poisoners of the well-springs of German public opinion . . . it is not mine to consider which one of them has suffered too severely: I have only to see to it that Germany's lot shall not be intolerable . . .

I am ready to undertake responsibility at the bar of history for the 24 hours in which the bitterest decisions of my life were made, in which fate once again taught me in the midst of anxious care with every thought to hold fast to the dearest thing which has been given us in this world—the German people and the German Reich.

Since June 4th Hindenburg had been living in seclusion at his Neudeck estate in East Prussia. He was suffereing from a bladder complaint which made his death likely within three months. Hindenburg hoped that his death would be followed by a restoration of the monarchy. But according to the constitution there should be an election for a new president, with the President of the Supreme Court acting as head of state in the interim. Hitler could easily have arranged his unopposed return in such an election, just as his single list had had an unopposed return to the Reichstag. But rather than do this, he decided to abolish the presidency altogether by merging it into the chancellorship he already held.

Exactly why he was so keen on this he never explained, but the motivation must have been that he wanted to get away from the conception of a 'president' with its republican overtones. Hitler wanted to occupy no constitutional 'office', with powers defined by law, but to be the mystical 'Leader' with unlimited personal power.

In arranging this, the Röhm purge was of some advantage. To be head of state entailed being also the focus of allegiance of the armed forces. By the summer of 1934, Hitler had attracted so much public opinion on his side and had suppressed his opponents so thoroughly that it would have been difficult for the generals to refuse allegiance. But by eliminating Röhm and his claims to take over the forces and by guaranteeing that the professionals would remain in charge, Hitler obtained the generals' readier co-operation. It was, in any event, the tradition of the German army not to meddle in 'politics'; had it done so in the conditions of 1934 there could only have been civil war, with conceivably the Communists being the ultimate victors.

On August 1st, the cabinet promulgated a law by which Hitler was to assume the presidential powers on Hindenburg's death. It was, strictly, illegal, as the Enabling Act had specifically excluded the presidency from the area in which the cabinet was empowered to amend the constitution by decree. The following day Hindenburg died and the law came into immediate effect, the armed forces swearing 'unconditional obedience' to Hitler by name.

After this had been accomplished, Hitler put the question to the German electorate for ratification by referendum. As with the elections and referendum of the previous November, it was not a free vote. Official instructions on how to behave in the polling booth and how to mark the ballot paper in some instances included an injunction to mark the 'yes' box, with no mention of the 'no' box. Anybody who voted 'no' faced the definite possibility of maltreatment by the National Socialists or, even, of being sent to a concentration camp. There was no right of opposition propaganda and it was made to seem actually unpatriotic to vote against the nation's 'saviour'. Under rigorous National Socialist organisation, the extraordinarily high proportion of 95·7 per cent of the electorate went to the polls. Of these, 2 per cent spoiled their ballot papers, presumably, in many cases, because they opposed Hitler but did not dare vote 'no'. Of the valid votes cast, 89·9 per cent were 'yes' and 10·1 per cent were 'no'. The 'no' voters—there were 4,294,654 of them—were far from evenly distributed across Germany. The highest 'no' vote—20·5 per cent—was in Hamburg. 'Red' Berlin came next with 18·5 per cent 'noes', and Catholic Cologne-Aachen with 18·2 per cent. The best areas for the regime were Pfalzel in the southern Rhineland, next to the French-occupied Saar, where there were only 3·4 per cent 'noes' and East Prussia where there were 4 per cent.

These figures would seem to show that Hitler had dropped three or four per cent in popularity since November, 1933, but, naturally, they cannot be taken in any detail as a meaningful expression of public opinion. Perhaps some of the courageous 'no' voters had switched that way because whereas they could tolerate Hitler taking emergency powers in an emergency but would not tolerate a situation in which there would be no President over him. Perhaps some were protests against the manner of the Röhm purge.

Hitler was delighted with the result. He told the party rally in Nuremberg that autumn: 'The German form of life is definitely determined for the next thousand years.'

12

Hitler acted with energy and success in tackling the overriding problem of Germany, that of mass unemployment. His government was the most efficient of any advanced industrial country in dealing with this result of the 1929 slump. Exactly which were Hitler's ideas for dealing with it and which were those of others is often difficult to tell, due to Hitler's habit of operating by word of mouth rather than by written instructions. However, the galvanism with which the National Socialist regime acted must be traced to Hitler's prodding and impatience. Especially in the early days of power, National Socialists liked to give an impression of activity and energy, with much stamping and doubling around, and this was often just play-acting; but it did signify a zest to get things done. Hitler's pledge to abolish unemployment had been crucial in edging him into power and it was one he had to keep both from his own conviction and from the need to keep up his prestige; it would have been impossible to hide failure in it.

The method was improvisation. Hitler had told the Industry Club at Düsseldorf in 1932 that it was no use to 'doctor around on the circumference of the distress' and that he intended to 'penetrate to the seat of the inflammation—to the cause'. In practice, though, he could find no 'cause' of unemployment which could be dealt with in a single stroke such as shooting Jews. He used a variety of expedients, tackling the symptoms piecemeal. Some programmes had already begun under Brüning and Papen— Hitler simply took these over. His approach was basically conservative with, at least in the early years, no attempt at deficit budgetting, as Roosevelt was doing in the U.S.A. (Here, of course, fear of inflation counted).

One method, and this was characteristically National Socialist, was to get women off the labour market. In a law promulgated in

211

June 1933 Hitler established a system of interest-free marriage loans, of 1,000 marks each, which were granted to young couples on condition that the wife was not in employment. These loans were intended, also, to stimulate population growth, presumably with a view to eventual German colonisation in the east. The birth of each child cancelled a portion of the loan and turned it into an outright gift. Obviously the setting up of new households through the marriage loans stimulated the building and furnishing industries and provided jobs in them. The cost of the loans was met by a tax on the single. A related measure was to allow employers of female domestic servants to claim allowances for them against income tax, up to a maximum of three, on the same basis as if they were children.

For giving up every ambition outside the home, Hitler offered women a kind of love-making. He promised in a speech at Nuremberg in 1937: 'Our men will be trained to become a hard breed. The German woman can be assured that the coming generations of men will be in very truth the shield and shelter of their women.'

In a very large number of individual cases the government put pressure on employers to increase their labour forces, even where this was uneconomic. Employers had to get government permission before laying off redundant workers. The government discouraged and even banned the introduction of labour-saving machinery, notably in the cigar, chemical and glassware industries. Public works schemes were designed so as to use the minimum of machinery and the maximum of manual labour. How many workers an employer would take on was an active factor in negotiating government contracts.

Then there was the 'voluntary' labour service, in which every young man was expected to work for six months. This had already existed before National Socialism but Hitler turned it into virtual civilian conscription. It was not designed merely to reduce unemployment nor for the public works it carred out but also to break down class conflict. Hitler wanted to win the allegiance of the manual working class and one method was the psychological one of stressing the 'dignity' of manual labour, which no one ought to be ashamed to undertake. The nation must come together and the middle class should not look down on the workers.

'We are determined', Hitler said in a speech in September 1933, 'to build up an idea of respect for work, whatever its external appearance may be . . . The people must understand that all work which is necessary ennobles the man who does it; only one thing is shameful—to contribute nothing to the community.' But in following this kind of line he could be careless with truth. 'I was myself a labouring man for years in the building trade,' he said in a speech in May 1933.

In wooing the industrial workers, Hitler did not forget the classes which had provided his previous bulk support. A significant little law of 1934 made it criminal for anyone to open a new retail shop without a government licence; the idea was that the licence would not be granted if it threatened existing shopkeepers. There was a rapid reorganisation of agriculture, which had been deeply depressed, especially in eastern Germany. It put up peasants' incomes by thirty per cent between 1933 and 1934 but at the same time provided power to expel them from their land if they were inefficient. Farms too small to provide a proper livelihood were amalgamated into larger units. A peasant lost the right to sell his land and had to bequeath it, intact, to his eldest son.

The 'respect for work' speech just quoted was delivered at a ceremony marking the start of work on the Frankfurt-Heidelberg motorway, the first of the motorway programme. It was to provide Germany with Europe's most efficient road system and to make significant inroads on unemployment. It affected not only the construction industry, which had the highest unemployment rate of all, but also the iron and steel industries, which supplied material for bridges and flyovers. Previous administrations had done preliminary planning for motorways but it was Hitler who jerked the programme into action. He was passionately interested. 'Magnificent roads,' he said, 'are better evidence of the civilisation of a people than the so-called freedom of the Press.' A 350 million mark programme was announced in June 1933 and that work had already started by September was an indication of the tempo Hitler could achieve. It was to be financed largely by taxes on motor fuel and lubricants.

Some conservatives saw the motorways as grandiose extravagance. The steel manufacturer Thyssen thought them insane. There could never be enough cars to make them worthwhile, Hitler thought otherwise and in some sense was the Henry Ford of Germany. He had been interested in cars since he was a young man and, with accurate assessment of human psychology, considered that cars could be an asset for him. One of his early acts was to abolish taxation on new cars. Neither propaganda nor terror, real as they both were, provided a sufficient prop for his regime. But to get every German family driving around in its own car would be a tangible result of National Socialism, and one in tune with the aspirations of the people. By 1937 Hitler was promising that he would ultimately provide one car for every five

213

persons. He had a good amateur technical knowledge of auto-mobiles and supervised in detail the design of his 'people's car'—the 'beetle Volkswagen'—which was intended for the masses, the price to be brought down by mass production. He specified that the engine must be air-cooled. Eva Braun had one of the earliest Volkswagens as a gift from him but the war delayed it coming on to the market. After 1945 it was a world best-seller.

A similar type of programme, on a smaller scale, was that for the mass production of radio sets to turn them from a luxury into a regular household item. There was a cheap 'people's receiver', capable of receiving only German stations. Here, of course, the use of the radio for political propaganda was significant, and Josef Goebbels the Propaganda Minister was active in promoting sales. 'With the radio,' he said, 'we have destroyed the spirit of rebellion.' Ownership of radio sets in Germany almost doubled in five years, from five million to nine million. National Socialism in its high days was not a distant autocracy but a personal type of leadership, with Hitler adulated as a saint and the ordinary people encouraged to feel a sense of participation. Anti-Nazi propaganda tended to avoid attacking Hitler personally, it being reckoned to be bad tactics to do so

Hitler best exemplified the sense of mystical communication he claimed to have with the people in a Nuremberg rally speech in 1936, part of which reads as if it were an imitation of the gospel according to St. John.

Once [said Hitler] you heard the voice of a man, and it struck deep into your hearts; it awakened you, and you followed this voice, though him who had spoken you never even saw. You heard only a voice and you followed it. When we meet here together, the wonder of our coming thus together fills us all. Not everyone of you sees me and I do not see every one of you. But I feel you, and you feel me.

Between 1933 and 1937 German unemployment fell from six million to one million. In the same period, taxation rose by five per cent.

This was by no means all due to Hitler's programmes. Trade revived and unemployment fell in every country as the industrialised world began to recover from the 1929 slump, and Germany had already been showing the first signs of the recovery before Hitler came to power. (The lowest point in the slump in Germany had been August 1932.) Some of the programmes Hitler used had been initiated before he came to power. He absorbed some labour by rearmament and enlarging the army but this was subsidiary, at least until 1936. The three fastest expanding industries between 1933 and 1936 were construction, engineering and automobiles, which increased their labour forces by 209 per cent, 106 per cent and 117 per cent respectively.

But if this triumph was not entirely attributable to Hitler and National Socialism, nor was it an accident. The energy and single-mindedness of the regime did make a difference. The psychology of National Socialist Germany would be a mystery were it not that the vast reduction in unemployment—far greater, proportionately, than in the comparable countries of the United States and Britain in the same period—brought a sense of national achievement. Even those, and they existed particularly in the older age-groups, who remained sceptical about Hitler's ideas, sensed a glow and felt an obligation to co-operate in the great task. Some, and of course particularly the capitalists, had a sharper incentive to co-operate; some of the Hitler measures were not in their short-term interest but they tended to believe that if Hitler failed the obvious alternative was Communism.

Speaking to the Krupp workers at Essen in March 1936, Hitler said:

The life of our nation has experienced a new order. Our economic life has reached a new level of prosperity. You yourselves, work-men here in Germany's greatest factory, can bear witness to this. You know how empty these halls used to be, how dead things were in so many of these steel cathedrals of industry. And you hear and see how life here today is humming with busy industry, not only in the armament-producing works, but everywhere throughout this giant concern . . . If you ask me, my German workmen, how this became possible, let me tell you that I did not need to spend a long time looking for a prescription, and there could not be, for the past had left only one prescription—how not to do it . . . No, I have had to travel by new and unknown paths. And the fact remains that in these three years nearly five million men were brought back into employment.

The actual standard of living achieved by 1936 and 1937 was not particularly high and thereafter it did not rise at all under National Socialism. The Germans were to do far better for themselves in the next generation, after 1945. Possibly, indeed, living standards under the National Socialists were no better than those of the previous boom-years 1926–8. But the propaganda about the National Socialist success was incessant, with no critical voice allowed.

215

Hitler had taken over the most divided nation in Europe—divided by religion, by regional loyalties, by class and by politics. He consciously and passionately tried to make a single nation, with a sense of national cohesion which was instinctive to the British and the French. To foreigners, unable to understand German, Hitler's platform speeches, shown on newsreels, sounded like hysterical paeans of hate. Sometimes they really were that but, also, they were very often passionate appeals to people to put loyalty to the whole community before loyalty to their class. He insisted that he wanted to build a system based upon leadership by merit.

He told the Labour Front at Berlin in 1933:

We do not regard any one class as being of paramount importance; such distinctions disappear during the course of centuries, they come and go. What remains is the substance, a substance of flesh and blood, our nation. That is what is permanent, and to that alone should we feel ourselves responsible.

In another speech at Berlin in 1937 he proclaimed:

'I, too, am a child of the people; I do not trace my line from any castle; I come from the workshop. Neither was I a general: I was simply a soldier as were millions of others. It is something wonderful that amongst us an unknown from the army of millions of the German people—of workers and soldiers—could rise to be head of the Reich and nation . . . We have removed the animosity which some strata in our society felt for the hand worker . . . But our education also trains men to respect intellectual achievement; we bring one to respect the spade, another to respect the compass or pen. All now are but German fellow countrymen and it is their achievement that determines their value. If a man is a genius, then assuredly I shall not employ him all his days in digging potatoes . . . For what is the meaning of socialism and democracy? Can there be anything finer than an organisation which draws from the people its most capable personalities and places them in positions of leadership? Is it not wonderful for every humble mother among our people and for every father to know that perhaps their boy may become anything—God knows what!—if only he has the necessary talent? That is socialism at its highest.

But the central condition for this apparent wonderland was that of absolute authority at the top. Hitler was contriving the most autocratic form of government that has ever existed in an advanced European state.

There must [he said in December 1934,] be a single will and a single will must lead. And when anyone says to me that I may make mistakes, then my answer is: I know that quite well, but if I make ten decisions and only one of them is mistaken then I can accept responsibility for that mistake. But as for the others [his predecessors in office] they did nothing: of ten decisions taken, not one was carried into execution.

There was no legal check on Hitler's will. Laws were promulgated by the 'cabinet', which he appointed: later, during the war, even this shred of constitutionality disappeared and Hitler assumed power to do anything he wanted by direct personal decree. But already in the Röhm purge he had asserted the right to execute people without trial and by administrative decision. The armed forces were bound to him by an oath of loyalty, to him personally and not to his office. His N.S.D.A.P. permeated civilian society. with even more accuracy than Louis XIV he could have claimed: 'The state, it is me.' In the Soviet Union, Joseph Stalin, although effectively dictator, was responsible in law to the Soviet constitution and the Communist Party; in theory he could have been removed from office at any time by a vote. Similarly in Italy, Mussolini was capable of being dismissed by the king and the Fascist Grand Council and this eventually did happen to him. Hitler, however, was subject to no limitations and there was no authority which, legally, could question his decisions or, still less, remove him from office. He was more absolute than an hereditary monarch in that he had power to nominate his own successor.

Such a system was essential for Hitler's style. He required the freedom of an artist putting brush to canvas. On occasion, however, he did ponder on the idea of creating a constitution for his new Germany. He told the Reichstag in 1937:

It will be one of our future tasks to give the German people a constitution which will be in harmony with the real life of our people, as that life has developed politically. This constitution will place its seal on this life for all time to come and will be an imperishable and fundamental law for all Germans.

What he had in mind was a constitution similar to that of the papacy and the college of cardinals. He mused aloud about it during World War II. The Leader should be an autocrat but he should appoint a 'senate' analogous to cardinals. Membership should be fluctuating and based upon holders of particular posts rather than upon individuals. On the death or resignation of the

Leader, the senate should meet to choose a successor; the election should be in private and in silence, with no debating allowed. 'Although a state founded on such principles can lay no claim to eternity,' mused Hitler, 'it might last eight or nine centuries. The thousand-year-old organisation of the Church is proof of this.' He did nothing practical about it and his designated successor, until the last days, was Göring and this was the obvious choice, with the advantage that Göring was never likely to try to take over by force.

Hitler's take-over of Germany was described by the N.S.D.A.P. at the time as the 'national revolution' but it is doubtful whether the term 'revolution' was really valid. What was being attempted was to bring the whole nation under the influence of a single method of thought and a single doctrine rather than to cause any fundamental change in the social order or in the distribution of property. Existing institutions were used rather than overturned, with extra institutions being grafted on to them. The better description, also much used at the time, was 'co-ordination' *(Gleichschaltung)*, and this meant in practice the supervision, or sometimes the absorption, of every facet of German political, social and cultural life by the N.S.D.A.P. Trade unions were absorbed into the Labour Front, with the right to strike removed; but Labour Front representatives did have genuine powers on the workers' behalf over wages, hours and dismissals. There were a few unofficial strikes, (the leaders of them faced the risk of a concentration camp) but, on the whole, within the limited period it functioned, the Labour Front was a success. Associated with it was the 'Strength Through Joy' movement which arranged much publicised recreations and holidays for the masses, including cheap tours abroad to Scandinavia and Italy; in one aspect the 'Strength Through Joy' movement was a precursor of the mass tourist industry in Europe which arose in the 1950s.

An auxiliary weapon in 'co-ordination' was the concentration camp, although it was probably an unnecessary institution once the initial 'revolutionary' period was over; ordinary prisons could have coped quite well. The number of people in 'protective custody' reached a peacetime peak of 26,789 (many held only for a matter of weeks) in July 1933. Conditions in the first concentration camps were chaotic with many prisoners being beaten up, and even murdered, by largely amateur guards. From 1934 onwards, the camps settled down into a more formal pattern with no more unofficial arrests and random brutality greatly reduced, although not, as in any prison system, eliminated. Most of the inmates were released. A special division of the S.S., the 'death's head' units, was recruited as professional guards; most of the rank and file were

218

men in the sixteen to twenty age-group and they were enjoined to be aloof from the prisoners and not to inflict informal punishments. Conditions in the camps were spartan but, by prison standards, there was an adequate diet and reasonable accommodation in dormitories. Discipline was severe. For example, guards were under standing orders to shoot to kill in the event of rebellion or attempted escape; by ordinary German law this was probably murder and there was a legal gap that was never properly plugged. Punishments for idleness or other ill behaviour included solitary confinement, dietary restrictions and floggings of twenty-five strokes—the floggings had to be authorised, in each case, from Berlin.

The camps were meant to be mysterious places, with a vague aura of terror; inmates, on release, had to sign undertakings not to reveal what they had experienced. More formally, they were meant to be 'educational'; by the late 1930s, also, they were beginning to be regarded as a reservoir of cheap labour and this became so on a very considerable scale during World War II. But the 'educational' idea was still subsisting as late as 1941. Stone-breaking and quarrying for Hitler's 'monumental architecture' was characteristic concentration camp labour in the 1930s.

The inmates were by no means all political martyrs. Indeed part of the psychology of the concentration camp was that it mixed together 'anti-socials' and 'politicals' so as to taint the latter. To make 'insulting' remarks about the state was a sufficient cause to be sent to a concentration camp. But so, also, was to be an 'habitual criminal', a prostitute, a homosexual, a pimp, a drunkard, or a beggar. From 1936 onwards there was a category of 'work-shy' prisoners; any unemployed person who, without good reason, had rejected two offers of a job became liable for the concentration camp. Jews, in these various categories, were more likely to suffer than non-Jews, but to be Jewish, as such, was not normally, in the 1930s, sufficient cause for being sent to a camp. However the International Bible Students (Jehovah's Witnesses) were locked up from 1935 onwards because of their refusal to accept military service.

The numbers inside the concentration camps declined between 1934 and 1937, reaching at their lowest point some 7,500. From 1937 onwards there was a tendency for the numbers to rise again. This was through the police chief, Himmler, ordering purges in every locality to arrest 'anti-socials' and also, in 1938, the incorporation of Austria and the Sudetenland into the Reich. There was a further rise on the outbreak of World War II in 1939 but it was not until 1941 that the camps began to reach really gigantic proportions. In the closing months of the war the system fell into

219

chaos with gross overcrowding and mass starvation, as at Belsen. In 1942–4, as described in chapter sixteen, camps in conquered territory in eastern Europe, but never within Germany itself, were used for a more or less systematic policy of mass murder of Jews and Gipsies. Allied with the concentration camp system in the 1930s Hitler had a policy of sterilising the incurably insane and even, although this was done discreetly, killing them.

The concentration camps existed alongside the ordinary penal system. Quite often an 'habitual criminal' was sent to a concentration camp after he had completed a gaol sentence which had been inflicted upon him through normal police and court procedures. There were, on occasion, tussles between the two systems; these arose, particularly, when public prosecutors attempted to intervene in cases of death and brutality in concentration camps and certainly, in the 1930s, they did succeed in mitigating some abuses. Hitler's personal bias, however, was deeply antipathetic to legal procedures, judges and lawyers; whenever he intervened it was on the side of arbitrary action. He took a sporadic interest in the more spectacular criminal cases and demanded harsh punishments. To supplement the ordinary courts, he created special 'people's courts' to try offences of a political or 'anti-social' nature; these had an informal procedure which could degenerate into bullying. Under the 1933 'emergency' legislation, the political police continued to possess and exercise a virtually unlimited power of taking people into 'protective custody'; in other words, sending them to a concentration camp. The only rights the prisoner had in such cases were those contained in the regulations framed by the police themselves from time to time; the principal one was the 'right' to have his case reviewed at regular intervals.

Under Hitler, and more particularly through the enterprise of Göring in his capacity of minister-president of Prussia, there was a sharp rise in the number of executions in Germany from 1933 onwards. The total number of legal executions, after trial by a civilian court, in Germany under Hitler's rule was some 32,600 people, the bulk of them during World War II. Göring, at one point, ornamented his office with a headsman's axe. The rise was due to more and more offences becoming subject to the death penalty and to a rigorous refusal of clemency: Göring gave only two reprieves and confirmed 212 death sentences in the period June 1933–June 1934. The Reichstag fire perpetrator, Marinus van der Lubbe, for example, was condemned to death under a law which, retrospectively, made arson a capital offence. His head was chopped off, before an audience, by a headsman wearing full evening dress. Later, for ease of operation, a guillotine was introduced. The trial of Lubbe and those accused of acting with him lasted for months at Leipzig before a normal criminal court and resulted in acquittals for all but Lubbe. It attracted the widest international attention; the Communist Dimitrov went on, after his acquittal and deportation, to become secretary of the international Communist association, the Comintern, in Moscow and after World War II to become ruler of his native Bulgaria. But it was by the Reichstag trial that Dimitrov's international fame was secured; he goaded Göring into losing his temper while on the witness stand. This was the only major state trial, with proper rights of defence, which ever took place in Hitler's Germany and it can only have deepened his dislike of legal processes. When the Röhm affair arose a few months later, Hitler acted as judge and executioner himself.

There were many cases under the National Socialists of petty 'anti-socials' and politicals pleading guilty before the people's court in the hope of getting a lighter sentence. But there was none of the brainwashing which, in Moscow in the same period, was producing spectacular 'confessions', with previously leading personalities accusing themselves of imaginary crimes. There were cases of injustice in the German concentration camp system, with prisoners locked up through malice or by mistake, but these were exceptional; whatever the rights and wrongs of the system, as it existed in the 1930s, most prisoners were in them because they had actually done what they had been accused of. In the vastly greater Soviet labour camp system, many, possibly a majority of the prisoners were innocent and were confined partly as a terror policy and partly because Stalin was a megalomaniac about plots against himself. Stalin, however, was operating during and in the aftermath of a genuine revolution in which actual property changed hands and a wholly new governing class came into existence; Hitler's 'revolution' was, in comparison, trivial. Also Stalin was operating in a country where arbitrary autocracy was traditional whereas Hitler was overthrowing a long-settled system of orderly justice.

Hitler could certainly show malice in individual cases. He loved revenging himself. There was Kahr, killed in the Röhm purge although he had long since retired from politics; Kahr was murdered as vengeance for having let down Hitler in 1923. A similar case was that of Hans Litten, a distinguished young lawyer, who in 1931 had cross-examined Hitler as a witness in a political murder trial. Hitler showed up badly under Litten's questioning and did not forget the experience. Litten was arrested in February 1933, and tortured to try to make him admit the guilt of one of his clients,

221

a Communist accused of murder. (Litten was not himself a Communist.) Later, under international pressure, he was somewhat better treated and given facilities for study, although still in Dachau. But eventually, after five years' confinement, Litten hanged himself. The case was an embarrassing one for German international diplomacy—it was widely publicised—and it could have been solved by the simple expedient of releasing Litten on condition that he emigrated. It would be difficult to forego the conclusion that Hitler valued revenge above his international good name.

On a much more substantial scale, in any event, Hitler was suffering in international reputation from his anti-Jewish policy. It was based, during the 1930s, on the principle of making life so uncomfortable for German Jews that they would emigrate, preferably leaving property behind them to pass into state ownership. Many did so but the majority could not believe that in a country, such as Germany, anti-semitism was more than a passing phase. They were a part of the real Germany, not the temporary one of Hitler's creation. It was not as if Germany were like Poland or Rumania (two other countries which were anti-semitic in this period) or the old Tsarist Russian Empire; for centuries it had been a home for Jews who were entirely German in outlook. Had it not been for Hitler's anti-semitism, the Jews would probably have split in much the same proportions for and against National Socialism as any other group in the population. Even as things were, there were a few Jews voting for Hitler in the days of contested elections.

Some Jewish businessmen benefited temporarily from the economic revival that came with Hitler. But the community as a whole had no share in the new prosperity. Jewish lawyers and doctors found increasing difficulty in practising and were eventually forced out of business altogether or confined to Jewish clients. Jewish businesses were subject to persecution and near-expropriation. Thus the great Ullstein Press, which published newspapers, magazines and books on a scale that made it the largest in Germany and was Jewish-owned, found its canvassers and street sellers being intimidated by the S.A. In 1934, the Ullsteins sold their business to Amann, the National Socialist business manager and publisher, for twelve million marks—about a fifth of the true value. (But as a result of the economic slump and National Socialist intimidation, the company had made a loss of over two million marks in the year preceding the sale.)

Immediately on Hitler's advent to power there were many individual cases of Jews being beaten up and packed off into 'wild' concentration camps run by the S.A. but with the restoration of calm in the spring of 1933 this kind of thing eased off. Persecution became calmer and more organised. The first formal anti-semitic act of the regime was a one-day boycott of Jewish-owned shops called for April 1st, 1933. This was in retaliation for a 'campaign' waged by Jews abroad against the National Socialist government. It was organised on a solely party basis, with S.A. men picketing the shops. Its effectiveness varied widely. A programme, planned by Streicher, to hold thousands of public meetings to support it was never carried out. A week later came a decree which dismissed every civil servant with at least one Jewish grandparent. This aroused Hindenburg, who was sensitive about Jews who had fought in the war. 'If they,' he wrote to Hitler, 'were worthy of fighting and bleeding for Germany, they must be considered worthy of continuing to serve the fatherland.' Hitler replied that his own followers had suffered too—'adherents of my movement, who were Germans, for years were driven from all government positions, and never mind if they had wives or children or what they had done in the war'; he claimed that Jewish officials were a 'mustard seed' of corruption because they had primarily a 'business' outlook. But Hitler accommodated Hindenburg's prejudice by exempting, until 1935, from dismissal civil servants who had fought in the war, or who had lost a father or son in the war or who had held office since 1914.

The next big step was the Nuremberg laws, which were passed by a special session of the Reichstag called during the annual party Nuremberg rally. They were the climax of a period of intense anti-Jewish propaganda by the regime. The laws cut off the Jews from the mainstream of German life. A new category of 'Reich citizenship' was devised for non-Jewish Germans. Jews remained German 'nationals' without the supposedly higher status of being 'citizens'. Intermarriage or sexual intercourse between 'Aryans' (the jargon for non-Jewish Germans) and Jews was made a criminal offence. This, of course, in a sense suited Jews of orthodox belief who disliked marriages outside their own community. But, obviously, there is a distinction between the voluntary customs of a community and the laws of the state. Moreover many, probably a majority, of German Jews were loose in religious practice and did not fully share orthodox prejudices about marriage. An odd appendix to the new laws was that no 'Aryan' woman aged under forty-five was to be employed as a servant in a Jewish household; here Hitler may well have been bearing in mind the stories about his own grandmother and the Jewish Frankenberger family at Graz.

At the time the Nuremberg laws seemed to be the worst that

Hitler could do. In his best-selling *Insanity Fair,* published in 1938, the British journalist, Douglas Reed, who himself had an anti-Jewish streak, wrote that Hitler's anti-semitism was a 'pricked balloon'. 'The Jews know it in their heart. They may hate National Socialism but they no longer fear it . . . The anti-Jewish laws of Nuremberg . . . were thought by the outer world to mark the climax of anti-semitism in Germany; actually they mean the end of the bluff.'

But Hitler was thinking of further measures and the possible mass imprisonment of the Jews. 'Fence them in,' he remarked privately at the time of the Nuremberg laws, 'somewhere they can perish as they deserve while the German people look on, the way people stare at wild animals.' For public, and especially foreign, consumption he was more moderate. He told an American United Press interviewer, who had asked him about the laws: 'The fundamental principle which governed the treatment of this question in Germany was that the German should be given that to which the German had a just claim and to the Jew that which the Jew could justly claim.' The report continued: 'He stressed the fact that this served to protect the Jew, and this was proved by the fact that since the passing of the restrictive measures anti-Jewish sentiment in the country had decreased.'

Anti-Jewish activity did in fact decrease in 1936 and this was partly due to the Olympic Games being held in Germany. There was a danger of the games being cancelled through international opposition to Hitler's policies. To conciliate foreign visitors during the games many anti-Jewish placards and signs were taken down. Once the games were over, there was a steady stream of new regulations, all tending to damage Jews. In 1938 all male Jews were ordered to use the first name 'Israel' and women Jews the name 'Sara' in business and legal matters, Jewish street names were removed. The Lord Mayor of Leipzig, Carl Goerdeler, resigned when the local party district manager removed a statue of Mendelssohn. Party-controlled local authorities banned Jews from public parks, swimming pools and sometimes, even, from public transport. There was even an attempt to suppress the fact that the words of *Lorelei,* Germany's most popular traditional song were written by a Jew, Heinrich Heine; under the National Socialists it was published with the words 'author unknown' at the bottom. In country villages, where there was no Jewish population at all, there were cases of party fanatics erecting signs: 'Jews come here at their own risk' or 'Jews get out, or else . . .' But these were sometimes held to be incitements to violence and were removed on the orders of the normal government apparatus—this is an example of how it continued to function alongside the party. There were cases of Jewish schoolchildren being persecuted and humiliated by National Socialist schoolmasters. Equally, however, there were many cases of 'Aryans' assisting Jewish friends, even at risk to themselves. Despite the propaganda, there seems to have been little hostility to the Jews among the ordinary 'Aryan' people, especially in the manual working classes; there was much indifference and the campaigns were run by party fanatics. Sympathy for individual Jews extended high up into the government—both Göring and Hess were capable of being mildly tolerant in individual cases and Schacht, until his resignation in 1938, tried to protect Jews working in his department.

Anti-semitism reached its pre-war climax on 'crystal night', November 9th–10th, 1938. 'Crystal night' was a pogrom definitely designed to persuade Jews to emigrate. The pretext for it was the assassination in Paris of a German diplomat by a seventeen-year-old Jewish refugee. The idea for it seems to have been Hitler's, but he remained in the background, and left the whipping up of the party militants to Goebbels. It was not an openly-organised party campaign but was presented as a 'spontaneous reaction of the German people'. (In practice, however, party leaders were instructed to see that demonstrations took place.) Some 7,000 Jewish shops were wrecked, synagogues were burned and ninety-one Jews were killed. Only a handful of the perpetrators were ever punished and those in some cases only because they had committed 'pollution' in raping Jewish women. More officially, some 30,000 Jews, mostly well-to-to, were arrested for their own 'protection' but in reality as an incentive to emigrate. The community was fined over a billion marks and the insurance payments for the damaged buildings was confiscated. Following 'crystal night', there were further restrictions on Jews, especially in the economic field, and the Jewish relief organisations were overwhelmed by mass poverty. There were many suicides.

Certainly the anti-semitism was a handicap to Hitler in his foreign relations. Germany seemed to be adopting the worst traditions of eastern Europe. Jewish communities outside Germany, notably in the United States and Britain, were vehemently hostile, and this was only to be expected. But, more significantly, the anti-semitism aroused distaste among much (but not all) public opinion at large in those countries. Whenever Hitler wanted to make a friendly gesture abroad, he tended to be handicapped by and distrusted for his anti-semitism at home. It was bad enough to the liberal-minded that he should lock up and kill individual political opponents but insufferable that he should persecute a whole section of his own nation. As Benito Mussolini put it in 1934: 'The anti-semitic question could turn Germany's enemies, including her Christian ones, against Hitler.'

In fact it was Christians in Germany who provided the strongest focus of resistance to Hitler and the major failures in 'co-ordination' were with the Churches. Hitler was not strong enough to tackle them outright, although he hoped he would one day be able to do so. In his early years of power, he made something of a point of stating in speeches that he was restoring 'Christian' standards, and in view of his private views this must have been conscious deception. The original causes of anti-semitism in Europe had been religious with Church leaders, over the centuries, in a persecuting role. But the National Socialists almost ignored the religious aspect and used a 'social' approach. Besides being generally undesirable, the Jews were liable to pollute the purity of the German 'race', and the 'race' was all-important for the future. The German Catholics, although many individuals among them were party supporters and even members, retained their independent organisation. A papal encyclical 'With burning anxiety', critical of some aspects of the regime was read aloud from Catholic pulpits on March 3rd, 1937. What the regime did against the Catholics, in practice, was to make a point of publicising Church scandals that happened to arise, particularly when they related to priests and monks failing to be chaste. The Protestants, who had traditionally regarded themselves as members of state Churches, might have been expected to be easier to deal with. In fact they were not. Hitler appointed a 'Reich Bishop' to 'co-ordinate' the Protestants but there arose immediately the 'Confessing Church' movement which insisted upon its independence from the National Socialist state and comprised the bulk of the abler and more pious Protestant clergy and laity.

Religion interested Hitler. Whether or not he was a monotheist is difficult to establish. In public speeches he sometimes implied that he had a special mission from God and some of those close to him reckoned that he believed this. However in his private conversation, as recorded, he made no such claim. Certainly he had little taste for paganism. Some National Socialists, notably Rosenberg, tried to revive the old nordic gods and held weird ceremonies. Hitler criticised this publicly and mocked it privately. He often, when in power, went on privately about the Christian religion, reckoning that it was a Jewish plot to soften the 'Aryans'. He regarded it as ultimately incompatible with National Socialism and sometimes he reckoned that it might have to be outrightly attacked. But, as with so much, it is difficult to pin Hitler down.

A possibly more settled view, which he also expressed privately, was that Christianity was withering away. 'Put a telescope in a village and you destroy a world of superstition,' he remarked privately in one of his more epigramatical moments. Before the splendour of National Socialism, he sometimes remarked, Christianity would be left only as a comfort for 'old women', and he did not bother about that. There was some tendency in the late 1930s for local party branches to hold parades on Sunday mornings and march past the churches, bands blaring, while services were going on.

Also the army and navy remained outside National Socialist 'co-ordination'. It had long been a rule that neither officers nor men should take part in political activity or belong to political parties. This rule was maintained even in the circumstances of a one-party state. Occasionally it was broken but then the army took disciplinary measures, including, on occasion, court martial. Thus the German army under Hitler was unlike the Red Army in the Soviet Union. The Red Army was a definitely political force and had commissars, political representatives, who were supposed to supervise the morale of the men and see that the military officers followed the party line. The German army and navy had no commissars but kept to their Christian chaplains. The air force, a National Socialist creation in defiance of the Versailles Treaty, did, however, have some political flavour and many individuals within it were party supporters. It was not until the last months of World War II that Hitler attempted to make the army 'political', and introduced the Roman salute.

It is often difficult to establish to what extent Hitler exerted detailed control over any particular aspect of National Socialist action. Thus, for example, he was prejudiced against too much university education and under him, there was a considerable reduction in the numbers of students. (This can be accounted for partly by a National Socialist prejudice against educating women but the numbers of men students also tended to go down.) Did Hitler directly and immediately cut down the universities, or was this something of which he merely approved and for executive purposes was outside his ken? There is no certain answer. Part of Hitler's skill was that he could delegate some subjects—really delegate them so that he felt no emotional involvement. At times he interfered in detail, as over the design of military weapons, at others he let his machine have its way, even in matters that concerned his personal life.

It was Hitler's method, and probably also instinct, to avoid creating a clear-cut hierarchy. National Socialist Germany became a welter of competing factions and interests with, often, several authorities doing virtually the same work at once. This was a support for Hitler's ultimate dictatorship; nobody but himself had final power. Often, however, he insisted that rival factions should compose their differences rather than come to him for adjudication. At the same time, and as a complement to this, some individual National Socialist leaders held a wide range of offices. The prime example was Göring who, in 1936, was minister-president of Prussia, commander-in-chief of the air force, president of the Reichstag, chief forester of the Reich, director of Reich television and chairman of the four-year plan. In none of these posts did he have final authority. As television director he was a rival of the propaganda minister Goebbels. As head of the air force he was partially subordinate to the armed forces supreme command. As chairman of the four-year plan, discussed more fully below, he clashed with the Economics Minister, Hjalmar Schacht. He had no single power base over which he had complete control and could have challenged Hitler, even if he had wanted to.

Göring was characteristic, also, of the corrupt side of National Socialism. His various salaries, alone, made him a prosperous man. 'Gifts' from industry, which were scarcely better than protection money, enabled him to live like a millionaire. There were so many controls and licences needed that a powerful friend, such as Göring, was a useful asset. He could reward his patron with what he had become sinecure honorifics, such as membership of the Prussian state council; more significantly, he could intervene deep down into the government bureaucracy to help a friend who was having trouble over some licence or contract. He could provide a commission in the air force for a patron's son. That Göring was greedy was well known and jokes about him, centring on the fact that he owned a galaxy of uniforms and was sometimes very fat, provided about the only light relief that existed in National Socialism; Göring seemed to enjoy the jokes himself and to encourage them. When he stumped past Hitler, at the head of his personal S.A. unit at the annual Nuremberg rally, Göring always drew an affectionate, amused cheer from the crowd. A typical joke of the time was that Göring had special rubber medals to wear in his bath. Another was that of Hitler dozing off during a performance of *Lohengrin,* awaking with a start, and shouting to a knight in armour on the stage: 'Hermann—you are going too far!'

Other leaders, notably Goebbels and, later, Ribbentrop also did well for themselves. Goebbels drew generous fees, on top of his salary, for his newspaper and magazine articles and his broadcasts. His job included supervision of the film industry and he threw himself into womanising among the stars and starlets. At one point he actually wanted to divorce his wife, Magda, and marry a Czech film star Lida Baarova but Hitler, who had long had a liking for Magda and had been best man at their wedding, vetoed the project. In the background, Max Amann became Germany's biggest publisher by using his party position to help him to take over newspaper, magazine and book publishing firms; he ran them with a clear eye for economy and profitability. Himmler, in the mid-1930s, although assuming more and more police power and building up the S.S., was personally unassuming and incorrupt and not yet a figure of the top rank. He lived a quiet, bourgeois form of life. He did reward industrialists with S.S. rank in return for subscriptions but did not appropriate the money for himself.

Lower down the hierarchy were the party area managers, who enjoyed considerable autonomy in their sphere and were often, but not invariably, corrupt. Hitler made a point of buttressing their authority. They were generally of a cruder type than the 'intellectuals' of the S.S., had been with Hitler since the days of 'struggle' in the late 1920s, and felt a sense of personal relationship with him. They were supposed to supervise all party activities in their districts but this was somewhat ambiguous, due to competing authorities. Quite often a party area manager was in conflict with civic authorities and did not invariably come out on top. He had some power over industry and labour in his district but could be cut across by orders from Berlin. The police and the S.S. could be influenced by him but were not fully under his control. (The political police (the Gestapo) and the S.S. were, incidentally, by no means the same thing. Most Gestapo men were drawn from the ordinary criminal police and only about a quarter of them held S.S. rank.) Streicher at Nuremberg was often, at the time, regarded as the archetypal area manager. He was a bully, sexually abnormal in that he liked to rape young girls and crazily anti-semitic. On occasion he personally beat up political prisoners held by the police. Scandal continually revolved around him and eventually he was relieved of his duties as a result of a rape; Hitler, however, insisted that he should continue as honorary area manager. But Streicher was really the most notorious of the area managers, rather than the most typical. More commonly, an area manager was an ex-N.C.O. from the army of World War I, who tended to feather his own nest and, following Hitler's lead, to try to bring about the erection of monumental public buildings to perpetuate his own fame.

So far as he was aware of corruption in his system, Hitler tolerated it. One reason for this must have been a gangster leader's instinct for keeping a hold over his lieutenants. If they became troublesome, he could always 'expose' them and ruin their reputations on entirely non-political grounds. Quite a point had been made of Röhm's homosexuality in justifying the 1934 blood purge. But to a considerable extent Hitler may well have been simply unaware of corruption; he had an unusually strong capacity for concentrating on what he considered to be the most vital matters, and cutting himself off from everything else. One of the catch-phrases among the ordinary Germans, especially women, was, at some example of corruption, cruelty or ineptitude, to sigh: 'If the Leader only knew . . .' And very often Hitler really did not know. (This is not to state that Hitler did not set a general tone. He is most clearly on record as believing that terror was a necessary and legitimate political weapon.)

But Hitler was not financially corrupt himself and took little interest in money. Some small point was made in National Socialist propaganda that the Leader took no salary. Hitler was, however, a rich man through the sales of *My Struggle*. The book had its political inconveniences, especially for foreign policy, and it was not well enough written to be much use as domestic propaganda. Amann boosted its sales from primarily commercial motives. It was bound in black, to make it look like the Bible, and, on a semi-compulsory basis was sold in bulk to schools. Municipalities bought stocks and distributed them as wedding gifts. It became a sign of good citizenship to have a copy of *My Struggle* in one's home. Amann handled the whole of Hitler's business affairs and investments and whenever Hitler wanted cash Amann was able to provide it. There was also an 'Adolf Hitler Fund', raised by public subscription, which Hitler could use at his discretion.

In 1935 and 1937, Hitler rebuilt his home on the Obersalzburg, Haus Wachenfeld, into a residence more suited to a head of state and renamed it the Berghof. It was by no means a palace and was designed for comfort rather than splendour, with plenty of easy chairs. The most striking feature was a picture window with views over the Alps and Hitler loved showing this to his guests. Here, from 1936 onwards, Eva Braun was head of the domestic side of the household, although she had to disappear from view when anybody outside Hitler's immediate entourage came to the house— she was not allowed to meet even Göring. In the early years of his power, Berchtesgaden and the Obersalzburg attracted many tourists who wanted to see Hitler in his mountain retreat and they did, sometimes, catch glimpses of him. If there were children, Hitler would sometimes come and chat affably to them.

The scene gradually changed as the Obersalzburg became almost urbanised. Martin Bormann, adjutant to Hess, Hitler's deputy for party affairs, was largely responsbile. Under Bormann's direction, land was purchased, roads were made, buildings and barracks were erected and these entirely changed the character of the place. Göring, Goebbels and Bormann acquired houses there and an hotel was erected for other official visitors. Fences and guards kept out the public. Hitler himself seemed somewhat irritated by the transformation but the positive step he took was to ban blasting explosions before noon, lest they interrupted his sleep. Fear of assassination may have had something to do with it, but really in this matter affecting his own personal surroundings, Hitler just let Bormann have his way. His, Hitler's, mind was on other things.

Bormann's most extraordinary construction was the Eagle's Nest on the peak of the Kehlstein mountain. Money was collected for it on the basis that it was to be a fiftieth birthday present to Hitler from the party and nation. The Obersalzburg area, where Hitler's house was, is 3,300 feet above sea level. The Eagle's Nest, at the top of the mountain, is 5,674 feet above sea level and before Bormann started work the site was accessible only on foot, after a stiff climb. Bormann brought in 3,000 labourers—their very existence, in a camp, was sufficient to disturb Hitler's seclusion. After nearly two years' work, and an expenditure of some twenty-five million marks, Bormann had constructed a road up to the Kehlstein, with five tunnels cut through the granite, to within 400 feet of the peak. Then he blasted a tunnel 400 feet into the mountain. From this he blasted upwards to form an elevator shaft leading to the peak where he erected the actual 'nest', a house of six rooms with panoramic views across the mountains. Due to snow, it is accessible only from May to October each year. (It now belongs to the German Alpine Club.)

Hitler visited the Eagle's Nest less than a dozen times and that only out of curiosity. He took the French ambassador there in 1938, to try to impress him. It is possible that Bormann took over-seriously some casual remark by Hitler that he would like a house at the top of the mountain where he could get away from everything. There was some idea, also, that it would symbolise the union of Germany and Austria. An explanation for Hitler not using it has been that the height made him dizzy. The better explanation is that Hitler never really wanted the place and that it is an example of his extraordinary capacity for cutting himself off from what did not interest him, even when it was an enormous constructional work on his own doorstep.

It was, thus, always the Berghof and not the Eagle's Nest that was Hitler's home. He spent as little time as possible in Berlin.

He enjoyed, up to 1939, making frequent visits around Germany, now using his special train in preference to car or air. But above all he liked to get to the Berghof, where he felt most free from official schedules. He remarked that he felt healthy there because the mountains were full of salt. He was unsystematic, preferred walking around to sitting at a desk, and drew up his own appointments list, which he frequently amended. Sometimes a visitor would wait several hours in an ante-room to see him and then be told that the Leader had changed his mind and was not keeping the appointment. (But he never did this when the visitor, or the reason for the visit, was really important.) He liked to be fed frequently with information, especially translations of articles in foreign newspapers; unfavourable ones would enrage him but he would still read them. He hated being alone. Lunch and dinner, eaten with a dozen or so intimates, each lasted up to two hours, with Hitler leading the conversation, which was usually unsophisticated and often banal. Then there was coffee and cakes in the late afternoon, usually in the 'tea house' some 500 yards from the Berghof, to which Hitler with Eva led his entourage on foot. In the evening after dinner there was often a film show—Hitler took a great liking to *Lives of a Bengal Lancer,* which portrayed the British in India and saw it repeatedly. Then there would be records, principally of Wagner, and then further talk extending until the small hours of the morning. When he had finally exhausted himself, Hitler would withdraw with Eva to their private quarters. He was prudish about appearing to sleep in the same room as her and very probably, in fact, often did not do so; it is unknowable. He rose late in the morning, often not appearing until noon. Hitler had vegetarian food for himself, carefully cooked but not luxurious. He served meat and wine to his guests, sometimes gently twitting them for eating 'flesh'. Bormann was considered a toady because when with Hitler he ate the vegetarian food and refused alcohol but, it was said, as soon as he got back to his own place he sat down to a *schnitzel* and a bottle of hock. Hess had individualistic ideas about an 'organic' vegetarian diet and, until Hitler found out and forbade it, would turn up to Hitler's table bringing his own food in a box.

When meeting a stranger, it was Hitler's habit to avoid taking the initiative himself. He would open the conversation with an interrogative '*Na?*' and then sit back to see what the visitor wanted, absorbing impressions as well as words. The visitor saw a well-built man between five feet nine inches and five feet ten inches in height, with a largish head and an artistic hair style, with a brown lock dropping over the left side of his forehead. His eyes, in repose, seemed to smoulder; when he was excited they seemed to blaze. Until the start of World War II he was accustomed to wear a lounge suit, not uniform, in private. As a conversation proceeded Hitler would begin to intervene and eventually would take over completely, using energetic gestures and speaking enthusiastically and without hesitations. He became an animated, dynamic figure. Although he expected to be treated with deference, Hitler was never pompous and used minor courtesies with visitors, such as seeing them to the door.

The lack of interest in the Eagle's Nest was not, of course, indicative of Hitler's attitude to construction work as a whole. Motorways were a subject on which he always became animated and he took a continuous and close interest in public buildings. Right back in the 1920s, when he had been only a minor opposition politician, he had sketched out designs for the buildings he would erect when in power. He disliked the atmosphere of Berlin and, at first, had some idea of creating a completely new capital somewhere in central Germany. Then he decided, for reasons of historical continuity, that Berlin should be retained. South Germans, such as himself, should be willing to recognise the Prussian contribution to German unity. But he planned an entirely new centre for Berlin which would have made it the most grandiose capital in the world. His assistant in this was Albert Speer, aged thirty in 1935, who came from the Troost office in Munich. Hitler sketched the rough designs and Speer, as the trained architect, turned them into proper plans, adding ideas of his own. Speer was very much Hitler's personal protégé and there was something approaching a father-son relationship between them. Hitler saw his new Berlin as a monument to remind future generations of his greatness. It would be like the pyramids of Egypt. 'Granite,' he said, 'will ensure that our monuments last for ever. In 10,000 years they'll still be standing, just as they are, unless meanwhile the sea has again covered our plains.'

Work on the new Berlin was planned to be completed by about 1950 but the outbreak of World War II prevented any major start. One feature of it was to be an enormous chancellery, where a visitor would have to walk for a quarter of a mile from the main entrance to reach the Chancellor's office. Hitler reckoned that he himself needed no such grandeur to sustain his authority but his successors would inevitably be lesser men who would need it. He would occupy the building himself but only for a short while, so as to sanctify it for the benefit of his successors. Another showpiece was to be the world's biggest assembly hall, capable of accommodating 180,000 people. Hitler had first begun sketching this as far back as 1925 and plans began to take final shape in 1936. It was to be circular, with a diameter approaching a fifth of a mile. Over it, starting at a height of 323 feet, was to be a fantastic dome, rising to 726 feet. Often the dome would have been among the clouds and the first glimpse someone arriving by air at Berlin would have had would have been of the dome in the sky.

Besides his buildings memorialising his own greatness, Hitler planned that they would symbolise his great new Germany, which, like the architectural plans, scarcely got off the drawing board. The achievement of curing unemployment was, in his view, only a start. Germany would go on to become the richest and most powerful nation on earth.

An initial effect of rising employment was to put foreign trade into deficit. Germany produced more goods than there was room for in the depressed world market and needed more raw materials than she could afford to pay for. The orthodox solution would have been a devaluation of the mark but this, because of memories of the inflation of 1923, was politically unacceptable. Had the Germans found that the value of the mark in their pockets was again beginning to crumble, they would rapidly have lost faith in the regime. Accordingly, Schacht, the Economics Minister, in what was described at the time as 'wizardry' manipulated the external value of the mark while keeping the internal value almost stable. This involved detailed controls over international transactions and it was difficult to establish what the true international value of the mark was; there were over a hundred different exchange rates for different types of transaction. Moreover Schacht eliminated money from some transactions altogether and negotiated, especially with the Balkan countries, straightforward barter deals by which they exchanged raw materials and food for German manufactured goods. Schacht, never a National Socialist, was a paradoxical figure. He was by temperament a conservative but in actual financial operations he pioneered new techniques which were to be widely imitated by other countries after World War II. Hitler understood very little of the details of Schacht's juggling; but it was an essential factor in the full employment policy.

In 1936, with the first phase of economic recovery over, Hitler announced a 'four-year plan', with Göring as chairman, and this was designed to make Germany economically self-sufficient and insulated from the vagaries of world trade. Instead of buying in the cheapest market, Germany would, for nationalist reasons, give preference to her own products. Thus there was plenty of oil in the world, produced from normal wells, but Germany was to set up a more expensive process for making oil from her own coal.

234

Göring took the 'self-sufficiency' so far as to toy with the idea of alchemy, of Germany manufacturing her own gold. All kinds of cranks wrote in with ideas. More substantially, Göring boosted the output of the iron and steel industry, running much of it at a loss, with state subsidies to make up the gap. Propaganda convinced most ordinary Germans that the project was as viable as the 'five-year plans' being forced through by Stalin in the Soviet Union but, in fact, German circumstances were different. The Soviet Union did possess the resources to become ultimately self-sufficient whereas Germany did not. Experts, such as Schacht, recognised this and Schacht resented Göring's authority cutting across his own. Moreover Schacht believed that Hitler was spending more on armaments than the economy could stand. In 1938 Schacht resigned, an event which somewhat shook Hitler; at their last meeting, Hitler accompanied Schacht all the way to the front door of the chancellery before shaking hands in farewell.

Hitler, of course, was not an idiot over self-sufficiency, and knew well that Germany within its then frontiers could never achieve it. Exactly how, or when, he did not know but he intended Germany to acquire new territories in the east which would be like the colonies of the British Empire. (His ideas on German autarky were similar to those of the British 'Empire Free Traders' of the 1930s, with the difference that Germany needed to conquer new territory whereas the British were wanting to make better use of what they already had.) The new 'Greater Germany' would, however, be stronger than the British Empire because it would consist of a continous mass of land. German settlers had been living in the Ukraine since the eighteenth century and they had kept their language. They would be the forerunners of a much greater movement.

The ambition was a hazy one and virtually nobody at the time realised how seriously Hitler took it. The key to foreign policy and questions of war and peace appeared to depend only on the relatively minor frontier problems left over from World War I.

13

'No matter what you attempt,' mused Hitler privately at about the time of his accession to power, 'if an idea is not yet mature, you will not be able to realise it. I know that as an artist and I know it as a statesman. There is only one thing to do: have patience, wait, try again, wait again. In the subconscious the work goes on. It matures, sometimes it dies. Unless I have the inner, incorruptible conviction: *this is the solution,* I do nothing. Not even if the whole party tries to drive me to action. I will not act: I will wait, no matter what happens. But if the voice speaks, then I know the time has come to act.'

It was above all else in his conduct of foreign affairs that Hitler applied this intuitive and essentially irrational method of taking decisions. His inner 'voice' was a primary cause of World War II, of his own downfall and of disaster for Germany and Europe.

What exactly were Hitler's long-term intentions at any given point of time is impossible to pin down. Certain negatives can, however, be clearly established. The main one was that Hitler never intended to fight a world war, and still less a prolonged world war. That war came, in the form it did, was a result of miscalculation on Hitler's part. He eventually managed to muddle himself into a position in which ultimate ruin was almost certain. Similarly, although Hitler was often irrational and over-confident of his own talents, he was never so vain as to see himself as the potential conqueror of the world. He was an extreme German nationalist who wanted to create a powerful, self-sufficient Germany which would be dominant in Europe and a super-power by world standards. He wanted for Germany something like the position occupied by the United States and the Soviet Union in the years after 1945, except that he had no particular desire to win non-German peoples to his ideology. He could go so far as to say that National Socialism was such a good idea that it would be an absurdity to export it and allow rival countries to get strong from it.

In 1933, Hitler's immediate task in foreign policy was to remove the disabilities placed upon Germany by the Versailles Treaty and to aim at some form of frontier revision. This was an idea common to virtually all German politicians of the time and the only difference was how it best might be realised. Hitler had won power partly on the argument that the democratic parties had failed at it. (Arguably, they had done none too badly.) But it is now clear from the start his thinking went far beyond the Versailles grievances. 'The re-creation of pre-war Germany is a task unworthy of our revolution,' he said privately in about 1933, and it was a point he had made already in *My Struggle*. He wanted, but only in a shadowy, undefined way, to create a new Reich, incorporating not only the old Hohenzollern Germany but also the Germans of Austria and Czechoslovakia of whom he himself was one, plus the Germans in Poland who had been lost to Germany as a result of Versailles.

For reasons of economic self-sufficiency and 'living space', this new Reich ought to aim at expanding eastwards. The process, thought Hitler, would be analogous to that of European expansionism in America, Asia and Africa in the immediately preceding centuries; it would be ruthless and based upon colonists of a 'superior race' taking over the land. It was a part of the law of nature. Hitler believed the Slav nations of eastern Europe to be technically inferior to the Germans and so capable of being conquered; in the Soviet Union, especially, they had been weakened by Communism, which Hitler saw not as a monolithic force, challenging the rest of the world, but as a form of decay.

Apart from a few paragraphs in *My Struggle*, which were so vague as to be almost incapable of being analysed in detail, Hitler made little reference to his eastern dreams, even in the privacy of his own circle. At no point did he ever lay down exactly what colonial territories he wanted to acquire, although presumably they included European Russia, the Ukraine and the Crimea. Perhaps the subject came to him sometimes while sleepless at Berchtesgaden he stared at the moon shining on the mountains but in his working moments in the 1930s it seems rarely to have been at the top of his mind. Certainly German military preparations in the 1930s were unrelated to the Leader's private dream.

Hitler's mind was powerful at envisaging a remote future. His tactical skill was considerable in immediate, practical problems. But he was deficient when it came to envisaging the middle distance.

237

In foreign affairs, he stumbled one step at a time with only his hazy grand design to guide him. Unlike, for example, Bismarck or even Neville Chamberlain, he could fail badly in making a realistic appreciation of what lay around the next corner. The best instance of this blindness was his declaration of war on the United States in 1941.

Although he wanted to avoid any prolonged war, Hitler was obviously not a pacifist. The sword, in his view, was probably necessary to undo Versailles and certainly necessary if the eastern empire were ever to be won. He thought in terms of swift war, undertaken only in circumstances which guaranteed overwhelming victory. 'Interlocked frontal struggles lasting for years on petrified fronts will not return. I guarantee that,' he said privately at about the time of his accession to power. Propaganda would be a vital weapon.

The place of artillery preparation for frontal attack by the infantry in trench warfare will in future be taken by revolutionary propaganda, to break down the enemy psychologically before the armies begin to function at all . . . Whoever has experienced war at the front will want to refrain from all avoidable bloodshed . . . I shall never start a war without the certainty that a demoralised enemy will succumb to the first stroke of a single, gigantic attack.

Hitler's idea of swift, surgical wars, started only when success was certain, was reflected in German military planning. In 1936, Göring made a widely-reported speech in which he said the German people must put 'guns before butter', but in fact almost precisely the opposite process was going on. Germany, while re-arming with modern equipment (scrutinised by Hitler personally) up to about parity with Britain and France, was avoiding 'in depth' preparation for the type of world conflict that actually came in the early 1940s. From the start of his political career, one of Hitler's basic propaganda points, in which he himself must have really believed, was that World War I had been lost for Germany by a collapse in civilian morale; thus his aim, far into World War II, was to ensure that in the next conflict the ordinary public suffered as little as possible. 'Guns before butter' was effective more for foreign consumption than for use in home propaganda. During his early years in power, Hitler became almost a bore on the subject of peace.

In his Reichstag speech of May 17th, 1933, his first foreign policy statement, he said that to have a war would be 'infinite madness' and that 'No European war could improve the unsatisfactory conditions of the present day. On the contrary, the application of violence of any kind in Europe could have no favourable effect on the political or economic position.' A new war would cause Europe to 'sink into Communistic chaos'.

We in this new Germany, [he said,] are filled with deep understanding . . . for the rightful claims to life of other nations . . . Our boundless love for and loyalty to our own national traditions makes us respect the national claims of others and makes us desire from the bottom of our hearts to live with them in peace and friendship . . . Germany wants nothing for herself which she is not prepared to give to others.

A few months later, in an interview with the London *Daily Mail* he was asserting: 'Our youth constitutes our sole hope for the future. Do you imagine that we are bringing it up only to be shot down on the battlefield?' In a proclamation to the German people for New Year's Day 1934, he explained that war could be 'only a new catastrophe for the peoples of a Europe that had become insane'. To the *Daily Mail*, again, in 1935, he said: 'When I talk of peace I am doing nothing but give expression to the profoundest and most sincere wishes of the German people. I know the horrors of war too well. No possible profits could justify the sacrifices and sufferings that war entails.' In his May Day proclamation for 1935 he stated: 'Just as we have to establish peace within our own people, so we want nothing less than peace with the world. For we all know that our great work can only succeed in time of peace.' To the American *Literary Digest* he declared in 1935: 'In the old days a deliberate maker of war may have been a patriot; today he is a traitor, leading his people in the valley of the shadow of death.' On May Day 1936 he proclaimed: 'It is not necessary for me to win esteem and respect from my people through any famous triumph which carries in its train millions of dead.'

It was scarcely possible, indeed, for Hitler to make any prolonged public statement in this period without mentioning 'peace'. And his early rearmament had actually the effect of weakening Germany. He inherited the small but highly efficient army of 100,000 men allowed to Germany under the Versailles system. Neither tanks nor military aircraft were allowed, although Germans had received some training with these by arrangement with the Soviet Union. By any standard other than that of Germany permanently accepting subjugation to second class status this was unsatisfactory but at least it was a viable, trained force. The idealists hoped that Germany would obtain parity by other powers disarming down to a similar level and this, in fact had been envisaged in the Versailles settlement. In October 1933, Hitler withdrew Germany from the League of Nations on the plea that disarmament negotiations had got nowhere and Germany was still condemned to inferiority. In leaving the League, Hitler said he was willing to disarm 'down to the last machine gun' if other powers would do the same. He had already decided to treble the German army from 100,000 to 300,000 men and to ignore the Versailles restrictions on weapons. The immediate result of such a rapid increase was somewhat to weaken the effectiveness of the army, too many trained men being used up in instructing recruits. (But at least Hitler had avoided the mass incorporation of the brownshirts into the army.) In March 1935, on the ground that France had extended her period of compulsory military service,* Hitler introduced conscription in Germany. This in terms of immediate military efficiency was almost catastrophic, particularly when a year later Hitler, against the wishes of the generals, doubled the period of conscription from one to two years. The needs of training used up almost the whole regular manpower and most of the actual fighting units existed scarcely more than on paper.

Hitler's calculation, which was justified, was that Germany need not fear outside attack while the new army was being trained. It was not as if foreign governments regarded the National Socialists as the arch-criminals of the age, to be extirpated at all costs. But his foreign policy generally had little relationship to the strength of his military forces at any given moment, and from an early stage he was liable to confuse paper strength with real strength. By 1939, by the constant proliferation of army units, Germany had reached the almost ludicrous condition of having 730,000 trained men in the active army but a paper establishment requiring 2,758,000 men to fill all vacancies. By the end of the war Hitler had become capable of issuing military orders to units which had ceased to exist altogether.

In the west, Hitler had no claims and wanted no war at all, of any kind. He reckoned, however, that France with her system of alliances encircling Germany from the east was likely to be an irreconcilable enemy which might have to be dealt with. Hitler repeatedly and specifically renounced any German claim to Alsace, Lorraine, which was the only direct territorial issue between Germany and France, but this was far from sufficient to guarantee peace. His political intuition, however, told him that France, exhausted by World War I and with bitterly quarrelling politicians,

* The French had increased their military service primarily because there were not enough men in the relevant age group to keep their army up to strength.

was now no more than a paper tiger. At the time Hitler came to power, France was in the midst of constructing the Maginot Line—a system of fortresses, tunnels and anti-tank defences—along her frontier with Germany and the faith she attached to this was indicative of a fundamentally defensive posture. (To the German generals, naturally, the supposedly 'invulnerable' Maginot Line, based upon the supposed lessons of World War I, posed an interesting professional challenge.)

But the really key power in the west was Great Britain, which still had an empire covering a quarter of the world, colossal self-confidence and an historic policy of wanting to cut down any power which threatened to dominate mainland Europe. Hitler was interested in the British, and in the naval tradition upon which they had apparently built up their strength. He saw them as ruthless and clever, particularly admiring their feat of having conquered India. Ideally, Hitler would have liked a form of alliance with the British; they should give him a free hand in Europe and he would not interfere with their empire, which was beginning to run into considerable difficulties. Despite the urgings of Schacht that, for economic reasons, Germany needed her pre-war African colonies back, Hitler showed relatively little interest in them. They were a fair price to pay for Anglo-German understanding.

While if he had been a more travelled man, and had met more British at first hand, Hitler's techniques for dealing with the British might have been more effective, he was really up against an impossibility in coming to terms with them. While French foreign policy was reasonably coherent and conducted according to clear. long-term principles, British policy lacked long-term planning and was virtually unpredictable. Stanley Baldwin, the dominant British politician during Hitler's first four years, believed that a new war would be the greatest conceivable evil but relied upon hope rather than action. His successor in 1937, Neville Chamberlain, was a totally different type of man, who believed that vigorous British initiatives were needed to sort out European disputes. But even Chamberlain, a generally clear-headed man, was in a muddle whether British policy should be altruistic or directed for motives of national self-interest.

Hitler's only real success with the British was the 1935 Anglo-German Naval Agreement, which limited the strength of the German fleet to thirty per cent of that of the British. The agreement (which Hitler later did not regard as sacrosanct) was a triumph in that the British Government formally and specifically recognised Hitler's right to break the Versailles Treaty, which had limited German naval strength to a much lower level. For Hitler this agreement was a crucial event. He knew well that naval rivalry had been a significant background cause of war between Germany and Britain in 1914; by apparently eliminating the possibility of the same rivalry re-arising, he had improved his chances of avoiding a new world war.

The German negotiator of the Naval Agreement was Joachim von Ribbentrop, the wine merchant in whose Berlin apartment Hitler had held important discussions with Oskar von Hindenburg immediately before being appointed Chancellor in 1933. Ribbentrop, who had lived in Canada as a young man, had a love-hatred for the British. He was intelligent, ambitious and devoted to Hitler. His weakness was vanity.

In foreign affairs, as in every other field, Hitler believed in working through a multiplicity of subordinates. He distrusted the official Foreign Office, which until 1938 was under the career diplomat, Baron Konstantin von Neurath, believing that it was out of date and wedded to the kind of doctrines that had led to catastrophe for Germany in World War I. So he had a second 'foreign office' under Rosenberg and this was an organ of the National Socialist Party. Rosenberg, with his Baltic background, shared Hitler's eastern ambitions. He thought he ought to be the real Foreign Minister instead of just a party official but he lacked the worldly capacity really to push his claim and at most he provided a useful implied threat for Hitler—if the Foreign Office did not toe the line, it might find itself under Rosenberg. Then there was a third 'foreign office' under Ribbentrop—the 'Ribbentrop Bureau', which was independent of both state and party and relied upon Hitler's personal patronage. Ribbentrop built up his organisation with much vigour as a kind of information clearing house. There was even, in minuscule form, yet a fourth 'foreign office' under the old stalwart from the early party days, 'Putzi' Hanfstaengl, the Munich and New York art dealer. Hanfstaengl was supposed to be in charge of relationships with the foreign press and had to fight off attempts by Goebbels to control him; his leading interest, in which he got nowhere, was to try to persuade Hitler that it should be a central aim to be on good terms with the United States. Rosenberg made a visit to London in 1934 but his dreamy, awkward manner made a bad impression and a wreath he had placed on the principal war memorial was thrown into the Thames.

That Ribbentrop, the following year, was able to go to London, be taken seriously and get the Naval Agreement was the making of his career with Hitler. He became German ambassador in London in which office he spent lavishly and became the most prominent member of the diplomatic corps but achieved no success in trying to persuade the British Government not to intervene in east European affairs. In 1938 Hitler appointed him Foreign Minister, in which office until 1945 he efficiently carried out Hitler's instructions. By his own account, he sometimes argued with Hitler but he certainly did what he was told and was an instrument rather than a maker of foreign policy. Unlike Göring or Goebbels, or even Hess, he had no real power base in the hierarchy; had Hitler died and Göring come to power, that would have been the end of Ribbentrop.

While Hitler was realistic enough to know that the best he could hope from Britain was neutrality and that an alliance was out of the question, he did expect that Italy would be Germany's ally. This was partly on general principle; he regarded Italy as being like Germany in that she was a power which had come relatively late on to the European scene and had not received a fair share of the pickings. A more immediate factor was his feeling of political kinship with Benito Mussolini, who had been Prime Minister of Italy when Hitler was still unknown. In 1933 Mussolini had already been eleven years in office and was a considerable figure in Europe; liberals and Marxists disliked him but he had many admirers on the right, including Winston Churchill. In terms of formal ability and knowledge, he was Hitler's superior; he was well read, had travelled and could speak French, German and English. He lacked Hitler's crippling delusion about the Jews. From almost the start of his political career, Hitler had admired Mussolini from afar and his National Socialist state owed much to the Fascist model. Hitler considered Mussolini to be a brilliant leader.

The problem was that Germany and Italy had been on opposite sides in World War I and that the turning point in Mussolini's political career had been his vigorous advocacy of Italian entry into the war. There was the rump state of Austria which Mussolini was determined to maintain as a buffer and which Hitler wanted to absorb into Germany. There were German claims to the South Tyrol. The initiative for friendship came from Hitler and at first went badly. He expected his first meeting with Mussolini to be 'the happiest day of my life' but when it took place at Venice in June 1934, it was almost a fiasco.

It was the first time, apart from his war service, that Hitler had ever been abroad.* He was ill at ease about the adventure, even to the extent of not knowing what to wear. The Foreign Ministry advised him that since he was going as Chancellor of Germany, and not as party leader, he should wear civilian clothes. Accordingly Hitler wore a grey, double-breasted lounge suit and

* Except a brief speaking tour in Austria in 1919.

over it a belted khaki raincoat especially bought for the occasion. When he stepped out of his aircraft at Venice, he was embarrassed to see Mussolini resplendent in full uniform. Fortunately for him, he did not hear Mussolini's first reaction which was a whisper to his son-in-law Galeazzo Ciano: 'I don't like him.' At a banquet, Hitler refused fine food and had only scrambled eggs. At another meal, some disgruntled servant put salt into his coffee. Mussolini went so far as to provide an insulting march-past of Fascist militia—he had them dressed in old uniforms, unshaven and marching out of step. Hitler, looking incredulous, had to salute them. The two leaders, speaking in German without an interpreter, quarrelled over Austria and, probably, also over the Jews and the prospect of a new European war. After the visit was over, Mussolini, privately, described Hitler as 'a garrulous monk'. Hitler, although continuing to admire Mussolini, lost the more naive side of his hero-worship and this was probably an advantage for practical dealings.

The loophole enabling Hitler to get Mussolini on to his side was the latter's expansionist foreign policy. Mussolini talked vaguely of creating a 'new Roman Empire' and wanted Italy, rather than France or Britain, to be the dominant power in the Mediterranean. This was partly Mussolini's inherent dynamism, he not being the kind of leader who could ever stand still, partly bombast and partly a belief that Italy, like France and Britain, had a 'civilising mission' in the non-European world. He had a robust pre-1914 view that a taste of war would toughen his people.

Another potential ally for Hitler, of particular value for a drive eastwards, was the autocratic new state of Poland, run by army officers of anti-semitic bias. The ethnic frontiers of Poland, both west and east, were far from clear. She had claims against both Germany and the Soviet Union, and, with about equal justification, Germany and the Soviet Union had claims against her. The fundamentals of her foreign policy were alliance with France and the maintenance of large armed forces. Her most prominent leader, Colonel Josef Beck, a man who often got drunk, tended to behave as if he were at the head of a major European power and to exaggerate Poland's strength. For German nationalists of traditionalist outlook, Poland was automatically an enemy. After World War I, she had acquired sacred Prussian soil, with a German majority population, to form her 'corridor' leading to the sea. The German-populated port of Danzig, at the head of the corridor, was under League of Nations control although the majority of the people would have preferred to be part of Germany as they had been up to 1919. The 'threat' from an aggressive Poland to disarm Germany's eastern frontiers had been a continuous theme of German nationalism in the 1920s. Hitler, however, as a south German felt less personal involvement than the Prussians in the Polish question: it had, of course, to be solved in the long run for reasons of basic nationalism but it ranked in his scale of priorities below that of the southern questions of Austria and Czechoslovakia. A possible answer, in the long run, could have been a joint German-Polish attack on the Soviet Union, with Poland relinquishing the 'corridor' in return for a chunk of White Russia or the Ukraine, or perhaps the Baltic states. Poland also had territorial aspirations against Czechoslovakia which could be supported by Germany. In the short-term, however, existed the fact that German-Polish relations had been bad ever since World War I.

Hitler acted with ruthless simplicity. As one of his earliest acts of foreign policy, he offered conciliation with Poland. It was agreed in an informal statement in November 1933, that the German and Polish governments would 'renounce all application of force in their relations with each other'. Two months later, on January 26th, 1934, this was formalised as a ten-year non-aggression pact. German public opinion at the time was, of course, suppressed by National Socialist autocracy and censorship and so it is difficult to assess how it reacted. Among liberal and left-wing circles, dissatisfied as they were with the eastern frontier situation, the pact would certainly have attracted a measure of support; but these were the very circles which had opposed Hitler. Among nationalists, however, it must have seemed almost incredible that a government which had come to power partly on a programme of a vigorous foreign policy to amend German grievances should be giving way to Poland, and should be renouncing the use of even the threat of force. In any atmosphere of open debate, Hitler's action would have been open to severe and damaging challenge.

By his own statements, Hitler regarded treaties as binding only so long as it suited all the signatories to observe them and he was willing to break his word. In view of his renunciation of the Polish treaty five years later, in the spring of 1939, and his attack on Poland the following September, it has been argued that he was carrying out a deep-laid cynical plot in concluding it in the first place. But that is reasoning from hindsight and is not evidence of his motives at the time. The pact had straightforward advantages in tending to separate Poland from France and in helping the attempt to build up Hitler on the international scene as a man of 'peace'. At the time he signed it, Hitler had no diplomatic triumphs to his credit and no certainty that he would ever go to war with

Poland. On their side the Poles, while by no means trusting unduly to German friendship, were glad to have come to terms with the vigorous new regime. Had they been willing to go on from friendship to being a junior partner, making accommodation for German grievances over the frontier difficulties, the pact could well have been permanent. But the Poles insisted on independence, with dominance over large non-Polish minorities, without the means of maintaining it.

A more remote potential ally was Japan, the only country outside the Euro-American complex to have built a modern technological society. Japan had defeated Russia three decades earlier in the war of 1904 and had been on the winning side in World War I, as a reward for which she had picked up some Pacific islands which had formerly been German property. Although her internal balance of power was a shifting one, she possessed a strong militaristic and expansionist party who thought Japan should be as ambitious in the Far East as the European colonising powers had been before her. Indeed it was on occasion held that the Japanese, as the most advanced nation in the Far East were its natural leaders; all that was needed was to drive out the British, the French and the Dutch. In 1931-2, on the not wholly false plea that civil disorder was disrupting her business interests, Japan declared a protectorate over the Chinese province of Manchuria and set up the Chinese Emperor (who had been deposed as a boy in 1912) as puppet monarch. It was the kind of thing that the European powers had done dozens of times in the nineteenth century but in the new League of Nations atmosphere, and the revulsion against war and aggression which had followed the experiences of 1914–18, it was no longer acceptable by world liberal opinion. The League of Nations condemned and expelled Japan. That Japan emerged unscathed from the condemnation must have confirmed Hitler's assessment that the League was ineffective.

In 1937 Japan embarked upon a full-blown war with China, which was in a chaotic condition, and won big victories. To Hitler this was similar to what he wanted to achieve in Russia and to what he believed the British had already achieved in India. The historic trend of German policy had been to support China and in the 1930s there were still many German officers and technical experts serving with the Chinese army. Hitler gradually reversed this trend and withdrew support, although in the initial stages of the Sino-Japanese war there were still Germans fighting on the Chinese side. The real prize in all this for Hitler was that Japan was in a more or less permanent state of hostility with the Soviet

Union, due to border disagreements, and in 1938–9 Japan and the Soviets fought what amounted to a war, although undeclared. Moreover Hitler, and still more the National Socialist ideologists, were able to trace apparent similarities between the virile traditions of the Japanese aristocracy and their own ideas of elitism. There was a disposition to declare the Japanese to be 'honorary Aryans', rather as in the 1970s in the Republic of South Africa they, but no other Asiatics, are privileged as 'honorary whites'. A joint German-Japanese onslaught upon the Soviet Union would have made sound strategic and some political sense.

It is contributory evidence that Hitler was not a genius in foreign relations that he never came near to establishing an intimate working alliance with Japan. Germany and Japan had it in common that they were expansionist, hostile to the Soviet Union and outside the League of Nations; in 1936 they signed the 'Anti-Comintern Pact', ostensibly designed to defend themselves against Communism and containing a secret protocol that they would come to each other's assistance if either were attacked by the Soviet Union. But the two countries continued to run wholly independent foreign policies, with no advance notice of each other's intentions, and ended up with Japan taking on the United States and the European colonising powers while Hitler was embroiled with the Soviet Union. Had they been able to agree to concentrate their forces together and take on one objective at a time, they would have been the more formidable.

While the Manchurian episode must have gone far towards supporting Hitler's belief that the League of Nations and the 'collective security' spirit associated with it was an illusion, the episode of Italy colonising Ethiopia in 1935–6 must finally have confirmed it. There was also the advantage that it tended to drive Italy, who lost friends by the venture, towards alliance with Germany and acceptance of German aims in Central Europe. Italy had long been interested in Ethiopia, which in 1935 was one of the only two African states to have maintained a formal independence of European colonisation. In 1896, a time when no protest on principle could have come from the European powers, the Italians had attempted to march inland from their colonies of Somaliland and Eritrea to annex Ethiopia but had been defeated at the battle of Adowa. This was a setback even worse than the British had suffered with the Zulus in South Africa and it rankled long with Italians. Mussolini had first tried to make Ethiopia an Italian client-state and in 1923 had sponsored her admission to the League of Nations; the British had opposed her admission on the ground that she still practised slavery. But the Ethiopians, despite various promises they made, including a treaty in 1928, failed to give the Italians the privileges they wanted. By 1932 Mussolini was planning to take over the country.

In 1934 came a muddled incident at the frontier post of Wal-Wal in which, largely accidentally, local Ethiopian forces fought Italian troops. The rights and wrongs of Wal-Wal are disputable but Mussolini had at least some case for declaring Ethiopia to be the aggressor. He decided to use the episode to clarify the situation beyond doubt. Unless the Ethiopians apologised and paid an indemnity for Wal-Wal and put their country under Italian suzerainty, Italy would go in for outright annexation. The young Emperor of Ethiopia, Haile Selassie, took the politic line, well-designed to appeal to liberal European opinion, that the Wal-Wal dispute should go to international arbitration. Mussolini put his army on a war footing, equipping it with poets to keep up morale. 'Proletarian and Fascist Italy,' said Mussolini, 'on your feet!'

Interestingly, Mussolini, for all his talk of 'the day of the lion', did not march straight in. Had he done so as the immediate consequence of Wal-Wal, with the vigour that reputedly belonged to Fascism, he might well have won Ethiopia with minimal international disturbance. Instead he went in for diplomacy with France and Britain, to try to get them to endorse his occupation of Ethiopia and, even, appealed to the League of Nations. This was because he still saw himself as an 'arbiter' in Europe, on good terms with all countries and able, in particular, to mediate between France and Germany. He also wanted to preserve Austrian independence against the quaint new Hitler in Germany. Mussolini came quite near to enlisting British and French Government support, both the French Prime Minister, Pierre Laval, and the British Foreign Minister, Samuel Hoare, being sympathetic, but in the end he failed. The reasons ranged across the spectrum from automatic liberal and Marxist resistance to anything fascist to orthodox imperialistic dislike of a new power establishing itself in Africa; also, supporters of the League of Nations, to which Ethiopia belonged, saw the matter as a test case of the League's authority. Churchill, however, in England carefully avoided expressing any view.

It was not until October 1935 that the Italian army crossed into Ethiopia and by then the dispute was part of world diplomacy. The League of Nations imposed economic sanctions on Italy and, given time, these might have worked; but the Ethiopian emperor lacked the forces to put up more than a token resistance and he was beaten in under six months. The speed of the war took Hitler as much by surprise as anyone else. One possibility that must have been in his mind was that the Italians would get so bogged down

248

in Ethiopia that they would cease to be a military factor in Europe and, in particular, unable to continue to back the independence of Austria. Although as a non-member, Hitler was not bound by the League of Nations sanctions, he cut down German trade with Italy on almost the same scale as if he had been. Musing aloud in private at this time, he wondered whether, after all, the British might be better allies for him than the Italians; the trouble was that the British were perfidious and liable to let one down. The rapid Italian victory changed perspectives. So far from being weakened by sanctions and an African involvement, Italy had emerged with military prestige. At the same time, however, she had found herself in conflict with most of the rest of the world and so needed an ally in Germany; the lines were beginning to be drawn of a cold war between the 'democracies' and the 'dictatorships'.

Hitler had scored an important little international success in the Saar plebiscite of January 1935. This was a rich German coalfield which, under the Versailles Treaty, had been placed under League of Nations control with France taking over the mines. The arrangement had been that after fifteen years the population could vote to become German again, to join France or to continue under the League. That the Saar was really German could not be doubted. Even the Communists, in the plebiscite campaign, used the slogan 'Germany but not Hitler' and the National Socialists executed another masterpiece of propaganda. The vote to rejoin Germany was 477,000 to 48,000 and this could only have boosted Hitler's self-confidence; he took the opportunity to reduce friction with France by announcing that although Germany now had the Saar back, she made no claim to Alsace-Lorraine. France, however, went on to conclude a mutual assistance pact with the Soviet Union which, although both sides were only half-hearted about it, gave Hitler some cause for alarm and, more significantly, an excuse for taking vigorous counter-action.

Under the Locarno Treaty of 1925, Germany, as part of a package deal which had got her into the League of Nations and guaranteed her against attack from France, had agreed to continue the Versailles system in keeping no army or defences in her territory on the west bank of the Rhine. The idea had been to form a buffer zone between herself and France. For Hitler to revoke Locarno and put his army into the Rhineland would be direct assertion of German independence and a challenge to France.

At least on paper, France in 1935 and 1936 was a far more formidable military power than Germany. Given will-power and reasonably competent leadership she could have destroyed in battle the new German army, which was outnumbered, ill-equipped and in near-chaos through rapid expansion. Hitler took the decision to occupy the Rhineland on his own intuition and with no seeking of advice from anyone. Mussolini's success in Ethopia may have had something to do with it. Hitler may have wanted to emulate Mussolini and have been encouraged by Mussolini's success in ignoring world opinion. The German generals, including Blomberg, the Defence Minister, were appalled at the military risks involved and, indeed, planned to retreat back behind the Rhine in the event of any French challenge. Hitler issued his secret orders to the generals on March 1st, 1936, and the occupation of the demilitarised zone began at dawn seven days later. Only token forces, at a strength of about three battalions, were used and according to his own later recollection, Hitler had only four brigades available altogether.

It was a gamble. Had the French indeed hit back and the Germans had retreated, it would have been a blow which would have imperilled Hitler's continuance in power. Certainly Germany would have had to have engaged in deeper rearmament before going in for any more expansionist moves: there would have been no hope of gaining anything by bluff. The French Cabinet was interested in intervening but their chief of staff, General Maurice Gamelin, apparently under the impression that 35,000 German troops were engaged, insisted that there would first have to be full-scale mobilisation. The French consulted the British who were inclined to let Hitler get away with it on the ground that he was only walking into his own back yard. The sheer propaganda effect of such events as the Nuremberg rallies, with thousands of disciplined men marching on parade and apparently full of aggressive enthusiasm, must have been some influence on Gamelin's caution. Like all Frenchmen, Gamelin dreaded a repetition of the 1914–18 disaster. Most Germans did, too, but in Hitler there seemed to be a miraculous leader who could get his way without fighting.

In after years, Hitler liked reflecting back on the Rhineland occupation and, with justification, reckoned that he had brought it off solely on his own skill at bluffing. 'What saved us', he reflected in 1942, 'was my unshakable obstinacy and my amazing aplomb.' It was the kind of risk, certainly, that few political leaders would have undertaken and the fact that it worked further strengthened Hitler's faith in his own destiny.

But Hitler was careful to follow it up with a new call for European peace. He abrogated the Locarno Treaty on the ground that the French had already broken it with their alliance with the Soviet Union but, on the day of the occupation, he summoned the

Reichstag to announce that: 'We have no territorial demands to make in Europe.' He called upon the deputies to take with him 'two sacred vows'. The first was that Germany would 'yield to no force' in the restoration of her 'honour'. The second was that Germany would seek understanding among the European peoples and would 'never break the peace'.

Hitler had embarked on a course during which in four years, with only minimal warfare, he was to make Germany temporarily the master of the bulk of central and western Europe.

14

In July 1936, four months after Hitler's garrisoning of the Rhineland, a civil war started in Spain: it was basically the army rising against the republican government. The two events were unconnected with each other but nevertheless they seemed to many outsiders at the time to form a pattern of 'fascist' expansion. The Spanish war, which lasted three years, helped to draw the battle lines for World War II. It was nothing to do with Hitler and he took little interest in it: Spain was not a country which had featured in his plans and musings.

The Spanish rebel leader, General Francisco Franco, had the support of the army, the Church and the quasi-fascist 'Falange' party in a rising against a 'popular front' government which had just been elected to power under the republican constitution. Mussolini eagerly supported Franco, seeing the war as a means of extending Italian power and influence. Hitler, however, disliked Franco's clericalism and regarded him as a 'reactionary'; he was to be preferred to the republicans merely as a barrier against Communism. A Communist Spain might lead to France going Communist also and so Germany would be confronted with a Communist power in the west as well as in the east. How seriously Hitler took this argument is difficult to assess. The matter was, in any event, peripheral to his main preoccupations. He sent some aid to Franco and here his motive was mainly to give the German forces, especially the air force, battle practice; Spain, to National Socialist Germany, was just a military laboratory. The strategic value of Spain as an ally, in the event of war between Germany and the Anglo-French, does not seem to have figured in Hitler's calculations. He was hoping to avoid such a war, if he could do so without modifying his major policies.

With Italy, and to some extent Germany, supporting Franco

and with the Soviet Union assisting the republicans, the civil war was not a private Spanish turmoil. Official British and French policy was to be neutral but the huge liberal and leftish forces in both countries were strongly pro-republican. Thousands volunteered to fight in the republican 'International Brigade'. They believed they were taking part in a world struggle of 'democracy' (which was often a code-word for socialism or communism) against international 'fascism'. Hitler could never quite understand this. He had no interest in spreading 'fascism' around the world. There was no 'fascist' equivalent of the communist 'Comintern' in Moscow which, despite Stalin's primarily nationalistic policies, did exist as an international body to propagate Marxist revolution. Hitler's aim was not to spread 'fascism' but to increase the power and territory of Germany. Any opposition to him which seemed to be based upon ideological rather than nationalist grounds he saw as a Marxist-Jewish conspiracy; or, perhaps, it had something to do with 'plutocrats', often 'Jewish', who resented Germany cutting herself off from normal international trade. The 'fascist' versus 'democratic' ideological struggle had little to do with the actual actions of world leaders except, conceivably, Roosevelt. But it had a powerful effect on ordinary public opinion outside Germany.

What immediately concerned Hitler at this time, having successfully established German 'equality' by garrisoning the Rhineland, was to bring about a union of Germany and Austria. This, naturally, had always been basic to his political thinking and, very possibly, it went back so far as his schooldays at Linz. The opening words of *My Struggle* are an affirmation of faith in German-Austrian unity. In 1919, on the dismantling of the Austro-Hungarian Empire, the German rump-Austria, under Social Democratic leadership, had wanted to join republican Germany. This had been vetoed by the allies for the sole reason that they wanted Germany to be as weak as possible. In 1931 Germany and Austria had wanted to establish a customs union but France had prevented this. There can be little doubt that at any time in the 1920s majority Austrian public opinion was in favour of union with Germany. After Hitler's advent to power, however, the two major Austrian parties, the Social Democrats and the Christian Socialists, struck it out of their official programmes.

Although Hitler's emotions were intimately affected by the matter, his approach was cautious and tentative. The overriding difficulty was that it had been basic Italian policy to maintain a weak, independent Austria. Precipitate German action could have led to war between Germany and Italy; Hitler wanted no such thing—his long-term aim was to have Italy as an ally.

In 1933 the Austrian Chancellor, Engelbert Dollfuss, a Christian Socialist, of peasant birth, inaugurated, in conditions of political and economic turmoil, a quasi-fascist system. He suppressed Parliament, ruled by decree and established his Fatherland Front as the only legal political party. Dollfuss, a tiny man of only four feet eleven inches tall and nicknamed 'Millimetternich', was an Austrian separatist and depended heavily upon Italian support. His regime was commonly described as 'black fascism' because of its clerical associations. Parallel with the growth of National Socialism in Germany there had developed a powerful Austrian National Socialist movement, which looked across the frontier to Hitler for ultimate leadership. In 1933 Dollfuss tried to bring the National Socialists into the Fatherland Front but negotiations broke down primarily because of Dollfuss's insistence upon an independent Austria. A complicating factor for Dollfuss was that he depended upon bourgeois and rural support but that his capital, the city of Vienna was Social Democratic. Nearly a third of the 6,500,000 Austrian population were Viennese. In February 1934, Vienna rose in revolt and Dollfuss suppressed it by force, shelling the working-class apartment blocks, which had been the pride of the Vienna Social Democrat municipality in the 1920s. Almost immediately he faced a further attack from a different direction. In July 1934, National Socialist fanatics, in an attempted coup, seized the chancellery building and assassinated him. The coup failed and Hitler was furious and embarrassed. It is unlikely that he had been consulted in any detail, if at all. But the new Austrian Chancellor, Kurt von Schuschnigg, another Christian Socialist, was an improvement for Hitler in that he was a definite German nationalist. Hitler sent Papen to Vienna as German ambassador with a brief to smooth out the scandal of the Dollfuss murder and to work towards intimate German-Austrian co-operation. In 1936 Germany and Austria signed a pact by which Germany recognised Austria's independence but Austria undertook to behave as a 'German state' in foreign policy. In contrast to this calm, Papen policy, there was an atmosphere of plotting within the National Socialists to bring about reunification by force— one plan was to assassinate Papen and use this as a pretext for Germany occupying Austria. Thus Hitler (and also Göring, who took a close interest in Austrian affairs) had alternative courses to choose from.

Hitler's planning kept changing. For example, in November 1937 he was declaring at a secret military conference that he intended to have a war in the period 1943–5 with a view to solving Germany's 'territorial problem', by which, he meant not his ultimate grand design for colonising the Soviet Union but the Versailles-derived problems of Austria and Czechoslovakia. (At this stage he was still in favour of friendship with Poland.) He would strike sooner if France got involved in a war, which would presumably be with Italy. He expected Italy to be acquiescent over a German occupation of Czechoslovakia but she might be troublesome over Austria. His thinking, at this conference, bore no relationship to what actually took place during the succeeding ten months. He was reacting to events as they arose.

A central factor in Hitler's basically aggressive planning was the attitude of Great Britain. France he regarded as being automatically hostile to any increase in German power but he did hope for an accommodation with the British.

He seemed to be particularly glad to meet British visitors, although he had only a few direct contacts at government level. He met Anthony Eden, the British minister for League of Nations affairs, in Berlin in February 1934. Eden, according to his memoirs, found Hitler 'much more than a demagogue' and that 'He knew what he was speaking about and, as the long interviews proceeded, showed himself completely master of his subject.' Hitler was quiet in manner and, at first sight, insignificant compared with the imposing figure of the Foreign Minister, Neurath. At a second meeting, a year later, Hitler impressed Eden less favourably and Eden summarised the atmosphere in his diary with the words: 'The old Prussian spirit very much in evidence.' The British Foreign Secretary, John Simon, also took part in this 1935 meeting. He noted that Hitler had 'the hands of a musician' and was alarmed at Hitler claiming, 'untruthfully', that the German air force had reached parity with Britain's. The same year Edward, Prince of Wales, (later Edward VIII and Duke of Windsor) visited Germany with a delegation from the British ex-servicemen's association, the aim being to build up friendly contact with German war veterans. Hitler was affable and Edward was impressed; in later years Hitler was to claim that there would not have been a war between Britain and Germany had Edward remained on the throne. (Edward had a further interview with Hitler in 1937.) But the Eden meeting of 1935 was the more significant; Eden definitely took against Hitler, and he represented what was to become the mainstream of British public opinion.

In September 1936, Hitler had what was psychologically his most interesting meeting of all. David Lloyd George, Prime Minister of Britain from 1916 to 1922, came to talk to him at the Berghof. Lloyd George, aged seventy-three, was past his prime and on the orthodox pattern of British party politics, as it had

255

developed, was remote from power. He still, however, possessed great energy and imagination and there was still some possibility, in special crisis conditions, of his again becoming a force. But it was for reasons of history and personality that Lloyd George and Hitler wanted to meet each other.

Lloyd George's supporters claimed for him that he was 'the man who won the war' and there is at least some truth in this. In 1914 Lloyd George had been undecided up to the last moment whether to support a war against Germany. He had considered going into retirement. But having plumped for war, he threw his whole energies into winning it. When he took over as Prime Minister at the end of 1916, there was a serious possibility of Britain being the loser, or at least of failing in her then objective of crushing Germany. Lloyd George's will-power, oratory and organising ability galvanised the British into a fresh effort; he could cut corners and he could be deceitful but he was like a dynamo in Downing Street. It was his considered view that the reason for German total collapse in 1918 was that there had been no figure in Berlin equivalent to himself. He reckoned that strong political leadership, capable of enthusing the German people, would have swung the balance; had such leadership brought the German armies back behind the Rhine and inspired the people with a sense of patriotism, then Germany would have been almost invulnerable and a compromise peace would have ensued. This line of reasoning, of course, was in line with Hitler's own. The starting point of his political career in 1919 had been his belief that the German soldiers had been let down by incompetent politicians. Hitler wanted to be the German Lloyd George and appears to have studied the British model quite closely. In speeches, Hitler on occasion used the words that he was 'a child of the people' and this, consciously or unconsciously, echoed a characteristic phrase of Lloyd George's.

On his side, Lloyd George in 1936 felt frustrated. His dynamism was unharnessed and power in Britain was in the hands of men he believed to be incompetent. In 1929 and 1935 he had put forward sweeping plans to reorganise the British economy to eradicate unemployment and had failed with both. Hitler's achievement in Germany in this field impressed him and had, in his view, proved what could be accomplished by intelligent political leadership.

Hitler and Lloyd George were fascinated with each other. Although in many respects their political outlooks were different (for example, Lloyd George supported the republican side in Spain), they had it in common that they were both imaginative men, capable of thinking unconventionally. Hitler could not keep

256

his eyes off Lloyd George and listened intently while Lloyd George was speaking as if he could understand the words before they had been translated. He presented Lloyd George with a signed photograph of himself, which Lloyd George said he would put on his desk next to pictures of Clemenceau and Foch. The two men exchanged several compliments. Hitler said the war had been won for the allies not by the soldiers but by 'one great statesman, and that was Mr. Lloyd George'. Lloyd George told Hitler that he was 'the greatest German of the age' and informed Hitler of a sentence in the final volume of his *War Memoirs*, which was published two months later: 'If in September, October and November 1918 Hitler had been Germany's Führer, a better peace would have been negotiated.' The meetings lasted for two days and the two men agreed that it ought not to be difficult to draw up a mutual security pact between Britain, France, Germany and Italy. The east was another question. Hitler claimed that Czechoslovakia had Soviet air bases on her territory, aimed at Germany. Lloyd George, who had taken a dislike to the Czechs at the 1919 peace conference, was non-committal. Hitler came passionately to life when the talk switched to motorways and explained to a fascinated Lloyd George how they were financed.

Summing up his impressions of Hitler in an article in the London *Daily Express* immediately after the meeting, Lloyd George termed him 'the George Washington of Germany'. In a private letter to a friend in December 1936, Lloyd George stated: 'I have never doubted the fundamental greatness of Herr Hitler as a man, even in moments of profound disagreement with his policy . . . I only wish we had a man of his supreme quality at the head of affairs in our country today . . . Mussolini is temperamentally an aggressor. I have never thought that Herr Hitler was and I do not believe it now.' In his comparison of Mussolini with Hitler, Lloyd George differed from his old friend and colleague Winston Churchill who also at the time was out of office, at odds with his party and apparently an elderly politician with no future. Churchill had some sympathy for Mussolini and had kept silent during the Ethiopian affair but advocated vigorous rearmament with a view to war with Hitler's Germany. Even Churchill, though, could write in a newspaper article in 1937 that he hoped that if Britain ever lost a war she would find a leader as great as Hitler.

The Hitler-Lloyd George meeting was one at which both men were truly interested in each other. When, however, six months later, Hitler met the British Socialist leader, George Lansbury, at Berlin, Hitler was probably less sincere. Lansbury was a pacifist and an internationalist—he had resigned the Labour Party leadership on these grounds in 1935—and so represented a political type Hitler had always detested. Lansbury was touring Europe on a 'peace' mission, to try to avert a new war. Hitler put on an act of being an innocent, naive person, under many pressures. Lansbury was enchanted and came to the view that Hitler would not go to war 'unless pushed into it by others'. To Lansbury, Hitler appeared to be 'distressed and lonely' and ripe to be converted to what Lansbury regarded as 'Christianity in its purest sense'. Lansbury's overriding aim, as he expressed it in a book, was to 'banish Hate and substitute Love' in international relations, an idea which would have tickled Hitler.

Lansbury and Hitler were remote from each other in outlook. Hitler was equally remote, but in a different way, from his next significant British visitor, Lord Halifax. An aristocrat and a churchman, Halifax had been Viceroy of India and was now, in November 1937, a cabinet minister with no departmental responsibilities. Officially he visited Germany to attend a hunting exhibition in Berlin but the real purpose of the trip was to sound out Hitler on behalf of the British government. The meeting started with what nearly became the social gaffe of the century. When Halifax arrived at the Berghof, he assumed that, according to protocol, Hitler, as a Head of State, would receive him inside the house. As Halifax climbed out of his car he saw a nondescript figure, in black trousers and brown jacket, holding out a hand. Halifax automatically assumed that this was a servant, come to take his hat. He removed his bowler and began to pass it towards the outstretched hand. Only a frantic whisper from his German escort: 'Der Führer! Der Führer!' prevented the hat reaching Hitler's hand and made Halifax realise that a welcoming handshake was being offered by the Leader of the German Reich.

Halifax, according to his notes of the time, felt a gulf of non-understanding between himself and Hitler.

It was not only the difference of outlook between a totalitarian and a democratic state. He gave me the impression of feeling that, whilst he had attained power only after a hard struggle with present-day realities, the British government was still living comfortably in a world of its own making, a make-believe land of strange, if respectable illusions.

The inner nub of the meeting was for Halifax to hint to Hitler that Germany might get her overseas colonies back, in return for behaving as 'a good European' and not being aggressive. This was something Hitler was prepared to talk about but not take too seriously; to him overseas colonies were only a luxury and Germany's future could not lie in them. Despite the lack of real contact, however, Halifax noted: 'I am sure Hitler was sincere when he said he did not want war.'

For all this kind of talk, the real diplomatic movement in Europe from 1935 to 1938 was a coming together of Germany and Italy. This had long been Hitler's aim and he had even postponed an Austrian settlement in order to achieve it. The initial Hitler-Mussolini meetings had not been happy. But Ethiopia and the Spanish war made Mussolini come to believe that Hitler's Germany was his only available ally. In September 1937, Mussolini toured Germany and was impressed by the apparent strength National Socialism had brought. He and Hitler were still not in harmony personally and up to 1939 British diplomacy was still working towards a by no means necessarily unattainable policy of separating them. But the Fascist and National Socialist systems had similarities with each other and both countries were expansive in outlook and felt a sense of grievance. Mussolini, in 1937, was the first to coin the phrase of a single 'axis' running through Berlin and Rome. During the Mussolini visit to Germany, Hitler put on a show of the two of them riding side by side in separate railway trains to symbolise that their paths were parallel. After this visit, Mussolini introduced the goose-step into the Italian army, and, more significantly, introduced a measure of anti-semitism which although mild by German standards, represented a reversal of his former policy. Mussolini had previously opposed anti-semitism and had been liberal in granting Italian visas to Jews who wished to go into exile from Germany.

By the start of 1938, therefore, Italy had become less of an obstacle to a solution of the Austrian question on lines suitable to Hitler. But Hitler still had no settled plan of how to act.

His opportunist approach was exemplified by the manner in which he took over the direct control of the armed forces at the start of 1938. As Head of State, Hitler was also commander-in-chief. But the practical control and administration of the forces was still in the hands of traditional authorities. By old custom, stretching back to the imperial days, the Minister of Defence was a general, not a politician. The army was supposed to be 'above' or 'outside' party politics. This was something of an inconsistency in a one-party state. Moreover the existence of the Defence Ministry meant that there was a rival centre of power; in case of conflict, many soldiers would have preferred orders coming through conventional Defence Ministry channels to orders direct from Hitler. In 1937 there was a rumour (almost certainly unfounded) among foreign newspaper correspondents in Germany that the army planned to surround the Reichstag while Hitler was addressing it, arrest him and the deputies and set up a military government. So long as the Defence Ministry existed, such ideas were bound to exist. Hitler's own predecessor as Chancellor, Schleicher, had come from the Defence Ministry.

Hitler's Defence Minister from the start had been General Werner von Blomberg, who was a pro-Nazi in that he regarded Hitler as the best available choice for leading Germany, but he was not a party member and had continued to ban political activity within the forces. Blomberg had been central in opposing Röhm in 1934 and, more or less as part of a bargain connected with the blood purge, had accepted Hitler becoming Head of State on Hindenburg's death. A Christian and a monarchist, Blomberg was impressed by the fact of Hitler's public popularity. He believed that the army must adjust itself to the reality of the 'national revolution'.

Constitutionally, Hitler could have dismissed Blomberg at any time but he waited until luck threw up a personal excuse for doing so. Blomberg, a widower, fell in love with his secretary, a woman much younger than himself, and decided to marry her. According to former convention she was socially not really fit to be a general's wife and he went around asking advice on the project. Göring definitely urged him to go ahead and Hitler also gave consent. It was a symptom of the 'classlessness' of National Socialism that a typist could marry the Minister of Defence. Hitler was a witness at the wedding on January 12th, 1938.

Then evidence came to light that Mrs. Blomberg had a police record as a prostitute. It has been suggested that Göring was aware of this when he had encouraged Blomberg to go ahead—it is the kind of thing Göring might have done. Hitler, however, had no prior knowledge. The fact came out, while the Blombergs were in Italy on honeymoon. An ordinary policeman, called Müller, came across the dossier in the files. He showed it to his superior who exclaimed, in horror, 'Good God, Müller, and this woman has kissed the Führer's hand!' For a presumably hard-bitten policeman to have reacted in such a way, is an indication of the sanctified status Hitler possessed.

Blomberg had to go but Hitler was puzzled and worried about what to do. Göring wanted the Defence Ministry for himself but, for one reason and another, Hitler did not warm to this. Possibly he feared that Göring had enough power already and might act too independently. The obvious alternative to Göring was Colonel General Baron Werner von Fritsch, commander-in-chief of the

260

army. Baron von Fritsch was a sensitive, intelligent man who hid his inner personality behind the mask of being a typical Prussian officer; he wore an actual monocle. He was a bachelor. As early as 1936 the Gestapo had been investigating him with a view to establishing that he was a practising homosexual. Even at first sight the evidence gathered was thin—it depended upon a single witness who claimed that Fritsch had committed a homosexual act with him at Potsdam Goods Station. Himmler had annotated the dossier with his green pencil and taken it to Hitler, who had replied with an instruction to burn 'this muck'.

The case remained, however, on the files and at about the same moment that the facts were uncovered about Mrs. Blomberg, Göring and/or Himmler told Hitler again about Fritsch's alleged homosexuality. This time Hitler summoned Fritsch and put the charge to him. Fritsch, on his word of honour, denied it. To his horror, Hitler did not automatically accept the word of honour but went on to confront Fritsch with the witness from the Potsdam Goods Station. The witness, who had served a prison sentence for an offence of homosexual blackmail, got some provable facts, including Fritsch's name, wrong; but he professed to identify him. Fritsch, dazed and shaken, demanded that he should be allowed to exonerate himself at a trial. This took place, with Fritsch acquitted, the following May but by then Hitler had made his new dispositions. Himmler, by one account, sat in a circle with senior S.S. officers, during the trial, with their fingers touching, to exert will-power to get the court to convict.

Hitler's solution was to abolish the Defence Ministry and to assume direct command himself of the armed forces. Once he had arrived at it, he was pleased with it and it seemed the most natural thing for him to do. But it had been the Blomberg scandal that had set the ball rolling, not Hitler's initiative. Under the new system the Defence Ministry organisation was replaced by a staff, the O.K.W. (Supreme Command of the Armed Forces—*Oberkommando der Wehrmacht*), working under and for Hitler. To be the O.K.W.'s chief of staff, Hitler brought in General Wilhelm Keitel, a hard-working staff officer, lacking in independence of outlook.

At the same time, in February 1938 and almost as part of the same operation, Hitler 'promoted' the Foreign Minister, Neurath, to be 'President of the Secret Cabinet Council'. There was no such body, except for a nameplate on a door, and Neurath was being put into salaried retirement. A professional diplomat of nationalist outlook, Neurath was becoming unsuitable for the kind of foreign policy Hitler had in mind and there had already been disagreements. In his place, Hitler appointed Ribbentrop, who had been making a great splash as ambassador in London.

It was while these changes were going on that the Austrian question began to boil up again. This was primarily due to the illegal Austrian National Socialist movement, largely financed from Germany, carrying out an anti-government reign of terror. The province of Styria was virtually in a state of civil war. The Austrian Chancellor, Schuschnigg, considered various schemes to buy off the campaign; one was to cede Hitler's birthplace, Braunau, to Germany. On February 11th, 1938, Schuschnigg set off for Berchtesgaden for a secret meeting with Hitler—he disguised it as a skiing trip and loaded himself with skiing paraphernalia. He joked that it was not he who ought to be seeing Hitler but Wagner-Jauregg, one of Vienna's leading psychiatrists. He certainly found Hitler in a maniac mood. Hitler raged to Schuschnigg that Austria had been failing to follow a 'German' foreign policy but was imprecise about details. 'The whole history of Austria,' he said, 'is just one uninterrupted act of high treason.' Schuschnigg asserted that Austria had made a full contribution to German culture and cited Beethoven. Hitler retorted that Beethoven had been a Rhinelander, to which Schuschnigg rejoined that Beethoven had chosen to live and work in Vienna. Back on the main point, Hitler said that Austria now had no friends. Italy would now support Germany. Britain was uninterested. France had missed her chance by not opposing the garrisoning of the Rhineland. He called in the uniformed Keitel to give an impression of military menace. Eventually Schuschnigg signed a document by which he promised to legalise the Austrian National Socialists and release such of their members as were in gaol, allow close collaboration between the German and Austrian armies and, above all, to agree to pro-Nazis joining his administration at the head of the interior, defence and finance ministries. The key appointment of these was to be of Artur Seyss-Inquart, a Vienna lawyer, to the Ministry of the Interior; a Catholic intellectual, friendly with Schuschnigg and not a National Socialist member, Seyss-Inquart saw himself as a middle-man who would reconcile the two sides. His aim was for Austria to be incorporated within the Reich but with a special status allowing internal self-government.

Back in Austria, Schuschnigg began to carry out the conditions he had signed but disorder from the Austrian National Socialists continued. He decided to assert continuing Austrian independence by a plebiscite putting to the Austrian people the question: 'Are you in favour of a free and German, an independent and social, a Christian and united Austria?' In its way it was quite a shrewd move; observers at the time reckoned that he would get a 70 per cent 'yes' vote. Schuschnigg made the most of Austrian nationalism; his speech announcing the plebiscite he made at Innsbruck wearing Tyrolean dress of loose grey jacket and green waistcoat and some of his sentences were in local, Tyrolean dialect. This speech was on March 9th and the plebiscite was to take place four days later, on March 13th.

Hitler felt he was being tricked and outwitted. The British ambassador in Berlin, Nevile Henderson, told Göring that Schuschnigg had 'acted with precipitate folly'. What was happening was that Schuschnigg was calling what he hoped was Hitler's bluff. Hitler either had to climb down, or proceed to extremer measures. He chose the latter and decided to occupy Austria to stop the plebiscite. It was Göring, who by his own account at Nuremberg, really forced the pace. He had had for some time a map on his study wall showing Austria as part of Germany and wanted to make it reality. (He had two sisters married to Austrians.) Göring faked a telegram from Seyss-Inquart which asked for German troops to 'restore order'. (Seyss-Inquart knew nothing about it until after it was published.) Schuschnigg, to try to stave off the occupation, cancelled the plebiscite. Then Göring, operating on the telephone from Berlin to Vienna, insisted that Schuschnigg should resign and Seyss-Inquart should become Chancellor. Schuschnigg tried to call Mussolini to ask for help but Mussolini did not come to the telephone. The Austrian President, Wilhelm Miklas, accepted Schuschnigg's resignation but refused to appoint Seyss-Inquart in his place. Meanwhile National Socialists were seizing control by informal coups in various localities. Seyss-Inquart, without the President's consent, formed a 'provisional government'.

On the morning of March 12th, German troops crossed the Austrian frontier, with bands playing in front of them. They met nil military resistance and on occasion were garlanded with flowers. Their mission, theoretically, was merely to 'restore order' at the request of the Austrian provisional government but doing so was no problem. It was as well for them that they did not have to fight. Their plans were only improvised and their tanks and vehicles kept breaking down; it was from this period the story dates that German tanks were fakes, constructed from cardboard.

Even at this late stage, Hitler was still not certain how the matter would end. He himself entered Austria in an open Mercedes at three fifty p.m. on March 12th, crossing at his birthplace, Braunau, where his father had been a customs officer. His status, as Göring put it at the time, was that of a 'tourist'. His welcome was that of

263

a conquering hero. Anti-Nazis stayed at home but many thousands poured on to the streets to cheer him. In one aspect, of course, he was a local boy who had made good. When the same evening he reached Linz, which he always regarded as his home town, there was a crowd estimated at 100,000 to greet him. Swastika banners hung from balconies and cars and taxis hooted in welcome. He visited his parents' grave. It was by instinct that Hitler had expected a good reception and once again his instinct had proved right; the occupation of Austria was one of the chain of events which, as time went on, more and more deepened Hitler's faith in his own intuition. But in the case of Austria there was more to it than that. Hitler was back again in the streets he had paced as an imaginative frustrated teenager and he was back as a great man. More or less on the spot he decided to beautify Linz and rebuild it on a grand scale, just as he had dreamed when young. Linz would become the twin of Vienna as a great German city on the Danube. Crowds, carrying flaming torches, serenaded him from outside his hotel. Germany's 'saviour' was to save Austria, too, and not only in a mystical sense; Hitler was the maker of the economic 'miracle', the man who had cured unemployment and economic depression. As he listened to the crowds, Hitler at last decided upon his final solution for Austria.

When, the same evening, Seyss-Inquart arrived at Linz to greet Hitler and to negotiate the detailed terms of association between Germany and Austria he eventually realised that there was nothing to discuss. Hitler had decided, at last, to incorporate Austria outright into his Reich, with no special status whatsoever. Indeed Austria was to cease altogether to exist as a separate unit and was split up to become two regions of Germany.

The next day, March 13th, Hitler went by road from Linz to Vienna. The 120-mile journey took six hours. This was only partly due to crowds, who cascaded him with flowers; another factor in delays was that the road was blocked by broken-down German army vehicles. As he approached Vienna, the Cardinal-primate, who had previously been anti-Nazi and had supported the Dollfuss-Schuschnigg line of an independent 'Christian-Social' Austria, ordered the church bells to ring and sent Hitler a message of greeting. In Vienna, to another huge welcome, Hitler announced the union *(Anschluss)* of Austria with Germany. Instead of the Schuschnigg plebiscite, the Austrians were confronted with a plebiscite on the question: 'Do you acknowledge Adolf Hitler as our Leader and the reunion of Austria with the German Reich which was effected on March 13th, 1938?' Even the Austrian Social Democrat leader, Karl Renner, although critical of Hitler's

264

methods, endorsed the appeal to vote 'yes'. The voting, which was apparently free and orderly, produced a stunning majority. Of an electorate of 4,484,000, 4,453,000 voted 'yes' and 12,000 'no'. There were 6,000 spoiled papers. The pro-Hitler majority was 99·73 per cent, the highest he ever achieved anywhere. The Hitler magic had worked even more strongly in his own Austria than his adopted Germany and the pan-Germanism of his youth had triumphed.

The absorption was quick and total. There were wholesale purges of civil servants. The Austrian general staff was dispersed. In the early weeks, apparently, there were 76,000 arrests of suspected opponents but most were soon released. The anti-Semites had a field day.

Vienna had the third largest Jewish community in Europe, after Warsaw and Budapest. There was no equivalent to it in Germany. It could trace its history back until at least the twelfth century and in terms of culture and achievement was probably the leading Jewish community in the world. Freud, Adler, Kafka, Mahler and Stefan Zweig were all Viennese Jews. There had been pogroms, from time to time, from the fifteenth century. In many aspects in 1938 the community—forming about ten per cent of the total population—was well integrated. But it had also been the birthplace of Zionism. The National Socialist take-over, not surprisingly, distinctly accelerated Viennese Zionism, thus contributing to conflicts which were still causing wars in the Middle East two and three decades later. Jews existed at all social levels in Vienna—about a third of them were manual workers—but it was the Jewish bourgeoisie of doctors, lawyers, traders and journalists which attracted the most attention. As Hitler must well have known from his experience in youth, it had long been a political factor that it was possible to whip up hatred among the non-Jewish lower middle class against the Jewish bourgeoisie. This had been so in Vienna on a scale that had not in the same period been so in Germany, until Hitler. Immediately on the German occupation in 1938, the Austrian National Socialists embarked upon crude and violent anti-Semitism on a scale which shocked some even of the German forces. Photographs of what happened, flashed around the world, gravely damaged German prestige and contributed to the climate of opinion that was to make World War II possible. The most widely-publicised atrocity was that of leading Jews, including the Chief Rabbi and the World War I veteran General Ernst Pick, being forced to scrub pro-Schuschnigg slogans off the streets of Vienna. Worse than this, were outright murders and beatings, plus arrests and committals to concentration camps. There was a wave of suicides in the Jewish community. Many lost their jobs and by September 1938 some 60,000 of the 190,000 Jews of Vienna were destitute. (Austrian Jewish communities outside Vienna also suffered but they were not of significant size.) Göring announced the extraordinary policy of making Vienna 'Jew-free' within four years; this, at the time, was taken to mean forced emigration. Possibly, but not certainly, Göring really intended expulsion rather than murder—but it was not a distinction that would particularly have interested him.

Hitler, by feeling his way gradually, had achieved a lifetime's ambition in incorporating Austria into his Reich. He had ceased to be a kind of foreigner in the country of which he was Leader. He had fulfilled an historic ambition of German nationalism. He could rebuild Linz, but there was a debit side which he gave no indication of recognising. Internationally the union of Austria and Germany was fully recognised; within three weeks of it, for example, the British withdrew their ambassador from Vienna and replaced him with a consul. However the methods Hitler had used in bringing about the unification, plus the anti-semitic excesses which followed it, aroused international distrust. It was directly consequent to the unification that the British first started to take rearmament seriously and to contemplate war. This was not just British dislike of a strong Germany, although that came into it, but also a revulsion against Hitler personally. Even the United States was affected; the Americans did not embark upon general rearmament but Roosevelt did inaugurate a strengthening of the navy.

15

Hitler seems to have had some premonition that he would die relatively young. He certainly believed that it would be a disaster for Germany if his death came before his designs were well on their way. He saw himself not just as the head of a particular generation but as a miraculous, or near-miraculous, turning-point which would affect German and world history for centuries ahead. He believed that he possessed not only political and propagandist gifts but that he was also capable of being a great general. War and strategy was a subject on which he apparently had read widely and he certainly displayed a detailed technical knowledge of and interest in weapons. With his cult of youth, he did not want to wait until he was an old man before waging war. He wanted war while he was still at his best. In 1938 and 1939 he was remarking quite frequently, in private, that he would prefer to have war now that he was only fifty, rather than wait ten years until he was sixty. The fact that Germany was not prepared for a major conflict did not deter him. His genius would make up for that and, he correctly assessed, potential opponents were even less prepared. By war, he meant swift, victorious campaigns and not a prolonged global struggle.

His long-term war aim, so far as he had one, was to create a great Germanic empire by colonising European Russia, the Ukraine and the Crimea. He genuinely believed Communism to be a disruptive and weakening force (the mass purges conducted by Stalin in 1934–9 must have been confirmatory evidence for him of this) and thought the Soviet Union must fall to pieces of its own accord; that, presumably, would have been his opportunity to seize territory. In the short run, the dynamics of his policy required him to solve the problems of the German minorities in Czechoslovakia and Poland. Particularly following the triumphant union

267

of Austria with Germany, nationalist feelings among these minorities rose to fever heat. While it had always been fundamental for Hitler to support and encourage such tendencies, he was far from fully in control of them. At times, and particularly in the case of the Polish-Germans, it was they and not he who dictated the pace. Because of his background, of course, Hitler was particularly interested in the Germans in Czechoslovakia; he was quick to believe every atrocity story about them.

It was only at the very last moment, after his entry into the country, that Hitler had decided to absorb Austria into the Reich and, similarly, he had no detailed, advance plans for how to deal with Czechoslovakia and Poland. He was an opportunist with them, but an opportunist prepared to fight.

Into this came a new force in the person of the British Prime Minister, Neville Chamberlain, who took office in May 1937. Chamberlain, a vigorous, autocratic man, wanted to avoid both war and German domination of Europe. In reputation he had long been overshadowed by his father, the imperialist Joseph Chamberlain, who among other things had shown anti-semitic inclinations, and his elder brother Austen Chamberlain who had negotiated the Locarno Treaty from the British side. (The ideologist H. S. Chamberlain was not a relation.) Neville Chamberlain, like Hitler, distrusted the workings of traditional diplomacy and believed in personal intervention by heads of government. He was somewhat like Hitler, also, in that he was capable of taking snap decisions without full consideration of the consequences. His approach was that of a businessman and he wanted to sort out Europe before it drifted into chaos. Chamberlain's method was a policy called, at the time, appeasement, and this meant satisfying reasonable German demands but resisting, to the point of war, demands that were unacceptable. There had been some British rearmament under Chamberlain's predecessor, Stanley Baldwin, but Chamberlain increased the programme. Chamberlain was not concerned, particularly, with the ideological side of National Socialism; or, at least, he considered it no greater an evil than Communism. Among his immediate entourage was a definitely anti-semetic element.* But Chamberlain did have a certain admiration for the Czechoslovak political system, which was run on bourgeois parliamentary lines and was akin to his own. It was of some influence with him that Czechoslovakia counted as a 'democracy', like Britain, the United States and France, as opposed to a 'dictatorship' like Germany, Italy or the Soviet Union. The

* During an interview in August, 1968, with the present author, Sir Horace Wilson, chief civil service adviser to Chamberlain 1937–40, said he could understand Hitler's feelings on the Jews and put the question: 'Have you ever met a Jew you liked?'

interaction of Hitler and Chamberlain was to be decisive in settling the form of the opening stages of World War II.

Following the incorporation of Austria into Germany in the spring of 1938, Czechoslovakia obviously faced difficulties. Until twenty years earlier, her whole territory had been part of the Austro-Hungarian Empire. The Czech heartland of Bohemia, although it had a natural defensive frontier of mountains, was now surrounded on three sides by Germany. On the Czech side of the mountains lived a long-established and rebellious German population, the Sudeten Germans. The state was based upon Czech nationalism but the actual Czechs provided only six million of the total fourteen million population. Their Slovak partners, totalling some three million, were less than fully enthusiastic about the state. The German minority numbered three million; there were also a Hungarian minority of 750,000 and a Polish one of 75,000 and both Hungary and Poland had territorial claims against Czechoslovakia. At the Versailles conference of 1919 there had been some idea that this new country, of mixed nationalities, should be run on the Swiss model as a loose federation of cantons. In fact, the brilliant Czech nationalists Thomas Masaryk and Edward Benes had made it a unitary state. Also, instead of following a Swiss neutralistic policy, they had based their external relations upon an alliance with France. Benes, who in 1935 had become President of Czechoslovakia, was a cultivated, vigorous intellectual; he was five years older than Hitler and felt nothing but scorn for him on the personal level.

The grievances of the German minority in Czechoslovakia were real. They had the democratic right to send deputies to Parliament in Prague but, like the Irish in the British Parliaments of the nineteenth century, were always in a minority. While the Czech-Germans were not outrightly persecuted, as were the Jews in Hitler's Germany, they suffered disabilities centring mainly on their language. Czech was the official language of the state and this meant that people who could speak only German were excluded from most state employment. It was common in otherwise German areas for the police to be Czech. Then, like every other industrial country, Czechoslovakia had suffered in the world depression; the German unemployed inevitably looked over the frontier to where Hitler had solved this problem.

Benes judged that Czechoslovakia should react vigorously to the situation created by the union of Germany and Austria. He must allow no impression to the outside world that his country was in a shaky condition and, as events were to show, liable to fly to pieces. He had an apparently efficient and well-equipped army. He had an alliance with France and he wanted to put up a show of firmness which would encourage the British, too, to support him. Benes believed that it was in Czechoslovakia that Hitler's expansionist ambitions could be stopped. On May 20th, 1938, he showed his teeth by mobilising his army, on the pretext that the Germans were on the point of invading Czechoslovakia. There was at that moment no such German intention, and Benes must have known it; his move was intended to attract the sympathy of France and Britain. The Soviet Union was scarcely a factor in Benes' calculations; she had no common frontier with either Czechoslovakia or Germany and Benes had some feeling that if Soviet troops ever did arrive in his country they might be a long time leaving.

The Czech mobilisation seemed to Hitler to be insolent provocation. He had always despised the Czechs and now they were daring to try to match Germany militarily. He would spit out the word 'Czech' as if it were an obscenity. Hitler's rages were sometimes simulated but over the Czechs in the summer of 1938 his anger does seem to have been real and extreme. Immediately after the Czech mobilisation he ordered plans to be drawn up for a real German invasion of Czechoslovakia, to take place by October 1st, and he set about making a series of hate speeches. The German Press and radio supported him with stories about Czech atrocities against Germans. There was, following the martial law proclamation, some rioting and disorder in the Sudeten areas and the Czechs did act with vigour, and some cases brutality, in suppressing them; to hear Hitler talk they were engaging in near-genocide. At times, Hitler seemed to go over the border of insanity in his attitudes to the Czechs. His generals were doubtful about the enterprise. Czechoslovakia on her own, with her army and mountain defences, looked like a tricky proposition and Germany was certainly did not seem to be equipped to take on Britain, France and, conceivably, the Soviet Union at the same time. One group of generals, centreing on the army chief of staff, General Ludwig Beck, planned to overthrow Hitler in the event of his actually starting war with Czechoslovakia. They debated among themselves what to do with him after they had seized power: to shoot Hitler out of hand might make him a martyr, to put him on trial would give him the opportunity to use his histrionic ability to defend himself. They settled for putting him in a mental hospital.

Undoubtedly, Hitler, following his intuition, believed he could beat Czechoslovakia and intended to make war. He was not bluffing. He believed that the Sudeten Germans urgently needed rescuing from intolerable conditions. France, despite her treaty obligations, was hesitant about supporting Czechoslovakia unless

Britain came in too. The British, partly from the habit acquired in 1914–18 and partly from a generalised distaste for aggression and dislike of an over-strong Germany, were disposed to fight but Chamberlain wanted to have a good try at keeping the peace. He sent a British delegation to Czechoslovakia to study the position in the Sudeten areas. On September 15th he followed this up by flying, at virtually nil notice, to meet Hitler personally at the Berghof. It took him seven hours in the air to reach Munich and then a further three hours by train to Berchtesgaden. He and Hitler plunged straight into negotiations and rapidly arrived at the key point that Hitler did not want to take over all Czechoslovakia but wanted only the Sudeten German areas, which were now in a condition verging on civil war, to be incorporated into the Reich. Chamberlain, who felt at this stage that Hitler was 'a man who could be relied on', seized this as a suitable compromise solution. Hitler was fond, at this time, of spitting out 'I do not want Czechs' and so the war scare ought to have been over. Chamberlain went home the next day expecting there to be an orderly procedure, which would take several months, of further consultations with the French, the Czechs and the Germans, the holding of plebiscites in the affected areas, drawing up new frontiers and so on.

But Hitler went straight on planning his armed invasion of Czechoslovakia. Perhaps he did not trust Chamberlain to keep his word. More probably, he wanted to win his first military victory and so prove himself a better general than the cautious professionals. He was full of nervous tension and some thought him on the edge of a breakdown.* He screamed such things as: 'The Germans (in Czechoslovakia) are being treated like niggers.'

A week after the Berchtesgaden meeting, Chamberlain flew to meet Hitler at Bad Godesberg, on the Rhine near Bonn. Chamberlain brought with him a plan which he expected Hitler to find acceptable. It had been drawn up in consultation with the French and the Czechs and envisaged the Sudeten areas being handed to Germany without even plebiscites; instead a commission consisting of a German, a Czech and a neutral member would draw up the boundaries. Czechoslovakia would thereafter become neutral, like Switzerland, with all powers guaranteeing her independence. The process would take about three months. It is evidence of Hitler's mental state at the time that he rejected this out of hand. Nothing less than the cessation by October 1st, nine days later, of areas which he pointed out on a map would prevent him going to war. October 1st was the date he had already fixed

* But he did not chew carpets. The idea that he did so came from the German term 'Teppichfresser' which in literal translation means 'carpet eater' but is really an idiom describing someone who paces a room excitedly.

for the invasion in his military planning. His only comfort for Chamberlain was that, after he had got the Sudeten areas, he would have 'no further territorial demands in Europe'.

War now seemed almost inevitable. Even by night, under blazing arc lights, work was pressed ahead on building a German defence system against France, the Siegfried Line. While the Siegfried Line was partly only a propaganda exercise, Hitler took a close technical interest in it, ordering modifications based on his own experience as a front line infantryman; it was necessary to assure the German public that the equivalent existed of the French Maginot Line. But German public opinion, so far as it could be expressed at all, was opposed to war. Neville Chamberlain drew significant applause in the streets. A parade of tanks in Berlin attracted only glum looks. Göring, although willing to defer to Hitler's judgment, thought that war would be a desperately risky enterprise; when Ribbentrop talked of the air force bombing London, Göring remarked sardonically that he would be happy to fly over London himself, providing that Ribbentrop were sitting beside him. The generals were opposed to war. The naval commander-in-chief, Erich Raeder, made a special visit to Hitler to advise him that the fleet was in no condition to take on Britain. In London, Chamberlain announced that the situation was 'fantastic'; with his businessman's mentality he could not believe that Hitler would really in the end reject a deal which in principle gave him all he wanted. But on September 26th, in a speech at Berlin, Hitler seemed to go right over the edge. He lashed himself into near-hysteria on the platform with abuse of Benes and the Czechs; he announced that he would get the Sudetenland by October 1st, five days later.

It was Mussolini and Chamberlain who between them saved the peace. There had been an attempt at mediation by Roosevelt but this could be brushed aside because he stated that in any event the United States would not intervene in a war. Mussolini had the edge in that Hitler was relying upon the Italians to pin down the French army. On September 28th Mussolini offered to 'mediate' on the Sudeten issue, pointing out that the differences on it were now 'very small'. He proposed a four-power conference of Germany, Britain, France and Italy. Hitler, who by this time was already showing some slight tendency to retreat from his war-at-any-price attitude, agreed to postpone his mobilisation for twenty-four hours, his first significant concession. He invited the other three powers to a conference at Munich on September 29th. Chamberlain received an ovation in the British House of Commons when he announced this.

The Munich conference phased the German occupation of the

Sudeten areas from October 1st to October 10th. The Czech representatives were not even allowed to attend the discussions—Hitler said he wanted no Czechs in his presence—but were merely told the result after agreement had been reached. Whereas Mussolini had been the key man in getting the conference called, it was Chamberlain who took the lead in agreeing to the German demands. The day after the agreement, Chamberlain called unexpectedly on Hitler in his private Prince Regent Square apartment in Munich. He sat on a sofa of which, Eva Braun afterwards amusedly recalled, she had affectionate memories. Chamberlain pulled out a piece of paper, in his own handwriting, which stated that 'consultation' would in the future be the method of settling differences between Germany and Britain and referred to 'the desire of our two countries never to go to war with one another again.' Hitler, on the spot, agreed to sign it.

On the face of it, Hitler had achieved an enormous triumph. With no loss of life, and still less without the risk of embarking upon a war which Germany might well have lost, he had united nearly three million Germans with the Reich. He showed some surface pleasure over this and toured the Sudeten areas, to an ecstatic reception, as soon as they were occupied. Filled with pastoral zeal, he asked to visit the hospitals where the victims of Czech brutality were being treated and was put out to learn that there were not any. It is evidence for his unusual mentality, however, that deeper down he felt that he had somehow been 'tricked' by Chamberlain at Munich. He harked back to the subject during what remained of his life and never with satisfaction. But the only 'trickery' really involved was that the French, and more particularly the British, did not regard the Munich settlement as being part of their normal behaviour, to be repeated as necessary. It was the limit of their tolerance of Hitler's pushful behaviour and of German expansion. Chamberlain pushed ahead with rearmament.

In Prague, Benes resigned office and with his departure Czech nationalist ambitions collapsed. The ceded areas included almost all the Czech mountain fortifications and so she ceased to be a viable country in terms of military defence. She also lost much of her industry and natural resources. The example of the Czech-Germans asserting their nationality was inspiring to the Slovaks and the other minorities. Within six months, without any particular prompting from Hitler, Czechoslovakia fell to pieces. The Slovaks declared their own separate republic, under German patronage, the Poles and the Hungarians moved in to claim the bits containing their nationals and Hitler got the Czech authorities to agree to a

German 'protectorate' over Czech Bohemia. All this followed inevitably from the Munich settlement but to the British, and notably Chamberlain, it seemed like a deliberate breach of treaty. So far from having 'no further territorial demands', Hitler had now taken over most of Czechoslovakia; moreover he was not merely incorporating Germans into the Reich but was taking over a non-German nationality. Where would he stop? Chamberlain introduced conscription into Britain, for the first time ever in peace, and began, almost at random, to distribute British 'guarantees' in eastern Europe. The first went to Rumania, on a groundless scare that Germany was about to attack her and seize her oilfield, and the next on March 31st, 1939, was to Poland.

Hitler had no emotional animus against Poland, as he had against the Czechs. His concern was to find a swift, compromise solution to frontier and minority problems. There was Upper Silesia, where ethnically the towns were German and the country-side Polish. Despite a plebiscite in which by an overwhelming majority the population voted to continue as part of Germany, the allies in 1921 had partitioned Upper Silesia and awarded a third of it, including most of its coal mines, to Poland. There was the 'corridor', which provided Poland with access to the sea at the price of cutting off East Prussia from the rest of Germany. At the head of the 'corridor' was the German-inhabited city of Danzig which was under League of Nations control and in which militant National Socialists had won the popular vote. The Danzig Nazis, inflamed by the example of the Sudetenland, vociferously demanded union with Germany and they were not a force Hitler could turn on and off like a tap.

Real problems existed and at the start of 1939 Hitler was far from wholly unreasonable about them. Friendship with Poland had long been a mainstay of his diplomacy. He hoped to do a deal. He offered to be satisfied with rail and motorway communications, under German sovereignty, through the 'corridor'. The obvious corollary would be that Poland would drift towards becoming Germany's subordinate ally, with a view to an eventual attack on the Soviet Union. It was only by way of Poland that Germany could get at the Soviet Union at all. But the Poles, whose national anthem included the words 'We have a lesson from Bonaparte, how to conquer all', refused concessions. Over-estimating their strengths, and the potency of Anglo-French support, they saw themselves as an independent great power; they went so far as to participate in the final dismemberment of Czechoslovakia.

Hitler struck menacing attitudes. In March 1939 he denounced his non-aggression pact with Poland. The following month he sent a peremptory ultimatum to Lithuania demanding the return of the German-populated coastal strip of Memel to Germany; the Lithuanians (who had for years been quarrelling with Poland) yielded. At about the same time Mussolini took over Albania; he used little force and really gained control by the simple expedient of paying the Albanian civil service their overdue salaries. But, again, it seemed in the west, and particularly in Britain, as if the 'dictators' were expanding everywhere and ought to be stopped. There was a definitely ideological feeling, which Hitler did not understand, that 'fascism' was a kind of infection with similar supra-national effects to those of 'communism'. Hitler might have got somewhere with the Poles by long, patient negotiation but his building up an air of crisis only made them the more intransigent, especially after their guarantee from Britain. They were not the kind of people to yield to threats and Hitler, disappointed that he had not been able to test his military genius in Czechoslovakia, was willing to turn threats into reality. In May 1939 he gave orders to his military staff to prepare an attack on Poland.

To Chamberlain, Hitler, by his occupation of Czechoslovakia, had lost all credibility. Chamberlain, supported by the bulk of British public opinion, was now prepared to fight to try to prevent Germany expanding any further and to force a change of German government. It was in many ways an unrealistic attitude, based upon emotion rather than upon strict calculation, and Hitler was at a loss to understand it; he fantasised that Britain must be under 'Jewish' control. France had no enthusiasm for war at all but had to go along with Britain, or else risk isolation. The only power capable of directly assisting Poland against Hitler was the Soviet Union and, with a touch of realism, Chamberlain did open negotiations in Moscow. He was, however, lukewarm about it and sent only a low-level delegation; Chamberlain, a firm anti-Communist, would have preferred Germany and the Soviet Union to be neutralising each other rather than ally himself with the Soviet Union to destroy Germany.

It was in this context that Hitler pulled off his greatest stroke in diplomacy, his pact of August 1939 with the Soviet Union. Formally National Socialist German and the Soviet Union were irreconcilable ideological enemies. To Hitler, Communism was a force of decay that had been introduced into the world by the Jews; from the very start of his public career in Munich, one of his basic propositions had been that the Soviet leaders were enemies of mankind. On the Soviet side, 'fascism' was regarded as the last-ditch stand of 'capitalism' before the inevitable world revolution. In practice, however, despite the continuing Marxist

275

dialectic on the international nature of the 'class struggle' and the 'fascist enemy', Joseph Stalin, the Soviet dictator, was thinking primarily in terms of Russian national interests. On his side, Hitler was prepared to make any bargain with anyone if it advanced his immediate interests; it could always be altered later, as necessary, for he did not regard treaties as binding.

The idea of the pact seems to have sprung from Hitler's intuition and to have been in his mind for some time. The earliest definite clue is that in a Reichstag speech in January 1939, he omitted his customary denunciation of Communism. While he regarded the Soviet system with contempt, Hitler did have a respect for Stalin, regarding him as an astute realist; he scented that a deal might be possible. Stalin, on his side, wanted above all to avoid war. He thought that eventually there would be world-wide revolution but the immediate task ought to be to build up the strength of the Soviet Union. He had territorial aspirations, both with a view to strengthening Soviet defences and to rectifying frontier grievances. Poland's eastern frontier with the Soviet Union was as disputable as her western one with Germany. In July Hitler sent Ribbentrop to Moscow. The very fact that he had sent his Foreign Minister whereas the British had sent only officials was evidence of his serious intentions. Stalin drove a hard bargain. Publicly, all that was concluded was a non-aggression pact but there were also secret clauses defining German and Soviet 'spheres of interest'. Under this the Soviet Union got Finland, half Poland and the Baltic states of Estonia and Latvia. Hitler besides being given a free hand in the rest of central Europe, including half of Poland, also got the Baltic state of Lithuania, which he hoped to make into an ally.

Hitler was plainly overjoyed by the conclusion of the pact. To be sure, he was going back on a lifetime's advocacy of anti-Communism but there could only be public relief in Germany in that he seemed to have avoided the danger of war with substantial powers on two fronts. The 1914 situation, in which Russian armies had poured into Prussia while the main German forces were tied up in the west, could not now recur. Moreover an alliance with the Soviet Union had been one of the doctrines of old-style German nationalism, back in the 1920s; Hitler had always opposed it but now, especially in the eyes of nationalist-minded army officers who remembered their days of friendship and collaboration with the Red Army in the Weimar period, he seemed to be coming around to common sense.

To the rest of the world the pact came as an enormous surprise. It was a possibility that had simply not been taken into account.

276

But, on the British, at least, it had little coercive effect. Hitler and Stalin seemed as bad as each other and at least it clarified things to have them in the same camp. Strict military realities came very little into Anglo-French planning at the political level.

In preparing war against Poland, Hitler faced little opposition from the generals; there was some plotting to remove him from power but on nothing like the scale of that which had taken place during the Sudeten crisis of the previous year. At Munich, Hitler had seemed to demonstrate that the British and French were paper tigers. Moreover, to Prussian officers the merits of the German case against Poland seemed to be stronger than that against Czechoslovakia. The most active force in trying to keep the peace was Göring, who had no objection in principle to tackling Poland but did not relish the idea of war in the west.

Any possibility, however, of another Munich-type settlement was ruled out by the fundamental attitudes of Hitler and Chamberlain. Hitler was intent on proving himself with a 'lightning war' and victory against Poland. He was not interested in bloodless compromise. By the summer of 1939 he was thinking almost entirely in military terms and scarcely went through even the motions of negotiation; he did not even present a coherent list of demands. He wanted to be in a position simply to dictate. He hoped that Britain and France would not intervene but intended to press on regardless. His propaganda machine thundered out, for home consumption, tales of Polish atrocities against Germans. Chamberlain, on his side, was determined to fight for Poland and had definite backing from British public opinion. While the mass British public (like, for that matter, the mass German and French publics) had no zest for war for its own sake and knew almost nothing about Poland, it regarded a renewal of war with Germany as almost an inevitability; Chamberlain would probably have lost office if he had weakened. Göring tried desperately to patch up a peace in the west through a Swedish emissary but given Hitler's and Chamberlain's basic attitudes it was hopeless. The only thing that made Hitler waver at all was Mussolini's announcement, almost at the last moment, that he would not come in on Germany's side.

Hitler used straightforward fraud and murder as a pretext for starting his war with Poland. A group of concentration camp prisoners were dressed in Polish uniforms and shot; their bodies were placed just inside the German frontier as if they had been a raiding party. On September 1st, 1939, the German army, supported by the air force, moved into Poland. Unlike in 1914 there were no cheering crowds in the German streets. The British and French sent Hitler ultimata to withdraw. When these expired on September

3rd, World War II had started. There were no cheering crowds in London or Paris, either.

There was little the British could do to assist Poland. They had no mass army capable of being a force on the European mainland. They did have bombers which could reach Germany and these were used to drop explanatory leaflets. Their major weapon, at the time, was the Royal Navy which was capable of cutting off virtually the whole of Germany's overseas trade. The British strategy, so far as it existed at all, was to avoid a repetition of the bloodshed of 1914–18 and to use the navy to conduct 'economic warfare'. But Germany, unlike in 1914–18, had supplies from the east.

The French did have the capacity to assist Poland. For purposes of his 'lightning warfare' in Poland Hitler had taken the risk of denuding his western front to a point at which there could have been no serious resistance to a French offensive. The whole of the German armour was reserved to Poland and only twenty-three properly-equipped divisions were left in the west, plus a further eleven reserve divisions which were under-equipped and under-trained. The French, on mobilisation, put eighty-five divisions into the field. They did advance fifteen miles into Germany, in the Saarland, and met no resistance at all beyond light skirmishing. But as Hitler had expected (and on this the calculations of the general staff supported him) they made no serious attack. There were various reasons for French hesitancy. Why should they be expected to do all the fighting? No British forces arrived in France until September 26th, and then only two divisions. The gibe that the British would fight to the last drop of French blood was a potent one in German propaganda. Then there was the deep French fear of a repetition of 1914–18, which seemed to have proved that offensive warfare resulted in vast casualties for no gain of ground. They trusted in their own Maginot Line and regarded the Siegfried Line as being equally invulnerable. The kind of war for which they had planned had been to hold the Maginot Line against German attack and they had made no provision for vigorous, swift offensive action like that of the Germans in Poland. They had declared war on Germany with no real intention of prosecuting it.

The British and the French had counted on the Poles holding out for six months or more. But the Poles, who were supposed to have the best cavalry in Europe, collapsed completely before a swift German pincer movement, based on the concentrated use of tanks and harassment from the air. Within a week German armour had reached Warsaw and the Polish defences were fragmented. Within a fortnight the Polish government itself had left the country and taken refuge in Rumania. On September 17th the Russians moved in to claim their part of the country. Eastern Poland was annexed outright to the Soviet Union, after plebiscites, as Western Ukraine and Western Byelorussia. There followed mass deportations to labour camps of 'class enemies'. In western Poland, Hitler annexed Polish Silesia, the 'corridor' and Danzig back to Germany and set up the remainder as a 'governor-generalship'. He agreed to transfer Lithuania to Stalin's 'sphere of interest'.

There had been some idea, from the Soviet side, of forming an independent, rump Polish state with a view to facilitating peace negotiations with Britain and France. Mussolini also advocated this. Hitler, however, wanted to use Poland for colonisation by German farmers; he had no further interest in the Poles as allies. Nor was Hitler at this stage particularly interested in peace in the west, although he did make perfunctory noises about it. Immediately after his Polish victory, he began planning an offensive against France with a view to knocking her and Britain out of the war. So long as they remained undefeated, he could not hope to get on with his basic strategy of winning more territory in the east. A merely patched-up peace, with Britain and France free to meddle again in his schemes whenever they felt like it, would be no use. Moreover a patched-up peace was not really attainable at all, as Sumner Welles, American Under-Secretary of State, found when he visited Berlin, Paris and London that summer. The British, at least, would have wanted some restoration of Czechoslovakia, as well as of Poland, and would have been doubtful of negotiating with Germany at all, so long as Hitler remained dictator.

In the Soviet Union, Joseph Stalin had no prevision that in only twenty months' time he would be at war with Germany. Nevertheless he did want to strengthen his defensive position and get back territories that had belonged to Tsarist Russia. He forced the three Baltic states of Estonia, Latvia and Lithuania to accept Russian garrisons and in the north he moved against Finland, demanding territory to strengthen the defences of Leningrad. The Finns resisted and Stalin attacked them. It turned out to be no 'lightning war' like Hitler's onslaught on Poland. The Finns resisted strongly before, after three months' fighting, they yielded to overwhelming superior force. Their plight attracted much sympathy abroad, especially in Britain, and early in 1940 there was a point at which the British nearly intervened on the Finnish side. Hitler, too, privately sympathised with the Finns, but considered it tactically best to keep strictly to his agreement that Finland was in the Soviet 'sphere of influence'. The poor performance of the Red Army, in the early weeks of the war, must have impressed

279

him; interestingly, though, the standard of Soviet generalship and tactics rose as the war continued. Another effect of the Soviet-Finnish war was to make Hitler jumpy about Stalin's apparently aggressive attitude. Suppose the Soviet Union attacked Germany while she was bogged down in the west? Stalin, so far as can be ascertained, had no such intention and was thinking only defensively; but it was natural for Hitler to impute to others what would have been his own reactions in their situation. While colonisation in Russia had always been Hitler's long-term aim, he also, almost paradoxically, feared a Soviet onslaught on Germany. At one moment, in his thinking, the Russians were an 'inferior' race and at the next they were a menace. Undoubtedly by the end of 1939 the germs existed in his mind of what would simultaneously be a 'preventive war' against Russian 'aggression' and also an opportunity for Germany to acquire Russian territory. While the 'preventive war' doctrine was essential for propaganda purposes, it was not entirely phoney, or, at least, Hitler himself, as often, was taken in by his own propaganda. As early as October 1939 he was instructing his generals not to rely upon more than a year of Soviet neutrality.

Hitler planned his offensive in the west, attacking France through Belgium, the Netherlands and Luxembourg. It was scheduled to start on November 12th, 1939. For both political and military reasons, the generals, including Walther von Brauchitsch, commander-in-chief of the army, opposed it. Politically, the violation of neutral states would make it the harder for Germany ever to negotiate a compromise peace. Militarily, it seemed to be a gamble; Germany might be defeated with enormous casualties. Under pressure from his staff, Hitler postponed the offensive and continued to do so almost week by week in the winter of 1939–40. Incidentals such as the weather and a set of German plans falling accidentally into Belgian and allied hands had something to do with it. Also Hitler was still, on military matters, to some extent open to advice; it was not until the victories of the summer of 1940 that he proved to himself for certain that he was a military genius. Above all, there was his sheer intuition; he would not take the offensive until he was in an emotional mood to do so.

Assassination is rarely an effective political weapon; it tends to whip up sympathy for the victim and so to strengthen the system for which he stands. Hitler, however, was a special case. The future of Germany and of Europe depended upon his emotional state and to have removed him would have meant sharp changes of policy. His designated successor, within the National Socialist system, was Göring who, although personally greedy and capable of brutality, had gifts of normal, high intelligence and common sense. It is not to make Göring a saint to assert that he was sceptical about the war; unlike Hitler he did not see himself as a miraculous turning point in history but only as a soldier-statesman. Some measure of reason and logic would have come with Göring into the conduct of German policy; it is difficult to suppose him gambling on war with the Soviet Union and the United States. While he was anti-semitic, he lacked the type of fanaticism on the subject that could lead to systematic mass murder. Of course the National Socialist system might have collapsed altogether with the disappearance of Hitler, with incalculable consequences beyond the fact that the first successor-regime could only have been a military one.

It would, therefore, have been reasonable Anglo-French planning, as a war tactic, to have tried to rub Hitler out. There was no individual on their own side whose elimination would have counted for so much. And on November 8th, 1939, Hitler very nearly was killed. The assassin, Georg Elser, was a carpenter who had, but only briefly, been a member of a Communist organisation. He was not quite such an oddball as van der Lubbe of the Reichstag fire but ostensibly acted on his own; he certainly had no connection with the main 'underground' resistance to Hitler.

Elser chose the occasion of Hitler's annual speech at the Löwenbräu (formerly Bürgerbräu) beer cellar, Munich, in commemoration of the 1923 attempted coup. He spent weeks in preparation. He took a job in a quarry which brought him into contact with explosives, of which he stole some. He also acquired, somehow, a grenade and took explosive from that. Inside the huge beer cellar he got at the wood panelling which sheathed one of the main supporting pillars for the roof, calculating correctly that an explosion in this pillar would literally bring the roof down. He planted his bomb inside the panelling and timed it to go off towards the end of Hitler's speech, or, as was Hitler's custom on these occasions, when he was chatting to old comrades after the speech was over. Such notabilities as Goebbels, Himmler, Ribbentrop and Rosenberg were also likely to be caught in the explosion. To have made and planted the bomb so skilfully and without detection suggests that Elser could well have had some outside assistance.

It was fog that saved Hitler. He flew down from Berlin to Munich for the meeting and had intended to fly back. But, almost at the last moment, he decided to return by scheduled train rather than risk his flight being delayed by the fog that was around. This entailed him leaving the meeting earlier than would otherwise have been the case and was his custom. Hitler arrived at eight p.m., spoke for an hour to an audience of 3,000, and left the hall at about ten past nine, to catch his train. Ten minutes after his departure the bomb, controlled by a time-clock, went off; the heavy ceiling collapsed, killing eight 'old fighters' and injuring more than sixty. Elser tried to get to Switzerland but was arrested the same evening at the border, where he was found to be carrying a picture postcard of the cellar, sketches of grenades and fuses and a Communist badge. He was locked up in Dachau as a 'special' prisoner, where he remained until in April 1945, when it was announced that he had been killed in an air raid. In fact he was murdered on instructions from Himmler, who specifically said that he was passing on an order from Hitler.

Immediately after the explosion and Elser's arrest, it was announced that it had all been the work of 'British agents'. But the difficulty, presumably, was to get enough proof to put Elser on trial; it would have been a good show-piece if such proof had been available. In fact the episode was so fishy that it has been much suggested that someone in the German administration, or even Hitler himself, planned it for merely propaganda reasons. It was desired to get a public wave of sympathy for Hitler. An embellishment of this is that Hitler wanted to get some of his 'old fighters' out of the way. It was certainly odd that Elser had such simple, incriminating evidence on him when he was arrested. It is even suggested that Elser admitted to fellow-prisoners in Dachau that he had been employed by the government for the plot. The weakness of this reasoning is that it would seem to be an extravagant and dangerous method of boosting Hitler's popularity. Better ways of doing so could easily have been contrived. Moreover Hitler himself, if he were in the plot, is unlikely to have chanced being present within ten minutes of the explosion of what by all accounts was an amateur time bomb. If it was 'old fighters' he wanted to bump off, he had ample other resources for doing so. The better explanation, but for which there is so far no evidence, must be that Elser really was mixed up with foreign intelligence and that he was held alive so long in Dachau because he was believed to possess valuable information.

At any rate, Hitler had been saved by fate, or luck from the Munich bomb. (Interestingly, he spoke little about it afterwards in his table conversation, as recorded.) He went on planning his offensive in the west. He settled German 'colonists' in Poland. Stalin prepared his next move against the Baltic countries. The French sat behind the Maginot Line and the British planned to win the war painlessly by economic means, although due to undisrupted German trade with the Soviet Union and Eastern Europe the British blockade was less effective than it had been in World War I. The big opportunity for the British seemed to be the iron ore which came from northern Sweden and was indispensible for the German economy. In the winter months when the Baltic was frozen this ore had to come out through the Norwegian port of Narvik and go by sea down the Norwegian coast to Germany. The British had at the time practically no army, by continental standards, but they had the world's strongest navy and one that was far superior to Germany's. Seize Narvik, the British navy minister, Winston Churchill, reasoned and the iron ore could be cut off and the war won. Churchill got the war cabinet to approve the plan, which involved blatant violation of Norwegian neutrality; British forces landing in Norway were to be instructed to try to be friendly and to fire only if first fired upon. The justifying argument was that Hitler was so evil that it was in the Norwegian's interests, as much as anyone elses, to defeat him. The British laid mines in Norwegian territorial waters, attacked a German prisoner-of-war ship in a Norwegian harbour and violated Norwegian neutrality by sending arms to Finland across her soil.

Hitler toyed with the idea of a political solution. Vidkun Quisling, leader of a fascist-style party in Norway, visited Berlin in 1939 and offered to launch an uprising against the government if he received German assistance. The new Norway, under Quisling's leadership, would become a German satellite. This is the type of thing that appealed to Stalin (he had attempted to set up a puppet government even in Finland) but Hitler was wary about it. With the possible exception of Slovakia, he was not in the habit of allowing power to nominally independent puppets. He decided upon a direct occupation of Norway, taking in Denmark on the way. Erich Raeder, the naval commander-in-chief, was well aware of the likelihood of the British getting in first and kept pressing for action. Apart from the purely preventive action of keeping the British out, the operation had the advantage of providing Germany with naval bases for use against Britain. (Of course the Netherlands and northern France were not yet occupied and so bases in Norway seemed to be really significant.)

Hitler was not involved in the detailed planning of the operation which, since it was carried out against superior naval opposition, was a brilliant success. Denmark, of course, was easy and she was occupied in a day. Her king and government protested but lacked any means to resist; under German occupation, the Danish civil administration continued to function, within limits, and the country even had a general election, the only one which ever happened in a country under Hitler's control. In Norway the king and government did resist and enlisted British support. But fighting continued for under three weeks. It was sheer vigour and efficiency in the Germans that counted. In the higher command there was relatively little co-ordination—the joke was that Germany had the Prussian army, the imperial navy and the Nazi air force—but at the middle and lower command there was excellent collaboration and improvisation.

The collapse in Norway forced a change of government in Britain. Chamberlain, ill and disappointed, lacked qualities of war leadership and had been unwise enough to announce a few days before the Norway invasion that Hitler had 'missed the bus'. He was replaced by an all-party coalition government under Churchill, but in which Lloyd George declined to serve. In his own way, Churchill was nearly as much a romantic as Hitler. He was a believer in the British world-empire and willing to take strategic risks in order to try to preserve it. (He did, though, possess a realism which enabled him to reverse his philosophy of a lifetime and pledge post-war independence for India.) Hitler regarded Churchill as a senile drunkard. 'I have never met', remarked Hitler privately in 1942, 'an Englishman who didn't speak of Churchill with disapproval. Never one who didn't say he was off his head.' As a basis for assessing his enemy's capabilities, such a judgment by Hitler was wholly inadequate. Churchill had oratory as good as Hitler's own and in war leadership he used it far more than Hitler did. He was at once pushful and cautious, single-minded about being on the winning side against Germany and, like Hitler himself, wholly opposed in this matter to consider surrender or even compromise. He was on excellent personal terms with Roosevelt in the United States. Traditional British nationalists joined with liberals and the left to form a near-unamimous public opinion in favour of fighting National Socialist Germany to the end. (Fascists and Communists, who both opposed the war, were insignificant in numbers.) The fervour was partly ideological. Bernard Shaw, a life-long opponent of wars, in a broadcast he wrote in June 1940, and was banned from delivering, stated:

I have no patience with the journalists and the tub thumpers who are breaking our spirits by snivelling about our being the victims of a foul and treacherous aggression. We are the challengers and the champion fighters for humanity . . . Nine tenths of what Mr. Hitler says is true . . . We must sift out the tenth point for which we are fighting and nail the enemy to that.

Shaw identified this 'tenth point' as Hitler's anti-Semitism, racial ideas and police methods. 'We ought to have declared war on Germany the moment Mr. Hitler's police stole Einstein's violin.' Although he was not, in fact, allowed to say this on the air, Shaw's pro-war fervour was indicative of the widespread support Churchill received in his own country. With Churchill in power, Hitler no longer had any option at all of a compromise peace. More plainly than ever, Hitler had either to conquer or go under.

On May 10th, 1940, the day Churchill became head of the British government, Hitler launched his offensive in the west. He had no numerical superiority in men or equipment and for this reason alone it was a gamble. Moreover the tactics Hitler selected for the attack was risky. In 1914, under the Schlieffen Plan, Germany had struck at France in an encircling movement through Belgium; it had almost come off and it seemed the obvious tactic to try it again. (There was no Maginot Line on the France-Belgium frontier.) Hitler, however, took up a plan conceived by the relatively junior General Erich von Manstein. It was that there should only be a feint attack across Belgium, designed to get the Anglo-French forces rushing northwards to repel it. Then, when the enemy was off balance dealing with the feint, the true German attack would come in the centre, in the Ardennes forest, and would press vigorously forward to split the allied forces. If it came off, Germany would win with most of the French army never having been engaged in battle. Failure would enable the enemy to strike across Belgium to the Ruhr; moreover by orthodox doctrine, the panzer divisions, on which the attack hinged, would be gravely hindered by having to operate in a forest.

Overriding any particular planning, the Germans were superior in speed and ruthlessness. Also they used their tanks in concentrated mass formations, whereas the French had theirs uselessly strung out along the whole line. (Hitler supported the concentrated use of tanks but it was not particularly his idea; it was part of the doctrine of the German general staff, worked out from the lessons of 1914–18.) Hitler added the Netherlands to his invasion list primarily because Göring wanted airfields there for use against Britain. Luxembourg was also on it because of her geographical position. Hitler dispensed with any preliminary ultimata and attacked Belgium, the Netherlands and Luxembourg at dawn on May 10th. It was a straightforward assertion of power, with no humbug about it. The conquest of the Netherlands took only five days and was a largely airborne operation, with extensive use of the novel weapon of parachute troops. The German reputation for terror was reinforced by the bombing of Rotterdam while surrender negotiations were already in train, with 980 people killed. The Dutch at the time claimed that 30,000 were killed and this made the Germans appear the more formidable. In fact the attack was largely an error caused by the general atmosphere of breathless speed and ruthlessness, plus confusion in signals.

On May 14th the main German armour, supported by dive bombers, took the enemy wholly by surprise by striking into France through the Ardennes. Within twenty-four hours there was a thirty miles wide breakthrough and the French army in the area had ceased to exist as an effective fighting force. Hitler screwed himself into extreme tension, on occasion screaming and raging at his staff; he was taking his biggest military gamble so far. But in five days his armour reached the English Channel and then he relaxed and began planning a peace treaty, which was to be Versailles in reverse. On May 26th, the British began evacuating their forces from Dunkirk, taking many French with them. On May 28th Belgium surrendered. On June 10th Mussolini declared war on France and Britain and attacked, ineffectively in the Riviera. Mussolini was worried about this and remarked privately, immediately after declaring war, that the conflict would last at least five years and that Hitler led only towards 'ruin'. His motive can only have been to claim a voice in the peace conference, and he had no backing in popular Italian sentiment for his action. On June 14th the Germans occupied Paris. On June 16th, Marshal Henri Pétain, the World War I hero of Verdun, took office as Prime Minister of France, and on June 17th Pétain asked for an armistice and this was signed on June 22nd in the forest at Compiègne, the same place where the armistice of 1918 had been concluded and in the same railway carriage. The symbolism of this was Hitler's own idea. He himself, with Göring, Hess and Ribbentrop, was present, but the actual negotiations and signatures were left to the generals.

In six weeks of fighting, Hitler had reversed the verdict of 1914–18. He was the dominant power in western Europe, with Denmark, Norway, the Netherlands, Belgium, Luxembourg and, under the armistice terms, northern France, including Paris, under his occupation. (He also had annexed Alsace-Lorraine outright.) He luxuriated little in his conquests. He made a fleeting visit to Paris, principally to see the opera house, which he already obviously knew intimately from pictures; he also stood some minutes in silence at the tomb of Napoleon I. Then, after a victory parade in Berlin, he retired to Berchtesgaden and began to dream of his next step. The victories so far had been only a preliminary proof that he was a turning point, such as came only once in a thousand years, in German and European history; his real work was still to come and that was to be the conquest for Germany of European Russia and the Ukraine. He had been seven and a half years in power and he seemed to have proved himself a military as well as a political genius.

16

The logic of Hitler's 'lightning war' doctrine would have dictated an immediate assault on Britain after the surrender of France, and the army and navy staffs did indeed automatically begin planning such an operation. Although the British had got the bulk of their trained men away at Dunkirk, they were in disarray and short of equipment. They had only one armoured brigade that was fully equipped. The experienced and victorious German panzer divisions would have had little difficulty in smashing major British land resistance if they had come to grips when the British were still militarily off balance. The British themselves expected invasion and, under the stimulus of Churchill's oratory, prepared to put up what fight they could. It was part patriotic fervour, part ideological distaste for National Socialism and part a widespread popular feeling that they were victims of aggression. Churchill, active and offensive-minded, had major units of the French fleet destroyed at Oran and ordered a token air raid, by night, on Berlin.

For both military and intuitive reasons, however, Hitler was none too interested in attempting to occupy Britain. Certainly by August 1940, and probably for two months before hand, his mind was concentrated far more on the grand project for colonising Russia. This, rather than another victory in the west, was to be his great contribution to history.

There had been no long-term German planning at all for an invasion of Britain and the fact that they were occupying the northern French coast was a surprise to them. The naval commander-in-chief, Raeder, first broached to Hitler the possibility of an attack over the Channel as early as May 21st, 1940, but Hitler showed little interest. Nevertheless the operation was a possibility that had to be considered and naval planning, and, in June, army planning went ahead. The central problem was superior

British sea power and the subsidiary one was that the British possessed an efficient air force. Whatever the German superiority on land, there was the gravest risk of their assault being repelled before it got ashore. Hitler, who was willing to take staggering risks when his intuition told him to, was never more than luke-warm about the enterprise. He tended to over-estimate rather than underestimate the significance of sea power. Although he took an interest in warship design and, by his own account, had done so since he was a teenager, he was timid about his capacity as a naval strategist. He rarely even saw the sea and had never done so at all until he was aged around forty. 'On land I am a hero. At sea I am a coward,' he once remarked to Raeder. He personally controlled the movements of the German battleships and cruisers, always with a view to caution. He would only occupy Britain if the operation were risk-free and such a situation did not exist.

There were also political considerations. Hitler had always hankered for an alliance with the British; he believed the British Empire to be a lasting and stabilising force in the world. To destroy British power at its centre might have incalculable consequences. He thought the British ought to be satisfied with their world-empire and, after their defeat in France and Belgium, ought to be content to stop meddling with his plans for the European mainland. On July 19th, in a speech before the Reichstag, he made a definite peace offer. He spoke moderately and thought-fully. He gibed at Churchill as an 'unscrupulous politician' who had no regard for the real interests of the British people; rather than be sensible and make peace, Churchill was exposing his people to 'great suffering'. Churchill was even proposing to continue the war from Canada in the event of German occupation of the British Isles, thus abandoning his people. 'Mr. Churchill ought perhaps, for once, to believe me when I prophesy that a great empire will be destroyed—an empire which it was never my intention to destroy or even harm.' He went on:

In this hour I feel it to be my duty before my own conscience to appeal once more to reason and common sense in Great Britain as much as elsewhere. I consider myself in a position to make this appeal since I am not the vanquished begging favours, but the victor speaking in the name of reason. I can see no reason why this war must go on.

Hitler named no specific terms but they could only have been British acceptance of his dominance on the European mainland. The British immediately, and almost certainly to Hitler's surprise, rejected the offer out of hand. It seems scarcely even to have been discussed in the British cabinet. Hitler, desultorily, turned again to his invasion plans but by September abandoned them. He decided to rely on air attack and submarine warfare to wear the British down. Which side started indiscriminate terror bombing by night is a subject capable of dispute but certainly, in the winter of 1940–1, Hitler was the first to employ it on a substantial scale. The results, in terms of military advantage, were meagre but undoubtedly the bombings stimulated the British towards their own mass, terror bombing of Germany in 1943–5. For submarine warfare, Germany was not yet fully equipped. At the start of the war, in September 1939, Hitler had possessed only twenty-two ocean-going submarines and in March 1940 he had actually reduced the construction programme from thirty to twenty-five a month. It was not until 1942 that the Germans were able to eliminate defects in their torpedo detonators and depth regulators, and by then Anglo-American shipbuilding capacity had greatly increased. The German navy, in the autumn of 1940, wanted a full-blown Mediterranean strategy against Britain, including the capture of Gibraltar and the elimination of British power in the Middle East. Hitler, however, was none too interested and failed to put real pressure on Spain. The Italians, in this area, had no grand strategy at all. They were unprepared for anything save a quick conflict and their East African empire, including their recently-acquired Ethiopia, stood in grave danger in a prolonged war due to communications problems.

The British mobilised their war effort on a scale never before attempted by a major industrial country. They conscripted their women. They built up and equipped their army and air force. While it was unlikely that Churchill, with no allies, would ever have attempted a direct confrontation on land in western Europe, the British were a continuing threat to Hitler's supremacy. Also they had generous material support from the United States; in the 'lend-lease' programme, from March 1941 onwards, this came virtually as a free gift. Roosevelt made no pretence of a neutral attitude and announced that his country was 'the arsenal of democracy'. In the event of the United States actually entering the war, Britain was the readily-available base for its armies. Hitler's deputy for party affairs, Hess, although not involved in major policy decisions, went so far as to fly, solo, to Britain in the hope of negotiating peace. The mission was eccentric and futile and Hess was merely held prisoner.

Hitler in formulating his major plans behaved almost as if this formidable enemy to the west of him did not exist. He could not understand why the British were fighting, felt that they ought to be taught a lesson but was unwilling to concentrate on them. From the summer of 1940 onwards his dominant idea was to get on with the conquest of European Russia and the Ukraine. Until his acquisition of Poland, this was never more than a distant dream. But now he had a common frontier with the Soviet Union, a battle-trained army and a reputation as a military genius. The existence of Britain could not be allowed to stand in the way of this crowning enterprise. 'Since I struggled through to this great decision, I again feel spiritually free,' he wrote to Mussolini. At the same time, however, he needed, for propaganda reasons, to make it seem that Germany would be acting defensively. Thus no preparations in depth were made for the attack and in the winter of 1940–1 the German economy returned to a semi-peacetime basis, which was a complete contrast to what was happening in Britain and an odd posture from which to tackle an enterprise which had defeated even Napoleon. Hitler nailed his entire hopes on another 'lightning war' which would destroy the Red Army within five or six months.

Stalin's pushful foreign policy gave some cloak of reality to the idea that Germany needed to fight a preventive war against him. In August 1940, he forcibly incorporated the Baltic states of Estonia, Latvia and Lithuania into the Soviet Union and forced, Rumania, under threat of war, to cede Bessarabia and Bukhovina. The latter aggression brought the Red Army to the edge of the Rumanian oilfield, which was essential for the German economy. At the same time, though, Stalin did genuinely attempt to avoid war with Germany, or, at least, to postpone it until 1942 when he considered that the Red Army would be ready for it. His thinking, unlike Hitler's, was primarily defensive.

Factors, which in Hitler's view were irrelevant to the main issue, kept coming in the way. In October 1940, for no clear reason and without consulting Hitler, Mussolini attacked Greece, which resisted strongly and successfully. Two months later the Italian army in North Africa was attacked by the British in a brilliant offensive which took the whole Italian province of Cyrenaica. Hitler, to his irritation, had to come in to help Mussolini. German fighter squadrons were based in Sicily and, in February 1941, Erwin Rommel arrived with German forces in North Africa. His generalship was temporarily to reverse the balance in North Africa and take him to the edge of British-occupied Egypt.

For allies in his attack on the Soviet Union, Hitler automatically had Finland and Rumania, who both had old scores to settle. Then there were Hungary, Slovakia and, of course, Italy. To complete the system it was necessary to bring in Bulgaria and Yugoslavia, or at least to neutralise them, and to finish off Greece. (With air bases in either Yugoslavia or Greece the British could have attacked the Rumanian oilfield, which was vital for Germany, and harassed the flank of the German drive against the Soviet Union). Bulgaria signed up with little trouble—Hitler got on well with the debonair King Boris. The Yugoslavs were more obdurate. They wanted the Greek port of Salonika as their price for neutrality and a guarantee against Italian or Hungarian attack. They sounded out Stalin, in the hope of obtaining his support, but received no response. Hitler was irritated; he regarded Yugoslavia as a weak, artificial state—and there certainly were strains between the Croats, the Serbs and the Slovenes—and thought it was overplaying its strength. Eventually, on March 25th, 1941, Yugoslavia signed a non-aggression pact with Germany, with a secret promise of the cession of Salonika after the war. Two days later there was a *coup d'état* in the capital, Belgrade. The circumstances of it are still not entirely clear. It seems to have been led by a group of air force officers. Hitler himself thought it had been inspired by Moscow. The new Yugoslav government did not denounce the non-aggression pact but crowds paraded in Belgrade to shout pro-British and pro-American slogans.

Hitler lost all patience. He was about to attack Greece, in Mussolini's support, and he decided to break up Yugoslavia at the same time. Significantly, the first air raid on Belgrade was named 'Operation Punishment'. Diplomacy had failed and Hitler, who was in a rage, fell back on force. The efficient German formations swept rapidly through Greece and Yugoslavia. Greece was placed under military occupation, but with Italy annexing the Ionian Islands and Bulgaria a frontier area in the north. Yugoslavia lost territory to Germany, Italy, Hungary and Bulgaria and was reorganised as the 'Kingdom of Croatia' (under an Italian duke who never visited it) and an 'independent' state of Serbia, both under German tutelage. Himmler recruited widely for the S.S. in Croatia and Serbia, seeking men of 'Germanic' stock; in many cases they could not even speak the German language.

Because of this Balkan attack, the campaign against the Soviet Union, which had been scheduled to start on May 15th, 1941, was postponed until June 22nd. This six weeks' delay was to prove, quite possibly, decisive and it had been the result of Hitler getting into a rage over the Yugoslavs.

The onslaught on the Soviet Union achieved complete tactical surprise. Over a front of 1,500 miles, and in three movements aimed at Leningrad, Moscow and the Ukraine, the German army raced in, supported by overwhelming air strength. The highest scores which have ever been made by fighter pilots were by Germans on the eastern front in 1941–5 but, in the opening stages, the bulk of the Soviet air force was destroyed on the ground. As late as nine hours after it started, Stalin seemed not really to believe what was happening and thought of negotiations which might get the attack called off. The training of the Red Army had been offensive rather than defensive. The overrunning of forward positions resulted in the capture of tens of thousands of prisoners to whom, Hitler decreed, the ordinary conventions of war should not apply; he ordered the execution out of hand of the 'political commissars', who were uniformed officers with primarily political and doctrinaire functions.

In many areas the German troops were greeted as liberators. Church bells rang to greet them. There were cases even of German tanks being festooned with flowers. The Communist revolution was only twenty-four years old and many opponents of it still survived in Estonia, Latvia, Lithuania and what had been eastern Poland it was a yet newer phenomenon. By the end of 1941, some 800,000 former members of the Red Army were serving with the German forces, some of them (notably Latvians and Estonians) in an actual combatant role. Peasants who disliked the collective farm system hoped to get their land back. Bishops hoped to restore 'Holy Russia'. In ordinary Russian homes appeared on the walls pictures of 'Hitler the Liberator'. This kind of thing, however, happened primarily in the rural areas and had little influence among industrial workers, save where there were special nationalist aspirations, as in the Ukraine.

Rosenberg, who since the early National Socialist days in Munich had been continually overtaken by other personalities, emerged into apparent prominence as Minister for the Eastern Territories. For all the dotty side to him, Rosenberg did know a lot about Russia and believed that the idea that Germany was 'liberating' the Russians should be pursued. He wanted a policy of conciliation, with the Germans recognising some legitimate Russian aspirations. But the real power in the occupied territories went not to him but to Himmler's S.S. organisation which followed closely behind the victorious armies and carried out a policy of undiluted harshness. According to Himmler's ideas, Russians were 'sub-human' and should be treated accordingly. Rosenberg, who even at his best was ineffective at executive action, stood no chance at all because it was the Himmler-type policy that Hitler himself supported. 'Our guiding principle,' he remarked of the Russians, 'must be that these people have but one justification for existence— to be of use to us economically.'

During the early weeks of the war, Hitler kept exulting away in private about his plans.

We'll take the southern part of the Ukraine, especially the Crimea, and make it an exclusive German colony. There'll be no harm in pushing out the population that's there now. The German colonist will be the soldier-peasant, and for that I'll take professional soldiers, whatever their line may have been previously. In this way we shall dispose, moreover, of a body of courageous N.C.O.s whenever we need them.

. . . What India was for England, the territories of Russia will be for us. If only I could make the German people understand what this territory means for the future . . .

The German colonist ought to live on handsome, spacious farms. The German services will be lodged in marvellous buildings, the governors in palaces. Beneath the shelter of the administrative services, we shall gradually organise all that is indispensable to the maintenance of a certain standard of living. Around the city, to a depth of thirty or forty kilometres, we shall have a belt of handsome villages connected by the best roads. What exists beyond that will be another world, in which we mean to let the Russians live.

. . . The Germans—this is essential—will have to constitute amongst themselves a closed society, like a fortress. The least of our stable-lads must be superior to any native.

. . . I shall no longer be here to see all that, but in twenty years the Ukraine will already be a home for twenty million inhabitants as well as the natives. In 300 years, the country will be one of the loveliest gardens in the world.

. . . We'll supply the Ukrainians with scarves, glass beads and everything that colonial peoples like.

. . . I don't see why a German who eats a piece of bread should torment himself with the idea that the soil which produces this bread has been won by the sword. When we eat wheat from Canada, we don't think about the despoiled Indians.

In designing this apartheid-type system in his private musings before the war was even won, Hitler stressed transport. He dreamed of enormous double-decker trains, on rails of ten-metre gauge, rushing across the steppes to link the new territories with the German homeland. Even more important, in his view, were motorways along which German families could bowl down to the Crimea in their Volkswagens for summer holidays. The motorways should be built on ridges so they would be swept by winds to clear them from snow. A motorway, he mused, was less 'impersonal' than a railroad. But, of course, only Germans would enjoy such facilities in the east. While capable on occasion, of remarking that it was 'to our interest' to allow the conquered peoples 'to live decently', Hitler was opposed to allowing them to be educated. They ought, perhaps, to be literate enough to read German orders but really the radio sufficed to give them necessary instructions. 'The sense of duty, as we understand it, is not known amongst the Russians. Why should we try to inculcate this notion among them?'

The Russian winter came early in 1941, in November, and halted the German advance before the primary objectives of Moscow and Leningrad had been attained. An earlier start to the campaign—the May 15th start rather than the June 22nd one—might have made all the difference. It is also debatable whether, in strict military terms, Hitler ought to have attacked in three directions at once, instead of concentrating on Moscow, which was a vital communications centre as well as a symbol. Hitler possibly underestimated the importance of Moscow but he was far from ignoring it. 'Moscow', he remarked in July 1941, 'as the centre of the [Marxist] doctrine, must disappear from the earth's surface, as soon as its riches have been brought to shelter.' At any rate, the German advance slowed and stopped with the onset of snow and ice. Hitler was fond of claiming that his experiences as a soldier in World War I had made him peculiarly sensitive to the needs of the ordinary fighting man but in his private conversation he showed no appreciation of the plight of his men who were stuck in a Russian winter without proper clothing or equipment for it. His orders, consistently, were that they were to hold ground at all costs. Dogmatically, almost hysterically, Hitler refused to countenance tactical retreat and this, in the particular conditions of 1940–1, was probably the most effective policy. But only someone of Hitler's will-power could carry it out. His fighting troops, sometimes literally freezing to death, held firm until the thaw enabled them to renew the offensive. In this situation Hitler behaved as if the war were already won and there was actually a degree of German demobilisation in the autumn of 1941.

It was while his forces were frozen down before Moscow and Leningrad that Hitler decided to declare war on the United States of America.

Public opinion, quite often misinformed, was a factor in the shaping of American policy in a way that it was in no other country. The prevailing view, from 1919 onwards, had been that of isolationism; the United States should avoid involvement in the affairs of Europe. Isolationism had been rather less meaningful in the Far East, where from 1937 onwards the Americans had been actively supporting China against Japan. The clash between Japanese and American interests in the Far East was such that it had to lead either to a compromise settlement or drift into war. Roosevelt, who was elected President in 1932 and re-elected in 1936 and 1940, developed gradually into an internationalist and a definitive opponent of National Socialist Germany. But in taking positive action he was hampered by public opinion and the isolationist-minded Congress. In 1937 Congress passed the Neutrality Act which made it illegal for any countries engaged in war to purchase arms in the United States; any other goods supplied to belligerent countries must be paid for in ready cash. This, obviously, hit primarily at Britain and France; the United States could never be a source for German war supplies if only because of the British navy. In May 1939, Roosevelt attempted to get the Act amended to the extent of allowing arms to be supplied to belligerents on a cash basis and it was a serious failure for him that the Congress refused. He himself believed that the refusal actually stimulated Hitler to proceed with an aggressive policy but there is no evidence of this from the German side.

On the start of the war in September 1939, Roosevelt proclaimed United States neutrality but made no attempt to disguise his hostility to Germany. 'I cannot', he said, 'ask that every American will remain neutral in thought.' He began evading the Neutrality Act by sending small shipments to the British and French by way of Siam and Honduras. In November the Congress passed the necessary amendment to the Act to make arms sales legal, although still on a cash basis. Roosevelt also got a conference of American states to agree to a 300-mile wide 'neutral zone' in the Atlantic off the coast of the northern and southern American continents, with the exception of Canada. This ought to have been a help for the British but in fact they refused to recognise it and it became a dead letter.

In June 1940 the appreciation of the United States chiefs of staff, backed by that of Joseph Kennedy, United States ambassador in London, was that the British would fail to hold out against the Germans and that aid for her would be a waste. It was more or less the personal decision of Roosevelt that the United States should in fact give the British vigorous support, even at the cost of denuding its own strength. At that time the United States army had only eight divisions capable of combat. Churchill's speeches seem to have had much to do with Roosevelt's action. There was, for example, an urgent British need for small firearms, and Churchill wanted the Americans to hand over what amounted to their entire available reserves. Roosevelt hesitated and then heard a speech by Churchill over the radio: 'We shall defend our island whatever the cost may be; we shall fight on beaches, landing-grounds, in fields, in streets, and on the hills. We shall never surrender.' Roosevelt turned off the radio and remarked: 'I guess they rate those guns'; in the following five months the United States sent Britain 970,000 rifles, 87,500 machine guns and 200,500 revolvers. In September 1940, in contravention of law, he handed over fifty old American destroyers to the British, in exchange for bases in British colonies off the American coast. By the end of 1940 the British were running out of cash and Roosevelt prepared American public opinion for further aid with a broadcast speech in which he likened the situation to a neighbour with his house on fire asking for the loan of a hose; in such circumstances one did not count the cost of the hose but simply handed it over the fence. Any reckoning of the cost would come later. This speech had a discernible effect on American opinion and resulted three months later in 'lend-lease' which meant virtually unlimited aid. Weapons and materials were 'lent' to the British, their only obligation being to hand back after the war what they had not used up.

Despite the fact that American intervention in World War I had been possibly decisive, Hitler in his own planning took relatively little account of the possibility of its recurring. Apart from anything else he was a victim of his own propaganda that the German collapse in 1918 had been due to Jews and Marxists undermining the home front and not to any external enemy. In the 1920s he expressed respect for American dynamism and had predicted in his unpublished 'second book' the possibility of a war to prevent American domination off the world. In the 1930s his views plainly changed. He saw American opposition to his regime as a plot by Jews and Freemasons. There was some little substance to this in that the American Jewish community was a force with some political weight and was inevitably hostile to him. But Hitler's ideas were inadequate as an analysis of the American political scene; even less adequate was Hitler's habit of describing Roosevelt as a 'lunatic' and a 'maniac', married to a woman of 'definitely negroid' appearance. By the early 1940s Hitler had come around firmly to the view that the Americans were so 'corrupted' by Jewish and African 'blood' that their only future could be one of decay. 'My feelings against Americanism', he remarked privately in January 1942, 'are feelings of hatred and deep repugnance. I feel myself more akin to any European country, no matter which. Everything about the behaviour of American society reveals that it's half Judaised and half negrified.'

While the United States was not a factor in Hitler's basic plans of 1939 and 1940, it would plainly be better for Germany if she kept out of the conflict. Accordingly, and despite Roosevelt's blatantly pro-British policy, Hitler did try to avoid provocation. On September 4th, 1939, a German submarine sank without warning the British passenger liner *Athenia*, apparently under the impression that she was an auxiliary cruiser; 128 Americans were among the dead. Hitler was furious at the incident and the German naval staff announced, at first under a genuine mis-apprehension, that it had been the work of the British, who had torpedoed their own ship to create German-American antagonism. It turned out later that a German boat had in fact been respon-sible. Hitler issued stringent orders against passenger ships of any flag being attacked by submarines. At the same time the personal abuse of Roosevelt, which had been part of the stock in trade of National Socialist journalism, was cut off. German funds backed an attempt to get Roosevelt defeated for renomination at the Democratic Convention of 1940. There was also German support for the 'America First Committee', which campaigned for continu-ing American neutrality; but this committee provoked a rival 'Committee to Defend America by Aiding the Allies'. A German propaganda offensive in Latin America met with virtually no success; with the possible exception of Brazil, the Latin American countries lined up on Roosevelt's side. By the winter of 1940–1 the restrictions Hitler had placed on his submarines to avoid provoking the United States were discernibly weakening his war effort against Britain. And, at the same time, there were incidents of American warships passing on information about German naval movements to the British.

By the spring of 1941, following the start of lend-lease, Hitler took it as almost axiomatic that the United States would soon enter the war directly. Probably he over-estimated American determination in this respect. At any rate, he lost faith in his appeasement policy and switched to a diplomacy aimed at trying to influence the form and timing of American intervention for his own best advantage. In particular, he wanted the Americans to stay out until he had destroyed the Soviet Union, a project he hoped to accomplish by the end of 1941. The key was Japan. From Hitler's point of view, the best that could happen would be for the Japanese to attack British possessions in the Far East, and, preferably, also the Soviet Union, while leaving the United States alone. He urged them to do this. It was what Churchill himself dreaded. The worst that could happen, from Hitler's viewpoint, was, of course, that the United States would enter the war against Germany with Japan remaining neutral. Hitler's problem in dealing with the Japanese was that their intentions lacked consistency and that the exact balance between war and peace factions varied. The Yonai cabinet of January 1940, wanted *rapprochement* with the United States. It was succeeded by the Konoye cabinet which zigzagged to the extent of losing both American and German confidence. Then in November 1941, came the Tojo cabinet which was in a hurry to settle with the United States; it what what amounted to an immediate free hand in the Far East, plus normal trade with the United States, or, as an alternative, war. The militancy of the Tojo faction had been much stimulated by the German victories in the west and the Soviet Union; they wanted to show that the Japanese could do equally well. But even under Tojo, the Japanese were concerned with their own interests, not those of Germany, a fact which Hitler failed fully to appreciate. There were no detailed consultations between the Germans and Japanese and certainly no advance notice of each other's intentions. There was some attempt in Germany to hail the Japanese as 'honorary Aryans' but Hitler had little interest in it. 'It goes without saying,' he remarked privately in January 1942, 'that we have no affinities with the Japanese. They're too foreign to us by their way of living, by their culture.'

While Hitler and the Japanese operated largely independently of each other, the co-operation between Roosevelt and Churchill grew closer. In May 1941, the Americans took over from the British the occupation of Iceland. It was a country which had common citizenship with Denmark and which the British had occupied in May 1940 as a result of the German occupation of Denmark. Lend-lease goods were virtually convoyed by the American navy to Iceland and actual fighting broke out between American warships and German submarines; the first shots fired were American. Roosevelt's specific intention, indeed, was to incite 'incidents'; if it could be made to look as if the Germans were firing at American ships, it would be the easier to get Congress to agree to intervene directly in the war. Hitler was furious at such provocation and also felt strongly about Iceland which, he felt, represented American aggression against Europe. Because of his predilection in favour of Britain and his detestation of the 'mongrel' Americans, he could not see the Anglo-American alliance lasting. 'It will be a German-British army that will chase the Americans out of Iceland,' he predicted privately. He reckoned that 'one day' Britain and the United States would go to war with each other, with Germany on Britain's side. The conflict would be waged 'with the greatest hatred imaginable'.

Under Roosevelt's 'new deal', the anti-Communism which had long been a powerful force in the United States had been somewhat muted. Thus Churchill's immediate declaration of support for the Soviet Union at Hitler's first onslaught in June 1941 did nothing to weaken Anglo-American collaboration. That Churchill had himself been a fanatical anti-Communist helped to make it more palatable and, in any event, Japan and Germany seemed to pose immediate threats to the United States whereas the Soviet Union did not do so. In August 1941, Roosevelt and Churchill met in warships off the coast of Newfoundland. Besides drawing up the propaganda document known as the 'Atlantic Charter', they, privately, came to the crucial decision that if the United States were involved in war simultaneously with Japan and Germany, she would concentrate her first effort against Germany. Roosevelt pledged himself to bring about a war between America and Germany as soon as he could.

In Japan, Tojo and his cabinet decided to break off negotiations with the United States and to start a war aimed at eliminating American and European power in the Far East. The first blow, in the opening moments of the war, was to be an air strike to destroy the United States fleet at Pearl Harbour in Hawaii. Through a communications' error, the attack took place immediately before, instead of immediately after, the formal declaration of war on December 7th, 1941. Hitler was given no advance notice at all. Militarily the attack was a complete success but the fact that it preceded the declaration of war stirred American public opinion. In a flash, 'isolationism' vanished, to be replaced with an upsurge of public hatred against the Japanese and their allies the Germans. Pearl Harbour brought extra bitterness into the conflict.

Hitler was none too pleased with the Japanese action. In particular he did not like the prospect of the British base at Singapore being captured. He went so far as to grumble, in private, that, through force of circumstances, Germany was fighting the wrong enemy and should be allied with the 'Anglo-Saxons'. Also he had no treaty obligation to come to Japan's support; the two countries were contracted to support each other only if either were attacked. Nor was it at all certain that in the aftermath of Pearl Harbour the Americans would declare war on him. In his speech to Congress on December 8th, Roosevelt attacked Japanese 'infamy' but made no mention of either Germany or Italy. Also Japan was specifically not helping Hitler against the Soviet Union—Japan and the Soviets remained at peace until August 1945. Roosevelt, although obviously wanting to go to war with National Socialist Germany, might well have been unable to do so; in the immediate aftermath of Pearl Harbour, the overwhelming trend of American public opinion was to go for the Japanese at all costs. A declaration of war on Germany would be, arguably, a diversion from this. Hitler, however, was actuated in part by sheer personal hatred of Roosevelt, which publicly he had kept long pent up. Then there was the not wholly unreasonable point that through Roosevelt's actions the United States was already, for most practical purposes, at war with Germany and a formal declaration would not make too much difference. The Americans would be too busy dealing with Japan to spare any extra effort against Germany. Even if they were not, the Soviet Union would have been defeated long before they could become a military force in Europe. Then Hitler did not want to take what he regarded as the risk of the Americans declaring war on him first— it would look too much like a repetition of 1917. For domestic consumption in Germany, it would look more like self-confidence for him to take the initiative. He specifically told the Reichstag: 'We will always strike first. We will always deliver the first blow.'

Hitler summoned the Reichstag for December 9th but at the last moment postponed the meeting for two days. Possibly his intuition was not yet clear enough about what to do, but, equally probably, he just wanted longer to prepare his speech. He mounted the rostrum on December 11th and started with an abusive attack on Roosevelt, whom he described as 'mad', being like 'an old freemason', and 'the main culprit in this war'. Roosevelt, Hitler argued, had fomented wars around the world in order to divert attention from the failures of his home policy. He had 'the diabolical meanness of Jewry' around him. He was seeking 'to destroy one state after another'. On a more rational basis, Hitler said that Roosevelt had violated the laws of neutrality and attacked German and Italian ships. He went on to announce that the American chargé d'affaires in Berlin was being handed his passports and his actual words declaring war were lost in cheering. The formal German note to the United States said that due to American actions a virtual state of war already existed.

Limited 'lightning war', which had been Hitler's original intention, had been turned into a global struggle.

The phrase in Hitler's speech about 'the diabolical meanness of Jewry' was not just an oratorical flourish or an appeal to prejudice. He meant it as a statement of fact. As he had stated much earlier in *My Struggle,* he held the view that the various Jewish communities were a form of poisonous bacteria in the world. He believed, as he put it in a private remark in February 1942: 'The discovery of the Jewish virus is one of the greatest revolutions that have taken place in the world. The battle in which we are engaged today is of the same sort as the battle waged during the last century by Pasteur and Koch . . . We shall regain our health only by eliminating the Jew.' In other words, mere persecution, segregation or deprivation of rights could never solve the Jewish 'problem'; the only answer, in Hitler's view, was physical extermination—and he was in a position to attempt it. Centuries of European anti-semitism had reached a climax.

Hitler was now seeing the Jews as a European rather than a solely German 'problem'. The German Jews were a small, dwindling community, cut off by the Nuremberg laws and subsequent repression from the rest of the nation. Of a German-Jewish population of 503,000 in 1933, some 207,000 emigrated in 1933–45 and, also, in the same period it had an excess of (natural) deaths over births. Hitler's eyes were on the much bigger target of the millions of Jews in eastern Europe, particularly in Poland, the Soviet Union and Rumania. The Jews of Germany were only a detail, as were those of France, Britain and other western European countries, who were included in draft extermination programmes to make them complete. (But there was no planning to deal with the Jews of the U.S.A.)

The immediate pretext for mass murder and one in which Hitler, in his tortured way, may well have believed sincerely, was that the Jews had been responsible for the war. He went so far as to hint at this publicly in the course of a speech to the Reichstag in January 1939.

'If the international Jewish financiers inside and outside Europe should again succeed in plunging the nations into a world war, the result will not be the bolshevisation of the earth and thus the victory of Jewry, but the annihilation of the Jewish race throughout Europe.'

Few or no people took these words literally, but Hitler at the very end of his life harked back to them with pride, as a pledge he had carried out. But in 1939 the National Socialist idea of a 'final solution' was still merely to pressurise Jews to leave Germany and Himmler's S.S. was working vigorously on this. Emigration was shading towards actual deportation. There was even an unexpected partnership between S.S. officials and Jewish Zionist extremists to try to get the German Jewish population moved *en bloc* to Palestine, which was then under British mandate. But the British, under Arab pressure, were severely restricting Jewish entry and in practice the majority of the Jews who left Germany went to the United States. On the National Socialist side, also, there were ideological objections to the Jews becoming numerous enough in Palestine to set up their own national state; a Jewish sovereign state would, according to this line of thinking, make the Jews more dangerous than ever.

The conquest of Poland added some two million further Jews to Hitler's subjects. There was, in 1940, some idea of making defeated France yield up Madagascar to become a Jewish national home, under German rule, and, in fact, preliminary surveys were made of Madagascar to assess the economic and geographical conditions. (The Polish regime of the 1930s, anxious to get rid of its Jews, had also considered Madagascar.) In 1939–40 there was also a German scheme to set up a form of Jewish reserve in the area of Lublin, Poland; Jews from all over Europe would be concentrated within it, again under German sovereignty. But this rapidly broke down because Hans Frank, Governor General of occupied Poland, complained, successfully, that there was scarcely enough food for Poles, let alone masses of Jewish immigrants.

It was with the attack on the Soviet Union in 1941 that Hitler's policy switched decisively to mass murder. Exactly when he made up his mind on this is not clear but, in all probability, he saw the destruction of 'Bolshevism' and the destruction of Jewry as related operations to be carried out simultaneously. The two things were inextricably mingled in his mind; to him, 'Jew' and 'Bolshevik' were almost interchangeable words. Interestingly, though, he did not regard the mass killing of Jews as a policy proudly to be proclaimed from the house-tops. It was something to be done, so far as possible, in secret, without involving German public opinion or, in particular, the morale of his fighting troops. Hitler was not closely involved with the details of the mass killings, although it is a fair assumption that he discussed them on occasion with Himmler who, through the S.S., actually carried them out. (But the S.S. as a whole was not involved, only specialised units.) On no occasion did Hitler actually witness any killings; his reaction, had he done so, would have shed useful light on his personality. Himmler, when he saw a mass shooting of Jews, felt physically ill; he was dottily convinced that the murders were necessary but he found them repugnant. Hitler, however, given his possible pathological sadism, might have found them actually enjoyable but this, unfortunately, is unknowable. For reasons connected with his public image as an inspired saint, he did not, with the sole exception of the Röhm purge, like to be connected personally with the bloodier aspects of his regime.

After World War II a view grew up in Germany, quite widely held at a popular level, that Hitler was actually ignorant of the mass killing of Jews and that the responsibility was Himmler's. This is sustainable to the extent that there is no evidence in government records to provide conclusive proof that Hitler knew what was going on. There is no such thing as a written order, signed by him, for European Jewry to be exterminated. But even the most cursory examination of the facts points to the extreme probability that Hitler was not only aware of the policy but was its active instigator, no matter how much or how little he knew of the practical details. To state less would be to underrate him as a practical politician. In all matters Hitler preferred to act verbally rather than in writing and the Jewish 'final solution' was a particularly delicate matter. While it is true that Hitler was good at delegating authority this only applied in areas that did not interest him. He was passionately interested in the Jewish question and it is virtually impossible to suppose any major decision being made upon it in the Third Reich without his initiative. Moreover Himmler, repeatedly and definitely, told his officials, according to the minutes of meetings, that the extermination programme was based upon the Leader's orders and Himmler was not a liar. Again, there were some men of influence in the National Socialist movement who learned what was going on and objected to it, the most notable case being that of Wilhelm Kube, professed anti-semite, party 'old fighter' and area manager who was made Commissar General of White Ruthenia. Kube, until his assassination by partisans, protected Jews, complained that mass liquidations were 'unworthy of a German or of the Germany of Kant and Goethe' and wrote detailed reports to Rosenberg. It is hard to see how Himmler could have concealed the killings from Hitler when this kind of thing was going on. And, yet again, there is strong evidence that Josef Goebbels and fair evidence that Hermann Göring knew, at least in outline, what was happening and could readily have enlightened Hitler, had he been uninformed. Finally, there are statements in Hitler's 'Testament' of 1945 in which he accounted the destruction of European Jewry as his achievement.

The first phase of the extermination policy was linked directly to the Russian campaign. Four special 'action groups' *(Einsatzgruppen)*, each of some 750 men, mostly S.S. members, were formed to operate behind the German front line to destroy political resistance. They were specifically charged with the duty of shooting Communist Party officials and, somewhat more vaguely, with shooting 'Jews'. In 1941–2 they liquidated about half a million in both categories, on occasion rounding up whole Jewish communities and shooting them, men, women and children. Members of the groups suffered a high proportion of nervous breakdowns and, apart from a minority of pathological sadists, service in them was not popular. The discovery of a mass grave at Katyn, near Smolensk, containing 10,000 Polish officers who had been shot in 1940 by the Soviets, did something to raise their morale. This was widely publicised and gave the 'action group' members the idea that they were fighting an enemy as ruthless as themselves. The 'action groups' developed a curious *camaraderie* within themselves, feeling that they were doing something the rest of humanity could not understand. They tended, when possible, to avoid purely arbitrary killings and to label their victims as 'resisters' or, even, to say they had to be shot to prevent the spread of epidemics. Code words, such as 'special treatment', 're-settlement' and, even, 'change of address', were used in place of 'killing'.

Alongside with the mass killing of Jews and Communist officials went a programme to eliminate the Gipsies. These are people of probable Indian origin who speak their own Romany language but customarily adopt the religion of the country in which they are living. They migrated into Europe in medieval times and in the 1930s were at the most numerous in south-eastern Europe where they lived at a low economic level as petty craftsmen. A few of them were conjurers, jugglers, fortune-tellers and musicians. They tended to live in shanty towns. They had a 'royal dynasty' which had arisen during the nineteenth century and in 1937 in Warsaw there was an actual coronation ceremony in which Janusz I was crowned King of the Gipsies by an Orthodox bishop. There was a congregation of 15,000 Gipsies and the regalia was borrowed from the opera house. King Janusz afterwards approached the League of Nations with a request for a Polynesian island which the Gipsies could make their national home. The community did have reason for wanting to leave Europe—it had often been persecuted. Hitler was not interested in Gipsies to anything like the same extent as he was in the Jews. If he thought about them at all, he would have dismissed them as 'riff-raff', 'alien' and a danger to 'race purity'.

The Jews at least had valuable skills, some money and powerful international connections. In Poland the extermination programme had in some places to be postponed because Jewish labour was essential in factories producing equipment, notably uniforms, for the German army. The Gipsies, in contrast, were poor, mostly illiterate and lacked powerful international connections. (American Gipsies had merged with the general population and had no sense of ethnic identity; British Gipsies lacked political influence.) There was thus no obstacle to decrees from Himmler that the Gipsies should be wiped out. In 1939 there were 18,000 Gipsies in Poland. By 1946, only 4,500 were left.

Although always improvised and, by its own criteria inefficient, the extermination programme moved into its most horrific phase in December 1941 with the opening of a gassing centre at an isolated country house near Lodz, Poland. This made the killing more 'impersonal' and so more bearable to the perpetrators. (The psychology of this was somewhat similar to that of mass terroristic bombing: the airmen who started the Hamburg fire storms did so impersonally; they would have found it repugnant had they been required to throw men, women and children into fire with their bare hands.) Gassing and subsequent cremation were a success and the major centre became Auschwitz (Oswiecim), a complex of concentration camps at a rail junction thirty-two miles west of Cracow, Poland. Interestingly, there were no outright exterminations within Germany itself. Many concentration camp prisoners in Germany did die through maltreatment and overwork—and in the closing phases of the war through starvation—but 'the final solution of the Jewish problem', in terms of deliberate mass killing, was carried out in seclusion in Poland. How far this was Hitler's personal decision is not clear. There was some feeling that the soil of Germany should not be polluted by mass killing and, also, some necessity to keep the German population in ignorance of what was going on; most Germans, when they saw their Jewish neighbours deported to the east preferred to think that they were merely being 'resettled'. (But there were nasty rumours going around.) The deportation of Jews from occupied western Europe had only mixed success. The Italians were unco-operative, Pierre Laval managed to save most Jews in France who had French nationality and the S.S. commander Werner Best collaborated in shipping the Jews of Denmark off to safety in Sweden.

It is impossible to arrive at a firm total of how many were murdered in the holocaust of 1941–4. The first estimates, after World War II, put it at eight million, this has later been reduced to six million and then to five million. Of these a high proportion died through general maltreatment rather than straightforward murder. But, and this was a fundamental of Hitler's policy, the numbers of men, women and children who were herded into gas chambers and murdered simply for being Jews did run into millions. In terms of numbers the principal victims were the Jews of Poland and they were mostly helpless; the great resistance was that in the Warsaw ghetto in 1943 where, for twenty-eight days, the Jewish community held out against superior German forces.

Some of the perpetrators of the 'final solution' were crazed anti-semites. Some were sadists. Many were swept into it, step by step, in the pressures of war and the feeling that Germany was fighting for survival and that orders at all costs must be obeyed. In the calmer, post–1945 atmosphere, many came to feel remorse. Presumably Hitler himself would have felt none. Most of his ruthless, aggressive acts had some reason behind them. It was against international comity and beyond German power, but his scheme for turning European Russia into a German colony was no more irrational than that of a man planning to rob a bank. The shuffling of millions of Jews around Europe and murdering them, in a time of desperate war emergency, was useless from any rational point of view. Hitler believed it was a 'cleansing' operation and an act of 'retribution'. In reality he showed how far superstition could still count in the high politics of the twentieth century.

17

In January 1942, at the start of his tenth year in power, Hitler was involved in a world war which he had never intended and for which German advance preparations had been inadequate. Instead of swift, surgical conquests to form a greater German Reich, there was now a global conflict with Germany, in terms of manpower and resources, on the weaker side. It rarely occurred to Hitler to question the wisdom of his own past decisions and there are some signs of puzzlement in his private conversation over the situation he had got himself into. He found the actions of such opponents as Roosevelt and Churchill inexplicable on any ground that, to him, seemed rational; they must be 'mad' or somehow suborned by 'Jews' and 'Freemasons'. While Hitler exerted no detailed control over anti-Jewish policy, the fact that in the 1942–4 period the 'final solution' of mass killing was in full swing, may well have been a reflection of Hitler's baffled anger at the way in which his enemies were behaving.

Nevertheless, Germany's position at the beginning of 1942 was far from hopeless. A Bismarck, or even an ordinary, prudent leader, might have made much from it. Even Hitler still had a gambler's chance. The Americans and the British were both reeling in the Far East against the first wave of Japanese victories. In the Atlantic, the German submarines were beginning to reach their peak performance. German and Italian troops were poised to seize British-occupied Egypt; Mussolini had gone so far as to arrange a white horse on which he was to ride into Cairo. There were capacities in the German economy which, as yet, had scarcely been mobilised for war at all. In 1942, production of consumer-goods in Germany was running only seven per cent below the peacetime rate. Above all, the possibility still seemed to exist of Germany being able to knock out the Soviet Union. The initial offensive of 1941 had come near to achieving this and Hitler's ruthless will-power kept his forces in position during the winter ready for a renewed attempt in 1942. Destruction of the Red Army would enable him to move seasoned fighting troops to the west in sufficient quantity to ward off any Anglo-American incursion.

Thus everything depended upon Hitler's generalship on the Russian front in 1942. He needed a fourth year of victories, to match those of 1939, 1940 and 1941. But the factors of luck, surprise and often local superiority that had been with him in those years were now missing and the end result was the disaster, for the Germans, at Stalingrad (now Volgograd). At first everything went well. A German offensive into the Crimea was a stunning success, and Rostov was captured with the Red Army running away almost in panic. The glamorous A. A. Vlasov, who had risen from private to army group commander in the Red Army and been prominent in the defence of Moscow, was captured by the Germans. He was a Communist Party member of peasant origin, had fought in the revolution and was six feet five inches tall; he was willing to work with the Germans to create a 'Russian National Army' which would aim at the overthrow of Stalin and the establishment of Russia as an 'independent' state with the distribution of land to peasant proprietors. Properly used, Vlasov could have been a considerable ally for Hitler but in practice he was scarcely more than a propaganda figurehead; to have allowed him actually to form a Russian fighting army would have been too much of a threat to Hitler's plans for colonisation. He and Hitler never even met. Such fighting Russian units as were formed were deployed mainly in the west, where they were puzzled at having to face British and Americans. Some Cossack units, however, were used in the east.

In July 1942, Hitler decided to go for two objectives at once in the south of the Soviet Union. He decided to strike northwards and seize Stalingrad, a major industrial city and communications centre. He wanted Stalingrad for itself and also as a base from which to attack Moscow from the south; also, in all probability, the very fact that the city was named after the Soviet dictator meant much to Hitler. At the same time, Hitler decided to strike southwards to seize the oilfields of the Caucusus and, he dreamed, ultimately to link up with the Japanese in India. To attempt the two things at once was beyond German capabilities; it was a gamble which could only come off with enormous good luck. Moreover, the Soviets themselves were at a turning point in morale. Stalin, a Georgian and a Marxist theoretician, succeeded in turning himself into a Russian nationalist leader. The war became 'the great patriotic war'. Stalin threw overboard much Marxist practice, reorganised the army on traditionalist lines, made a *rapprochement* with the Church and appealed to Russian patriotic history. He found brilliant generals in Ivan Konev and Georgi Zhukov. The fact that the Germans had acted as predators rather than liberators—and this had been Hitler's policy, carried out in opposition to the advice of many of his experts—helped to consolidate Russian patriotism behind Stalin. The Germans had refrained, even, from distributing collective farm land back to individual peasant-proprietors on the ground that the collective system was the more efficient. Stalin was also receiving significant supplies from the United States and Britain and had overwhelmingly superior manpower.

Hitler, in the summer of 1942, behaved as if he were convinced that the Soviet Union was in the final stages of collapse. He actually refused to listen to intelligence reports which indicated that exactly the opposite was happening, that the Stalinist regime had already touched its lowest point and was now reviving. As the army chief of staff, Franz Halder (dismissed in October 1942) put it, Hitler acted on impulse 'which recognised no limits to possibility and which made wish-dreams the father of its acts'. The German forces smashed successfully into the Caucasus and northwards into Stalingrad, but exposed enormous flanks to counter-attack. An adventurous mountaineering group planted the German flag on the highest peak of the Caucasus, an episode which aroused Hitler's anger as being a waste of energy. Then, in the autumn of 1942, the Russians counter-attacked with the result that the German sixth army, of 320,000 men at its peak, was cut off in Stalingrad. By orthodox military doctrine it ought to have conducted a fighting retreat so as to link up again with the main German forces, and it was the unanimous advice of the generals that it should do so. It was sitting besieged in a ruined city and there was no possibility of keeping it supplied with ammunition, food and fuel. (Göring did, rather casually, say the air force could fly in supplies but the aircraft available were disastrously insufficient.) Hitler had a dream of a 'fortress Stalingrad' which could hold out through the winter as a German stronghold behind the Russian lines. He promoted the army commander, Friedrich von Paulus, to field marshal in an attempt to keep up morale. It was, really, sheer murder with the sixth army starving, freezing and being shot to death; it finally surrendered, to Hitler's fury, on February 2nd, 1943, when it was down to a strength of 91,000, including twenty-four officers of general rank. It was indicative of Hitler's thought-process that he considered Paulus should have committed suicide rather than go into captivity. Hitler talked almost mystically about Stalingrad as a form of blood-sacrifice which in the long run would inspire the German race. It would have been better if he had shot himself.

Stalingrad was the worst German defeat since Jena 137 years earlier. In the form it happened, it was due solely to Hitler's generalship, and in particular to his using faith and will-power as a substitute for rational judgment. It was a disaster for Germany in its own right and was also the turning-point of World War II in Europe; all that remained was two years of German retreat, before overwhelmingly superior forces. Stalingrad was matched, too, on a smaller scale by the battle of El Alamein on the frontier of Egypt in which superior British forces smashed the Germans and Italians under Erwin Rommel. The catastrophe would have been the worse had not Rommel specifically disobeyed orders from Hitler to hold ground at all costs. Rommel withdrew in some kind of fighting order but the balance of power in North Africa was finally decided by the American landing in Tunisia in November 1942.

Hitler's expert skill, during his rise to power and consolidation of it, had been as a publicist. He had exerted passionate personal leadership before the German people and preached a form of crusade of healing social divisions and strengthening the nation. No politician in the world had appeared more frequently before his own people to convince them of his suitability for power. During the war, however, Hitler, almost like Philip II of Spain burying himself in the Escorial, shut himself up in his military headquarters and at Berchtesgaden and rarely appeared in public. He took ever more detailed control of the war and of military tactics, believing that only his personal genius could save Germany. It must, in some ways, have been paradise for Hitler. In World War I, as a corporal, he must often have looked critically at the higher command; now, he was master of the war machine. In the autumn of 1941 he assumed the position of commander-in-chief of the army (this was in addition to his position as commander-in-chief of all the armed forces). In the early stages of the war he had relied on and rewarded his generals—he created the unprecedented number of twelve field marshals after the fall of France—but as things began to go badly, he raged at his subordinates. He complained that there was not enough 'National Socialist spirit' in the forces. At one point he refused to eat meals with his military staff, regarding this as a punishment for them. He kept seeking out new commanders. Of the thirty-six officers who served during the war in the rank of colonel-general, seven were killed in action, three were executed, two were expelled from the army in disgrace and twenty-one were relieved of their commands. (Colonel-general was the highest rank attainable by normal promotion; the next step, to field marshal, was a special honour.)

In Wilhelm Keitel, chief of staff to the supreme command of the armed forces (O.K.W.), Hitler was fortunate to have a hard worker, an uncritical admirer and a man who could put up with moods. Keitel came from a farming family in Brunswick but in appearance he looked like a Prussian aristocrat—Hitler, on occasion, slipped, incorrectly, into calling him 'von Keitel'. He was a Protestant Christian and had the O.K.W. staff sing 'Now Thank We All Our God' before Hitler to celebrate the victory over France; Hitler listened in silence. While in his private views he had been a monarchist, Keitel came to believe that Hitler's will-power, military knowledge and original methods added up to genius. He always had an air of being overburdened and in a hurry. 'See that field marshal scurrying past, with his adjutant bringing up the rear with measured tread,' joked one officer at headquarters of him. Keitel was really a super-clerk who translated Hitler's decisions into precise orders. A rather more independent person-ality in Hitler's military entourage was the Bavarian Alfred Jodl, chief of the supreme command operations staff. He was capable on occasion of standing up to Hitler in military matters and getting orders changed; he was capable of facing, unmoved, Hitler's rages. So far as there was any directing brain behind German strategy, other than Hitler's, it was largely Jodl's. Both Keitel and Jodl ended up being hanged in Nuremberg for having passed on atrocity orders from Hitler, notably those for executing some categories of prisoners. Keitel, at least, found it incomprehensible that Hitler should not have stayed alive to assume total responsibility for the orders. From the winter of 1942–3 there was a division between the O.K.W. and army staffs. O.K.W., instead of being the supreme command for all the forces, concentrated on the war on all fronts save the Russian, while the army staff ran the Russian war. Hitler found no Keitel or Jodl (both of whom served him continuously from 1938 to 1945) to run the army staff. He ran through army chiefs of staff at an accelerating rate—Halder, Kurt Zeitzler, Heinz Guderian, Hans Krebs.

By his own account, Hitler spent ten hours a day thinking about the war and half an hour making decisions. He was in the histori-cally novel position of being a supreme commander able by radio and teleprinter to control in detail operations anywhere in the world. Yet, despite his definite skill as a map reader, he had almost no first-hand knowledge of the terrain where the battles were taking place. Jodl was fond of describing Hitler's headquarters as being partly a monastery and partly a concentration camp and the atmosphere, with concrete bunkers and barbed wire was a depressing one. In the two years of retreat that followed Stalingrad (there was one final attempt to advance on the Russian front in the summer of 1943) Hitler visibly aged into an old man, looking far more than his age, which in 1943 was still only fifty-four. This was largely due to psychosomatic but real illness. He became bent and pale and his limbs trembled. His eyes lost their glow. To some it seemed as if his symptoms were those of Parkinson's disease, but the medical records do not bear this out. His mind and memory remained intact but he had lost some of his charisma and probably, also, his sense of driving intuition. His eyesight was worsening and he bent over his maps with a magnifying glass. By 1944 some who had previously known him well, but had not seen him for three or four years, found him almost unrecognisable.

World War II was a politicians' war in that the political leaders took the strategic decisions and many of the tactical ones also. Apart, possibly, from in Japan, there were no equivalents to Haig or Ludendorff who in World War I had acquired independent authority. In Britain, Churchill paid the closest attention to military questions and functioned, virtually, as commander-in-chief as well as Prime Minister. In the Soviet Union, Stalin took active command and secured his promotion to the actual rank of marshal. In the United States, Roosevelt had the constitutional position of commander-in-chief; he took the key decision to concentrate on victory in Europe before victory over Japan and was instrumental in lifting Dwight D. Eisenhower, who had been only a brigadier-general in 1941, to high command. Hitler assumed the most detailed control of all and in his own terms he was right to do so. From Stalingrad onwards, eventual German defeat was a near-certainty, which could only be averted by some form of miracle and the only available provider of miracles was Hitler himself. Orthodox leadership could have looked only for an early negotiated peace but, to Hitler's mind, defeat could only mean the total annihilation of Germany. He was supported in this by the Casablanca declaration of December 1943, that the allies would insist on the 'unconditional surrender' of their enemies. This declaration was made on Roosevelt's initiative. Both Churchill and Stalin considered it unwise and it was later watered down with pledges that the German people would be treated fairly. But it was the phrase 'unconditional surrender' that stuck and Goebbels made the most of it in his propaganda.

The puzzle must be why he did not use his oratory to whip up the war spirit. When Britain had been in danger of defeat in 1940, Churchill's oratory had been a definite factor in raising morale.

313

Roosevelt spoke often and eloquently. Hitler, however, from 1941 onwards kept largely silent. This was particularly surprising in his attitude to the mass bombing of German cities, which was started by the British in 1942. The raids were frankly terroristic and aimed at breaking German civilian morale. A single attack on Hamburg on July 23rd, 1943, killed 56,000 people, many of them dying in 'fire storms'. Hitler steadily, and despite the pleas of Goebbels, refused to visit the bombed cities. This was in sharp contrast to what had happened in Britain in the bombing of 1940–1. Although the British had a King and Queen who could and did visit the victims, Churchill, too, despite his preoccupations with running the war, made a point of going.

It has been suggested that Hitler was actually afraid to visit and mix with the bombed Germans, that he thought he would get a rough reception. This would seem to be improbable if only because Goebbels, who did make morale-raising visits, suffered no difficulties. At one point Goebbels, when Berlin was under heavy air attack, set up his desk in the street so that people could see him and approach him. Hitler, who could exert personal charm and had been regarded by many Germans as a saint-like figure, could undoubtedly have done even better than Goebbels. The better explanation must be not that he was afraid to visit the bomb victims but that he was not particularly interested, especially as the bombing had relatively little effect on war production. Hitler could shut himself off from unpleasant realities. There was, for example, an episode when his train happened to halt beside a hospital train. The wounded soldiers could look into the dining car and see Hitler and his staff, in comfort, at table. Such a charismatic leader as Hitler might have been expected to wave to the men or even enter their train to make an impromptu visit and shake their hands. In fact he merely ordered the blind to be drawn.

Hitler's reaction to the bombings was to think in terms of retaliation. Against the advice of his experts, he ordered the first jet fighter to be converted into a bomber. As a fighter, it would have served in some measure to protect the German cities against the overwhelming Anglo-American air superiority. As a bomber it was futile because its load was so slight. But what mattered to Hitler was to hit back. In one of his rare broadcasts—it was of his annual Löwenbräukeller speech in November 1943—he proclaimed 'The hour of revenge is nigh'. The new 'secret weapons' with which he hoped to swing the balance in his favour were termed 'vengeance weapons' *(Vergeltungswaffen)* and given the initial 'V'. They were the 'V–1', a pilotless aircraft which functioned as a self-propelled bomb, the 'V–2', which was a rocket on which has been based all subsequent space flight, and the 'V–3', a super-gun with a barrel 416 feet long. The 'V–3' was never finished and the 'V–1' and 'V–2' had the weakness that they were not accurate enough for battlefield use and suitable only as terror weapons against a large city such as London. They were deployed only against Britain. (There were plans for a huge intercontinental rocket, capable of reaching New York, but these reached only the preliminary design stage.) The 'V–1' could be shot down by con-ventional fighter aircraft or caught by barrage balloons but to the 'V–2' there was no antidote whatsoever. It merely landed out of the stratosphere, with a sound like a double clap of thunder. Hitler talked of launching 5,000 'V–2s' at once at Britain and so forcing her out of the war. But allied bombing delayed the production of the weapons and when, in the summer of 1944, they came into use they were destructive but far from decisive. In any event they could not affect the Soviet armies rolling in from the east.

The only weapon that could really have made a difference to Germany's position would have been a nuclear bomb. Had that been available to Hitler and not to his enemies, he might well have continued longer as master of Europe. Germany did have some nuclear research but Hitler did little to encourage it. He said he was nervous lest a nuclear explosion set off a chain reaction which would destroy the world. More substantially, he did not grasp fully the potentiality of nuclear weapons; even the British and Americans did not appreciate until after they had been used in Japan how destructive they were. Then Germany had lost, through emigration, certain Jewish physicists who were specialists in the nuclear field. Above all, however, in 1941 and 1942, when certain areas of choice were still open for Hitler, he laid down the rule that work should be undertaken on no new weapon that could not be available within two years. There was sense in this because Germany had to win either quickly or not at all. But it ruled out nuclear weapons which, it was estimated, could not be ready before 1947 or 1948.

In these last two years of World War II, Germany, paradoxi-cally, kept going both because of Hitler and in spite of him. He was now an elderly man, filled with disappointment and with no real plans for the future. There was nobody among his enemies who would have dreamed of negotiating with him. In some sense he was mad; or, at least, the ideas of which he dreamed did not fit the real world. The temporary period in the mid–1930s when his dreams had coincided with a reality was over. Yet he could still, by a form of hypnotic power, convince some in his entourage that out of the mess he could still pluck a miracle. He could be impressive to visitors, especially to officers from the front who came to him to receive decorations. Speaking with an apparent frankness which impressed them and made them feel they were being let into secrets, he would explain how the alliance between the Americans and the British on the one hand and the Soviet Union on the other could not last and that eventually the Anglo-Americans would link up with the Germans. For the meantime, it was necessary only to hold the front. Germany kept going because of him for the reason that compromise was not in his nature. It kept going in spite of him for the reason that, although he had the occasional successful idea, he was operating in a dream world. Whether it was running an extermination camp in Poland, reviving the municipal administration in Hamburg, experimenting with 'V–2' rockets or running a regiment in retreat before overwhelmingly superior Soviet forces, it was ordinary Germans, with an instinct for order and a sense of duty who kept things ticking over. Germany was like the supposed chicken which can continue to run around after its head has been cut off. There was much improvisation and 'muddling through'.

Most deeply of all, Hitler could not use his oratory to his people because, when it had worked, that oratory had been based upon honest convictions which had shown through to an audience. He had not, as a great platform speaker, been a conscious liar. His sincerity had burned through. But in 1941–5 he was engaged upon secret enterprises, which could be justified only by success and subsequent rationalisation. The attempt to exterminate the Jews was not something he could shout from the housetops. He thought, in his odd way, that it was right but had the political sense to know that it was not the kind of thing that would warm the German people to him. Also he could not orate about Russia. His ambition had been to make European Russia a German colony but propaganda had convinced the German public that the Soviets were the aggressors or, at most, that Germany was fighting a preventive war against Slav and Bolshevik invasion. To have gone on to a public platform and orated sincerely about his aims in regard to the Jews and the Soviet Union would not have worked. Also he could not have orated on the theme that, victory now being impossible, the only reason in prolonging the war was to prolong his own life.

He lived his own odd life. He was Eva Braun's lover in that he telephoned her nearly every day and for an occasional fortnight or month went to Berchtesgaden to relax, where she was mistress of the household. Stalin, and to a considerable extent Churchill, were controlled alcoholics who ended the day with heavy drinking. Hitler ended it with coffee, and now, in this period, an occasional beer, and with conversation which lasted far into the night. To new-comers his talk seemed to be original and interesting but people who attended at length found it repetitive. Martin Bormann, who from 1941 onwards acquired authority as head of party affairs, had the patience to sit it out; this was a factor in his increasing influence. The programme was for Hitler to rise at noon, or shortly earlier, and to go straight into his major conference. He heard reports, looked at the maps and dictated orders which, as time went on, became less and less real. Their followed a long luncheon, with Hitler controlling the conversation. Then Hitler had a nap. If he was at Berchtesgaden, he took exercise by walking to the tea house before nodding off. At his military headquarters—mainly Rastenburg in East Prussia—he took his nap having had no exercise at all. There followed a supplementary military con-ference in the evening and then supper, plus hours of Hitler monologue. He exhausted himself in private talk before feeling able to go to sleep. Even in the most serious circumstances, it was not permissible to wake him when he had once gone off. It was noon, when he had awakened normally, that Hitler was first told in 1944 that the Anglo-Americans had landed that morning at dawn in Normandy.

Meanwhile Hitler had lost his ally, Mussolini, who had had a poor war. Instead of establishing a new 'Roman Empire' in the Mediterranean, Mussolini had been humiliated in Greece and had lost all his African colonies, including the newly-acquired Ethiopia. The Anglo-Americans were poised, in the summer of 1943, to cross over from North Africa and invade Italy itself. Mussolini's not unreasonable idea of a remedy for the situation was for Hitler to drop his Russian ambitions, patch up what peace was possible with Stalin and concentrate on holding the west, and especially Italy, against the Anglo-Americans. This was in line with arguments that Goebbels was putting to Hitler and it could, possibly, have worked except that Hitler had no idea of surrender—peace with the Soviets after Stalingrad could only have been obtained on humiliating terms; moreover it would have been an unsafe posture to fight on in the west and leave the east unguarded. Anything Stalin had failed to gain in a peace treaty he would be liable to grab at a moment of German weakness. So far as Stalin needed any lessons at all in power politics he had been taught them by Hitler. In April and July 1943, Hitler had meetings with Mussolini and tried to stiffen his morale but it was hopeless. Public opinion in Italy had always been dubious about the war and was now frankly hostile, with the army itself almost disintegrating. Mussolini himself was plainly dispirited and took no precautions to maintain himself in power. On July 10th, the Anglo-Americans landed in Sicily. Two weeks later the Fascist Grand Council censured Mussolini and the King dismissed him. A new, perfectly constitutional government was set up under Marshal Pietro Badoglio. Mussolini, driven off into custody in an ambulance was obviously taken by suprise but he accepted the dismissal quietly. Later, on Hitler's initiative, Mussolini was rescued by air from a mountain hotel where he was being held and set up as ruler of the 'Italian Social Republic' in the north. Hitler was keen on this partly for propaganda and morale reasons; it must not look as if dictators could be overthrown. But it was also a factor that Hitler's personal respect for Mussolini, going back to the 1920s, still subsisted.

In the tricky situation of a new Badoglio government existing in Rome, Hitler acted swiftly and decisively. He was at his most effective. Without awaiting complete reports from Rome, he ruled that Badoglio must be treated as hostile. There were eight German divisions in Italy which were in danger of being cut off if Badoglio negotiated peace. Hitler seized the Alpine passes and poured all the reinforcements he could muster into Italy. His intuition was correct. Badoglio did initiate negotiations but he and the allies were much slower than Hitler. It took six weeks to conclude an armistice—the 'unconditional surrender' phrase was one stumbling block—and in that time the Germans had built up a strong position in the northern half of Italy.

On the announcement of the armistice on September 10th, the Germans were able to disarm much of the Italian army. Even in this crisis, Hitler was unwilling to broadcast to the German people and only pressure from Goebbels induced him to do so. He made no ringing 'backs to the wall' appeal but concentrated on asserting that there were no 'traitors' in Germany and that his personal position as leader was secure.

In fact Hitler's position was far from secure and there was an element of sheer luck in his being alive at all.

It would be difficult to envisage Hitler being overthrown by his own party colleagues as Mussolini had been. Göring, Goebbels and the party area managers who would have comprised a National Socialist 'grand council' had pinned their whole lives and careers to faith in Hitler's unique genius. Himmler, for all that he commanded the police and S.S., was becoming slightly more independent; his outlook widened somewhat with experience and he was beginning to think of himself as a statesman as well as an administrator. He collected a dossier to show that Hitler was in ill-health and fumbled with the idea that he, Himmler, would be indispensable for maintaining order in the event of Hitler's disappearance.

However no 'grand council' existed for the National Socialists and, still less, a head of state who, like the Italian King, could have endorsed Hitler's dismissal.

The only way to get rid of Hitler was to assassinate him. Apart from anything else, this would immediately dissolve the personal oath of allegiance which every army officer had sworn to him. The German resistance to Hitler was widespread but kept well underground by the police and the networks of party informers. There were, however, occasional episodes of it breaking spontaneously to the surface. The University of Munich became in 1943 a centre of student unrest, which spread to other universities. The brother and sister, Hans and Sophie Scholl, Munich students, circulated the 'white rose' letters calling for an end to the war and the overthrow of National Socialism. They, and others in their group, ended up by being beheaded but not before they had succeeded in mounting a demonstration in the public streets of Munich. Some Communists cells continued to operate and had occasional minor successes in disrupting war production. Roman Catholic bishops, notably Count Galen of Munster, kept up resistance to National Socialist ideological teaching.

The main conspiracy against Hitler, however, was based upon the Prussian military aristocracy, with strong Protestant Christian connections. Winston Churchill was under the impression and quite often said that National Socialism was a manifestation of a 'Prussianism' that had to be destroyed. But he was really thinking in terms of the propaganda of 1914. National Socialism was a south German movement controlled almost entirely by south Germans. 'Prussianism' was its effective opponent if only because the code of honour and mutual loyalty that bound the Prussian officer class facilitated conspiracy; it was easier to trust a member of one's own caste than any outsider.

Hitler had come within discernible distance of being removed from power by the army in September 1938. In November 1939, he had nearly been blown up in the Munich beerhall explosion. Further attempts followed. In March 1943, Hitler visited the central army group headquarters at Smolensk where the chief of staff, Henning von Tresckow, was a leader in the main conspiracy. Tresckow, with the knowledge of his commander, Guenther von Kluge, had prepared a bomb. He and other staff officers actually passed it to one another while seated at the dinner table with Hitler. They disguised it as a parcel, supposed to contain two bottles of Cointreau, and got it on to the aircraft in which Hitler was flying back to East Prussia, together with a timing device which ought to have exploded it after Hitler had been thirty minutes in the air. But it failed through a fault in the detonator. The conspirators tried again a few days later. The only certain method of assassination was to find someone with access to him who was willing to sacrifice his own life by detonating a bomb concealed on his own person while standing close to Hitler. (Mere shooting would not have been enough, as vigilant bodyguards would have been liable to intervene; a failed attempt, with the perpetrator caught, would have been worse than no attempt at all.) The conspirators enlisted Colonel Baron von Gersdorff, an intelligence chief, who besides being adamantly anti-Hitler was also in a depressed state through having recently become a widower. He was, heroically, prepared to render a last service to his country by killing Hitler and himself simultaneously.

It was beginning to seem as if Hitler had a charmed life and, certainly, it seemed as if he almost smelled danger in the Gersdorff attempt. The occasion was the annual 'heroes' day' ceremony at the Berlin Arsenal where Hitler was to speak, with Gersdorff in his entourage. The proceedings began with the Berlin Philharmonic Orchestra playing the first movement of Bruckner's eighth symphony. Then Hitler spoke from the rostrum. Gersdorff was there with two bombs, one in each overcoat pocket, but during the music and the speech could not get close enough. Then Hitler moved among wounded soldiers in the front row; now Gersdorff could get near him but he did not want to involve the wounded in the explosion. He reckoned his chance would come at the next stage when Hitler was due to inspect an exhibition of captured trophies from the eastern front. Hitler finished with the wounded and went to the trophies. He was scheduled to spend half an hour with them but instead he gave them only a perfunctory glance before suddenly hurrying, almost running, out to his car, followed by his startled staff and bodyguards. Gersdorff was left standing with his bombs still in his pockets.

Further assassination plotting continued and knowledge of it was widespread among the army staff and higher command. It was haunted with misfortune. At one point an enemy air raid destroyed the stock of assassination explosive. Many, in high rank, would have liked to see the end of Hitler and an attempt to negotiate a peace, with Germany still intact and undefeated. As subsequent events were to show, such a Germany would have been a useful counterweight to the Soviet Union. It was obvious that Hitler himself could not negotiate a peace even had he wanted to; he was personally unacceptable to the enemy powers. On the other hand, and this is unmeasurable, there was some feeling that the 'unconditional surrender' gave Germany no choice but to carry on

320

fighting and so there was no use an individual taking personal risks to get rid of Hitler. How far 'unconditional surrender' was merely a post-war excuse for not acting and how far it was a real factor at the time is a subject capable of argument. The effective conspirators were not the generals but the staff officers of middle rank, about that of colonel, who were well-informed about the progress of the war, tired of the regime (and in many cases morally affronted by it) and eager to act. Their superiors, the generals, mostly would have been happy to accept the results of a coup but were not themselves ready to participate too deeply in the dirty work. The generals mostly, of course, owed their positions to Hitler and had been selected personally by him.

Among the plotters the outstanding personality was Colonel Count Claus von Stauffenberg, who was aged thirty-seven in the summer of 1944. He had an electric personality, physical courage and, ultimately, a sense of destiny. From 1936 onwards he had talked among his friends of the need to overthrow Hitler, to whom he referred as 'the buffoon'. Like Hitler, he had as a youth considered becoming an architect, but instead became a regular cavalry officer. He was not a Prussian but a Swabian and he was a Roman Catholic; after the Nazis came to power, he made something of a point of wearing his officer's uniform while taking his children to church. Under the influence of the poet Stefan George, whom he had known well as a young man, Stauffenberg probably ceased to be a dogmatic Christian in his inner convictions; but he remained a definite churchman for partly political reasons. He thought the Church should be maintained as an independent force in the National Socialist state. There is some indication that he actually went to confession and communion immediately before attempting to murder Hitler in July 1944. It would have been possible for him to find a confessor who would have endorsed his intention—there were bishops as well as priests (especially Jesuits) who knew of the conspiracy—but it did pose an interesting moral problem. Protestants also had scruples. One was so devout that he endangered the safety of his companions by declaring he would regard it immoral to tell lies in the event of his being arrested. The theologian Dietrich Bonhoeffer was of special value in such cases, being able to argue that in certain circumstances political murder could be justifiable; it was a decision he had reached with difficulty and one which he believed would ruin his worldly career as a pastor.

Up to 1941, Stauffenberg took the view that the war, although foolish, needed to be won before there was any attempt to overthrow Hitler. It would be unpatriotic to split the nation in wartime.

He began to change his mind in 1941 and 1942 because of what he, as an informed staff officer, regarded as Hitler's inefficiency and wanton atrocities. He was involved with organising Russian volunteers into German units and believed that it was only by treating Russians as equals that they would work with Germany to overthrow Communism. Like Rosenberg, the nominal Minister for Eastern Territories, he was appalled by the harshness of the occupation policy but unlike Rosenberg, who contented himself with protests, he was willing to do something about it. By the autumn of 1942, he was talking, unguardedly, of the need for someone to put 'a revolver to the brute's head'. In the spring of 1943 Stauffenberg was posted to North Africa where, almost immediately, he was nearly killed in an air attack. As it was, he lost his left eye, his right hand and two fingers of his left hand. There was doubt whether his right eye would survive and he spent three months in hospital. It was during his recovery that he began to acquire a sense of destiny, a feeling that as a thanks-offering for his life he should eliminate Hitler.

Stauffenberg learned to write with his mutilated left hand and eventually returned to active service, being promoted to full colonel and made chief of staff of the 'replacement army', the organisation of reserve, training, and holding units in Germany. This post gave him occasional direct contact with Hitler. But Stauffenberg was not just a potential assassin but also, from the autumn of 1943 onwards, became the mainspring of the entire anti-Hitler conspiracy; he had capabilities of drive and leadership. He drew up a peace programme by which German forces would retreat to the frontiers of 1914. These would include Austria and the Sudetenland but not Alsace-Lorraine. A freely-elected German government would collaborate in the reconstruction of Europe and punish 'criminal' acts committed by the National Socialists. His candidate for the chancellorship was the socialist, Julius Leber. He recognised, however, that his terms might be unacceptable to the allies and envisaged a negotiation in which the new German government would necessarily be in a weak position. Germany would, however, maintain a 'defensive capability' in the east and this would have been a useful bargaining factor.

The aim was to kill Hitler and set up a temporary military regime before the Anglo-Americans invaded France. Stauffenberg accepted his 'replacement army' post with this specifically in mind. His chief, Colonel General Friedrich Fromm, knew what he was up to and advised that it was important to deal with Keitel as well as with Hitler; but Fromm, who still used the 'Hail Hitler' greeting, was ready to identify himself with the conspiracy only

322

after it had succeeded. The successful Anglo-American landing in Normandy in June 1944, threw the conspirators into disarray. Stauffenberg saw that the war was now lost and wondered whether it might not be best for Hitler to remain in power so that it would be clear to history that he and not any opposition group was to blame.

In point of fact the allied cross-channel invasion was a desperately tricky operation. The supreme commander of it, Dwight D. Eisenhower, had prepared in advance the communiqué he would issue in the event of failure. Were the Germans able to concentrate against the allies before the latter had been able to build up their strength, the allies might well have been driven back into the sea. (The situation was not like that of 1940 when the British had been almost wholly lacking in equipment to deal with an invading force, had it managed to cross the water.) The commanders on the spot, Gerd von Runstedt and Rommel, favoured the immediate use of reserves for a counter-attack but this was vetoed by Hitler. Anglo-American intelligence had put out the fake information that the Normandy attack was only a feint and that the main assault was to come in the Calais area. Exactly what effect this had on Hitler is hard to assess but certainly his intuition told him that Normandy was a feint and he withheld the reserves until it was too late for them to be any use. Once they had consolidated their Normandy base, the Anglo-Americans were able to ferry over superior forces and exactly when they would overrun France and reach Germany was scarcely more than a matter of detail.

Hitler was unwilling to come west. That the Anglo-Americans were so far from breaking with the Soviet Union as to be launching a vigorous offensive was unpalatable for him. There had, in particular, still been some hope in his mind that the British, when they had been weakened by the 'V' weapons, would come to an accommodation. Hitler could not see it as a British interest to allow the Red Army to come sweeping westwards. It was not until eleven days after the Normandy invasion had started, and then only at the urgent prompting of Rundstedt and Rommel, that Hitler came to the new western front. He occupied a headquarters at Margival that originally had been constructed as the base from which he was to direct the invasion of England in 1940. He looked unwell and desperately tired. He kept fiddling with pencils. Rommel, in particular, was in a tough mood; he said the allies were overwhelmingly superior and were landing two or three fresh divisions daily. How, asked Rommel, was the war going to end? Hitler had no reply beyond an injunction to Rommel to concentrate on the fighting and not bother about politics. It was at

323

this point that Rommel finally decided that Hitler must be over-thrown but soon afterwards he was put out of action by wounds resulting from an enemy air attack near Caen. (Rommel had favoured the arrest and trial of Hitler, rather than assassination.)

There had been some idea that besides conferring with the generals, Hitler should also visit the fighting men in the west. But during his first night at Margival one of his own flying bombs landed just outside the bunker in which he was sleeping. It was, presumably, an accident rather than an attempt to kill him—the flying bombs were being used before they had been perfected and could not be aimed at any exact target. Nobody was hurt but Hitler decided to leave immediately; he went first to the Berghof and then to his headquarters at Rastenburg, East Prussia, to try to cope with the Russian offensive. This was probably not cowardice in any simple sense but more a feeling that he was in danger of death—he must have sensed the hostility that came from Rommel, for instance. Hitler, with reason, believed that his own death would also be the death of the Germany he had attempted to create.

It was at Rastenburg, on July 20th, 1944, at twelve twenty-eight p.m., that Hitler had his narrowest escape from assassination. The effective leader of the conspiracy, Stauffenberg, did the deed himself. Because of the Anglo-American offensive, the original plans had now been modified; the new German regime would break off the fighting in the west, withdraw to the Rhine and send all battle-worthy units to the east. Stauffenberg was visiting Rastenburg in his capacity of chief of staff of the 'replacement army' and attended Hitler's noon conference. This was normally held in a concrete bunker, underground, but on July 20th, because it was a hot day, the venue was switched to a hut, mostly wooden, above ground. The windows were open.

When Stauffenberg entered the hut, Hitler greeted him with a handshake. Stauffenberg placed a briefcase containing a bomb under the table, close by Hitler. Shortly afterwards, on the pretext that he had to telephone to Berlin, Stauffenberg left the hut. The bomb went off and Stauffenberg saw the hut apparently blown to pieces; believing that Hitler must certainly be dead, he flew straight off to Berlin to direct the takeover of the government.

But Hitler was not dead. The force of the explosion threw him to the ground and ripped his trouser legs to shreds. He suffered superficial cuts and burns and his eardrums were damaged. Keitel helped him back to his feet. What had saved Hitler was that the force of the explosion had been dissipated on the wooden hut; had it happened underground, he could not have survived. More-over at the moment the bomb went off, Hitler had been leaning far over the table and this had shielded his body. Others in the hut were not so fortunate. Four received wounds from which they afterwards died; one of them, a stenographer, had both his legs blown off. Nine others received wounds that required major medical treatment.

In Berlin, the conspirators tried to take over the government. The key figure was Friedrich Fromm, the commander-in-chief of the 'replacement army', whose troops were an essential part of the mechanism. Fromm, a cautious man who had been propelled into the plot by Stauffenberg, was prepared to act only if Hitler really were dead. He believed that a living Hitler would be able to rally the masses against any *coup d'état* and, even, to appeal to ordinary soldiers over the generals' heads. When told of the explosion and Hitler's apparent death, his first act was to telephone Rastenburg and check; Keitel told him that Hitler was still alive. When Stauffenberg arrived in Berlin, Fromm advised him to shoot himself. Stauffenberg and other conspirators locked Fromm in his office and tried to exercise command of the 'replacement army' themselves but, really, they had lost their main hope. Also Goebbels, the senior 'political' figure in Berlin acted decisively. He realised that a serious coup was being attempted—it was an eventuality which he must have often considered. When Major Otto Remer, commander of the troops that guarded the government area, came, on the conspirators' orders, to arrest him, Goebbels contacted Rastenburg by telephone and got Hitler to talk to Remer to confirm that he was alive. (Remer had recently met Hitler to be decorated.) Hitler, on the spot, gave Remer command of all troops in and around Berlin and by nightfall Remer had freed Fromm and secured complete control. Stauffenberg and three other leading conspirators were shot after an emergency court martial during the night, their executioners being auxiliary troops of the army fire brigade.

His near-miraculous escape from death gave Hitler an extra injection of faith in his own mission and destiny. In this he was encouraged by Goebbels. He sent immediately for Göring, who had been out of favour but whose presence was reassuring in a crisis. The same afternoon Mussolini arrived on a visit that had been arranged before the explosion. Hitler looked extraordinarily pale but had control of himself and was able to meet him at the station. He took Mussolini to inspect the wrecked hut. In the night Hitler broadcast to the German people and spoke mostly of punishment and revenge. He was almost self-pitying. 'I have,' he said, 'lived through countless days and sleepless nights only for my people.' The assassination attempt was 'a crime unparalleled in Germany's history'. It had been the work of 'a gang of criminal

325

elements which will be destroyed without mercy'. He regarded his escape as 'a confirmation of the task imposed upon me by providence'. The effect of the broadcast seems to have been depressing rather than inspiring. Nor were German ambassadors abroad particularly inspired by a message from Ribbentrop ' . . . Providence saved the Leader for us as by a miracle . . .'

The purge continued until the end of the war, although in the last months it tended to flag as individual Gestapo officers began thinking of the future. For example, Konrad Adenauer, the former mayor of Cologne, (who had had no contact with the July 20th conspiracy) was arrested and at one point nearly executed; but he was released in November 1944. Altogether some 10,000 people were arrested or investigated and some 5,000 executed. Rommel was bribed to commit suicide by promises of an honourable funeral and pension rights for his family. Even Fromm, who had played a possibly decisive role in impeding the conspirators, was sentenced to death, although he was allowed a firing squad rather than the hanging most of the conspirators suffered. The trials, before the Berlin 'People's Court', were hysterical, with the judge, Roland Freisler, a former Communist, shouting abuse at the prisoners. The proceedings were so undignified that Goebbels had to abandon a project for showing a film of them as propaganda.

It is an indication of Hitler's mentality that he took the closest interest in the trial and execution of his enemies. The normal death sentence on a German citizen was to be beheaded if he were a civilian and shot if he were a soldier. Hitler, however, devised a special form of hanging for the July 20th victims; they were to be strung up on meathooks and to die of strangulation. He had a film made of one group of ten (including a field marshal and three generals) being hanged in this way and watched it as a form of entertainment. It seems to have given him actual pleasure, although whether it was primarily sadism or merely joy in revenge is unknowable.

Once he had got over the first shock of the explosion, Hitler fell into a depressed state. 'I am no longer afraid of death,' he remarked to a secretary. 'Since my youth, misery and anguish have been my constant companions.' There were periods when he lost interest even in the military situation. More definitely than ever before, he trusted no one. He raged against his generals. By the end of 1944 the Russians in the east and the Anglo-Americans in the west had reached German soil.

18

Hitler's final attempt to save himself and National Socialist Germany was the Ardennes offensive in the snow of December 1944. For the last time, the panzer divisions rolled forward on the attack. They were the most experienced fighting men in Europe and they achieved tactical surprise. The aim was to inflict a major defeat on the United States and, possibly, even sweep the Anglo-Americans off the European mainland altogether. It was a gambler's throw but it was only by gambling that Hitler could hope to retrieve his situation at all. He was still, at bottom, the same person as the teenager who had pinned everything on winning a lottery or the immature politician who had hoped to seize power in 1923 by an armed demonstration in Munich. Having beaten the Americans he could turn his forces around to fend off the Soviets, who were entering Germany from the east; there might even have been a prospect of a separate peace. During the first week the offensive was successful; it gained ground and disorganised the American third and sixth armies. But resources of fuel, manpower and equipment were insufficient to keep up the momentum and within a fortnight the allies had the situation under their control. For them it was just a passing setback during an inexorable progress towards the occupation of Germany.

Short of a miracle, for which Hitler tried to force himself to hope, the war was hopelessly lost. He carried on with the fighting because he thought it better than surrendering. 'They may exterminate us,' he said, 'but they will never lead us to the slaughterhouse.' As always, he was inconsistent. He told Speer that Germany was entirely finished and that the future belonged to 'the stronger race from the east'. In other moods, however, he asserted that defeat would only stiffen the German people. 'The more we suffer, the more glorious will be the resurrection of eternal Germany.'

The continued fighting he did not intend as just a token. He ordered the destruction of bridges and industrial machinery in order to deny them to the advancing enemy and ordered executions of officers who yielded. In fact these kind of orders were widely evaded. What he did not do was to broadcast to his people to inspire them or, even, to explain what was happening.

In the early months of 1945, Hitler dictated a series of statements in which he envisaged defeat and which he intended as his testament to Germany and the world. They are impromptu, disorganised documents, impressionistic rather than logical. He was a man under enormous strain. His sleep was down to three hours in the twenty-four. At times he fell into apathetic depression but then he would goad himself into a new frenzy of interest in the war. Eva Braun, who in October 1944 made her will, feared that even if the war were won, the effort involved would kill Hitler. But he still kept architectural magazines by him and the plans for rebuilding Linz. His 'testament' was something he threw out in odd moments when he felt like summarising the situation.

One theme, indeed the only definite theme which runs right through it, is the Jews. Hitler reckoned that, however else he had failed, he had made an imperishable contribution towards the future welfare of humanity. 'National Socialism,' he said, 'can justly claim the eternal gratitude of the people for having eliminated the Jew from Germany and Central Europe.' He really regarded this as a benefit and, of course, it was in line with his idea, stretching back to the 1920s and earlier, that the Jews were a 'bacillus' infecting and corrupting the rest of the human race. The fact that he referred to Central Europe, and not just to Germany, is evidence that he was referring to mass killings and not merely deportation. There had been 'an essential process of disinfection, which we have prosecuted to its ultimate limit.' He remembered and referred to his Reichstag speech of 1939 in which he had declared that if the 'Jews' started war, he would eliminate them from Europe. This had been a reasonable warning which the 'Jews' had chosen to ignore. 'I have always,' he said, 'been absolutely fair in my dealings with the Jews.'

Interestingly, though, he was still a bit puzzled about anti-semitism and the nature of the Jews. It was as if the rational part of his mind were still wrestling with prejudice. What exactly were the Jews? He pondered aloud on the question. Like every extreme anti-semite he had decided long ago that they could not be regarded as merely a religious group. At the same time, though, they were not a 'race' either. 'I promise you,' said Hitler, 'that I am quite free of all racial hatred' and it had not been for

328

'racial' reasons in the ordinary sense that he had attacked them. The Jews were a 'community', not a 'race'. They were 'a race of the mind' and this was something more durable than a race based upon blood. 'There in a nutshell,' he remarked, 'is the proof of the superiority of the mind over the flesh.' And, yet, he could not let race and blood be ignored altogether; inconsistently, he went on: 'Every Jew in the world has some drop of Jewish blood in him.'

So far as, in his 'testament', he admitted error, Hitler reckoned that it had lain in his alliance with Italy. Mussolini himself was a great man, a 'Roman', but the Italians had been hopeless material for him to work on. It was because Germany had had to assist Italy in the Balkans in 1941, that the attack on the Soviet Union had been delayed for a crucial six weeks. Had the attack been on time, the war would have been won in 1941. Hitler made no apology for having gone to war with the Soviet Union but was silent on his plans, about which he had spoken and even written generously in earlier years, to make European Russia and the Ukraine into German colonies. It was not the need for 'living space' that had impelled him to attack but merely defensive considerations. It had been a preventive war. Had the Russians been allowed to take the initiative they would have flooded into Germany along the motorways. 'It was absolutely certain that one day or other she would attack us.'

Hitler saw himself as a 'European' standing against both Asiatic Bolshevism and American 'gangsterism'. 'I have been Europe's last hope,' he said. The condition for forming a united, independent Europe was to destroy old institutions. 'Europe can be built only on a foundation of ruins. Not material ruins, but on ruins of vested interests and economic coalitions, of mental rigidity and perverse prejudice, of outmoded idiosyncrasy and narrow-mindedness.' Britain's guilt was that, Jew-ridden, she had chosen to link up with the United States and the Soviet Union rather than with Europe. He had hoped to work with the British but they had been 'perverse'. He now hoped they would all die of tuberculosis in their 'accursed island'.

The future of Bolshevism was unpredictable but the United States was a mess with little chance of survival.

The fact that they [the Americans] combine the possession of such vast material power with so vast a lack of intelligence evokes the image of a child stricken with elephantiasis. It may well be asked whether this is not simply a case of a mushroom civilisation, destined to vanish as quickly as it sprang up ... It will soon become apparent that this giant with the feet of clay has, after its spectacular rise, just sufficient strength left to bring about its own downfall.

Hitler did not predict, in any detail, the 'cold war' that was to come between the Soviet Union and the west, beyond noting that the alliance was 'incongruous'.

As always, he was egotistical. National Socialism, he implied, was not a creed which, like Marxism, could go forward irrespective of individuals. The grand design had to be carried out in Hitler's own lifetime or not at all; there was nothing he could leave for a successor because no successor could possess his genius. Ideally he should have spent a further twenty years building up the National Socialist spirit in Germany before going to war. As it was he had had to rely upon 'petty bourgeois reactionaries' for generals and diplomats instead of upon trained National Socialists and this was one reason why the war had gone badly. As it was, however, even the delaying of war from 1938 to 1939 had been a loss of precious time.

In a document dated February 6th, 1945, he displayed the last of his real eloquence, the eloquence that had turned him from an unknown soldier into 'saviour' of Germany, although now it was reserved for private dictation.

. . . The situation is serious, very serious. It seems even to be desperate. We might very easily give way to fatigue, to exhaustion, we might allow ourselves to become discouraged to an extent that blinds us to the weaknesses of our enemies. But these weaknesses are there, for all that. We have facing us an incongruous coalition, drawn together by hatred and jealousy and cemented by the panic with which National Socialism fills this Jew-ridden motley. Face to face with this amorphous monster, our one chance is to depend on ourselves and ourselves alone; to oppose this heterogeneous rabble with a national, homogeneous entity, animated by a courage which no adversity will be able to shake. A people which resists as the German people is now resisting can never be consumed in a witches' cauldron of this kind. On the contrary; it will emerge from the crucible with its soul more steadfast, more intrepid than ever. Whatever reverse we may suffer in the days that lie ahead of us, the German people will draw fresh strength from them; and whatever may happen today, it will live to know a glorious tomorrow.

The will to exterminate which goads these dogs in pursuit of their quarry gives us no option; it indicates the path which we must follow—the only path that remains open to us. We must continue the struggle with the fury of desperation and without a glance over our shoulders; with our faces always to the enemy, we must defend step by step the soil of our fatherland. While we keep fighting, there is always hope, and that, surely, should be enough to forbid us to think that all is already lost . . .

Hitler had conducted the Ardennes offensive from a headquarters at Bad Nauheim in the Taunus hills. On January 16th, 1945, he returned to Berlin and was never again to leave there. He quite possibly already had some distant premonition that he would die in Berlin but his options on this were still open. There was a plan of forming a 'national redoubt' in the Bavarian mountains in which the regime and its remaining forces would have made a final stand. Nothing could have been more natural than for Hitler to have placed himself at the head of this final resistance. By the Berghof at Obersalzburg had been built an elaborate system of bunkers for him, which had taken months of work by a labour force of 3,000. They included kitchens, dining-rooms, guard rooms, dog kennels, and suites of living quarters, with tiled bathrooms, for Hitler and Eva. There was air conditioning and hot and cold running water. But for all his apparent fanaticism about fighting until the last, Hitler did have some remnants of political reality left. So long as Germany, or the bulk of it, existed as an independent entity under his rule, he was a figure of European stature. To become a mere guerilla leader in the mountains, with the bulk of his country occupied by the enemy, was a different proposition. Hitler was prematurely aged and desperately tired. His will-power could keep him on his accustomed path until the last moment but he would have been incapable of adopting any new role.

In January 1945, the Reich Chancellery had suffered only superficial damage and Hitler could easily take up residence there. For him was constructed, in a hurry, a relatively primitive underground bunker for use during air raids—it was not nearly so elaborate or luxurious as that at his home, Obersalzburg. Whether the Americans or the Russians would reach Berlin first and whether either would be able to capture it still appeared to be an open question. The Russians, certainly, regarded it as a most serious operation and the cautious Zhukov took two months to prepare it. Hitler, correctly, foresaw that his enemies were likely to fall out with each other and banked on their doing so before his Germany was defeated.

His woman friend, Eva Braun, was versed in neither politics nor military strategy but through normal common sense she realised that the end was near. In October 1944, aged thirty-two, she had made her will, not that she had much to leave. Hitler fussed about her welfare and instructed her to sleep in the shelter at Obersalzburg. He fell into a neurotic habit of remarking that only she and his dog Blondi were truly loyal to him. This was a ludicrous thing to say, if only because of Keitel. Moreover Himmler, although seriously considering taking over the government and negotiating peace with the west, still had a dotty sense of loyalty; Himmler knew that things were bad and that Hitler was ill but he could not shake off the possibility that perhaps the Leader had some 'plan' that would save everything. Then there was Goebbels, who like all really successful propagandists believed in his own product; Goebbels was prepared to stick by Hitler until the very end.

Eva arrived in Berlin determined to die with Hitler. There had long been a suicidal tendency in her, to match Hitler's, and she was possibly also worrying about his health and comfort. At any rate, she was going to claim her place at his side. Hitler had specifically told her not to come to Berlin. She belonged to his off-duty moments and not in his command post. But, once he had got over an initial irritation at having been disobeyed, Hitler was obviously glad to have her.

By every account, Hitler was now in an appalling state and it is understandable that he should have been so. His hands shook, he had a shambling walk and his eyes kept filling with tears. All he had achieved in twelve years of self-imposed supreme responsibility was a ruin. He did not worry about having to answer for his actions but only about being exposed to ridicule in 'Moscow zoo'; here he was stating with ingenuity what would hurt him most.

The final fantasy, in which he was egged on by the desperate Goebbels, related to the British writer Carlyle's account of Frederick the Great. In the bad, although not yet finally disastrous, months of January-February 1945, Goebbels occasionally took to reading the Carlyle narrative aloud to Hitler. The key to it is that when all seemed lost for Frederick, and he was on the point of committing suicide, the Czarina Elizabeth died and the anti-Prussian alliance dissolved. On April 12th, 1945, Franklin D. Roosevelt died unexpectedly, aged sixty-three. Goebbels was transfixed with joy and even Hitler seemed to find some encouragement in the event. Goebbels produced a horoscope which seemed to show that by August peace would have been negotiated. In fact it was far too late for the death of Roosevelt to have any effect at all on the course of the war. Had he died in 1940, there might, arguably, have been significant differences in American policy but now overwhelming American opinion favoured the total overthrow of Germany and Japan. There is no evidence that Hitler seriously thought otherwise or that his intuition really told him that the death of Roosevelt made any difference. It was just that the only policy he had was to keep on fighting in the hope of something cracking in the enemy and any crack, however small, was something to be welcomed.

Hitler celebrated his last birthday, his fifty-sixth, in the bunker on April 20th. On that day also he made his last public appearance, an inspection of boy soldiers from the Hitler Youth who, about 1,000 in numbers, had been enlisted to hold the Berlin bridges against the advancing Russians. Hitler wanted the bridges for a counter-attack to drive the Russians back but the units that were supposed to make the counter-attack now scarcely existed. Virtually the whole of the German arms industry was now in enemy hands and this meant that the forces that did still exist could fight only for as long as their immediate stocks of weapons and ammunition lasted out. There is no report of Hitler saying anything to the boys; he appeared before them swathed in an overcoat, but without walking stick or spectacles.

On April 22nd, at his last real military conference, Hitler realised that Berlin was not going to be relieved and accepted that the war was lost. He summoned his reserves of strength to fly into a terrifying rage, in which he screamed, shook and foamed at the mouth. It was a display of self pity by a man whose will-power had finally broken. He had, he said, been betrayed by incompetence and treachery. He would stay in Berlin and die there. Since Berlin was on the point of being cut off this meant, in effect, that he was abdicating. Keitel, for one, was shattered; he thought that Hitler, as the responsible commander-in-chief, should carry on until the end. The decision to stay in Berlin was, in Keitel's eyes, little better than desertion in face of the enemy.

There were three obvious candidates to take over from Hitler, assuming that in no circumstances would he hand over to the generals, whom he believed had betrayed him. There was Göring who had become a peripheral figure in the regime but still, on paper, held a range of high offices. Göring, moreover, was Hitler's legal successor, having formally been designated as such back in 1939 and 1941. Then there was Himmler, who in terms of his practical power over the police, appeared to be indispensable. Himmler had seriously considered arresting Hitler on the 1945 birthday, declaring that he had retired through ill-health and assuming power in the state. There was Goebbels, well-known to the German people through his broadcasts and writings; but

Goebbels was determined to stay with Hitler in Berlin where, among other things, he was the party area manager. 'The area manager of Berlin dies in Berlin,' he said. In addition to these three there was Bormann, who would have loved to take over himself but lacked the public stature to do so. Bormann's aim was that Hitler's successor should be someone he could influence and this ruled out, for his purposes, all three obvious candidates and especially Göring. It is indicative of the unusual mentality that could exist in Hitler's entourage that Bormann seriously thought that, by manipulation, he might still have a political future.

During the great rage of April 22nd, Hitler tossed off a remark to the effect that all that remained was to negotiate a peace and for that task Göring was well suited. Göring, at Obersalzberg, had this reported to him and, genuinely, did not know whether or not this meant that Hitler had abdicated and that he, Göring, was to fulfil his legal duty of taking over. Göring was prepared to negotiate what peace terms he could and had gone so far as to adopt a quiet type of uniform which looked somewhat like that of an American general. He had the idea of flying to General Eisenhower's headquarters and thrashing out the problem man to man, the aim, of course, being to get as much of Germany as possible under American rather than Soviet occupation. But before taking action, Göring decided to check that Hitler really had abdicated and sent him a respectful telegram of inquiry. Hitler retaliated by dismissing Göring from all his offices and ordering his arrest; here, in all probability, Bormann's influence had been significant and Bormann may well have planted in Hitler's head the idea the Göring was behaving traitorously. Thus from April 23rd, the day of Göring's dismissal, to April 30th, when Hitler made his will and testament, no legal successor existed at all. Communications between what remained of Germany and its absolute dictator depended upon a single radio balloon flying above the bunker. In the circumstances it seemed that the only person who could take over was Himmler and Himmler certainly thought so; he was puzzled when, in negotiations through the Swedish Count Bernadotte, he learned that the western allies regarded him as unacceptable. Hitler learned what Himmler was up to on the night of April 28th-29th and, again, reacted as if it were treason. He had shot out of hand, Hermann Fegelein, who was not only Himmler's liaison officer in the bunker but also Hitler's prospective brother-in-law; Fegelein was married to Eva Braun's sister Gretl and Hitler had attended the wedding.

Until the last weeks in the bunker, it is unlikely that Hitler had ever given much consideration to whether or not he would ever marry Eva. But she herself naturally wanted a public acknowledgment of her status; although a far from bad-tempered girl she had, over the years, thrown out wry remarks such as 'I am Miss No-private-life'. Perhaps she had looked forward to Hitler retiring after the war, marrying her and settling down to a quiet life in Linz and, perhaps, even to having children by him, despite Hitler's reiterated statement that he would never have children. In the bunker circumstances she could, up to a very late stage, have got out and left Hitler to die alone; her memoirs would have commanded wide interest. But, so far as is known, no alternative existed in her mind to her staying and dying with Hitler. On his side, Hitler found her fidelity the more remarkable because so many others were 'deserting' him; even his protégé Speer had been countermanding his directives to destroy German industry. (That Hitler did not execute Speer is an indication that somewhere in him was a softer side to his nature. Speer had been something approaching a son to him and in the last days he had had the courage to come to the bunker and confess his disobedience.) Eva deserved to be rewarded for fidelity and the best thing he could give her was a wedding ring. Moreover, despite the tortured condition of his mind, Hitler still had some capability of thinking rationally, and for a man of his propaganda skill the advantages of marrying Eva could seem considerable. It indicated to history that he was not a eunuch but a red-blooded man. It would underline his previous celibacy and indicate how he had 'sacrificed private happiness' for the sake of Germany. It would appeal particularly to women—and this was a type of consideration which had counted with him back in the early 1930s when he had been campaigning for power. Moreover it would make the practical task of suicide somewhat less difficult to have a partner in it. Hitler, incidentally, repudiated automatically any idea that he should leave the bunker and fall fighting with his troops against the Russians; this was because of his dread of capture and undignified treatment. One reason for Fegelein's execution had been a fantasy that he had been involved in a plot with Himmler to hand over Hitler's corpse to the enemy.

The marriage took place in the early hours of the morning of April 29th, before an official of the Berlin municipality, especially summoned to the bunker. It was almost certainly never consummated. After the brief ceremony Hitler and his wife, together with the Goebbelses, Bormann and Hitler's two women private secretaries, opened champagne and reminisced, relaxedly, about the older party days. Then Hitler dictated a personal will, leaving his property to the N.S.D.A.P., and a political testament in which he had another go at the Jews and, more significantly, appointed Grand Admiral Karl Dönitz, the submarine commander who had become naval commander-in-chief, as his successor. Dönitz was to be the new 'President' of Germany with Goebbels as 'Chancellor'. Dönitz had not had the least inkling that this was going to happen. Presumably, after the 'treachery' of Göring and Himmler and the 'failure' of the army, Hitler felt only the navy had been loyal; he had been interested in battleships since he was a boy.

Hitler was a married man for less than forty-eight hours. On the afternoon of April 29th he tested a cyanide tablet by having his dog, Blondi, poisoned with it. The results were effective. Early in the morning of April 30th he shook hands in silent farewell with what remained of his staff. Russian advanced parties had reached within 300 yards of the bunker. At noon Hitler received his last military reports; they were about further Russian gains in Berlin. He lunched, calmly, with his secretaries and his vegetarian cook, with his wife not present. After lunch Eva appeared from her private quarters and she and Hitler had a further silent handshaking ceremony with the staff. At three fifteen p.m. they retired into their private sitting-room. Almost immediately Eva killed herself by cyanide and Hitler either shot or poisoned himself (or conceivably both). Their bodies were carried out to the Chancellery garden and partly burned by gasoline. The charred corpses were then buried in a shell hole.

Three days later, the Russians dug up from the Chancellery grounds the charred corpses of a man and a woman and conducted autopsies. Whether in fact they were the bodies of Hitler and his wife is disputable; the 'Hitler' body, in particular, was burned so badly as to be most difficult to identify. It was monorchic, whereas other evidence, from doctors who had treated the living Hitler, asserts that Hitler was normal in this respect. The corpse had no bullet wound in its head and apparently had died of cyanide poisoning. The unanimous German evidence, from the bunker, is that Hitler shot himself. Some have regarded it really significant whether Hitler died a 'soldier's death' with a revolver or merely took poison as if it would somehow affect his historical reputation. What is of greater true significance, symbolically, is that Hitler's burial place was on the frontier between West and East Berlin, a frontier which, a quarter of a century later, still existed as one of the most rigorously guarded in the world and the most vivid symbol of the division between the Communist and non-Communist worlds. Hitler had been the direct cause of this frontier.

In 1940–4, western Europe, with the notable exceptions of Britain and Spain, had the experience of living as a single economic and political unit, with only marginal independence for the French, Danish and, even, Italian governments. This had nothing to do with any dream of Hitler creating a 'United Europe'. It was German colonisation in the east which interested him and he had occupied the west only for military reasons. His only policy for western Europe was to put down resistance movements with maximum terror and to exploit the economies of the subject-countries for Germany's benefit. Anything like the future European Economic Community was alien to Hitler's way of thinking. Even while he was alive, some of the more intellectual National Socialists, who were interested in the west rather than the east, were uneasy that absolute German control was not consistent with free co-operation between the European countries. Thus, but only in a negative sense, Hitler was one of the creators of the E.E.C. By taking nineteenth-century nationalism to an extreme, he killed it. His own country, which he had loved so passionately and which he had led to both great military achievement and to infamy, he left in ruins.

He had been, above all, the product of World War I.

Bibliographical Note

With an insignificant exception, noted below, this book is based upon published sources. Very many books—the total must run into thousands—deal directly and indirectly with Hitler's career, particularly that during World War II. The selected works cited here are of central biographical importance. Wherever possible, British editions are cited. Works marked by an asterisk are translations from German originals.

1. Books recording Hitler's own words

*Adolf Hitler, *Mein Kampf* ('My Struggle'). First published in two parts at Munich in 1925 and 1926. First published as a single volume in 1930. Tr. by James Murphy, London 1939. Tr. by Ralph Manheim, London 1969.

Adolf Hitler, *Die Südtiroler-Frage und das Deutsche Bündnis-probleme* (Munich, 1926).

*Adolf Hitler: untitled book written in 1928 and first published in 1961. The English version is *Hitler's Secret Book* tr. and ed. by F. Gilbert, New York, 1962.

*Adolf Hitler, *The Testament of Adolf Hitler*. This is a series of statements dictated by Hitler at the end of his life. It was published in London in 1971, ed. by F. Genoud.

Hermann Rauschning, *Hitler Speaks* (London, 1939), gives samples of Hitler's private conversation at about the time of his accession to power.

Henry Picker, *Hitler's Tischgespräche im Führerhauptquartier* (Stuttgart, 1963).

*N. Cameron and R. H. Stevens (tr.), *Hitler's Table-Talk, 1941–4* (London, 1953).

Max Domarus, *Hitler. Reden und Proklamationen 1932–45* (Munich, 1965).

*Norman H. Baines, *The Speeches of Adolf Hitler, April 1922— August 1939* (London, 1942).

F. Gilbert, *Hitler Directs His War* (New York, 1950).

*H. R. Trevor-Roper, *Hitler's War Directives 1939–1945* (London, 1964).

Andreas Hillgruber, *Staatsmänner und Diplomaten bei Hitler* (Frankfurt am M., 1967 and 1970).

2. Biographies

Biographies of Hitler are surprisingly few. (This was the prime reason for the present author undertaking the present book.)

For long the field was dominated by Konrad Heiden: *Adolf Hitler* (London, 1936), and *Der Fuehrer* (London, 1944). Heiden was an exiled opponent of his subject. Although he did his best to get his facts right, he should now be read as a sample of the literature of the time.

Alan Bullock, *Hitler—A Study in Tyranny* (London, 1952, revised 1964). This was for long the most authoritative biography, but it now requires further revision on some points of detail.

Werner Maser, *Adolf Hitler. Legende, Mythos, Wirklichkeit* (Munich and Esslingen, 1971). This is a work of enormous but necessary pedantry which concentrates primarily on the obscurer points of Hitler's life. The present author is particularly indebted to this and other works, as cited, of Dr. Maser.

*Franz Jetzinger, *Hitler's Youth* (London, 1956). This contains important material but should be read with caution, particularly on the matter of Hitler's ancestry.

*August Kubizek, *Young Hitler* (London, 1954). This is a vivid and significant first-hand account, but written many years after the events it describes.

Bradley F. Smith, *Adolf Hitler. His Family, Childhood and Youth* (Stanford, 1967), is the most authoritative work in English, on its subject.

H. R. Trevor-Roper, *The Last Days of Hitler* (London, 1947), remains the standard authority on its subject.

Lev Bezymenski, *The Death of Adolf Hitler* (London, 1968), gives Russian autopsy reports on Hitler and others. But in the case of Hitler the Russians seem to have got the wrong body.

*Nerin E. Gun, *Hitler's Mistress Eva Braun* (New York, 1968), is the biography of Frau Hitler. It is based primarily, apparently, on material from the Braun family.

3. Selected autobiographies, memoirs and diaries which contain accounts at first hand of Hitler

Earl of Avon, *Facing the Dictators* (London, 1962).

Earl of Birkenhead, *Halifax* (London, 1965).

B. Brandmayer, *Mit Hitler Meldegänger* (Überlingen, 1940).

Otto Dietrich, *Mit Hitler in die Macht* (Munich, 1934).

*Otto Dietrich, *The Hitler I Knew* (London, 1957).

Keith Feiling, *The Life of Neville Chamberlain* (London, 1956).

André François-Ponçet, *The Fateful Years* (London, 1954).

Hans Frank, *Im Angesicht des Galgens* (Munich, 1953).

*Josef Goebbels, *The Early Goebbels Diaries 1925–6* (ed. H. Heiber) (London, 1962).

*Josef Goebbels, *Goebbels's Diaries 1942–3* (ed. Louis P. Lochner) (London, 1948).

*Heinz Guderian, *Panzer Leader* (London, 1952).

Franz Halder *Kriegstagebuch* (Stuttgart, 1962).

Ernst Hanfstaengl, *Hitler, the Missing Years* (London, 1957).

Ernst Hanfstaengl, *Zwischen Weissem und Braunem Haus,* (Munich, 1970).

Neville Henderson, *Failure of a Mission* (London, 1940).

*Heinrich Hoffmann, *Hitler Was My Friend* (London, 1955).

*Wilhelm Keitel, *The Memoirs of Field-Marshal Keitel* (tr. and ed. David Irving) (London, 1965).

K. W. Krause, *Zehn Jahre Kammerdiener bei Hitler* (Hamburg, 1949).

Kurt Luedecke, *I Knew Hitler* (London, 1938).

Otto Meissner, *Staatssekretär unter Ebert—Hindenburg—Hitler* (Hamburg, 1950).

Adolf Meyer, *Mit Hitler im Bayerischen Reserve-Infanterie Regiment 16 List* (Neustadt, 1934).

Oswald Mosley, *My Life* (London, 1968).

*Franz von Papen, *Memoirs* (London, 1954).

Raymond Postgate, *The Life of George Lansbury* (London, 1950).

*Joachim von Ribbentrop, *Memoirs* (London, 1954).

Ernst Röhm, *Die Geschichte eines Hochverräters* (Munich, 1933).

Alfred Rosenberg, *Das politische Tagebuch Alfred Rosenbergs aus den Jahren 1934–5 und 1939–40* (ed. H-G Seraphim) (Göttingen, 1956).

*Hjalmar Schacht, *Account Settled* (London, 1949).

*Hjalmar Schacht, *My First Seventy-Six Years* (London, 1955).

*Paul Schmidt, *Hitler's Interpreter* (London, 1951).

*Albert Speer, *Inside the Third Reich* (London, 1970).

*Otto Strasser, *Hitler and I* (London, 1940).

A. J. Sylvester, *The Lloyd George I Knew.* (This author was present at one of Lloyd George's meetings with Hitler and the author has consulted his as yet unpublished diary.)

Fritz Thyssen, *I Paid Hitler* (London, 1941).

Fritz Wiedemann, *Der Mann, der Feldherr werden wollte* (Velbert, 1964).

A. Zoller, *Hitler Privat. Erlebnisbericht seiner Geheimsekretärin* (Düsseldorf, 1949).

4. Selected secondary works

Richard Collier, *Duce* (London, 1971).

*Andreas Dorpalen, *Hindenburg and the Weimar Republic* (London, 1964).

*Saul Friedländer, *Prelude to Downfall. Hitler and the United States 1939–45* (London, 1967).

Walter Goerlitz, *History of the German General Staff* (New York, 1953).

C. W. Guillebaud, *The Economic Recovery of Germany 1933–39* (London, 1939).

John Gunter, *Inside Europe* (London, 1936).

Oron J. Hale, *The Captive Press in the Third Reich* (Princeton, 1964).

Peter Hoffmann, *Widerstand, Staatstreich, Attentat* (Munich, 1969).

*Heinz Höhne, *The Order of the Death's Head* (London, 1969).

David Irving, *The Mare's Nest* (London, 1964).

*Joachim Kramarz, *Stauffenberg* (London, 1967).

*Helmut Krausnick and Martin Broszat, *Anatomy of the S.S. State* (London, 1968).

Burton H. Klein, *Germany's Economic Preparations for War* (Harvard, 1959).

Werner Maser, *Die Frühgeschichte der N.S.D.A.P.* (Frankfurt am M/Bonn, 1965).

*Werner Maser, *Hitler's Mein Kampf: An Analysis* (London, 1970).

Erich Matthias and Rudolf Morsey (ed.), *Das Ende der Parteien* (Düsseldorf, 1960).

E. A. Mowrer, *Germany Puts the Clock Back* (London, 1933).

Anthony Nicholls and Erich Matthias (ed.), *German Democracy and the Triumph of Hitler* (London, 1971).

R. J. O'Neill, *The German Army and the Nazi Party 1933–9* (London, 1966).

Dietrich Orlow, *The History of the Nazi Party 1919–33* (Pittsburgh, 1969).

Edward N. Peterson, *The Limits of Hitler's Power* (Princeton, 1969).

*E. P. von der Porten, *The German Navy in World War II* (New York, 1969).

Douglas Reed, *Insanity Fair* (London, 1938).

Gerald Reitlinger, *The Final Solution* (London, 1953).

S. H. Roberts, *The House that Hitler Built* (London, 1937).

*Wilfried Strik-Strikfeld, *Against Stalin and Hitler* (London, 1970).

A. J. P. Taylor, *The Origins of the Second World War* (London. 1961).

*Fritz Tobias, *The Reichstag Fire* (London, 1963).

E. B. Wheaton, *Prelude to Calamity* (New York, 1969).

Index

347